OTTO NEURATH'S ECONOMICS IN CONTEXT

VIENNA CIRCLE INSTITUTE YEARBOOK [2007]

13

VIENNA CIRCLE INSTITUTE YEARBOOK [2007]
13

Institut 'Wiener Kreis'
Society for the Advancement of the Scientific World Conception

Series-Editor:
Friedrich Stadler
University of Vienna, Austria, and Institute Vienna Circle/Institut Wiener Kreis

Editorial Address:

Institut Wiener Kreis
Universitätscampus, Hof 1
Spitalgasse 2-4, A–1090 Wien, Austria
Tel.: +431/4277 41231 (international)
or 01/4277 41231 (national)
Fax.: +431/4277 41297 (international)
or 01/4277 41297 (national)
Email: ivc@univie.ac.at
Homepage: www.univie.ac.at/ivc/

The titles published in this series are listed at the end of this volume.

Elisabeth Nemeth • Stefan W. Schmitz
Thomas E. Uebel
Editors

Otto Neurath's Economics in Context

Springer

Editors
Elisabeth Nemeth
University of Vienna
Austria

Stefan W. Schmitz
Institute Vienna Circle
Vienna, Austria

Thomas E. Uebel
University of Manchester
United Kingdom

Gedruckt mit Förderung des *Österreichischen Bundesministeriums für Wissenschaft und Forschung*
Printed with financial support of the *Austrian Ministry for Science and Research*
In co-operation with the *University of Vienna*

ISBN 978-1-4020-6904-8 e-ISBN 978-1-4020-6905-5

Library of Congress Control Number: 2007940849

Printed on acid-free paper.

9 8 7 6 5 4 3 2 1

springer.com

Otto Neurath's Economics in Context

Elisabeth Nemeth, Stefan W. Schmitz, and Thomas E. Uebel

Promotional Text

Otto Neurath (1882–1945) was a highly unorthodox thinker both in philosophy and economics. He proposed a radically expanded scope of economic analysis that would facilitate a comparative and systematic study of the impact of a great variety of economic and political measures on a population's well-being. Neurath regarded the controversial and widely misunderstood concept of calculation in kind as an indispensable instrument for anyone (economist or politician) who sought to analyze economic relationships from a wider perspective than that of price formation under market conditions. What is the impact of alternative (economic, political or organizational) measures on living conditions? What are the appropriate methods to compare and to rationally choose among alternative measures? In Neurath's opinion, answers to these questions are crucial for every democratic government. The contributions to this sparkling new book conclude that Neurath touched on many of the most critical problems of economic theory during its formative years as a modern discipline; his economics provides insights into the foundational problems of modern economics and should encourage contemporary economic theorists to critically reflect their own hidden presumptions. Neurath's arguments continue to challenge the foundations of today's neo-liberal approach to political-economy. They have also been rediscovered by researchers in the fields of ecological economics and of sustainable development as visionary and original. His comprehensive theory of life conditions and life quality anticipated the questions development economists and the general public meet today.

Contents

Part I
Neurath's Economics in Context

Introduction

Elisabeth Nemeth, Stefan W. Schmitz, and Thomas E. Uebel

After several decades of neglect, Otto Neurath's writings on the theory of science have come to be considered by many to be among the most interesting on the subject in the philosophical tradition of Logical Empiricism. His writings on economics, by contrast, have remained widely neglected.[1] That Neurath was a highly unorthodox thinker both in philosophy and economics suggests, however, that a new look at his economics might prove profitable.

Neurath proposed a radically expanded scope of economic analysis: he sought to develop methods that would facilitate a comparative and systematic study of the impact of a great variety of economic and political measures on the highly complex phenomenon of a population's well-being. As a doctoral student of Eduard Meyer and Gustav Schmoller in Berlin he shared the interest of the "Younger German School of Economics" in history and macro-economics. At the same time, he felt a close affinity to Josef Popper-Lynkeus's radical individualism. The individual's well-being constituted for him the ultimate foundation of economic analyses. Neurath also agreed with the "Austrian School of Economics" that some of the theories expounded by the "historical school" did not meet the standard of modern disciplines and he maintained that economics could only become a real field of study with the help of mathematical methods. Then, at the end of World War I, he became a prominent advocate of planned economies – and this coloured his reputation as an economist ever since.

That Neurath's economic contributions have begun to be discussed again seriously may even seem surprising, given his reputation, but there are at least three good reasons for the renewed interest.[2] First, Neurath's engagements with Mises and Hayek in the socialist calculation debate feature arguments that continue to challenge the foundations of today's neo-liberal approach to political-economy.

---

[1] We have looked at a rather arbitrarily composed sample of eight books on the history of economic thought: Backhouse (1993), Blaug (1996, 1997), Herz, Weinberger (2006), Kolb (1997), Priddat (2002), Srepanti and Zamagi (2005) and Stavenhagen (1969). Neurath is not mentioned in any of them.

[2] A selection of recent publications in economic journals and books that explicitly discuss Neurath's contribution to economics includes: Martinez-Alier (1987), Rosier (1987), Chaloupek (1990), O'Neill (1998), Leonard (1999), Uebel in Neurath (2004), Uebel (2005), Greenwood (2006) and Leßmann (2007).

E. Nemeth et al. (eds.), *Otto Neurath's Economics in Context.*
Vienna Circle Institute Yearbook [2007]. Volume 13.

A number of contributions to this book clarify and elucidate Neurath's original contributions to this issue and interrelate it with his studies on the war economy and on his visions for a socialistic economic order, the economy-in-kind (*Naturalwirtschaft*). In Neurath's view all "thinking in dichotomies" was the result of intellectual lassitude or "pugnacity among scientists". The radical thrust of his proposals can be traced back to his attempt to overcome traditional dichotomies by means of a profound reflection of the underlying foundational questions. This is also true for his idea of calculation-in-kind (*Naturalrechnung*) which was widely misunderstood already by his contemporaries. Neurath regarded it as an indispensable instrument for anyone (economist or politician) who sought to analyze economic relationships from a wider perspective than that of price formation under market conditions. Neurath was aware that every community, which refuses to let the living conditions of the population be determined exclusively by the logic of the market, is confronted with the following questions. What is the impact of alternative (economic, political or organisational) measures on living conditions? What are the appropriate methods to compare and to rationally choose among alternative measures? Importantly, for Neurath it was not the objective of economic theory to make the profoundly political choices with respect to the optimal economic policy – political decisions cannot be delegated to experts. It aims, however, at developing instruments and methods which can be used to analyse and compare the likely consequences of alternative political measures as well as to communicate the results to promote an informed discourse among those whose living conditions are affected by the measures, the general public. In Neurath's opinion, such instruments are crucial not only for socialist governments, but for every democratic one. In this sense, he considered "Planning for Freedom" (1945) as a necessary prerequisite for the further development of democracy.

The second reason for the renewed interest in Neurath's economic writings lies in that some of his arguments in the socialisation debate have also been rediscovered by researchers in the fields of ecological economics and of sustainable development as visionary and original (e.g. Martinez-Alier, Munda, O'Neill 1998). A further third reason can be found in the fact that Neurath developed a comprehensive theory of life conditions and life quality. In doing so, he anticipated the questions which met with renewed interest at the end of the twentieth century among development economists and the general public, as exemplified by the approach taken in the United Nations Human Development Report.

The present book aims at clarifying which of Neurath's ideas remain of relevance today and how these are interrelated. The method chosen is to elucidate their biographical and general historical background and to put them into the framework of the academic and political controversies of their time. This contextual approach yields results that are not just of antiquarian interest. It also enables the reconstruction of the theoretical thrust and continuing practical relevance of a thinker whose ideas were obscured by the catastrophes of the twentieth century. Neurath wanted to demonstrate by his own work in economics that scientific thinking always offers a number of different alternatives and that one must proceed towards applications in full awareness of this fact. In this respect, Neurath's thought is unusually demanding.

With perplexity in political and intellectual life becoming ever more widespread as the twenty-first century progresses, it strikes us as very useful to step back and reconstruct a type of thinking in the social sciences that goes back to the discussion on the big conflicts of the twentieth century but which does not accept as inescapable the intellectual alternatives seemingly cemented in these conflicts.

The book is structured so that it first addresses the question why the study of Neurath's contributions to economics in the context of his time is a worthwhile endeavour today. After all, the overwhelming majority of today's economists regard his contributions as out-dated and largely irrelevant for the continuing development of their discipline.

In the opening essay, *Nemeth* answers this question by drawing on recent results of the modern philosophy of science. Neurath's economic writings are of interest precisely because of their context – the specific constellation of economic theory development up to the end of World War I. At that time the debate about the foundational problems was very lively and controversial. It was only in the 1920s and 1930s that some of the previously debated assumptions and paradigms began to form the academic consensus which is regarded today as the foundation of modern economics.[3] During the time Neurath took part in the academic debate (until the end of World War I), these assumptions were still contested. His early economic papers therefore must be interpreted as one particular manifestation of a larger set of potential foundational problems and paradigms, most of which are no longer considered relevant by present-day economists. Nemeth then goes on to discuss one particular aspect of this contested terrain by focussing on Schumpeter and Neurath who both critically reflected the foundational problems of economics. Nemeth concludes that despite their common reference to Mach's theory of knowledge, they interpret Mach in different ways and arrive at different conclusions with respect to the foundational problems of economics.

Nemeth also provides evidence of a fundamental break in Neurath's academic biography at the end of World War I. He pursued a career as academic economist after his graduation but stopped doing so in 1919, when he turned towards political publications and activism. Neurath's engagement as socialisation commissioner in the Munich "Räterepublik" (Soviet Republic) in 1919 led to his expulsion from the University of Heidelberg where he received his habilitation (a junior professorship) in economic theory only in 1917. This put an end to his academic career before it fully began. As a political activist in the 1920s and 1930s, he rather aimed at integrating his economic ideas into the project of establishing a socialistic order of society. He argued that such an order can only be conceptualised as centrally planned economy in kind, a position that earned him fierce criticism from both sides of the political spectrum, from his socialist fellow-travellers as much as from his liberal opponents (anti-socialist). As already noted, until today Neurath's economic writings are predominantly associated with his concept of an economy-in-kind.

[3] These paradigms emerged during the "Years of High Theory" and stressed individualism, subjectivism, and the analysis of equilibrium in competitive markets in micro-economics, and monetary and macro-economic dynamics in macro-economics (see Mooslechner in this volume).

The remaining contributions in this book are grouped to reflect both this break in Neurath's career as an economist and the predominance in how he is remembered of his radical stand in the calculation debate. Neurath's politico-economic writings after 1919 (i.e. the socialist calculation debate) are considered first, then Neurath's academic research before 1919 (i.e. monetary analysis and utility theory) is looked at, and finally at Neurath's political activities (i.e. the Museum of War economy and his work on ideology and culture). All these contributions are devoted to our main second topic: which of Neurath's economic arguments are of relevance today?

Uebel scrutinises the concept of "in-kind-calculability" and shows that it possesses three interpretations: very weak in-kind calculability (i.e. an economy in-kind does exist in certain sectors of the economy where other than monetary profitability criteria are used for planning decisions), weak in-kind calculability (i.e. an economy in-kind exists in sectors where markets alone do not achieve the efficient allocation of resources and other than monetary profitability criteria must be used for planning decisions), and strong in-kind calculability (i.e. an economy in kind exists only where an economy operates without markets altogether). Arguments in support of all three interpretations can be found in Neurath's writings and he emphasised different ones at different stages of his lifetime. Uebel then argues that Neurath did not possess a valid argument for the non-necessity of monetary calculation, but one that only demonstrates the indispensability of in-kind calculation and the insufficiency of monetary calculation and he refers to this argument as an "ecological argument … against the exclusive role of money-calculation in economic matters." Uebel emphasises the necessity to differentiate between an economy-in-kind (as a model of a socialist economic order) and calculability-in-kind (as a conceptual framework for a theoretical research programme). While Neurath seemed to have dropped the idea of an economy in kind at later stages of his life, he adhered to the concept of in-kind calculability as indispensable instrument in comparative economic research. In addition, Uebel uncovers a number of *prima facie* surprising commonalities between Neurath and the Austrian School of Economics, in particular the strict dichotomy between a monetary market economy, on the one hand, and an economy-in-kind, on the other: "The Austrian position on this issue was 'either-or': either a free market with money or central planning without money. Call this the 'Austrian exclusive disjunction.' It is upon this that not only Mises and later Hayek built their alternatives of freedom or serfdom, but Neurath likewise rested his proposals for marketless socialism on it."

Chaloupek confronts Neurath's concept of an economy-in-kind with the critique that was put forth by contemporary socialist theorists (e.g. Helene Bauer, Otto Leichter). Neurath emphasised – in both his political activities in the Munich "Räterepublik" and in his theoretical articles – that a socialist economic order should be established in one step as "total socialization". By contrast, "the leading social-democratic politicians … and also most theoreticians of socialization were advocates of '*Teil*sozialisierung' (partial socialization)" and consequently of a gradual process of the transformation of society. Most socialist theoreticians regarded Neurath's concept of an economy in kind as politically infeasible and economically unrealistic. They warned of the problem of bureaucratization which they saw as a problem for socialism in general but considered completely unmanageable in Neurath's economy in kind. Chaloupek points out that "Neurath's critique of the capitalist money accounting system anticipates the critique of the SNA (System of National Accounts) developed during the 1960s and 1970s which became one of the theoretical foundations of the environmental movement." Finally he shows that Neurath was not aware of the leading contribution in the academic literature of his time that dealt with the issues he emphasised, namely A. C. Pigou's *The Economics of Welfare* of 1920. It also stressed the welfare effects of market imperfections (i.e. negative externalities) of capitalist systems and the importance of the distribution of income and of material well-being on social welfare.

O'Neill investigates an important politico-economic aspect of Neurath's concept of economic planning which is surprisingly topical, namely, his emphasis on pluralism. Hayek's critique of Neurath's economy in-kind – that a centrally planned economy in-kind would inevitably lead to totalitarianism – is chosen as starting point for the analysis. O'Neill demonstrates that Neurath was strongly committed to a pluralist alternative to totalitarianism. His research agenda on the establishment of a socialist order of society included the research question: what institutional structures allow for and are conducive to pluralism? Neurath's thinking is fundamentally pluralistic in a number of dimensions: pluralism of normative practice, of language, of welfare, institutional pluralism, belief pluralism and decision pluralism. O'Neill argues that belief pluralism in various forms stands at the centre of the debate between Hayek and Neurath. After providing a brief overview of Hayek's criticism, he then goes on to demonstrate that Neurath's concept of an economy in kind does not have the technocratic implications Hayek attributes to them. Rather Neurath's concept is pluralistic along two dimensions, in the future possibilities of social development and in the search for institutional conditions for pluralism in an envisaged socialistic order of society. While Hayek's solution to the coordination problem in a pluralistic society with dispersed knowledge is a non-discursive one (all information is communicated via relative prices), Neurath's solution has a discursive character (Actors derive at common decisions through a discourse based on a social lingua franca.). O'Neill then discusses Neurath's thoughts concerning the characteristics of such a social lingua franca and the characteristics of the proposed discursive institutions for the coordination of action. In addition, Neurath maintains that the coordination problem does not only arise in societies but also in complex organisations. Based on this observation, he criticises Hayek on the point that the latter reduces the set of institutional forms that can address the problem of coordination to the market. Finally, Neurath's analysis of the coordination problem in science is briefly discussed. O'Neill concludes that pluralism in a number of dimensions was a cornerstone of Neurath's concept of a socialistic order and that he was convinced that a plurality of institutional forms prevails in modern societies to address the coordination problem.

Mooslechner investigates Neurath's monetary thought. It has received surprisingly little attention so far, given that a proponent of an economy in kind and of in-kind calculation could be expected to embrace a very critical position towards money.

Mooslechner investigates the papers Neurath wrote before 1919, i.e. when he still considered himself an academic economist. The central question is how Neurath's studies in monetary economics relate to the prevailing academic debate of the time. Around the turn of the century the foundational problems of modern monetary economics emerged. Did Neurath take them into account? Mooslechner provides an overview of the state of the debate on monetary economics at the time. The contributions of Menger, Wicksell, Mises, Keynes and Schumpeter provide the background for the contextualisation of Neurath's work. Mooslechner uncovers four different lines of Neurath's thoughts on money. The most important one was the role of money as a unit of calculation in the economy, followed by money as an institution and the productivity of money, by the role of money in a war economy and by the role of money in the macro-dynamics of a market based economy. In the next step, Mooslechner examines how Neurath related to the academic literature on monetary economics of his time. He argues that the works of the above mentioned authors had strong (personal and/or topical) relationships with the academic discourse in Neurath's Vienna. Therefore, Neurath was very likely to have been aware of the modern developments in monetary economics. Nevertheless, Mooslechner concludes that Neurath did not show much interest in them, although some of his writings contain very interesting lines of argumentation which can be qualified as early forms of Keynesianism and modern Post-Keynesian.

The subject of *Leßmann's* contribution to this volume are the very modern lines of Neurath's economics which are mainly to be found in the pre-1919 writings. "Neurath begins in 1911 by exploring the possibility of *social* preference ordering on the basis of ordinally measurable utility. ... In 1912, then ... Neurath confirms that the resulting social preference ordering often is incomplete." After summarising Neurath's work on social preference orderings, Leßmann compares them with Sen's seminal work on the subject. Both investigate similar issues, namely the comparability and measurability of utility and the conditions of life and the elements of life situation. Both search for solutions to the problem that interpersonal comparisons of well-being are impossible on the basis of ordinal utility concepts. They study the method of analysing the lives people lead, the resources that are available to them, the state of various components of their lives that can provide hints at their well-being. Leßmann carefully carves out how the different terms both of them use relate to each other. Nevertheless, they conclude that the multidimensionality of the concept of well-being poses a serious problem for their approach and they suggest dominance orderings to cope with it in applied work, at least as a starting point. Finally, Leßmann stresses that there are important differences between both research agenda. While Neurath considers conditions of life as a means to approach the objective of measuring well-being in terms of utility, Sen regards it as an alternative. He wants to replace the focus of welfare economics on utility (or resources). Neurath integrates his approach to measure well-being into his concept of an economy in kind, while Sen has a strong leaning towards freedom of choice and free markets. Leßmann suggests, interestingly enough, that Neurath's awareness of the importance of time and its limited availability might be related to his greater project of Unified Science.

Vossoughian focuses on a facet of Neurath's economic oeuvre that has received very little attention so far, namely, his directorship of the German Museum of War Economy in Leipzig in 1919. It is an important example of the break in Neurath's biography which Nemeth discusses in her contribution. He turned from an academic career and an academic audience to political activism and the general public as target audience of his economic and societal visions. Since 1910 he had become interested in the war economy and had studied the sociological conditions during the Balkan Wars. During WWI he had managed to convince the Austrian Ministry of War to establish a commission devoted to the study and documentation of the economic experiences during the war. These activities lead to Neurath's contacts that eventually resulted in the foundation of the War Museum in Leipzig which opened in 1918. His concepts for the museum forestalled many ideas which Neurath realised at the Museum of Society and Economy in Vienna which he founded in Vienna in 1924. He wanted to demonstrate the repercussions different economic and social conditions in society had on the conditions of life of everyday people. The focus rested on the impact of the war on the supply of goods and services to the general public. As Vossoughian shows, these were described "in-kind": "One wall illustrated the impact of the leather shortage on various segments of the economy; how cobblers had to make due with more abundantly available resources like wood, how rabbit skin could serve as a material for clothing…, and how homemakers were becoming more conscientious recyclers." Vossoughian clarifies that Neurath's engagement at the German Museum of War Economy constituted an important link between his interests in modern museum education, the war economy, and the economy-in-kind within his political activism.

In the final contribution *Sandner* investigates how Neurath defined his relationship with Marx, Marxism and Austromarxism in the 1920s and 1930s. Although Neurath was "a very active intellectual in the Austro-Marxist milieu…, he was never an important political theoretician within the Austrian Socialist Party." His view of Marxism combined Epicurus and Marx, which did not fit with Max Adler's Kantianism. For Neurath, the most advanced form of materialism was *Empirical Sociology* (1931) which he conceived of as a framework for "dealing with human behaviour within a spatiotemporal order." In this framework the Marxist questions (for instance the relationship between base and superstructure) would be put in a new, fruitful way. Sandner shows that Neurath developed a sociological approach to culture which was non-deterministic but assumed a "coherence of customs." "He assumed that, in human society, there is always a coherence of mode of production, social structure and ideology." Cultural issues play an important role in this concept, particularly the democratisation of knowledge which also featured prominently in Austromarxism. Finally, Sandner presents evidence that Neurath's approach to culture displayed a number of similarities with the early British cultural studies in the 1950s and 1960s.

Can we draw conclusions from the book? While we cannot do justice to the wealth of new insights brought to light by the various contributions, we can conclude that Neurath's economics turn out to be worth studying even if his work provided insights only into the foundational problems of modern economics. To be sure,

Neurath's contributions to the socialist calculation debate are not done justice by judging them against the background of academic rigour, for they were published when he turned his back to academia and were intended for the general public within the framework of his political activism. Moreover, Neurath's writings were moving targets for his critics in that he kept developing his ideas and was not always coherent in his terminology throughout his long career. This analysis of his economics has a familiar ring to Neurath researchers: he focused on many different issues at the same time and seemed not always to devote the time necessary to study the entire relevant literature or to develop his thoughts with the necessary perseverance. However, the sheer wealth of original ideas and his overall vision are impressive. Most of all, Neurath touched on many of the most critical problems of economic theory during its formative years as a modern discipline. Neurath's "out-of-date" economics may encourage contemporary economic theorists to critically reflect their own hidden presumptions.

In closing, the editors would like to express their gratitude to the Viennese Chamber of Labour and to Oesterreichische Nationalbank for their financial support for the conference "Otto Neurath's Economics in Context" (organised by the Institute Vienna Circle, Vienna 29 Sept—1 Oct 2005) on which this volume is based; to the participants of the conference and the lively debate from which our project has profited immensely. Finally, they also wish to thank Robert Kaller and Dr. Karoly Kokai for their invaluable organisational and editorial assistance.

References

Backhouse, R. E. (1993) *Economists and the Economy*, Blackwell, Oxford

Blaug, M. (1996) *Economic Theory in Retrospect*, Cambridge University Press, Cambridge

Blaug, M. (1997) *Great Economists Before Keynes*, Edward Elgar, Cheltenham

Chaloupek, G. (1990) "The Austrian Debate on Economic Calculation in a Socialist Economy", *History of Political Economy* 22 (3), 659–675

Greenwood, D. (2006) "Commensurability and Beyond: From Mises and Neurath to the Future of the Socialist Calculation Debate", *Economy and Society* 35 (1), 65–90

Herz, D., Weinberger, V. (2006) *Lexikon ökonomischer Werke*, Verlag Wirtschaft und Finanzen, Düsseldorf

Kolb, G. (1997) *Geschichte der Volkswirtschaftslehre*, Vahlen Verlag, Munich

Leonard, R. J. (1999) "'Seeing Is Believing': Otto Neurath, Graphic Art, and the Social Order", *History of Political Economy* 31 (Supplement), 452–478

Leßmann, O. (2007) *Konzeption und Erfassung von Armut. Vergleich des Lebenslage-Ansatzes mit Sens* "Capability"-Ansatz, Duncker & Humblot, Berlin

Martinez-Alier, J. (1987) *Ecological Economics. Energy, Environment and Society*, Blackwell, London

Martinez-Alier, J., Munda, G., O'Neill, J. (1998) "Weak Comparability of Values as a Foundation for Ecological Economics", *Ecological Economics* 26 (3), 277–286

Neurath, O. (1931) *Empirische Soziologie*, Springer, Vienna, excerpts trans. "Empirical Sociology" in O. Neurath, *Empiricism and Sociology* (ed. by M. Neurath and R.S. Cohen), Reidel, Dordrecht, 1973, 319–420

Neurath, O. (1942) "International Planning for Freedom", repr. in O. Neurath, *Empiricism and Sociology* (ed. by M. Neurath and R.S. Cohen), Reidel, Dordrecht, 1973, 422–440

Neurath, O. (2004) *Economic Writings Selections 1904–1945* (ed. by Thomas E. Uebel and Robert S. Cohen), Kluwer, Dordrecht

O'Neill, J. (1998) *The Market. Ethics, Knowledge and Politics*, Routledge, London

Priddat, B. P. (2002) *Theoriegeschichte der Wirtschaft*, Mohr, Tübingen

Rosier, M. (1987) "Otto Neurath, economiste et leader du Cercle de Vienne", *Economies et Sociétés* 21 (3), 113–145

Srepanti, E., Zamagi, S. (2005) *An Outline of the History of Economic Thought*, Clarendon, Oxford

Stavenhagen, G. (1969) *Geschichte der Wirtschaftstheorie*, Vandenhoeck & Ruprecht, Göttingen

Uebel, T. E. (2005) "Incommensurability, Ecology, and Planning: Neurath in the Socialist Calculation Debate, 1919–1928", *History of Political Economy* 37 (2), 309–342

"Freeing up One's Point of View": Neurath's Machian Heritage Compared with Schumpeter's

Elisabeth Nemeth

1 Preliminaries

Why concern oneself with Otto Neurath's economic thought in its historical context? Could anything be more out of fashion than a theory proposing a centrally managed planned economy? Than the views of a theorist whose ideas on in-kind economic planning drove the notion of economic planning to its utmost extreme (ad absurdum, as most would say)? Indeed, Neurath's ideas appeared too radical and utopian even for the social democrats of the 1920s.[1] So why give even a second thought to them today? Would it not be better to follow the advice a colleague gave me in the 1980s and to pass over Neurath's "youthful sins" silently so as not to tarnish the reputation that – finally, after a lengthy delay – has been accredited to Neurath for his impressive philosophical achievements within the framework of logical empiricism?

In the years since the 1980s, however, Neurath's economic writings have attracted much more interest than anyone would previously have suspected. Today we are aware of the fact that Neurath formulated ideas at an unexpectedly early stage that are currently relevant in ecological economy, social choice theory and developmental economy. And that his reflections vis-à-vis "associational socialism" could provide interesting impulses for a new theory of socialism.[2] Viewed from this perspective, Neurath's status is secure as a precursor of theoretical developments and debates that are in full swing today. But is that enough? After all, if the role of the precursor is an endearing one, isn't it also quite thankless? For even in the areas in which Neurath can be regarded as a precursor, the relevant questions are posed today with far greater precision and with reference to current facts – so why should anyone concern oneself with a precursor whose fundamental assumptions differ so greatly from those of the overwhelming majority of economists working today?

---

[1] Cf. Chaloupek (1990) and in this volume, Sandner in this volume.

[2] Cf. Martinez-Alier (1987), O'Neill (1998, 1999), Uebel (2005a), Leßmann (2007) and in this volume.

E. Nemeth et al. (eds.), *Otto Neurath's Economics in Context.*
Vienna Circle Institute Yearbook [2007]. Volume 13.

I would like to propose a justification for such an undertaking that draws upon ideas presented by the philosopher of science James Lennox. In a talk given in 2001, Lennox argued that historical research plays an essential role in clarifying fundamental questions in the sciences, namely because "the foundations of a particular scientific field, and (though a wider lens is needed) of science generally, are shaped by its history, and to a much greater degree than many of the practitioners of a science realize. There is more conceptual freedom in the way theories – even richly confirmed theories – may be formulated and revised than is usually realized. Studying the way they actually came to be formulated, and revised historically, can be of considerable value in doing philosophical work."[3]

Lennox took his examples from the theory of evolution and genetics.[4] But it is true not only of biology that there is "more conceptual freedom in the way theories may be formulated and revised than is usually realized." The same can be said about any other discipline, including economics. "A reasonably mature science," Lennox argued, "is the result of a number of decisions made, at various historical nodes, as to which, among a variety of possible options, ought to be taken."[5] Most of those decisions have been forgotten, though, and it is precisely this lack of historical consciousness that characterizes the state of science Lennox called "reasonably mature." In a "mature" science, most of the practitioners agree on the central concepts and methods of their field and therefore do not see any need for reconstructing the possible options that were passed over during the history of their field. Nevertheless, any scientific field has its puzzles, its unsolved problems, and what Lennox calls its "conceptual muddles." The questions arising from them are what philosophers of science are interested in. They "look for the hidden presuppositions of different approaches, or for their logical virtues and flaws, or … draw out imaginatively the consequences of different ways of conceptualizing or formulating a theory or a problem."[6] In reconstructing the historical origins and development of those problems, philosophers of science may achieve, Lennox argued, a much better understanding of them. Note that, in Lennox's view, better understanding of the *philosophical* problems in a particular scientific field might be achieved by a *historical* reconstruction that situates the current theory in the space of alternative options that were articulated and discussed before the current theory became the dominant one. "As one traces back through the history of a current theory, one finds various alternatives. This historical research opens up a space of theoretical possibilities that were earlier rejected, or not considered, but in the light of current problems, may seem interesting and suggestive."[7]

Remarkably enough, Neurath expressed quite similar views on theory formation and on the part history of science can play in philosophy of science.[8] But this is not

---

[3] Lennox (2001, p. 4).

[4] They highlight the difficulty of giving a clear empirical meaning to concepts such as "fitness and "selection."

[5] Lennox (2001, p. 7).

[6] Ibid. p. 4.

[7] Ibid. p. 7.

[8] For instance in Neurath 1915 (1973).

our subject here. Our concern is Neurath's economic theory and the question why we should be interested in it. Lennox's paper gives another hint regarding this question. From his point of view, it is not just any alternative theory that showed up at any time in history that deserves the philosopher's attention, but primarily those theories the foundational problems of which were discussed by competing scientists before the current theory was accepted. "[I]t is often true that at that point, those involved in the scientific debate will be quite self-conscious of problems that a couple of generations later submerged as unquestioned, unanalyzed presuppositions of the field's common set of concepts and methods."[9] Thus, the historical point to which Lennox suggests tracing theories back is the point where scientists themselves still acted, so to speak, as philosophers: when they consciously discussed their conceptual and methodological assumptions. This is not to say, however, that scientists of former periods were *per se* more philosophically minded than those of later generations. The important point is, rather, that before the basic assumptions of today's "reasonably mature" science were established, scientists had quite a lot to gain from criticizing competing assumptions and convincing the scientific community that their approaches were sounder than competing ones. It is in this way that epistemological questions play a crucial part in the development of a scientific field. Since epistemological conflicts and their outcomes have deeply shaped the way current theories conceive of their subjects and problems, philosophers of science – and philosophically minded practitioners – might learn something from reconstructing the space of theoretical possibilities within which the current way of conceptualizing subjects and problems was only one possibility alongside several others.

2 Neurath as a Theorist of Socialism? Clearing up a Misunderstanding

There is one major controversy in the history of economics in the twentieth century in which Neurath's ideas on economics were rather widely discussed – namely, the calculation debate in the 1920s and 1930s. Neurath's radical conception of socialism was one of the major points of reference in the discussion, and a very contested one too. As it happened, his view that socialism was only conceivable as a centralized planned economy was rejected by the overwhelming majority of the participants in the discussion. But it was not only declared enemies of socialism – such as Mises and Hayek – who criticized Neurath's ideas. Even most of the socialist economists found that his concept of a planned economy was an extreme and unfeasible version of a socialist economic order.[10]

---

[9] Ibid. p. 23.

[10] Meyer (1932), Mandelbaum/Meyer (1934) give an overview of the literature on the debate on economic planning. Neurath's position is presented as being at one extreme of a spectrum of possible conceptions of socialist economics.

Recent research has demonstrated that there is much to learn from Neurath's contributions to this debate.[11] Nevertheless, it would be misguided to reconstruct Neurath's economic theory only from the perspective of the debate on socialization. From this perspective, Neurath's work prior to 1919 would appear to be nothing but a prelude to his theory of socialist economics. To a certain extent, Neurath himself invited such a construal through the publication of his book *From War Economy to Economy In-Kind* (*Durch die Kriegswirtschaft zur Naturalwirtschaft*) in 1919. The book, which contains a selection of earlier writings as well as a few new articles, can create the impression that Neurath's economic views were developing according to an inner logic beginning with war economics and reaching its natural conclusion in Bayern's and Sachsen's models of full socialization. But I think that this impression is misleading. In the preface, Neurath himself attests that the end of the war marked a major change for him,[12] that he had decided to end his career as scholar and scientist and to begin a new "life of action."[13] Hence, the 1919 book is, in contrast to Neurath's earlier economic writings, deliberately not addressed toward the scientific community. In fact, it constitutes the first major publication within Neurath's political project aiming to build up socialist society. The earlier writings that were included in the book were selected for their immediate relevance to this new political project.[14]

Neurath, however, was not born with a proclivity for political engagement. It is no mere rhetoric when he says that he had "long doubts" about his move in this direction. Indeed, Neurath's wife, Olga Hahn-Neurath, who vehemently opposed his shift into politics, was able to appeal to his own earlier efforts to maintain a clear distance from politics. Before the war, in fact, he had had a reputation for being difficult to position with respect to political camps.[15]

The transition into politics had far-reaching consequences for Neurath.[16] After the disbandment of the Munich Soviet Republic in 1919, he was arrested and

[11] Of course it is highly debatable what can be learned from this, as attested by the contrary views presented by Chaloupek (in this volume) and O'Neill (1999).

[12] Cf. Paul Neurath (1994).

[13] "The hesitations and the vacillations of those called upon to act, the advice of my friends and sundry accidental circumstances, finally moved me, after much reflection, to conclude my life of contemplation and to begin one of action. After many incidents I was entrusted, as President of the Central Office of Economics, with socialization of Bavaria. What hitherto I had yearned for as the future, I can now myself help to fashion in the service of the people, and soon, I hope, in the service of the free world." Neurath 1919 (1973), p. 124.

[14] Vossoughian (in this volume) demonstrates that characteristic features of Neurath's political activism were already apparent during the First World War in the context of the Museum of War Economy in Leipzig.

[15] One of his students remembered him as "a perfectly obscure character, said to be either socialist or a friend of the industrialists.... Only one [of the teachers EN] continued to be an enigma to the students of the Academy, politically and, in the last resort, also personally: Dr. Otto Neurath... he opposed any political activity vigorously... attacked Marxism, and socialism generally, with sarcastic words." Neurath (1973, p. 11). Otto Bauer also discusses Neurath's distant attitude toward politics (quoted in Paul Neurath 1994, p. 49).

[16] For biographical information, see Paul Neurath (1994), Fleck in Cartwright et al. (1996).

charged along with the other participants, and finally dispatched to Austria. He was forbidden to return to Austria and removed from the list of docents at the University of Heidelberg, where he had completed his habilitation in economics in 1917, thus putting an end to his academic career before it had properly begun. The letters that he addressed to the faculty of philosophy in Heidelberg bear eloquent witness to the significance this had for him and to the importance he placed on getting reinstated at the university.[17] Such a premature end to his career as a theorist of macroeconomics obviously disappointed the plans Neurath had been seeking to realize.

During the debates about the possibility and concrete form of a socialist economic order in the twenties and thirties, he presumably continued to view his role as that of a social scientist, albeit of one who had become a political actor and was applying his theoretical knowledge of economic planning to the project of changing society. In this period, he revised and qualified some of his views, incorporating ideas from various other socialist theoretical writings. His readings on English guilds, for example, led him to become critical of the tendency toward state centralism that characterized central European socialist thinking (including his own), and to favor models of self-management.[18] Moreover, he attempted to highlight the continuities between his own theories and those of Marx and Engels.[19] In short, his efforts to anchor his economic views in a political context and to reflect on their relation to socialist theory and practice more generally helped Neurath to arrive at some new formulations of his views.[20] But this ought not occlude the fact that what Neurath saw as his contribution to economics had been worked out by 1917 – that is, before his turn to socialism – and was never fundamentally changed. He was no longer an active participant in theoretical work in economics during the "years of high theory" in the twenties and thirties.[21] Surely this cannot be explained solely by his having been excluded from the University of Heidelberg. When he completed his habilitation in 1917, Neurath regarded himself as an expert on all questions of "directed economics" – i.e. not only on governmental direction of economics in wartime and in socialism, but also on various elements of state intervention and

[17] Universitätsarchiv Heidelberg, A-219 Neurath, Otto.

[18] Neurath (1921, 1922a,b). This new orientation reveals itself also in his work for the housing movement. See Novy (1983), Nemeth (1999a). After this point, Neurath held that "self-government and freedom and other social relations belong to the happiness conditions of human beings" (O'Neill in this volume).

[19] E.g. Neurath (1925). See Sandner (2006) and Sandner (in this volume) on Neurath's specific position within Austrian Marxism. See Chaloupek (in this volume) on Neurath's pragmatic attitude with respect to Marx and Engels.

[20] On the intimate connection among Neurath's intellectual projects within Viennese social democracy in the 20s and 30s, see Sandner in this volume.

[21] For the "years of high theory" see Mooslechner in this volume. The first work in which Neurath takes up his reflections on the nature of economic theory again is the 1935 "What is meant by Rational Economic Theory?" (Neurath 1935 (1987)). It is symptomatic that this return to questions of the foundations of theoretical economics that he had posed before 1918 occurred only when Neurath was in exile in Den Haag and could no longer pursue the political activities that has shaped his life between 1918 and 1934. Mormann (1999) has shown that Neurath's philosophy of science after 1935 contains elements that he had worked out before the First World War.

regulation.[22] From his perspective, the reasons for rejecting any economic theory that placed money at the center of attention were of a theoretical nature. It is therefore hard to imagine that Neurath could have gone along with the re-appraisal of the role of money in the economy and the resultant turn to dynamic macroeconomics even if he had continued fine-tuning his theories as a private docent in Heidelberg. Of course, his "relationship with the predominant economic thinking"[23] in the twenties and thirties was extremely weak; he seems not even to have been aware of the alternative economic theories that were closest to his, such as Pigou's "Economics of Welfare."[24] In the period before the First World War, on the other hand, Neurath was a highly ambitious young researcher who was able to make quite unorthodox contributions to the debates on fundamental questions in the social sciences of his time. He consciously sought to avoid the polarization between the Historical School and the Austrian School of macroeconomics and articulated his views with a mind to positioning them with respect to leading theorists in Germany, England and France.[25]

It is above all this discursive situation before 1914 that must form the primary basis for a reconstruction of Neurath's economic thought, and only secondarily the debate on socialization in the twenties and thirties. That does not mean that Neurath's active engagement in favor of the "full socialization" of Bavaria and his theoretical work on socialist economics should be taken less seriously. But it is important to understand that Neurath's understanding of socialist economics was based upon a theoretical framework that had already been formulated before the First World War.[26] In other words, long before Neurath the political activist claimed that a socialist economy would have to be constructed as a centrally managed economy in kind, Neurath the economist had already conceived of what he called "calculation in kind": a broad research program in which systematic comparisons would be made between the effects that various forms of economic organization under certain conditions have upon the well-being of the population.[27]

Neurath's theoretical conception of "calculation in-kind" as a comprehensive research program arose at the end of the "long nineteenth century" (which, following

[22] Cf. his writings on differentiated prices, e.g., 1911c and 1912b

[23] Mooslechner in this volume.

[24] Cf. Chaloupek (in this volume).

[25] Neurath's (1911b) work is especially important in this respect. Uebel (2004) recently presented an overview of these complex relations; the present volume brings out additional aspects.

[26] Leßmann points out in her contribution to this volume that it would be shortsighted to view Neurath's proposals for a transition from capitalism to socialism as a purely political program. Neurath was also attempting to act upon theoretical conviction that he had worked out in the years before 1918. Leßmann writes: "He argues in favor of a planned economy because he is convinced that it will work more efficiently than a market economy in terms of providing a good life for everybody."

[27] For the distinction between "economy-in-kind" and "calculability-in-kind" see Uebel in this volume. O'Neill (in this volume) distinguishes several forms of pluralism in Neurath's thought and shows that pluralism is not a result of the later Neurath giving in, but, on the contrary, was a characteristic feature of Neurath's ideas on economic planning from early on.

Hobsbawm, ended only at the beginning of the First World War). During what Hobsbawm called the "short twentieth century" (1914–1991) politics and social theory were marked by the rivalry between liberalism and socialism. Historically, this rivalry produced a fragile balance between the two camps that lasted until its definitive end in 1991. Seen from the perspective of the present, the discursive situation that preceded the unique constellation of the "short twentieth century" could be of more interest than it was just a few decades ago. After all, the economic theories of the inter-war period, "which have completely altered the orientation and character of economics"[28] were children of their time. As responses to the enormous economic difficulties arising in the twenties, they were of urgent political necessity: "in the end, policy relevance was the crucial point in making the revolution in economic thinking successful."[29] On the other hand, a historical reconstruction of the earlier situation before the "short twentieth century" can reveal a "space of theoretical possibilities" that was no longer explored by the "mature science" of economics in the twentieth century – and which, as Lennox emphasizes, there was no longer any obvious need to explore. At least for as long as the "puzzles" and "conceptual muddles" arising in theoretical economics as in other sciences do not become all-too intractable.

Neurath himself would probably press this point further than Lennox. He would presumably be in favor of exploiting the "space of theoretical possibilities" before we are confronted with immediately pressing conceptual difficulties. He repeatedly emphasized that we never know what part of our ship of knowledge will prove not to be water-tight. Besides, we cannot know whether the conditions under which we are sailing will remain more or less the same or undergo fundamental change. According to Neurath, it is not possible for science to predict the individual storms and icebergs with which it will be confronted, but it is possible to draw attention to the fact that the fundamental assumptions of any human practice – including the assumptions of scientific theories – rest upon prerequisites that did not always and will not always obtain. It is possible and advisable to conduct what Neurath called "utopistics": to conceive of the prerequisites of our thought and action as constituting a single case within the "space of possibilities" and thereby to gain flexibility in shaping the present and the future.[30]

3 What is the Object of Inquiry of "Theoretical Economics"?

Neurath's writings before the First World War are not only voluminous but also thematically quite broad. They deal with ancient economic history, didactics of economics, sociology of religion, value theory, war economics, theory of social science, history of optics and philosophy of science.[31] That Neurath also produced

---

[28] Mooslechner in this volume.

[29] Ibid.

[30] For the pluralistic utopianism characteristic of Neurath, see Nemeth 1982 (1991) and 1994, Nielsen and Uebel (1999) and O'Neill in this volume.

[31] See Uebel (2004).

a series of writings on the topic of money between 1909 and 1913 does not fit neatly into the typical picture. Moreover, these writings do not offer a critique of money, as one might expect on the basis of his contributions to the debate on socialization. Rather, they are for the most part investigations of the monetary system in Austro-Hungary.[32] In these works, Neurath reveals himself as an expert on questions related to banking and finances and also as a pragmatist – which also became apparent later on through his activities in the socialization program in Munich.[33] There are some surprising theoretical elements related to the topic of money[34], but it would be futile to search for a consistently worked-out theory of money. Neurath in fact never produced any such theory and, in fact, presumably regarded his works on the topic as belonging to "applied economics," in which – as Neurath writes in his 1910 *Textbook of Economics* – theoretical material is combined with various details that have not yet properly been researched and therefore cannot be included in a purely theoretical presentation.[35] Neurath's ambition, however, did not lie in "applied" but in "theoretical economics," which deals with questions of a highly general nature, comparable to those of geometry, as Neurath puts it in his 1910 textbook:

> Some scholars who work on economic questions abstracted from the circumstances of any individual population, much as one disregards the color and weight of a body, and much else besides, in doing geometry. They sought to study the causes that generally make a

[32] The issues addressed here include the development of marketable giro money (Neurath 1910/1911a) and the "psychological behaviour of the population with respect to particular sorts of money" (i.e. to metal and paper money, as well as to gold circulation) Neurath 1910/1911b. Neurath discussed currency and bequest politics in Austro-Hungary and wrote also a thorough examination of the Austro-Hungarian bank's balance sheets: "Yearly balance and weekly bank returns of the Austro-Hungarian bank" (1911a). Another main point of interest in the early writings was the role of the state in price formation, e.g., the effect of "differentiated prices" on economic affairs (Neurath 1911c and 1912b).

[33] Consider the "bank ordinance" that was enacted on Neurath's prompting in 1919 in Munich, and which was later to provide the basis of the charge of treason against Neurath. "This ordinance had established that only limited sums could be withdrawn each week and that large monetary transactions could only be conducted with checks and under supervision – all of which measures intended to prevent the flight of capital and a general run to the banks. The accusation charged Neurath with having illegally encroached upon private property, which was affirmed by a bank director who had been called as an expert witness. This point of the accusation was undermined in a somewhat surprising manner: Eugen Umrath, the commercial chairman of the AEG (Allgemeine Elektrizitäts-gesellschaft) in Chemnitz, who had come to Munich to help his friend Neurath, explained to the court that he himself had already enacted a very similar ordinance in Chemnitz on November 9, 1918 (the day of the declaration of the German Republic) in pursuance of the same goal as Neurath in Munich:to prevent the collapse of monetary transactions that was otherwise to be expected. But he was foresighted enough to attain confirmation from the director of the Reichsbank and the chairman of the bank assembly in Chemnitz of how useful this 'intervention in the sphere of private property' was at the time. After this account by Eugen Umrath and the presentation of a copy of the written confirmation, the invited bank director took back his statement and the state attorney dropped this point of the accusation." (Paul Neurath 1994, p. 47 f.)

[34] See Mooslechner in this volume.

[35] Neurath (1910b), in GS 4, p. 254.

> group of people richer when they stand in particular relations to one another, conduct business within a market, introduce tolls, etc. The science that was thereby established is what we call *theoretical economics*.[36]

What is introduced in passing here, by way of a textbook definition of theoretical economics, is in fact a shorthand formulation of the theoretical project which Neurath began to work on between 1910 and 1917. In this period, he formulated the basic principles of his theory of wealth, which was to re-define the range of objects of inquiry of economics and make it possible to conduct investigations that would present the "highpoint of scientific generality."[37] The conceptual and methodological framework for this theory was to be so broad that it could encompass elements from the Historical School as well as the Austrian School. Such an ambitious program demanded a theoretical foundation, which drew first and foremost from the discussions later recounted by Philipp Frank and now referred to as the "first Vienna Circle."[38] Neurath was especially influenced in his development of ideas in the area of theoretical economics in this phase by Ernst Mach's critique of Newton's concept of absolute space and by the new conception of gravitation that Mach formulated as a consequence of his critical re-sideration of Newton's. In a letter addressed to Mach (probably written in 1915), Neurath wrote:

> I have heard with great interest about the latest developments in relativity theory which can be traced to your conception that gravity as a function depends on the total distribution of mass and remains constant toward certain transformations (for example, rotation). It was this idea in your *Mechanics* which has never left me since my first reading, and has influenced my own intellectual development and by indirect paths even economics itself. It was your tendency to derive the meaning of particulars from the whole rather than the meaning of the whole from a summation of the particulars, which has been so important. It is in value theory in particular that these impulses have benefited me through indirect paths.[39]

It is perhaps not immediately clear what Neurath's value theory has in common with Mach's conception of gravity as a function of distribution of mass. One thing at least becomes clear from Neurath's remarks: he wanted to continue the holistic approach of the Historical School (sc. asking "the question of how *the total situation of a group of people* is conceived of" and putting "the concept of *life in its entirety*" at the centre of discussion"[40]), though in the conceptual and methodological framework of Ernst Mach's physical holism. To what extent this attempt can be

---

[36] Ibid.

[37] Neurath (1911b), in GS 4, p. 471.

[38] These conversations of a group of young researchers in a Viennese café in the years around 1910 – in which, according to Frank, Neurath participated – revolved around the dramatic scientific upheavals in physics, mathematics and logic beginning in the late nineteenth century. The goal envisioned by the members of the group was a new philosophical conception of scientific knowledge that was to be oriented toward Mach, Poincaré, Duhem, Hilbert and Einstein.

[39] An undated letter (probably from 1915) from Neurath to Ernst Mach, Engl. trans. in Blackmore et al. (eds.) 2001, Dordrecht: Kluwer, 117p. For Neurath's holism in relation to Mach's see Stöltzner 2001, 106p.

[40] Neurath 1909 (2004), 293p.

considered successful is another question that exceeds the scope of this article and could only be assessed in the context of interdisciplinary cooperation.[41]

At any rate, Neurath was not the only economist working in Vienna at that time whose writings reveal the influence of Ernst Mach.[42] I will confine myself here to one other example, namely to Joseph Schumpeter's 1908 *The essence and the main content of theoretical economics (Das Wesen und der Hauptinhalt der theoretischen Nationalökonomie)*, which is especially clearly oriented toward the ideas of Ernst Mach.[43] Years later, Schumpeter himself no longer regarded this first book of his very highly,[44] although it had made him famous as an economic theorist almost overnight – perhaps because it did not fit into the world theoretically captured in the "High Years of Economics." The 1908 book is expressly constrained to providing a closed system that describes the logic of exchange relations and refers exclusively to the area of theory construction that Schumpeter called economic "statics." It explicitly ignores the area that was to take center stage in economic theory construction in the twenties and to which Schumpeter himself was to devote his attention, namely economic dynamics.[45] All the more pressing, though, is the book's demand for a clear answer to the question of what the content of economic theory is:

> A critique of the foundations of our science with the goal of working out the exact content of all the loquacious claims that confront us at the threshold of economics and are offered in response when one asks about the foundations of theoretical economics – that is what we are seeking to contribute.[46]

In a systematic enquiry of the content of theoretical economics published 3 years later, in 1911, Neurath mentions Schumpeter repeatedly and criticizes him in the central passages in which he attempts to demonstrate a method for studying the "wealth" of an individual or a subpopulation without referring to the mechanisms of price formation. It seems that Neurath regarded the theoretical economics defined in 1908 by Schumpeter as an especially important rival conception.

---

[41] The meaning of "physicalism" in Neurath's work can only be explained by appealing to Mach. The problems that Chaloupek (in this volume) has with physicalism can by no means be dismissed easily. But they are in part due to a misunderstanding to which Neurath's own programmatic tone contributed. It is important to realize that Neurath did not want to introduce the explanatory model of classical mechanics into social science but, rather, the critique on this model as worked out by Mach. From Mach's perspective, it is pointless to talk about a "causally completely determined closed system" (Chaloupek towards the end of his article in this volume). With regard to "physicalism in the social sciences, see Uebel (2005b) and O'Neill (in this volume). An important point is raised by Leßmann (in this volume), namely that the physical interpretation of the social sciences helped Neurath to appreciate the significance of time and its limited availability in the economy.

[42] Hayek (1966), trans. in Blackmore et al. (eds.) 2001, 123p.

[43] On the commonalities between the conceptions of science espoused by Schumpeter and Neurath, see Uebel (2004, 33p). In a paper presented at the conference "Neurath's Economics in Context" in Vienna 2004, Hermann Rauchenschwandtner hinted at some further parallels between Schumpeter 1908 and Neurath 1911.

[44] Swedberg (1991) 1994, p. 50.

[45] See Mooslechner in this volume. Neurath does not mention Schumpeter's 1910 work.

[46] Schumpeter (1908) 1998, p. 26.

It is, however, no contradiction that the conceptions of science underlying the two viewpoints coincide in several respects, as I will elucidate shortly. Opposing positions are, from a sociological perspective, constitutive of scientific fields. They not only express the differing views espoused by scientists within a field, but also formulate rival normative conceptions of science. Fundamental scientific conflicts always concern also the criteria according to which problems are formulated, methodologies selected and results justified. Hence, even the fiercest rivals are also in a certain sense allies. In feuding over existing or new principles and standards, they also negotiate the preservation or realignment of the boundary between questions and problems that are regarded as having a legitimate place within a scientific field at a given time, and those that are excluded.[47]

In this respect, Neurath acted in a highly self-conscious manner in 1911 in positioning his viewpoints within the core of the conflict over the definition of the essence of economics and presenting them as a clear alternative to the "newest theorist" of pure economics.[48] His aim was to gain scientific acknowledgement for a new type of investigation, and thereby to expand the space of legitimate economic problems drastically. Neurath argued that elements that had been forgotten in the course of the discipline's history ought to be regained as resources for theory construction. He appealed, for example, to Aristotle's conception of "wealth" as the essence of pleasure or pain for individuals or groups. Economists ought to concern themselves again – as many classical economists did – with *all* institutions, measures and processes that go into making people rich or poor in Aristotle's broad sense, and not only with the exchange relations represented in monetary currency. These relations are for Neurath only one particular organizational form of economic behavior, and ought to be compared with other forms in view of their effects upon wealth and poverty.[49] Such a broad demarcation of the object of inquiry of economics posed a stark contrast to Schumpeter's aim, namely to cleanse economics of all inessential elements[50] and so to lay bare its core: the investigation of relations of exchange and their laws of movement.[51] For Schumpeter, price theory therefore assumes a central position. It is applicable not only to "exchange economies" but also to the "purely economic processes of isolated economies without exchange." Indeed, it presents "a systematic logic of economic affairs."[52]

Neurath, on the other hand, considered this conception of the "logic of economic affairs" to be a problematic restriction. He regarded Schumpeter's

---

[47] See Bourdieu (1975). I treated this more thoroughly in Nemeth (1999b).

[48] Neurath's "On the Theory of Social Science" from 1910 is thematically quite close to the work from 1911. There he refers to Schumpeter as the "most recent theorist" to address the question of measurability in the theory of value 1910a (2004), p. 279 and as a "modern proponent of the theoretical direction" (1910) 2004, p. 283.

[49] On Neurath's conception of "life conditions" in sociology, see Leßmann (2007) and in this volume, Amann (1996). These topics are addressed in some of my earlier publications, e.g., in Nemeth (1981, 1996, 1999a,b, 2006).

[50] Schumpeter (1908) 1998 p. 145.

[51] Ibid. p. 187.

[52] Ibid. p. 260. See also p. 49.

program as extending a trend that had long been developing in the history of economics, but as going too far in making the "exclusion of the theory of wealth" one of its central theoretical principles.[53] Such a restriction is in Neurath's view wholly unjustified. It is important to differentiate here between, on the one hand, Neurath's critique of the restriction of theoretical economics to the reconstruction of the system of price relations and, on the other hand, that of Schumpeter's other opponents. The latter argued that economics ought to pursue social aims, such as increasing the well-being of the population, and thus should not be formulated as abstractly as Schumpeter intended.[54] To Neurath, however, the normative discussions about the "aims" of political economics were misleading distractions from the real problem of the theory of wealth.[55] The real problem was rather of a philosophical nature, namely the question whether the wealth or poverty of a population could be made into the object of objective scientific study. Neurath answered this question in the affirmative and attempted in numerous writings to demonstrate "that wealth is in itself, as the result of certain conditions, an appropriate object of inquiry for a scientific discipline, and that it has nothing to do with 'goals', 'aims', 'shoulds' etc."[56] This does not mean, of course, that the study of wealth could not be conducted in such a way as to bear on practical questions. But wealth is, as an object of inquiry, no more closely linked to social aims than the objects of any other scientific inquiry.

> The content of theoretical economics is not "ethicized" if one uses the results to respond to problems which are selected according to criteria external to theoretical economics itself, just as chemistry is not "hygenicized" if one investigates how a certain poison can be destroyed. There is nothing that speaks against interpreting this observation as maintaining a distinction between theoretical and practical economics, *but it must be emphasized that the theory of wealth belongs not to applied but to theoretical economics*.[57]

So Neurath insisted on attributing to his investigations on wealth and poverty the status of a highly abstract theory constituting a part of theoretical economics and abstracting from the conditions of any individual population "much as one disregards the color and weight of a body, and much else besides, in doing geometry."[58] In short, he regarded his approach as being just as abstract as the "pure economics" espoused by Schumpeter and, indeed, as outdoing the latter in generality.

---

[53] "While many political economists have preferred price theory and downplayed the remaining problems, others have simply liberated themselves of the actual object of inquiry of political economics." And explicitly referring to Schumpeter Neurath comments: "The theory of wealth is explicitly excluded" Neurath (1911b) GS 4, p. 500.

[54] For this point see Uebel (2004), p. 30, Swedberg, p. 50. (The pagination corresponds to the German text).

[55] Neurath (1911b) GS 4, p. 502. See also 1910a (2004), p. 282.

[56] Ibid. p. 503. For Neurath in the "Methoden- und Werturteilsstreit" see Uebel (2004).

[57] Ibid. p. 504.

[58] See footnote 37.

4 "True Science Consists in Systematically Examining all Possible Cases"[59]

In his 1911 work on value theory, Neurath referred explicitly to Schumpeter in four different places. We have already encountered the first of these.

1) Schumpeter explicitly excludes wealth, as understood by Neurath, from economic theory. Thus, Neurath recognizes in Schumpeter's 1908 book a paradigmatic alternative position.[60]
2) Schumpeter claims to be able to demonstrate theoretically that indirect exchange – and thereby money – is economically necessary. But this, according to Neurath, is a mistake. The demonstration of necessity does not strictly follow unless one assumes restrictive conditions from the start. But as widespread as it may be to neglect phenomena that do not comfortably fit into one's picture, it is all the same not scientifically justified.[61]
3) Schumpeter criticizes the attempts of recent political economists to achieve progress in economic theory by freeing economic processes from the "monetary shroud." Neurath dissents in this assessment and maintains that the view "behind the monetary shroud" requires special theoretical efforts which hardly any economist has undertaken.[62]
4) Neurath points out that Schumpeter himself sees clearly that pure price theory does not take everything into account that de facto plays a role. Schumpeter himself had listed a series of objections that demonstrate "that the conditions of transfer of goods do vary at different times, that aspects other than pure price theory bear upon price formation..." But these objections failed to make Schumpeter aware, according to Neurath, that "one has to expand the range of conditions under consideration." So Neurath criticizes Schumpeter for contenting himself with declaring that "we describe what is often the case."[63] With this, Schumpeter has, according to Neurath, sacrificed his claim to generality and reduced theoretical economics to grasping "what is often the case," which for

[59] Neurath 1910a (2004), p. 278. And Neurath continues: "Exact political economy has not achieved this until now, it does not even encompass all actual cases."

[60] Neurath adds that in this respect Schumpeter stands in contrast to Carl Menger: Neurath (1911b) GS 4, p. 500.

[61] "The theoretical analysis by no means leads to the 'demonstration that indirect exchange is necessary...that there must be goods that one acquires not for their own sake but in order to use them in later exchanges, hence the phenomenon of money', as for example *Schumpeter* claims [...] 1908, p. 277. Highly restrictive conditions would be necessary to demonstrate the indispensability of money. Neglecting direct exchange involving more than two people is quite common in the economic literature, see Oresmius, Tractatus, c.I, Smith, Wealth of Nations I, ch.4." (Ibid. p. 484).

[62] The footnote with the reference to Schumpeter was erroneously omitted from the Gesammelten Schriften Bd.4 (1996) It can be found in the original from 1911 on p. 86. Since there are also quite a few further mistakes in the 1996 edition, some of which obscure or alter the meaning, it is worth consulting the original article from 1911.

[63] (1911b) GS 4, p. 493.

> Neurath is wholly unsatisfactory. As Neurath saw it, Schumpeter was stuck halfway between the simple assessment of empirical facts – which he had abandoned with good reasons – and a truly general theory. Although Schumpeter had admitted that he could finally justify his approach – pure price theory – only by referring to "what is often the case," he maintained his claim "that pure price theory is more suitable than any other in explaining the facts," and did "not seriously take a second option into consideration."[64] What Schumpeter's approach thereby missed was Neurath's attempt to attain "a free point of view." But what did Neurath mean by that?

I hope that this idea will become somewhat clearer at the end of this paper. In the context of Neurath's criticism of Schumpeter in 1911, he describes what he means by the "free point of view" which theoretical economics should attain in the following way. In his view, it is "only the elements and the elementary relations" that are fundamentally empirical – in economic studies as in any other science. "If we endeavor to produce all possible combinations of the elements that are given to us empirically, we arrive at types that present an approach that comes more or less close to reality."[65] The complex forms of organization that arise via abstraction and combination of elements in the course of scientific progress are historically realized only in part. "It is not always immediately clear what results of theoretical research are historically given. We can by no means claim that every theoretical presentation of relations describes real results even approximately."[66] For Neurath a truly general theory therefore has to be unrealistic in a certain sense. It has to develop a schema in which the combination of elements that "is often the case" can be compared systematically with other possible combinations, whether they are historically realized or not.[67]

In his criticism of Schumpeter Neurath is employing a series of intellectual figures that play a central role in the work of Ernst Mach: "elements and elementary relations," "expanding the range of conditions," "freeing up one's point of view," considering the possibility of a different explanation. Indeed, it appears that Neurath is demanding of Schumpeter that the latter pay heed to the fundamental principles of Mach's epistemology. It is important to note here that the traces of Mach in Schumpeter's book are so ubiquitous and obvious that Neurath can hardly have overlooked them. And if he was indeed responding to these traces, then it seems that Neurath was playing his own interpretation of Mach against Schumpeter's. Whether he did so consciously or not is not decisive for our discussion. In any case, I think that we can better understand what was at stake in the dispute between Neurath and Schumpeter if we see how they differed in the way in which they were

[64] Ibid. p. 494.

[65] Ibid. p. 493.

[66] Ibid.

[67] Against this backdrop we can better understand how Neurath conceived of the highly abstract theoretical economics as being related to practice: "Theory best serves practice when it is unrealistic in a certain sense: when it is ahead of reality, not just following it." (Neurath, cited by Uebel 2004, p. 33).

drawing upon Mach's epistemology. In reconstructing this differential influence of Mach upon Neurath and Schumpeter, there is a wealth of material I could analyze, but I will confine myself here to a few provisional points.

For Mach, ignoring the conditions under which we came upon particular findings is the primary source of error – within science and without.[68] By failing to bear in mind the conditions under which one made one's observations and developed one's concepts, one easily falls prey to the tendency to

> ...hypostasize concepts one created oneself, to ascribe to them a reality outside of one's consciousness. (...) Even scientists like Newton were, despite their fundamental principles, not always sufficiently careful. (...) Newton's conception of "absolute time" and of "absolute space" etc., arose in a fully analogous fashion.[69]

For Mach, the dissolution of hypostasized concepts is an indispensable prerequisite for furthering knowledge. In his *Mechanics*, which first appeared in 1883, Mach subjects Newton's concept of absolute motion to a critique that was to be one of Mach's greatest scientific achievements. In the 1908 edition, he remarks that many physicists had come to share his view "that 'absolute motion' is a senseless concept with no content and no scientific utility." The point, Mach adds, is not only to accept this critical insight but to use it to "give the law of inertia an understandable sense." Mach sees two ways of doing this:

> (1) The historical-critical way, which involves taking a fresh look at the facts upon which the law of inertia rests and considering the limits of its validity and perhaps also a new formulation of it. (2) To assume that the law of inertia in its old form acquaints us sufficiently with motions and to derive the right coordinate system *from* these motions. The presentation I give here is an example of the first method. It also contains an indication of modifications of expression which it now becomes necessary to introduce by expanding experience. Surely, the second way is psychologically more appealing in view of the trust that mechanics enjoys as the most exact natural science. In fact this way has often been pursued with more or less success, and I myself tried to do so before I came to believe it necessary to prefer the other way.[70]

These remarks contain a key, I think, first, to Neurath's understanding of the "free point of view" which theoretical economics is to attain, and secondly, to the question posed earlier, namely how Schumpeter and Neurath came to such divergent interpretations of Mach's epistemology.

Let us first take a look at a few motifs in Schumpeter's and Neurath's writings – without any pretension of completeness – that reveal common ground in their understanding of Mach. Both start out with a critique of the fundamental concepts of the

---

[68] Mach (1905, p. 10): "All such 'mistakes' result from ignorance of the conditions under which a finding was obtained, or from neglecting them, or from presupposing *other* conditions than the actual ones."

[69] Mach 1918 (1981), p. 51.

[70] Mach 1883 (1908), p. 257. In the 1912 edition, Mach abbreviated this passage and named Newton himself as an example of the "first way."

social sciences. They were both convinced that the contemporary debates about method in the social sciences had been driven to a dead end by abstract concepts created by social scientists – e.g. by the concept-pairs "individual and society," "egoism and altruism," "laws of nature and free will" and "economic and non-economic motives."[71] Schumpeter does not think that any of the problems expressed in these concepts and in the corresponding dichotomies will ever admit of clear and precise resolutions: "they belong partially to the realm of metaphysics, of course, and this alone makes true exactness impossible. Like thick fog, then, the unclearness blocks our way and prevents us from attaining a free point of view."[72] Beyond this, Schumpeter and Neurath also agree in drawing social scientists' attention to the fact that there is no need for a scientific endeavor to begin by defining the essence of its object of inquiry.[73] Against this backdrop, both also considered the stark opposition of "historians" and "theorists" to be exaggerated and misleading,[74] and to belie the essential continuity of scientific research – also a central motif in Mach's thought. Moreover, both hoped that conceptual and methodological reflection on the natural sciences would lead them out of the dead end.[75] The most important guiding idea in this respect came from Mach, who took a scientific explanation to be nothing other than a description of the connection of elements among each other. Accordingly, economic explanations consist for Schumpeter as well as for Neurath in the description of functional relations of dependence between elements.[76]

But as close as Schumpeter and Neurath draw to one another in diagnosing senseless concepts with neither content nor utility and in seeking ways of avoiding them, they part company abruptly when it comes to the question of how to give the general claims of macroeconomics, as Mach puts it, an "understandable sense." Schumpeter makes a plea for determining the meaning of general statements on the basis of results that have already been attained in economic research, particularly in monetary theory. With respect to these results, the question to be addressed is, as Schumpeter puts it:

> how we come to attain them with the least possible burden of presuppositions and general claims… In other words, we investigate what services each of the presuppositions and general claims renders our theory and whether these services could be rendered in a different, more innocuous way. Or, to put it in yet another way, we investigate *what economists*

---

[71] Uebel (2004) shows that the conceptual tools Neurath developed "represent the skeleton of a thoroughly de-psychologized theory of goods transfers." (33p.) Indirectly referring to Schumpeter, Neurath acknowledged "that even pure price theory can do away with motivations, but has rarely done sofar."(Neurath 1910a (2004) p. 278)

[72] Schumpeter (1908) 1998, p. 23.

[73] Schumpeter (1908) 1998, p. 32, Neurath (1911b) GS 4, p. 503.

[74] But in a different passage, Schumpeter clearly forced this opposition quite strongly. See Streissler (1990, 40p).

[75] Neurath in fact explicitly emphasizes this commonality with Schumpeter 1910a (2004), p. 288 (footnote 9).

[76] The "method of variation," which both employ in a quite different way though, is also a Machian legacy.

want to achieve with them, what they actually do when they formulate general claims of such a nature.[77]

Schumpeter is arguing here in an entirely Machian vein. Mach understood his epistemology as nothing other than the attempt of a natural scientist to achieve clarity with respect to his own activity – on the one hand in the sense of an empirical theory of epistemic processes, on the other hand in the sense of a logical clarification of general concepts. The principle of economy of thought, which was to guide Mach's critical studies of concepts, returns in Schumpeter's thought: the latter asks how to attain concrete results in pure economics with the "least possible burden of presuppositions and generic claims." Neurath, for his part, also takes his point of departure from Mach's "principle of economy" in elaborating his theory of wealth: it is a matter of "establishing how far one can get with a minimum of presuppositions."[78] But Neurath did not think that theoretical economics as developed up to that time "acquainted us sufficiently"[79] with the motions economists describe in order to derive the right coordinate system *from* them. Schumpeter, on the other hand, appears to have thought exactly that. The theory of balance – which is the core of his statics – is intended to be a sort of "right coordinate system" that can be attained from the description of "certain relations of dependency or functional relations."[80] What he has in mind is a closed system with universal validity, for which, according to Schumpeter, a direct empirical equivalent is immediately available: "the price, or, rather, the *exchange relation*. Practically all goods stand in this relation to each other."[81]

Neurath's approach, on the other hand, can be much better understood along the lines of Mach's "historical-critical way." Neurath was trying, as Mach put it, to "take a fresh look" at the "facts" which economists' theories refer to. By appealing to Aristotle and classical economists such as Smith and Ricardo, his aim was to recall the fact that economists at bottom are concerned with differential effects upon the well-being (pleasure and pain) of individuals and groups.[82] Analogously to Mach, Neurath deemed it necessary to consider a new formulation of the central propositions of theoretical economics in order to "expand the experience" which theoretical economics takes into account. This is precisely what he intended to achieve with the formulation "changes in wealth" (*Reichtumsveränderungen*) by means of which it would be possible to comprehend a much broader range of conditions that make people richer and poorer than price theory could.

"In principal, we do not limit ourselves to conditions of any kind. Cases can be taken into consideration in which different individuals are subjected to different

[77] Schumpeter (1908) 1998, p. 25.

[78] Neurath (1911b) GS 4, p. 474.

[79] See the Mach-quotation (footnote 71).

[80] Schumpeter (1908) 1998, p. 33

[81] Ibid. p. 49.

[82] Sen's demand that economists consider the way in which people lead their lives (Leßman in this volume) can be interpreted as an attempt to take a fresh look at the facts. Moreover, Sen brought out the "historical-critical" side of this undertaking quite clearly (Sen 1987, 16p., 20pp.).

rules, as well as to cases in which different rules are applied at different times. In short, anything that causes changes in distribution of wealth can be the object of inquiry of theoretical economics."[83]

Exchange relations would of course have a place within the framework of the theory of wealth, appearing as a particular type of changes in wealth, the effects of which would be systematically compared with the effects of other such types (e.g. gifts, theft, war, and various political strategies and changes of ecological conditions…)[84] Only by starting out from an expanded pool of experiences will economists come to realize how narrow the limits are within which heuristic constructions such as the *homo oeconomicus* are justifiable.

> Abstraction in theoretical economics can take cases into consideration in which all kinds of tendencies, errors, etc. cause changes in wealth, and can then endeavor to establish what effects on wealth are thereby brought about. *In doing so, it can disregard the concrete tendencies, the concrete errors;* it speaks of tendencies toward a, b, c; speaks of the error of taking a to be more valuable than b although it produces less pleasure. This kind of abstraction is suitable for yielding a schema of reality, not so the kind that produces *the homo oeconomicus* as the only economic abstraction, which is in our view a special case that is not very frequently applicable even under an improved interpretation.[85]

As I emphasized above, Schumpeter's balance schema, which was to comprehend the functional relations between distributions of goods at a given point in time, was also directed against the abuse of heuristic concepts like that of the *homo oeconomicus* and stands directly in the Machian tradition.[86] But for Schumpeter, this schema arose through an investigation of the epistemological presuppositions of the economic theories delivering *exact results*. It is "the arsenal of our exact results," according to Schumpeter, that "points out the right way."[87] Let us recall that exactitude also plays a role in Mach's presentation of the two ways in which we can make sense of the law of inertia. Since mechanics enjoys such great trust "as the most exact natural science," the assumption "that the law of inertia in its old form acquaints us adequately with motions" is psychologically the most appealing. It is important not to lose sight of the fact that this assumption is in Mach's view by no means disqualified. Mach regards our great trust in exact results as not only

[83] Neurath (1911b) GS 4, S. 482.

[84] It is true that Neurath – in contrast to Sen – is "skeptical of the effectiveness of the market" (Leßmann in this volume). However, Neurath explicitly admits that under specific circumstances a market economy may turn out to be more efficient than a planned economy: (1917a) 2004, 244p. And Sen, on the other hand, admits that a planned economy may produce better effects on functioning's and capabilities than a market economy, though only in particular respects (see the comparison between India and China in terms of the enhancement of the living standard (Sen 1987, 34pp.).

[85] Neurath (1911b) GS 4, p. 479. On Neurath's critique of the *homo oeconomicus* from a Machian perspective see also Nemeth (1999a).

[86] Schumpeter also places value on not building his theory upon agents' tendencies and motives: Schumpeter (1908) 1998, p. 541.

[87] Schumpeter (1908) 1998, p. 24.

an *explanation* of our readiness to accept the law of inertia in its old form but also as a *justification* for doing so. For Mach, all our concepts – including scientific ones – are above all instruments that serve practical purposes, and the exactitude of these instruments is eminently important. But Mach does not think that science serves *only* practical ends.

> Mature scientific thought creates its own goals, seeks to satisfy itself, to dispose of all *intellectual* discomfiture. Having matured in the service of practical goals, it becomes its own master. Vulgar thought does not serve purely epistemic ends, and therefore suffers from particular shortcomings that also plague the scientific thought that arises out of it. The latter frees itself from these shortcomings only quite gradually.[88]

When Neurath claims that Schumpeter has failed "to attain a free point of view," it sounds initially quite foreign. "Pure economics," of all things, has supposedly not distanced itself sufficiently from an assessment of purely empirical data? – I think that a look at Mach can help us to see more clearly what is at issue in Neurath's critique. In fact, it is in Neurath's view exactly the process of freeing economics from the practical aims in the service of which it matured that is insufficiently developed in Schumpeter's approach. Presumably, Schumpeter would not even have resisted this assessment. He saw the continuity of his theory with everyday economic thinking as an advantage[89] – and, indeed, could also appeal in this respect to Mach. To the Mach, that is, who regarded science as part of an evolutionary process in which human nature and history advance.

But there is also a Mach who saw in scientific thinking a force that frees itself from the practical aims that compel our thought in the direction imposed by existing natural and cultural developmental processes. This intellectual liberation, of course, does not lead us to a point of view outside of history but to what Mach calls "artificial naiveté." One does not start out in science with this artificial naiveté, rather, every scientist "stands in the middle of a developmental process and has to begin with the incomplete knowledge gained from predecessors…"[90] If one wants to go about completing and correcting this knowledge, one ought to bear in mind that it was easier

> to establish first provisionally and roughly the mutual dependency of whole complexes of elements (of bodies). In this process, it was chance, practical needs, and earlier findings that determined *which* elements appeared most important and to which attention was therefore drawn, and *which* elements remained neglected.[91]

So if we want to approach more closely the ideal that Mach proposes – namely, directly to describe "the multifarious and ubiquitous relations of dependency obtaining between the elements"[92] – then we must look not only forward but also

---

[88] Mach (1905), p .2.

[89] Schumpeter (1908) 1998, p. 580.

[90] Mach (1905), p. 16.

[91] Ibid.

[92] Ibid. p. 15.

backward. At any given time, one can observe that previous research contains one-sided construals and errors that cannot be uncovered without reconstructing the way in which particular complexes came to be considered relevant and worthy of further study. Hence, we have to dissolve the complexes into elements "beyond which we for the time being cannot progress,"[93] in order to attain a point of view that in a certain sense lies *prior* to those "complexes" which for historical and cultural reasons formed our starting point. Of course, this is not to say that we will ever achieve a "perfectly naive point of view."

> Thus, if we seem today to return to a *primitive* point of view in order to guide the discussion to newer and better pathways, then this is an *artificial* naiveté. It does not give up the advantages won during the course of a long cultural trajectory but, rather, applies insights that presuppose a very high level of physical, physiological and psychological thinking. Only at such a level is a dissolution into 'elements' conceivable. It is a matter of returning to the *starting points* of research with the deepened and enriched insights gained by the intervening research.[94]

It is precisely this sort of striving for artificial naiveté, proposed by Mach as a means of renewing the natural sciences, that Neurath brings to bear upon social science. Surely he was aware of the risk one thereby runs: "returning" to an apparently primitive point of view is also a return to formulations that, in comparison to the exactitude of contemporary theories, are bound to seem a bit vague.[95] Such a step may well seem implausible and unappealing to those who see successive progress in the shift from one scientific theory to the next – and it is often renowned and successful researchers who think this way. After all, this "step backward" always betrays a belief that there is a theoretical reserve beyond the explanations that appear at any given moment to be the most advanced, and constitutes an effort "to take a further possibility into serious consideration."[96] It does not necessarily amount to challenging hard-won scientific findings (both Mach and Neurath believed that descriptions of functional relations of dependency retain their value even in new theories), but it does express the conviction that the path we are on is not the only possible one.

5 Closing Remarks

Why concern oneself with Neurath's economic theory in its historical context?

The conceptual and methodological considerations that Neurath introduced into discussions of the foundations of the social sciences were not developed significantly further after the First World War. At the outset, I offered some general reasons why the

---

[93] Ibid. p. 12.

[94] Ibid. p. 16.

[95] Leßmann (in this volume) sees in the deliberately vague formulations of Neurath and Sen a further commonality.

[96] Neurath (1911b), GS 4, see footnote 61.

reconstruction of Neurath's project – which emerged during the decade before the "short twentieth century" – could be of interest to philosophy and economics. The contributions to this volume respond to this issue by presenting a variety of highly interesting facets of Neurath's economic and sociological thought.

By embedding Neurath's approach within the context of Schumpeter's and Neurath's differing receptions of Mach, I have tried to show that the orientation of economic thought toward the natural sciences – which both Schumpeter and Neurath draw from Ernst Mach – can lead to very different results. I believe that a more precise reconstruction of these two conceptions can yield insights into Neurath's economic and philosophical views – for example into his understanding of "physicalism." Beyond this, the different ways in which Neurath and Schumpeter exploit Mach's scientific and epistemological insights demonstrate that these insights offer an unexpected wealth of impulses for research today. Philosophy and history of science, having been established as independent disciplines in the twentieth century, appear to be struggling now, at the beginning of twenty-first century, to complement one another in a mutually productive way – not to mention the sciences they investigate, for which they rarely play a greater role than to provide charming words for the occasional public speech. In the person of Ernst Mach – one of the major figures that shaped the intellectual situation at the close of the "long nineteenth century" in Europe – scientific practice, philosophical reflection and historical reconstruction of scientific practice were combined in a way that has generally been underappreciated and misrepresented by generations of more specialized scholars. Perhaps the time is ripe to take a step back and reconstruct a discursive situation that can shed light on how the relationship between science, the history of science and the philosophy of science came to the impasse at which we find it today. We may find that Neurath's work has retained its freshness precisely because of the Machian conception of science that its author – stubborn as he was – never ceased to defend as a guiding principle of logical empiricism.

Translated from the German by John Michael. Thanks to Thomas Uebel for helpful advice.

References

Amann, Anton, 1996: Theories of life conditions since Otto Neurath – some fragments, in: Nemeth and Stadler (eds.), pp. 215–220

Blackmore, John, 2001, R. Itagaki, S. Tanaka (eds.): *Ernst Mach's Vienna 1895–1930. Or Phenomenalism as Philosophy of Science*, BSPS Vol. 218, Dordrecht: Kluwer

Bourdieu, Pierre, 1975: The specificity of the scientific field and the social conditions of the progress of reason, in: *Social Science Information* 14(6), pp. 19–47

Cartwright, Nancy, Jordi Cat, Lola Fleck, Thomas E. Uebel, 1996: *Otto Neurath: Philosophy between Science and Politics*, Cambridge: Cambridge University Press

Chaloupek, Günther K., 1990: The Austrian debate on economic calculation in a socialist economy, in: *History of Political Economy* 22, pp. 659–675

Hayek, Friedrich von, 1966: Diskussionbemerkungen über Ernst Mach und das sozialwissenschaftliche Denken in Wien, Symposium aus Anlass des 50.Todesjahres von Ernst Mach,

Freiburg im Breisgau trans. as: Ernst Mach and Vienna Social Science, in: Blackmore et al. (eds.), 2001, 123p.
Lennox, James, 2001: Conference: Pitt-London Workshop in the Philosophy of Biology and Neuroscience, September 2001, http://philsci-archive.pitt.edu/archive/00000378/
Leßmann, Ortrud, 2007: *Konzeption und Erfassung von Armut. Vergleich des Lebenslage-Ansatzes mit Sens "Capability"-Ansatz. Volkswirtschaftliche Schriften* Heft 552, Berlin: Duncker & Humblot
Mach, Ernst (1883), 1908: *Die Mechanik in ihrer Entwickelung historisch-kritisch dargestellt*, Leipzig: Brockhaus
Mach, Ernst, 1905: *Erkenntnis und Irrtum*, Leipzig: Barth
Mach, Ernst, 1918 (1981): *Die Prinzipien der Wärmelehre, historisch-kritisch entwickelt*, Frankfurt/Main: Minerva
Mandelbaum, Kurt und Gerhard Meyer, 1934: Zur Theorie der Planwirtschaft, in: *Zeitschrift für Sozialforschung*, Paris, Jahrgang III, S. 228–262
Martinez-Alier, Joan, 1987: *Ecological Economics*, Oxford: Blackwell
Meyer, Gerhard, 1932: Neuere Literatur über Planwirtschaft, in: *Zeitschrift für Sozialforschung*, Jahrgang I, Paris
Mormann, Thomas, 1999: Neuraths anticartesische Konzeption von Sprache und Wissenschaft, in: Nemeth und Heinrich (eds.) pp. 32–61
Nemeth, Elisabeth, 1981: *Otto Neurath und der Wiener Kreis. Revolutionäre Wissenschaftlichkeit als politischer Anspruch*, Frankfurt am Main, New York
Nemeth, Elisabeth, 1982: Otto Neuraths Utopien. Der Wille zur Hoffnung, in: Stadler 1982 (Hg.), S. 94–99, Engl. trans. by T.E. Uebel in Uebel, 1991, pp. 285–292
Nemeth, Elisabeth, 1994: Empiricism and the norms of scientific knowledge: some reflections on Otto Neurath and Pierre Bourdieu, in: Pauer-Studer, Herlinde (ed.): *Norms, Values, and Society*, Vienna Circle Yearbook 2, Dordrecht/Boston/London: Kluwer
Nemeth, Elisabeth, 1996: Otto Neuraths vision of science, in: Nemeth and Stadler (eds.), pp. 7–14
Nemeth, Elisabeth, 1999a: Auf dem Weg zur Wiedergewinnung eines wissenschaftlichen Gegenstands, in: Nemeth and Heinrich (eds.), pp. 146–166
Nemeth, Elisabeth, 1999b: *Denken in Beziehungen. Beiträge zur Ortsbestimmung der Erkenntnisphilosophie*, Habilitationsschrift, Wien 1999
Nemeth, Elisabeth, 2003: Gesellschaftliche Tatbestände sichtbar machen. Otto Neurath über den Gegenstand der Wirtschaftswissenschaft und seine Visualisierung, in: *Philosophie an der Schwelle des 21.Jahrhunderts*, hg. von Ewa Czerwinska-Schupp, Bd. 4 von Dia-Logos, Frankfurt/Main: Peter Lang, pp. 181–207
Nemeth, Elisabeth, 2006: Socially enlightened science. Neurath on social science and visual education, in: Mélika Ouelbani (réd.): *Thèmes de Philosophie Analytique*. Université de Tunis, Tunis, pp. 83–112
Nemeth, Elisabeth, and Friedrich Stadler (eds.) 1996: *Encyclopedia and Utopia. The Life and Work of Otto Neurath (1882–1945)*, Vienna Circle Yearbook 4. Dordrecht: Kluwer
Nemeth, Elisabeth, and Nicolas Roudet (eds.) 2005: *Paris-Wien. Enzyklopädien im Vergleich.* Wien-New York: Springer
Nemeth, Elisabeth, and Richard Heinrich (eds.) 1999: *Otto Neurath: Rationalität, Planung, Vielfalt.* Wien Berlin: Oldenbourg
Neurath, Otto, 1909 (2004): Diskussionsbeitrag über die Produktivität des Geldes, trans. as Remarks on the productivity of money, in: Neurath 2004, pp. 292–296
Neurath, Otto, 1910/11a: Kurantes Girogeld, in: *Der österreichische Volkswirt,* in: GS 5, S. 427–432
Neurath, Otto, 1910/11b: Die Unbeliebtheit des Metallgeldes in Österreich, in: *Der österreichische Volkswirt*, in: GS 5, S. 433–434
Neurath, Otto, 1910a (2004): Zur Theorie der Sozialwissenschaften, trans. as On the theory of social science, in: Neurath 2004, pp. 265–291
Neurath, Otto, 1910b: *Lehrbuch der Volkswirtschaftslehre*, GS 4, pp. 239–396
Neurath, Otto, 1911a: Jahresbilanz und Wochenausweis der Österreichisch-Ungarischen Bank, in: *Zeitschrift für die gesamte Staatswissenschaft*, in: GS 4, S. 435–469

Neurath, Otto, 1911b: Nationalökonomie und Wertlehre, eine systematische Untersuchung, in: *Zeitschrift für Volkswirtschaft, Sozialpolitik und Verwaltung*, Bd.20, in: GS 4, S. 470–518
Neurath, Otto, 1911c: Zur Frage der Preisdifferenzierung, *Zeitschrift für Handelswissenschaft und Handelspraxis*, 4.Jg.,H.5, in: GS 4, S. 533–543
Neurath, Otto, 1912a: Das Problem des Lustmaximums, trans. as The problem of the pleasure maximum, in: Neurath 1973, pp. 113–122
Neurath, Otto, 1912b: Sonderrabatte und Reingewinn, in: *Zeitschrift für Handelswissenschaft und Handelspraxis*, 5.Jg., H.1, in: GS 4, S. 544–547
Neurath, Otto, 1913b (2004): Über die Stellung des sittlichen Werturteils in der wissenschaftlichen Nationalökonomie, trans. as On the role of moral value judgements in economic science, in: Neurath 2004, pp. 297–298
Neurath, Otto, 1915 (1973): Prinzipielles zur Geschichte der Optik. *Archiv für Geschichte der Naturwissenschaften und der Technik*, trans. as On the foundations of the history of physics, in: Neurath 1973, pp. 101–112
Neurath, Otto, 1917a (2004): Die Wirtschaftsordnung der Zukunft und die Wirtschaftswissenscha ften, trans. as The economic order of the future and the economic sciences, in: Neurath 2004, pp. 241–261
Neurath, Otto, 1917b (2004): Das Begriffsgebäude der Wirtschaftslehre und seine Grundlagen, trans. as The conceptual structure of economic theory and its foundations, in: Neurath 2004, pp. 312–341
Neurath, Otto, 1919 (1973): *Durch die Kriegswirtschaft zur Naturalwirtschaft*, München: Callwey, partly trans. as Through war economy to economy in kind, in: Neurath 1973, pp. 123–157
Neurath, Otto, 1921: Von der Gildenfront, in: *Der Kampf. Sozialdemokratische Monatsschrift*, Bd.14, S. 416–420
Neurath, Otto, 1922a: Reichsgilden, in: *Der Kampf*, Bd. 15, S. 330–337
Neurath, Otto, 1922b: *Gildensozialismus, Klassenkampf, Vollsozialisierung*, Dresden: Kaden
Neurath, Otto, 1925: *Wirtschaftsplan und Naturalrechnung. Von der sozialistischen Lebensordnung und vom kommenden Menschen*, Berlin: Laub
Neurath, Otto, 1935 (1987): *Was bedeutet rationale Wirtschaftsbetrachtung?* Wien: Gerold, trans. as What is meant by rational economic theory? in B. McGuinness (ed.): *Unified Science*, Dordrecht: Kluwer 1987, pp. 67–109
Neurath, Otto, 1973: *Empiricism and Sociology*, ed. by Marie Neurath and Robert S. Cohen, Dordrecht: Reidel
Neurath, Otto, 1981: *Gesammelte philosophische und methodologische Schriften*, hg. von Rudolf Haller und Heiner Rutte, Wien: Hölder-Pichler-Tempsky (GS 1, GS 2)
Neurath, Otto, 1983: *Philosophical Papers 1913–1946*, ed. by Robert S. Cohen and Marie. Neurath, Dordrecht: Reidel
Neurath, Otto, 1991: *Gesammelte bildpädagogische Schriften*, hg. von Rudolf Haller und Robert Kinross, Wien: Hölder-Pichler-Tempsky (GS 3)
Neurath, Otto, 1994: *Otto Neurath oder Die Einheit von Wissenschaft und Gesellschaft*, hg.von Paul Neurath und Elisabeth Nemeth, Wien-Köln-Weimar: Böhlau
Neurath, Otto, 1998: *Gesammelte ökonomische, soziologische und sozialpolitische Schriften*, hg. Von Rudolf Haller und Ulf Höfer, Wien: Hölder-Pichler-Tempsky (= GS 4, GS 5)
Neurath, Otto, 2004: *Economic Writings. Selections 1904–1945*, ed. by T. E Uebel and R S. Cohen. trans. by R.S. Cohen. Marie Neurath, C. Schmidt-Petri and Thomas E. Uebel. Dordrecht: Kluwer
Neurath, Paul, 1994: Otto Neurath (1882–1945). Leben und Werk, in: Otto Neurath, 1994, S. 13–96
Nielsen, Camilla, and Thomas E. Uebel, 1999: Zwei Utopisten in einer gescheiterten Revolution. Otto Neurath und Gustav Landauer im Vergleich, in: Nemeth and Heinrich (eds.), S. 96–122
Novy, Klaus, 1983: Selbsthilfe als Reformbewegung. Der Kampf der Wiener Siedler nach dem 1. Weltkrieg, in: *Genossenschafts-Bewegung. Zur Geschichte und Zukunft der Wohnreform*. Berlin: Transit, S. 22–58
O'Neill, John, 1998: *The Market. Ethics, knowledge and politics*. Routledge, London

O'Neill, John, 1999: Socialism, ecology and Austrian economics, in: Nemeth and Heinrich (eds.), pp. 123–145
Sandner, Günther, 2006: *Engagierte Wissenschaft. Austromarxistische Kulturstudien und die Anfänge der britischen Cultural Studies*. Münster, Hamburg, Berlin, Vienna, London: Lit Verlag
Schumpeter, Joseph A., (1908) 1998: *Das Wesen und der Hauptinhalt der theoretischen Nationalökonomie*, Berlin: Duncker & Humboldt
Sen, Amartya, 1987: *The Standard of Living. The Tanner Lectures* 1985, Cambridge: Cambridge University Press
Stadler, Friedrich (ed.), 1982: *Arbeiterbildung in der Zwischenkriegszeit. Ausstellungskatalog mit Forschungsteil*, Wien-München: Löcker
Stadler, Friedrich, 2001: *The Vienna Circle – Studies in the Origins, Development, and Influence of Logical Empiricism*. Wien-New York: Springer
Stöltzner, Michael, 2001: "Otto Neurath 1913-1915", in: Blackmore J. et al. (eds.), 105–111
Streissler, Erich W., 1990: The influence of German economics on the work of Menger and Marshall, in: *Carl Menger and his legacy in economics*, Annual supplement to volume 22, *History of political economy*, ed. by B.J. Caldwell, Durham and London: Duke University Press
Swedberg, Richard, 1991: *Joseph A. Schumpeter. His Life and Work*, Cambridge: Polity Press, dt. Übersetzung von J.G.Pankau als Joseph A. Schumpeter. Eine Biographie. Stuttgart: Cotta 1994
Uebel, Thomas E., 1991: *Rediscovering the Forgotten Vienna Circle. Austrian Studies on Otto Neurath and the Vienna Circle*. Dordrecht: Kluwer
Uebel, Thomas E., 2004: Introduction: Neurath's economics in critical context, in: Neurath 2004, pp. 1–108
Uebel, Thomas E., 2005a: Incommensurability, ecology and planning: Neurath in the socialist calculation debate, 1919–1928, in: *History of Political Economy*, 37(2), 309–342
Uebel, Thomas E., 2005b: Social science in the framework of Neurath's physicalist encyclopedia: some anti-reductionist concerns allayed, in: Nemeth/Roudet (eds.), pp. 221–240

Department of Philosophy
University of Vienna
A-1030 Vienna
Universitaetsstrasse 7
elisabeth.nemeth@univie.ac.at

Otto Neurath as an Austrian Economist: Behind the Scenes of the Early Socialist Calculation Debate

Thomas E. Uebel

Otto Neurath is well known as a founding member of the Vienna Circle, one of several points of origin of logical empiricism or neopositivism.[1] While Neurath's distinctive contribution to the philosophy of science and epistemology in general has come to be recognised after long neglect, his economic thought remains relatively unexplored. A striking fact has thus remained long obscured: Neurath is not the "positivist" economist one might expect. To throw this point into further relief, the question I want to explore here is whether and to what extent, if any, it makes sense to look at Neurath as an "Austrian" economist. Aware of the danger of treading a thin line between blatant absurdity and Pickwickian banality, my hope is that this way of proceeding will unlock some of the still topical originality of Neurath's economics.

What would seem to render my leading thought absurd is, of course, the acrimonious debate between Ludwig von Mises and Neurath (and later, mostly unpublished, that between Neurath and Friedrich August von Hayek).[2] This early phase of the socialist calculation debate pitched Neurath very much against third-generation representatives of the so-called Austrian School of Theoretical Economics. And what seems to render my leading thought Pickwickian is the unspectacular fact that Neurath was of Austrian nationality. It is true, of course, that he was a self-consciously "Austrian philosopher", but that does not make him an Austrian economist in the relevant sense.[3] Yet when we delve into the depths of the debate with Mises, things begin to look quite different.

Concerning Neurath's stance in that debate, interpreters are also faced with a puzzle. While Neurath possessed all along what I think is an excellent if long-neglected argument against Mises' claim that in the absence of a market there cannot be economic rationality, that argument does not establish what Neurath

[1] See Stadler (1997) for a reliable account of the Vienna Circle as a whole with bibliographies of primary sources.

[2] Here my concern is mostly with the first debate; for a discussion of Neurath's debate with Hayek, see O'Neill (2004, 2006).

[3] On Neurath's adoption of the idea of a distinct Austrian tradition in philosophy, see Haller (1986) and Uebel (2003).

E. Nemeth et al. (eds.), *Otto Neurath's Economics in Context.*
Vienna Circle Institute Yearbook [2007]. Volume 13.

seems to have claimed for it. Two questions arise here. First, how to explain Neurath's apparent lapse of judgement; second, how to explain the remarkable fact that both the successful argument and the apparently problematic extrapolation from it are present in his work already before he was confronted by Mises' challenge? Both questions remain pretty much unanswerable unless Neurath's Austrian context is taken account of.

1 An Interpretive Puzzle and Some Distinctions

To lead us into the conceptual territory at issue consider Neurath's central notions of economy in kind (*Naturalwirtschaft*) and calculation in kind (*Naturalrechnung*). While often appearing to be more or less cognate notions they can and should be separated. And even though he did distinguish these notions elsewhere – "economy in kind" pertained to a certain type of social institution and "calculation in kind" pertained to a certain type of decision procedure for economic problems – Neurath can also be found to be mixing them up. Consider:

> If no longer sums of money, but things themselves are taken as the basis for our decisions, then we cannot speak of monetary economy but only of economy in kind (1920b [2004, p. 383]).

Note the multiple ambiguity here. Does Neurath claim that (a) an economy in kind exists whenever there are sectors where, as a matter of fact, criteria other than monetary profitability are used for planning decisions? Or does he claim (b) that an economy in kind exists whenever there are sectors where the market cannot work and where therefore non-monetary criteria are used for planning decisions? Or does he claim that (c) that an economy in kind exists only where an economy operates without a market altogether?

Clearly, in the period of his advocacy of total socialisation, 1919–1925, it was (c) that Neurath argued for. In later writings, however, since about 1935, it is primarily calculation in kind that Neurath argued for. Calculation in kind, of course, can find employment not only in marketless economies, but also selectively in separate sectors of an economy, as in (b) and (a). It follows that an argument for calculation in kind does not yet in itself establish the claim for total socialisation. Claim (c) expresses the ideal of marketless socialism, whereas claim (b) merely opposes its opposite, the ambitions of market fundamentalism (the idea that the market can solve all social coordination problems) and claim (a) even more minimally states the availability of an alternative to profit calculation in selected sectors of an economy.

Neurath's critics allege, of course, that he did not have a good argument for (c), nor for (b). In complex economies, rational decisions concerning production goods can only be effected on the basis of monetary cost-benefit calculations. According to these critics, Neurath had a point with claim (a), but he illegitimately extended its reach to (b) and even further to (c). From this perspective, Neurath's apparent shift from arguing for an economy in the sense of (c) to one in the sense of (b) still missed the point. Now I do not think that these critics are correct. Building on the work of Juan Martinez-Alier and John O'Neill, one can show that Neurath all along was in possession of a good argument for (b) – as I will in the next section.[4]

But even on this reading we are still left with a puzzle: what about Neurath's advocacy of an economy in the sense of (c), namely, marketless socialism? For even if we were to grant Neurath his argument for (b), it seems he did take it to be an argument for (c). Neurath appears to have fallen victim to a modal confusion, mistaking an argument for the indispensability of in-kind calculation and the insufficiency of monetary calculation in certain cases for an argument for the non-necessity of monetary calculation altogether. Against this unprepossessing appearance I shall argue that we must distinguish different stands of argumentation in Neurath. While it does appear that Neurath was in the process of shifting the emphasis of his argumentation by 1935 from one for marketless socialism to one against market fundamentalism, he did not simply overcome an old confusion. Rather, throughout he responded to changing dialectical situations. Here my concern is to show that, at least in part, he responded to changing argumentative positions held by Austrian economists. To put things most sharply, Neurath's arguments for marketless socialism proceeded from a platform which he partially shared with the Austrian economists, just as his argument against market fundamentalism was by no means voiced in opposition to all of the members of the Austrian school.

To facilitate our argument, let us replace the cryptic talk of claim (a), (b) and (c) by talk of assumptions of different strength concerning the notion of calculability in kind. Let us call the idea that the rational employment of production goods can be ensured entirely by in-kind considerations, the "*strong in-kind calculability assumption*". (This assumption corresponds to claim (c).) This is to be distinguished from the "*weak in-kind calculability assumption*", the idea that monetary calculation is not sufficient in all cases for rational economic decisions. (This assumption corresponds to claim (b).) Lastly, we can also distinguish the "*very weak in-kind calculability assumption*", which says merely that there are some cases where in-kind calculation can ensure the rational disposition of production goods but leaves it open whether these cases could also have been dealt with by monetary calculation. (This assumption corresponds to claim (a).) So whereas the strong in-kind calculability assumption says that alternative uses of production goods can be assessed as fully as is required for rational decision making by quantitative in-kind labour and production technology statistics – money calculation is not even necessary – the weak in-kind calculability assumption only claims the insufficiency of monetary calculation for all cases (and the very weak in-kind calculability assumption – which I will neglect here – claims even less).

As is evident from his address to the Munich Workers' Council in January 1919, Neurath held to both, the strong and the weak in-kind calculability assumption, as shown by his call for marketless socialism and his references to the provision of

[4] See Martinez-Alier (1987), O'Neill (1993, 1998) and Uebel (2005).

health and educational services, respectively.[5] Equally clearly, supporting the idea of marketless socialism requires making the strong in-kind calculability assumption, whereas an argument against market fundamentalism only requires the weak in-kind calculability assumption to be made. With these distinctions in mind, let us now reconsider Neurath's stance in the socialist calculation debate with Mises. What we must ask is how Neurath supported these different assumptions and what he took the arguments to prove in which he relied on these assumptions.

2 Neurath and Mises in the Socialist Calculation Debate, 1920–1928

What was wholly distinctive of Neurath's stance in the socialist calculation debate was his opposition not just to calculation in units of money or specific goods or services, but any universally applicable units of a means of measurement. His idea of calculation in kind was not met by substituting for money some other commensurating unit, whether it be socially necessary labour time or even more obviously physical measurements. This point lies at the heart of Neurath's call for a marketless socialism and it was this that prompted Mises' response in the socialist calculation debate.

Given the prominent rise of various conceptions of market socialism in that debate soon after, this point also remained the most radical one of Neurath's programme, for it also speaks against the idea that markets could be partially retained (say for consumer goods) or their action be simulated (to fix factor-pricing for production).[6] What distinguished Neurath's position, in other words, was not just the view that socialism would bring a moneyless economy. That was standard amongst socialists, but typically was accompanied by the idea that the commensurating role of money could be filled by labour time units so as to calculate the cost and benefit of production and regulate its distribution. Precisely this had been proposed already shortly after the turn of the century by Karl Kautsky's in his *On*

---

[5] "In a large-scale economy in kind, in a socialised economy, money no longer is a driving force. No longer is there a 'net profit' for which production occurs. Money could remain at best as a token for a claim on all sorts of goods and services which the individual consumer is given to enable him to arrange his consumption.... The greater or lesser economic efficiency of a system of measures can be ascertained only be comparing total plans.... There are no units that can be used as the basis of such a decision, neither units of money nor hours of work. One must directly judge the desirability of the two possibilities. To many it seems impossible to proceed in this manner, and yet it is only in this field that we are not used to it. For even in the past one has not started from units of teaching or sickness in order to decide whether new schools or hospitals should be built; rather one directly set over against one another, even if only at general outlines, the totality of changes caused by schools and those caused by hospitals" Neurath (1919 [1973, pp. 145–146]).

[6] For a discussion of the debates in Austria, see Chaloupek (1990), for the later international debates, see Lavoie (1985) or Vaughn (1994).

the Morrow of the Revolution (1902). Neurath's schemes for "total socialisation" from the start argued against both liberalism and socialist alternatives to marketless socialism (and so required argumentative support for the strong in-kind calculability assumption).

Importantly, Mises agreed with Neurath that a properly socialist economy would have to be marketless, but he disagreed with him in declaring this to preclude rational economic calculation altogether. His celebrated counterargument drew attention to the distinction between lower- and higher-order goods, between consumption and production goods. While Mises agreed that it was indeed possible to arrive at reasoned judgement concerning the rational deployment of lower-order, consumption goods without reference to a neutral measure like money, his critical point concerned higher-order, production goods: modern capitalist economies are simply too complex to allow the economical use of their production goods to be assessed in terms directly related to the use-values of consumption goods.

> Calculation *in natura*, in an economy without exchange, can embrace consumption-goods only; it completely fails when it comes to deal with goods of a higher order. And as soon as one gives up the conception of freely established monetary price for goods of a higher order, rational production becomes completely impossible. Every step that takes us away from private ownership of the means of production and from the use of money also takes us away from rational economics (1920 [1935, p. 104]).

Accordingly Mises' criticism – like Weber's (1921 [1978, p. 103]) – was that Neurath's plans only make sense within the circumference of a more or less directly surveyable household economy. Rational calculation in modern capitalist economies required the medium of a universally commensurate measure, money. Since without a market, it is meaningless to speak of prices, what is needed therefore is a market in production goods – just what socialism precludes.

Neurath's response to Mises' objection remained opaque for some time. It was not until *Wirtschaftsplan und Naturalrechnung*, a small book of 1925, that Neurath appeared to attempt to confront his challenge explicitly. There Neurath was able to demonstrate that in some cases Mises too employed something like calculation in kind and that in the health and education sectors it is often employed as a matter of course (1925a [2004, pp. 428–429, 446]). But was that enough to establish that it could always be employed or even independently of market calculations elsewhere? Not surprisingly, Mises' brief response (1928, p. 188) was scathing. He denied that what he admitted in the case of monopoly goods must be admitted in other cases too, namely, that the utility of varying the production of different substitutable goods can be judged directly. In general, direct judgement was possible only for consumption goods in concrete cases – not when the utility of the entire stock of a type of good was at issue. In short, Mises claimed that Neurath had failed to answer his criticism.

However, Mises did overlook an important aspect of Neurath's reasoning, his ecological incommensurability argument. This did not only make a brief appearance in his *Lebensgestaltung und Klassenkampf* of 1928 (1973, p. 263) – too late for Mises to have taken it into consideration in his own 1928 review (just cited) – but it was fully treated in a short article of 1925 in *Der Kampf*, the theoretical journal of the Austrian social democratic party. There Neurath asked directly: "Now how can this 'best use' be calculated in a socialist economic order? For a socialist calculation there does not exist a unit of the sort which capitalism finds in 'money'" (1925b [2004, p. 468]). To convince us of the good sense of his claim that commensuration by any single unit will not work, Neurath asked three rhetorical questions:

> Some had the idea to introduce a certain amount of labour as a unit. But how could this make it possible for the excessive exploitation of a coal mine to figure as a negative entry in the balance? How could a quantity of electricity which a river provides us with be entered as an increase in amounts of labour units? Or the increase in wind power used in the running wind mills? (ibid.).

Consider how ecological reasoning figures here. The first example trades on incommensurabilities of precisely the sort that environmental issues throw up: "the excessive exploitation of a coal mine" involves considering the intergenerational context and having to determine how much to discount future costs and benefits. No objective facts are available that could determine this rate of discount. The second and third examples trade on incommensurabilities in the case of assessing present-day but counterfactual costs and benefits, and here too we need a political decision about the value of the type of labour at issue, and, more generally, a hierarchy of needs (sometimes also of the needy).

Against the claim that monetary algorithms could overrule the incommensurability of different needs and values in a population stands the realisation that they would require a prior non-algorithmic weighing up of competing needs etc. and their determination in monetary values. It is this thought that justifies for Neurath the view that socialist calculation is moneyless, that socialist economic plans are designed by multi-criterial evaluation.

> 'Costs' in the capitalist sense and the 'negative quantities' of socialist calculation do not come to the same thing.... The 'positive quantities' of the socialist order also do not come to the same thing as the 'profit' of capitalism. Savings in coal, trees, etc., beyond amounting to savings in the displeasure of work, mean the preservation of future pleasure, a positive quantity. For instance, that coal is used nowadays for silly things is to be blamed for people freezing in the future. Still, one can only give vague estimates. Saving certain raw materials can become pointless if one discovers something new. The future figures in the balance sheets of the capitalist order only in so far as the demand is anticipated. The freezing people of the future only show up if there is already now a demand for future coal. Just as before, capitalism would cut down the forests even if the consequence were karstification in a hundred years. In the tropics, and elsewhere, capitalism engages in over-exploitation without any disturbance. In short, for it savings would be a loss of profits. (1925b [2004, pp. 470–471]).

Thus, when it comes to showing that the very logic of capitalism consists in the wrongful absolutisation of the profit motive as definitive of economic action, it is ecological incommensurability that Neurath invoked. Rather than pointing to areas where even Mises and his supporters would acknowledge the possibility of alternative calculations, it is this ecological argument that was Neurath's main argument against Mises' market fundamentalism. Unlike in the case of in-kind calculation in embedded welfare sectors of the economy, considerations of sustainability and ecological incommensurabilities cannot be waved away as easily as riding piggyback on monetary profit calculations elsewhere. (The arbitrariness in setting shadow prices, for instance, is insurmountable.) Market fundamentalism fails the ecological challenge.[7]

But how far does this argument get us towards socialism, indeed a moneyless economy? Neurath's ecological incommensurability claim says that only comparative and holistic in-kind evaluation enables one to deal with ecological and related issues. Socialist economics can deal with the incommensurabilities involved there, because it allows for such in-kind calculation, it is not bound to monetary calculation. In that respect Neurath did possess a limited argument for socialism. The argument says nothing, however, about what other role money may still have to play. Thus all that the argument establishes is thesis (b) that there are dimensions of economic decision making where market principles cannot work. But it says nothing about thesis (c) that the market is not needed for anything. Note then that Neurath's ecological argument is an argument against the exclusive rule of money-calculation in economic matters, but it is not an argument that establishes the exclusive rule of in-kind calculation. Neurath's ecological argument is an argument in support of the weak in-kind calculability assumption. It does not support the strong in-kind calculability assumption presupposed by Neurath's advocacy of marketless socialism. Neurath did possess a strong argument against market fundamentalism, but not for marketless socialism

Note, however, that on the textual evidence so far we cannot yet conclude that Neurath committed the modal fallacy, that he mistakenly derived the possibility of a moneyless economy from the fact that money calculation is not ubiquitous in economic decisions. He frankly stated that "[t]he present task is to create the foundations for such studies of moneyless economics. This is not easy." (1925a [2004, p. 446]) This suggests his strong in-kind calculability assumption must be understood to trade on the future achievement of a research programme called "calculation in kind." Here we must ask how reasonable that hope was: had Mises' counterargument not laid bare its desperate hopelessness?

3 Neurath and Mises in 1919

Neurath's ecological incommensurability argument was not new in 1925, however, but was first published in 1919 in a co-authored work with Wolfgang Schumann.[8] This means, of course, that *all along* Neurath's response to Mises' counter that

[7] It is this point that packs a punch against Mises who was unable to account for "extra-economic elements"; for further discussion of this see Uebel (2005).

[8] "[W]e ask whether the free market economy is as economical as an economy should be in the light of the limited resources of the earth and our limited lifespans – and as it could be given at least the same output. That it is not! In the first place, it wastes raw materials. In quite a few countries coal will last only for another few decades. From coal one can produce the most valuable

socialism was impossible for its in-kind calculation rendered impossible rational economic calculation turned on the claim that in-kind calculation was unavoidable in any responsible economic decision making concerning non-renewable resources. On pain of failing this dimension of economic reasoning altogether, economic rationality was bound to do without or go beyond calculation with monetary units – even when it came to production goods.

But note in addition that Neurath and Schumann also argued as follows:

> One last question remains to be answered. How is the content of the total economic plan to be determined? Not infrequently, one hears it said that a socialist economy is impossible in practice because it has no measure for what is good and useful to do with the raw materials, machines, labour power, etc. What is missing is the net profit which served as measure so far.... it is not of the essence of human decision making that it is arrived at by percentages of money sums. Many small and some very far-reaching decisions in the field of production have long been made on the basis of direct considerations of outcomes. From given means a school or a hospital could be built and it was not net profit that decided in favour of one or the other, but a judgement, undoubtedly imprecise in many respects, about the expected advance in education with all its consequences on the one hand and, on the other, the gain in health (Neurath and Schumann 1919, pp. 45–46).

This raises our old concern again. Even read in conjunction with the ecological incommensurability argument, Neurath and Schumann here presented an argument that only supports the weak in-kind calculability assumption, but not the strong one. Yet they seem to have thought, as this passage suggests, that they were presenting an argument for marketless socialism. Can we again use the charitable interpretation and hold that Neurath did not fall victim of the modal fallacy of mistaking non-sufficiency for non-necessity, but that he instead banked on the future results of a research programme? Even if we do so, this raises only another question. What prompted Neurath in 1919 not only to advocate such a programme, but to do so in response to the charge that what floors marketless socialism is the problem of rational accounting for production goods? Wasn't *this* the main point of Mises' argument in 1920?

Obviously, Neurath responded to a calculation argument of sorts, but what was it? Was the "not infrequently" heard argument that without money as commensurating measure no rational economic calculation is possible? Or was it that without private ownership in the means of production and the profit motive there is nothing to constrain and render rational the disposition of production goods? Neurath and Schumann explicitly singled out "the net profit" as that "which served as measure

---

and permanently useful chemicals which one does not know how to produce without it. Still, what are we doing with coal? We 'heat' furnaces and locomotives and other spaces and so waste it. One could provide heating in a different way, e.g. by means of gas or electricity. But that would be 'more expensive' which means: the entrepreneurs, the joint stock companies would not make as much profit from them. So they exploit coal mines and sell coal for heating because they value their net profit more highly than humanity's need for coal in the future. It is the same with other raw materials. We do not even stop to think whether we should conserve materials for the sake of future generations, but let the decision be made by the desire for net profit on the part of a few of our contemporaries" Neurath and Schumann (1919, p. 15).

so far". Now if one supposes that Neurath only yet responded to the argument against abolishing private ownership of means of production, then the point of the introduction of Neurath's strong in-kind calculability assumption becomes apparent. Multi-criterial calculation in kind was Neurath's answer to the claim that only the profit motive could ensure the rational organisation of a nation's economy!

Note that, since Neurath and Schumann did not yet respond to Mises' argument for the inescapable need of a commensurating measure like money, they can hardly be accused of the modal confusion that we worried about in Neurath's later writings. They did not claim the general non-necessity of monetary calculation on the basis of its occasional non-sufficiency for the rational disposition of production goods; rather, they claim that there already existed an alternative decision procedure to profit calculation that can be generalised (and so lay the ground for Neurath's research programme). Note that this sets the stage for Mises rather nicely: his point now becomes that Neurath's in-kind calculation alternative won't work in principle!

For all the sense this reading makes of tangled matters, it may strike readers familiar with Mises' *Theory of Money* of 1912 as incongruous. In that book Mises promulgated arguments that appear identical to those in his reply to Neurath in 1920.

> Therefore, if he is to obtain the maximum utility from his resources, the individual … needs some help in finding his way among the confusing multiplicity of the exchange-ratios. Money … is pre-eminently suitable for this. It would be absolutely impossible for the individual, even if he were a complete expert in commercial matters, to follow every change of market conditions and make the corresponding alterations in his scale of use- and exchange-values, unless he chose some common denominator to which he could reduce each exchange-ratio. Because the market enables any commodity to be turned into money and money into any commodity, objective exchange value is expressed in terms of money. Thus money becomes a price-index, in Menger's phrase. The whole structure of the calculations of the entrepreneur and the consumer rests on the process of valuing commodities in money. Money has thus become an aid that the human mind is no longer able to dispense with in making economic calculations (Mises 1912 [1953, pp. 48–49]).

However, *despite* the appearance created by the footnote reference to his *Socialism* immediately following this passage – a footnote that was added only in the second edition of *Theory of Money* (1924) – there are weighty reasons already in the text to suspect that in the first edition of 1912 Mises did not yet make the argument that money is indispensable for economic calculation *tout court*, but only for an economic system based on private ownership of the means of production.[9] What supports this

[9] That the economic system of capitalism provided the basic parameter of his discussion was stated clearly in the opening paragraph of the book: "Where the free exchange of goods and services is unknown, money is not wanted. In a state of society in which the division of labour was a purely domestic matter and production and consumption were consummated within the single household it would be just as useless as it would be for an isolated man. But even in an economic order based on division of labour, money would still be superfluous and impossible if the means of production were socialised and the control of production and the distribution of the finished product were in the hands of a central body." (Mises 1912 [1953, p. 29]); translation altered to agree with the first edition.)

reading even more strikingly, however, is a little book of his from 1919, his *Nation, Staat und Wirtschaft* in which Mises first sounded his characteristic clarion call for the return to true liberalism.

There his arguments against socialism were that without private property in the means of production, an economic system was condemned to reduced productivity; that the political exigencies of a socialist state made the progressive accumulation of capital highly unlikely; and the Malthusian claim that overpopulation would follow the adequate provision of all regardless of their economic contribution. "These are the objections against the socialist society which everyone must consider before advocating socialism." (1919, p. 156) To be sure, Mises also cited the unbridged abyss separating individual self-interest and the interest of communal welfare as critical for socialism and accused it of rendering victorious the interests of the producers over those of the consumers – characteristically denouncing socialism's "turn away from the rational conduct of the economy and impedance of all economic progress" (ibid., p. 163). All the standard arguments against socialism familiar since Schäffle's *Quintessence of Socialism* (1875) were renewed here. Most notable about Mises' argumentation, however, is that any trace of his calculation argument against socialism is missing. Instead, we find Mises writing in the conclusion:

> It may be the case that socialism represents a superior form of the organisation of human labour. Those who make this claim are obliged to furnish proof by reason. If the proof should succeed, a world democratically united by liberalism would not hesitate to realise the communist commonwealth. For who in a democratic state could resist a reform that would bring advantage to the overwhelming majority? Political rationalism does not reject socialism in principle (1919, p. 182).

Clearly, Mises did not yet take himself to be in possession of a knock-down argument against socialism. Since he was not at all shy about saying so in 1920 and ever since, his silence on this account in 1919 is telling. As yet, Mises did not yet see that the indispensability argument for money in systems with private property of the means of production could be enlarged so as to furnish an argument against socialism *tout court*.

4 Neurath's Austrian View of the Market

But even if in 1919 he did not as yet face Mises' in-principle critique, what good reasons did Neurath have in support of that research programme, in support of the strong in-kind calculability assumption which backed up his call for marketless socialism? This question divides further. First we must ask why he believed that programmes like those for market socialism as mooted by Kautsky in 1902 could be simply dismissed. Having established this, we may then ask for Neurath's positive reasons for the strong in-kind calculability assumption.

Neurath's reasoning in his counter to the claims that "a socialist economy is impossible in practice" generally turns on an argument from consistency. If one wishes to do away with the market because of the perceived failure of capitalist economies, then one had better *not* help oneself to organising principles and tools that force one's hand to operate an economy in the traditional way. Money calculation is essentially tied to the profit motive that is the driving force of capitalist market economies. What systematicity the "anarchy" of the free market possesses is owed entirely to the intimate relation between money, prices and property, especially property in means of production. Without a market, prices are but arbitrary figures and without capital markets, money calculations of efficient uses of production goods are meaningless. So an alternative to money calculation had better be found.

Clearly, however, questions like the most efficient use of available raw materials, labour, means of production, etc., did not disappear with the abolition of markets, as prior contributions to the debate about the viability of socialism had stressed ever since Gossen's originally neglected book of 1854.[10] Yet short of going back on his word about implementing socialism as he understood it, Neurath was unable to invoke anything like prices for this purpose. In this dialectical position, there was *nothing but* the strong in-kind calculability assumption that he could possibly field at this point. What the strong in-kind calculability assumption amounted to for Neurath already in 1919 was a make-or-break research programme according to which what is most economical has to be established by detailed studies of production and labour technologies whose in-kind results could not be converted back to monetary terms. What direction an economy was to take was to be decided by "the people" on the basis of multicriterial assessments of alternative economic plans for meeting perceived social needs, based on reasonably comprehensive production and consumption statistics.

Even before Mises' counter, this was a stunning proposal to make. So why was Neurath so convinced that another substitute for money, say mere "accounting-prices" or labour units, could not be found?[11] That, after all, was the orthodox party view ever since Kautsky's *On the Morrow of the Revolution* (1902). Why did Neurath feel so sure that the issue boiled down to the "either-or" of unfettered free market vs. moneyless central planning (money vs. strong in-kind calculability)? To answer this question we must briefly touch not only on the interesting Austrian pre-history of the socialist calculation debate, but also consider Neurath's own debts to the Austrian School of economics.

Having taken his doctorate in 1906 with Gustav Schmoller as one of his examiners (whose seminars he had attended regularly), Neurath returned to Vienna where he began to attend Eugen von Böhm-Bawerk's seminars, contributed papers and participated in the discussions. (There his interventions soon occasioned his fellow

---

[10] Excerpts from the second edition of Gossen's book (1882) were reprinted in Neurath and Anna Schapire-Neurath's reader (1910) in the history of economic writings (albeit not the anti-socialist argument.)

[11] For this see especially Neurath (1925a [2004, pp. 430–447]) reprising debates with fellow Austrian socialists Helene Bauer and Käthe and Otto Leichter.

participant Mises' displeasure, as it were, setting a pattern.)[12] As is evidenced by some of his early essays, Neurath soon became well acquainted with the major writings of the Austrian School (if he had not been familiar with them already). Given his training in the Historical School, of course, his relationship to the Austrian School was not unconflicted. Neurath rejected and actively sought to overcome the dichotomy of abstract-theoretical and concrete-historical methodologies, which some of its representatives were concerned to perpetuate; moreover, he rejected Menger's explicitly apriorist methodology and what he considered the absolutism of Menger's conception of social scientific laws.[13] That noted, however, consider the possibility that Neurath also shared important aspects of the Austrians' general conception of economic phenomena. A popular statement of the Austrian conception by Böhm-Bawerk helps to characterise these equally succinctly.

Böhm-Bawerk noted that understanding the "modern economic order" meant that, "first, as in Crusoe's economy, we must understand the relation of our interests to external goods; second, we must seek to understand the laws, according to which we pursue our interests when they are entangled with the interests of others" (1891, p. 379). The key to both, Böhm-Bawerk stressed, lay in the marginal utility theory of value. As a subjectivist conception, it not only opposed the labour theory of value but all objectivist theories of value and stressed that the only thing it made scientific sense to focus on was the exchange-value of goods and services. More than that, "the price or 'objective value' of goods is a sort of resultant of the different subjective estimates of the goods which the buyers and sellers make in accordance with the law of final utility" (ibid., p. 367). Böhm-Bawerk was well-aware that, on the one hand, "the price which can be asked in the market is influenced by the estimate which the buyer sets upon the goods", while on the other hand, "in many cases the buyer's estimate is influenced by the state of the market" (ibid.). The market was constituted in part by the expectations of the individuals who participated in it and adapted their courses of action to the signal it provided.[14]

The signal function which the market assumed in this broadly decision-theoretical conception was given a clear expression also in Friedrich von Wieser's *Natural Value* (which Neurath knew well).

> Although no one is able, and even though no one should attempt, to figure out the amounts of supply and demand, value shows, with numerical exactitude and down to the finest gradations that people usually make in practical life, the relation between supply and demand in so far as these tend to make themselves felt in exchange. Value shows the effect of causes which in themselves are hidden. And through the fact that we adapt ourselves to this effect, this value, it finally becomes possible to adapt ourselves to the causes, the amounts of supply and demand, and thus to regulate an economy with due regard to economic laws (1888 [1893, p. 212]).

---

[12] See the recollections in Mises (1978, p. 36).

[13] See the discussion in Uebel (1999).

[14] On the decision-theoretical nature of Austrian economics ever since Menger, see Streissler (2002).

Whatever is "objective" in economics is constructed out of subjective valuations.[15] Needless to say, Neurath later objected to such seemingly determinate and ontological value-talk and it is unlikely that he ever agreed with this way of putting matters. Once we abstract from this, however, what we get is precisely the conception of the "modern economic order" that also informed Neurath's reasoning about the market. This is significant not in the least because this conception also informed ideas of whether there could be any alternative to the market and what it would have to be. The Austrian position on this issue was "either-or": either a free market with money or central planning without money. Call this the "Austrian exclusive disjunction". It is upon this that not only Mises and later Hayek built their alternatives of freedom or serfdom, but Neurath likewise rested his proposals for marketless socialism.

The moneyless economy that Neurath came to envisage may well employ a system of tokens to mark differential values in the exchange of goods or services between individuals or groups and between these and society as a whole. But no such system, Neurath was adamant, was able to determine the price of the goods or services, it could only indicate one that was fixed independently. The money that Neurath rejected was the all-commensurating money that allowed profit calculation in purely formal terms and set the price-relations of the market. Any substitutes for that commensurating unit value of money were at best money by another name or they were arbitrary combinations of figures. If money by another name was adopted, then a market was still in existence and its organising principle of production for profit still ruled. If merely some kind of shadow-pricing was attempted, the question would be what these figures were shadowing. Neo-classical economists for whom markets "clear" by definition and who can construct a market wherever there are goods and respective needs, however unconnected their occurrence, were able recreate a market for accounting purposes even where there was none (as in market socialism). By contrast, the Austrians were unable to do so. Unlike the neo-classicists, the Austrian economists did not believe in equilibrium as an essential feature of the market and so were unable to use the mathematics of supply and demand to calculate prices if there wasn't a market to begin with.[16]

Neurath shared this disbelief in market equilibrium. When developing his programmes for total socialisation with calculation in kind (as well as his ecological argument) in 1919, Neurath agreed with Mises' position that without a market the notion of price makes no sense and in this respect was in well-considered agreement with the Austrian School as such. Quite generally, Neurath shared their subjectivism as far as the conception of economic value was concerned and opposed objectivist

[15] "Objective value or price is not in the least the expression of the economic valuation of goods, even when it is the result of economic competition and of the individual valuations of all the different members of the economic community. Price is a social fact, but it does not denote the estimate put upon goods by society" Wieser (1888 [1893, p.52]).

[16] Mises in the English translation of *Socialism* ([1951, pp. 137–142]) and Hayek (1935b, 1940) give clear expression to this opposition to "the artificial market as the solution of the problem of economic calculation". On Wieser's problematical position in this respect, see below.

conceptions like Marx's labour theory (upon which Kautsky's market socialism was based).[17] Despite these significant agreements, however, Neurath opted for the second term of the Austrian exclusive disjunction: the research programme of strong in-kind calculability. He did not believe that the market was the only solution to the economic coordination problem. Instead, his ecological incommensurability argument convinced him that certain problems it could not solve at all.

5 Wieser in the Pre-1919 Socialist Calculation Debate

In the debates about the viability of socialism that preceded his argument for marketless socialism of 1919, Neurath found a wayward Austrian inspiration for his unusual approach to the Austrian exclusive disjunction.

Note first that it would remain something of a mystery why Mises did not yet take the additional step that distinguished his indispensability arguments of 1912 and 1920, were it not for the fact that before Neurath's advocacy of total socialisation this additional step appears not to have been needed. Yet stressing the indispensability of money as opposed to the profit motive is not quite the natural step that it may appear, as can be seen from the theory developed by Friedrich von Wieser. Already Wieser gave an anti-socialist calculation argument that anticipated aspects of Mises' later argumentation, but it did not yet close the case against socialism completely.[18]

In his *Natural Value* Wieser noted that it was "the possibility of calculating utility in terms of value which first puts us in a position to draw out exact economic plans and to foresee their necessary limitation. Thus value comes to be the controlling power in economic life" (1888 [1893, p. 36]). Amongst other things, Wieser concluded:

> ... in any larger economy whatever, particularly in such a one as has the compass of a national economy, and is based upon a complicated system of production, it is quite impossible to dispense with value if we wish to have any clear notion of the utility of goods. A Robinson Crusoe does not require the aid of value; he can arrive at a right decision in every instance by simply testing what manner of treatment is likely to secure him the greatest amount of utility on the whole. In a national economy, on the other hand, with a complicated system of production, it is impossible in any way to make the necessary economic

[17] For Neurath's endorsement of the subjectivist conception of economic value, see his (1910a, p. 1).

[18] There is much interpretive thicket here. Note the claim by Vaughn that Mises "reasserted and elaborated upon Wieser's earlier argument" and in doing so "went further" (1994, p. 42) and that Hayek once noted that Mises was one of Wieser's students (1926 [1929, p. xvi]). Streissler (2002) suggests that Hayek's merely passing mention of Wieser in his (1935, p. 25) and Mises' studied complete neglect of Wieser's argument in his own (1920) and (1922, all eds.) are wholly inadequate. Yet whether it was animadversions against Wieser's economic interventionism – not all economists of the Austrian school were anti-interventionist – or something else that blinded them to the groundwork that Wieser had performed for the calculation debate must be left undiscussed here. On Wieser see also Hutchison (1953, pp. 153–164) and Steele (1992, pp. 74–77).

> decisions by testing the utility of goods on the whole.... By the socialist programme it is proposed to manage the counting of stocks and calculation of demand, in the state of the future, by means of government statistics. Could this plan be sufficiently carried out it would be so far possible to dispense with marginal value. On the other hand, it can never be dispensed with where the finding of an expression for the utility in the individual good is concerned. To dispense with it would be equivalent with giving up the attempt to determine utility in the individual case, and being content with making a general determination as to the direction of production and consumption, leaving out of consideration the quantities which it is desirable to gain or consume (ibid., pp. 210–211, 213]).

Statistical assessments, so Wieser, were far too coarse to allow fine-tuned policies for the deployment of production goods by naming specific quantities as production targets for consumption and other production goods. Socialism thus did not escape the need for calculations of value, a need which neither statistics nor its labour theory of value – where "pretty nearly everything is wrong" (ibid., p. 66) – was said to be unable to fulfil.[19]

Yet while Wieser claimed the indispensability of "value calculation" – "The natural principles of valuation are indispensable, because they serve indispensable economic purposes" (ibid., p. 163) –he did not argue that rational calculation would be impossible in socialism. To be sure, he clearly stressed the importance of production goods for his argument, but his argument apparently left it open for a socialist central authority to help itself to marginal utility calculation in disposing of its production goods. What made this possible was Wieser's notion of "natural value" as an original type of value which "arises from the social relation between amounts of goods and utility"; this was "value as it would exist in a communist state" or what "has been hitherto called social use value" (ibid., p. 60). By abolishing private property one merely neutralised the distorting effects of differentials in purchasing power. "In natural value, goods are estimated simply according to their marginal utility; in exchange value, according to a combination of marginal utilities and purchasing power" (ibid., p. 62). By ordering its affairs according to natural value, a socialist commonwealth was able to act rationally, at least in principle.

One concern that Wieser's argumentation concerning natural value raised was whether he did not allow for price equivalents where there was no market. If "[e]xchange value, even when considered as perfect, is, if we may so call it, a caricature of natural value" (ibid.), then how was that social utility to be calculated? To this end, Wieser recognised, alongside the marginal utility calculations of "private economy", what he called "national economic valuation" where the former kind of valuation "will be to a great extent abandoned" (ibid., p. 227). But Wieser had to admit that when it came to natural value, exact calculation was no longer possible. "It is the exact calculation and the incalculable but actually observed influences that, together, make up the full value of goods" (ibid., p. 231).

---

[19] For discussion of a still earlier formulation of the anti-socialist calculation argument in Wieser's habilitation of 1884, see Streissler (2002). Consider also Wieser's later reprise in: "A central prompter of this sort [like a communist administration] could never be informed of the countless possibilities, to be met with in every individual case."

Nevertheless, due to his own rejection of Menger's attachment to political and economic "individualism of the classical school", as he put it later (1921 [1929, pp. 123–124]), and his recognition of the need for the "formation of collective bodies" to secure "the carrying out of collective actions" (1888 [1893, p. 222]), Wieser concluded: "It is a matter of the first importance – one without which no decision can be arrived at – to recognise that there is a sphere within which the estimate of exchange value is applicable and another in which it is not" (ibid., p. 232).

Wieser's ideas did not find universal acclaim. Hayek preferred to characterise Wieser's argumentation here as a merely expository device (though it is unclear for what) (1935a, p. 25), but that Wieser seemed to allow for value where there was no market occasioned the caustic criticism of Gustav Cassel:

> Already the title *Natural Value* suggests a fundamentally mistaken conception which finds expression in the work itself by Wieser's investigation of the 'communist state'. Against all such foggy notions I must expressly stress that 'imputation' in Wieser's sense presupposes as a practical necessity a system of private property and a fully developed system of exchange. It is precisely the great fundamental defect of the 'communist state' that it can never evaluate rightly the different factors of production, and therefore can never be in a position to direct the production in the right way. To overlook this is to fail completely to understand the activity of the business man of our day. The idea that the productive contribution of different factors can be rightly accounted for is indeed only a fiction which takes on a definite meaning solely through the process of price formation, for the prices of the elements of production express simply what the market imputes to them (1899, pp. 456–457).

Cassel left the matter with these suggestive remarks, but given the pre-World War I prominence of his paper his suggestions may well have travelled.[20] Consider again Mises in his book of 1912. Following the remarks later marked out as anticipating his calculation argument of 1920, he noted:

> If in this sense [objective exchange value is expressed in terms of money] we wish to attribute to money the function of being a measure of prices, there is no reason we should not do so. Nevertheless it is better to avoid the use of a term which might so easily be misunderstood as this. In any case the usage certainly cannot be called correct – we do not usually describe the determination of latitude and longitude as a 'function' of the stars (Mises 1912 [1953, p. 49]).

Mises may well have intended criticism of Wieser when he corrected Menger's talk of the "price-index" and explicitly rejected the idea that prices measured a value independent of the market: his remarks certainly have this effect. He is also likely to have approved of Cassel's criticism in as much as it expressed – and reaffirmed against deviations by one of its most prominent practitioners – the Austrian conception of economic processes. Even so, Mises did not discuss Cassel in the context of the socialist calculation argument, aside from technicalities of price theory.[21]

[20] Hutchison claimed that "[t]hese ideas were, of course, developed much further by Mises" (1953, p. 247).

[21] Incidentally, Hayek also did not mention Cassel with regard to his calculation argument.

Interestingly, Neurath did comment on Cassel. He objected that Cassel had "by no means sufficiently justified" his claim that Wieser was wrong to assume a communist state as background for his investigation. Instead, Neurath argued "that it should become the task of a separate and comprehensive scientific investigation to determine whether the money economy really is superior to all possible forms of economies in kind, independently of issues of social order and distribution" (1911 [1998, p. 499]). Neurath did not here intend to defend Wieser's own position; rather, he opposed the idea that the indispensability of money and markets had been established still before modern forms of calculation in kind had been sufficiently developed to attempt a comparative assessment. It is also telling that Neurath objected to Cassel's rejection of intersubjective utility comparisons (which left but monetary values for economic calculations), announcing by contrast that "a common measure is not a necessary condition for comparison" of goods and pointing to his own in-kind calculus of merely ordinal comparability then under development (ibid., p. 472 n).

Significantly then, both the young Mises and the young Neurath can be seen to take divergent paths in pursuing their disagreements with Wieser's conception of economic calculation. Both rejected his idea of natural value. But where Mises absolutised marginalist value theory, there Neurath took issue with Wieser's contention that calculation in kind was too limited in principle to serve as an indicator for the direction of production in socialism and began to develop an alternative calculus for in-kind value calculations that, as he put it, sought to "stay unaffected by the still unsolved problems of [Austrian] value theory" (ibid., p. 518).

Now Wieser himself had stressed that whether socialism was possible in actuality was not his concern: "Natural value is a neutral phenomenon, the examination of which, whatever may come of it, can prove nothing for and nothing against socialism" (1888 [1893, p. 63]). Meanwhile, his appreciation of capitalism was not without ambiguity. Since exchange value guides economic decisions in the market and measures a combination of utility and purchasing power

> ... production is ordered not only according to simple want, but also according to wealth. ... It is therefore the distribution of wealth which decides how production is set to work, and induces consumption of the most uneconomic kind: a consumption which wastes upon unnecessary and culpable enjoyment what might have served to heal the wounds of poverty (ibid., p. 58).

Thus Wieser reserved considerable room for the state to carry through "just such economic tasks as could not be justified by their money return" even though they are "justified by their utility" (ibid., p. 53). In the end, however, he invoked what has since become known as the trickle-down argument:

> It may very well be that private property gives rise to great inequalities in the satisfaction of wants while it, nevertheless, secures, even to those who receive the smallest share in the general distribution, an enormously increased satisfaction of want on the whole – the reason being the enormously increase in productive return which it allows and brings with it (ibid., p. 241).

That this left unsatisfied Neurath who appreciated Wieser's observations about the distortions inherent in exchange-value and the need for collective bodies for the provision of public goods is easily seen, but also that Mises felt emboldened to reject Wieser's interventionism on account of the underlying conception of natural value. As differently motivated reactions to Wieser's position, both Neurath's embrace of the idea of calculation in kind in marketless socialism and Mises' turn to market fundamentalism become readily intelligible.

6. Conclusion

Clearly, Neurath was not an Austrian economist in any straightforward sense. But I hope readers will agree that by appreciating what Neurath shared with the Austrian school of theoretical economics and by noting his close familiarity with its internal disputes, we can gain insight into the nature of Neurath's rather different ideas. To reinforce this conclusion, I return to the question raised earlier: why did Neurath persist with the strong in-kind calculability assumption and pledged allegiance to it as a research programme still after Mises had mounted his calculation argument of 1920? Was it their political values alone that accounted for the opposition between Mises and Neurath? Here we must note one very sharp methodological difference that throws interesting and unusual light on a well-known feature of Neurath's general philosophy of social science. Neurath's tenacity in his pursuit of the idea of in-kind calculation is at least partly explained on philosophical grounds. As is hinted at already by his principled opposition, his and Mises' ideas clashed on account both of their conceptions of rational action and of the methodology of social science.

First, for Mises, at least as he is naturally read, the central point is that rationality in complex economies requires commensuration of all values onto a common one.[22] The possibility of just that, of course, is what is denied by Neurath's ecological argument: rationality is not renounced just because we have to make do with merely partial orderings of alternatives, moreover, with a plurality of those. What appears to be a presupposition of rational action for Mises was for Neurath but a recipe for pseudo-rationalism.[23] The very determinacy of action that Mises appeared to insist on, was anathema to Neurath in that it set an illusory standard that was rarely if ever

---

[22] That universal commensuration was a central point for Mises is also seen from the fact that Mises referred in both (1920) and (1922, all eds.) to Gottl-Ottlilienfeld (1914, p. 216) as an instance of the indispensability argument of economic calculation. Gottl-Ottlilienfeld derived from the technological demand that effort should be minimised the necessity to commensurate all efforts of different kinds so as to compute the most efficient course of action. "[T]hat technology must always calculate with prices… follows with strict necessity. One the one hand, technology must commensurate efforts of all kinds so that they can enter into the same calculation. On the other, it remains the task of economics to turn the required calculability into a fact.… This commensurate calculability is necessarily required not, as may be thought, in order to tell economists what an hour of horse power use really costs, but rather in order to facilitate the consistent realisation of the principle of rationality inherent in technology itself." (Ibid., pp. 215–216)

[23] For Neurath on pseudorationalism generally see his (1913 [1983]), on pseudo-rationalism in economics see his (1935 [1987]).

met. So for Neurath, Mises's charge was highly problematic. (By contrast the point of Hayek's elaboration of it was much more readily appreciable.)[24]

Instead, Neurath can be seen to be aiming for a different understanding of rationality altogether. What Neurath's often repeated juxtapositions of plan vs. profit amount to, is the claim that the economic systems of capitalism and socialism do not share the same concept of economic rationality, of "*Wirtschaftlichkeit*".[25] Given certain production goods, economic rationality in capitalism pertains to asking which of their possible employments is most profitable for their owner. Thus by some invisible hand mechanism, the many single agent rationalities are said to coalesce in social rationality. By contrast, for Neurath, economic rationality in socialism pertains to asking, from the start, which employment would provide the most use-value to the population as a whole and, then, how that particular employment could achieve the highest yield possible in terms of some product-labour expenditure ratio. This social rationality was not determined by the aggregation of individual preferences.[26] Moreover, whereas monetary economic rationality is determinative, typically singling out one alternative, the in-kind economic rationality is merely indicative by presenting the alternative opportunity costs that any one action would incur. Whereas monetary rationality is predicated on the automatism of the market, in-kind rationality requires deliberation and for these deliberations, Neurath's projected calculus of in-kind calculation was to provide the tools.

Second, for Neurath, economic planning by calculation in kind remained a legitimate aspiration, because in his view its supposed irrationality was arrived at by Mises on methodologically suspect grounds. What, for instance, justified Mises' unargued-for supposition that the concept of making "economic calculations" only applied to the actions of individuals in a market economy, but not to those of isolated Robinson Crusoes or members of household economies or, indeed, actions by the

---

[24] Hayek, after all, rendered Mises' bald complexity considerations such that the data-gathering task of Neurath's "universal statistics" was impossible to achieve since it would require the explication and codification of what are not only widely dispersed pieces of knowledge but also essentially tacit knowledges sensitive for their operation to highly local conditions. Compare Mises (1920 [1935, p. 102]; 1922 [1951, pp. 117–118]) and Hayek (1935b [1948, p. 155], 1940 [1948, p. 202], 1945 [1948, pp. 77–91]).

[25] This is particularly clear in the echo of his 1919 argument in his "System of Socialisation": "The general economic plans will have to replace net profits in regulating the economy. In a free market those enterprises were undertaken that yielded the highest money profits. The profits occurred automatically, as it were, and one obeyed to the relevant demands like players obey an acknowledged rule of a game. At certain points of economic life, profits were disregarded in the common interest. On behalf of the state, schools, hospitals etc. were built that did not yield any profit. How mistaken it was to take profits as indicating efficiency may be seen from the fact that certain commodities widely needed were not produced at all, because the masses of the population did not have the money to buy these goods and were thus unable to 'produce' this profit. Nonetheless, the production of these goods would have produced more happiness than not producing them, it would have been more efficient" Neurath (1920a [2004, p. 355]).

[26] For Neurath's reasoning on this and related points see his fundamental and far-reaching (1912).

central economic authority in marketless socialism (see 1912 [1953, 29])? Neurath saw in Mises' conclusion but the consequence of the a priori intuitions foundational to the distinctively *geisteswissemschaftlich* science of society.

In the Introduction to the first edition of *Socialism*, Mises explicitly declared his hand: "Social science… finds its objects within, not in the external world. We are related to it entirely differently than in the cognition of what is intrinsically alien to us, what we can only know but cannot experience. In this sense too the question must be answered – no longer of importance today – whether social science belongs to natural science or *Geisteswissenschaft*. Social life is part of what we tend to call *Geist*" (1922, pp. 11–12). That Mises dropped this passage in later editions and instead devoted entire books to the matter is less notable than that to Neurath, it indicated clearly which philosophical wind was blowing.[27] Neurath never made this criticism of Mises' methodology explicit, but it follows from his own early opposition to the categorical distinction of *Natur-* and *Geisteswissenschaften* (1910b [2004, p. 267]) and is fully in line with his advocacy of unified science and the rejection social science separatism ever since his Vienna Circle days (and Mises' opposition to it).

Now it is plain that, in order to convince, such a methodologically based counter to Mises needs proof both of the indispensability of *geisteswissenschaftlich* separatism for his anti-socialist calculation argument and of the untenability of such separatism. However, while he did develop in his Vienna Circle days the appropriate methodology of physicalist unified science, Neurath never produced a conclusive proof that such *geisteswissenschaftlich* separatism was essential to Mises' 1920 argument. So that argument remains to be made. Yet it is very suggestive that in their later works, ostensively unconcerned with the socialist calculation debate, Hayek inveighed against physicalism as passionately as Mises did against the idea of unified science.[28] Did they too believe that their argument of the impossibility of socialism depended on the idea that economics is a *Geisteswissenschaft*? (Again, Hayek's argument appears far less vulnerable to this objection than Mises', but this issue may be left open here.)

In sum: associated with Neurath's and Mises' different conceptions of political economy are different conceptions of rationality, and associated with these were very different methodological assumptions. Rather than raise the question of which of these conceptions possesses priority, I shall simply note that they are mutually reinforcing – and that each in turn is independent of what Neurath and Mises (and Hayek) did share: the subjectivist conception of market values. Thus one may, on account of Hayek's knowledge-based elaboration of Mises' complexity arguments, reject the ambitions of marketless socialism, just as, on account of Neurath's ecological incommensurability argument, one may reject market fundamentalism – and

---

[27] Prior to Mises, not only Menger but also Wieser indicated his *geisteswissenschaftlich* allegiance in his (1911) and affirmed in his (1913 [1927, p. 8]).

[28] See Mises (1933, 1962) and Hayek (1942–1944).

this position too is compatible with a subjectivist conception of market values. It must be left for another occasion to investigate whether the fully-fledged Austrianism that regards the market as the only rational mechanism for social coordination does indeed require what Neurath rejected: a metaphysical distinction between realms of being that is underpinned by an apriorist epistemology of intuited essences.

References

Böhm-Bawerk, Eugen von, 1891, "The Austrian Economists", *Annals of the American Academy of Political and Social Science* 1, 361–384

Cassell, Gustav, 1899, "Grundriss einer elementaren Preislehre", *Zeitschrift für die gesamte Staatswissenschaft* 55, 395–458

Chaloupek, Günther K., 1990, "The Austrian Debate on Economic Calculation in a Socialist Economy", *History of Political Economy* 24, 659–675

Gottl-Ottlilienfeld, Friedrich von, 1914, *Wirtschaft und Technik*, 2nd ed, 1923, Mohr, Tübingen

Gossen, Hermann Heinrich, 1854, *Entwicklung der Gesetze des menschlichen Verkehrs*, 2nd ed, 1889, Prager, Berlin

Haller, Rudolf, 1986, "Zur Historiographie der österreichischen Philosophie" in *Von Bolzano zu Wittgenstein* (ed. by J.C. Nyiri), Hölder-Pichler-Tempsky, Vienna, trans. "On the Historiography of Austrian Philosophy", in *Rediscovering the Forgotten Vienna Circle* (ed. by T.E. Uebel), Kluwer, Dordrecht, 1991, 41–50

Hayek, Friedrich August von, 1926, "Friedrich Freiherr von Wieser", *Jahrbücher für Nationalökonomie und Statistik* 70, repr. in Wieser 1929, v–xxiii

Hayek, Friedrich August von, 1935a, "The Nature and History of the Problem", in Hayek 1935c, 1–40

Hayek, Friedrich August von, 1935b, "The Present State of the Debate", in Hayek 1935c, 201–243

Hayek, Friedrich August von, ed., 1935c, *Collectivist Economic Planning*, Routledge, London

Hayek, Friedrich August von, 1940, "Socialist Calculation III: The Competitive Solution", *Economica* 7, repr. in Hayek 1948, 181–208

Hayek, Friedrich August von, 1942–1944, "Scientism and the Study of Society", *Economica* 9–11, repr. in *The Counter-Revolution of Science. Studies in the Abuse of Reason*, Free Press, New York, 1952

Hayek, Friedrich August von, 1945, "The Use of Knowledge in Society", *American Economic Review* 35, repr. in Hayek 1948, 77–91

Hayek, Friedrich August von, 1948, *Individualism and Economic Order*, University of Chicago Press, Chicago

Hutchison, Thomas, 1953, *A Review of Economic Doctrines 1870–1929*, Clarendon Press, Oxford

Kautsky, Kark, 1902, *Die soziale Revolution Bd. II: Am Tage nach der Revolution*, Dietz, Stuttgart, trans. in *The Social Revolution and on the Morrow of the Revolution*, London, 1907

Lavoie, Don, 1985, *Rivalry and Central Planning. The Socialist Calculation Debate Reconsidered*, Cambridge University Press, Cambridge

Martinez-Alier, Juan, 1987, *Ecological Economics. Energy, Environment and Society*, Blackwell, Oxford

Mises, Ludwig von, 1912, *Theorie des Geldes und der Umlaufsmittel*, Duncker & Humblot, Munich-Leipzig, 2nd ed. 1924, trans. *The Theory of Money and Credit*, Cape, London, 1934, enlarged ed. 1953

Mises, Ludwig von, 1919, *Nation, Staat und Wirtschaft. Beiträge zur Politik und Geschichte der Zeit*, Manz, Vienna

Mises, Ludwig von, 1920, "Die Wirtschaftsrechnung im sozialistischen Gemeinwesen" Archiv für Sozialwissenschaft und Sozialpolitik 47, trans. "Economic Calculation in the Socialist Commonwealth", in Hayek 1935c, 87–130

Mises, Ludwig von, 1922, *Die Gemeinwirtschaft. Untersuchungen über den Sozialismus*, Fischer, Jena, 2nd ed, 1932, trans. *Socialism. An Economic and Sociological Analysis*, Johnathan Cape, London, 1936, enlarged ed. 1951

Mises, Ludwig von, 1928, "Neue Schriften zum Problem der sozialistischen Wirthschaftsrechnung", *Archiv für Sozialwissenschaft und Sozialpolitik* 60, 187–190

Mises, Ludwig von, 1933, *Grundprobleme der Nationalokonomie*, Jena, trans. *Epistemological Problems of Economics*, van Nostrand, New York, 1960

Mises, Ludwig von, 1962, *The Ultimate Foundation of Economic Value*, 2nd ed, Steed Andrews and McMeel, Kansas City, 1978

Mises, Ludwig von, 1978, *Notes and Recollections*, ed. by M. v. Mises, Libertarian Press, Spring Mills

Neurath, Otto, 1910a, *Lehrbuch der Volkswirtschaftslehre*, Hölder, Vienna.

Neurath, Otto, 1910b, "Zur Theorie der Sozialwissenschaften", *Jahrbuch für Gesetzgebung, Verwaltung und Volkswirtschaft im Deutschen Reich* 34, trans. "On the Theory of Social Science" in Neurath 2004, 265–291

Neurath, Otto, 1911, "Nationalökonomie und Wertlehre, eine systematische Untersuchung.", *Zeitschrift für Volkswirtschaft, Sozialpolitik und Verwaltung* 20, 52–114, repr. in Neurath, *Gesammelte ökonomische, soziologische und sozialpolitische Schriften I* (ed. by R. Haller and Ulf Höfer), Hölder-Pichler-Tempsky, Vienna, 1998, 470–518

Neurath, Otto, 1912, "Das Problem des Lustmaximums", ", *Jahrbuch der Philosophischen Gesellschaft an der Universität Wien 1912*, trans. "The Problem of the Pleasure Maximum", in Neurath 1973, pp. 113–122

Neurath, Otto, 1913, "Die Verirrten des Cartesius und das Auxiliarmotiv: Zur Psychologie des Entschlusses", *Jahrbuch der Philosophischen Gesellschaft an der Universität Wien 1913*, trans. "The Lost Wanderers of Descartes and the Auxiliary Motive (On the Psychology of Decision)" in Neurath, *Philosophical Papers 1913–1946* (ed. by R.S. Cohen and M. Neurath), Reidel, Dordrecht, 1983, 1–12

Neurath, Otto, 1919, "Wesen und Weg der Sozialisierung", in Durch die Kriegwirtschaft zur Naturalwirtschaft, Callwey, Munich, 209–220, trans. "Character and Course of Socialisation", in Neurath 1973, 135–150

Neurath, Otto, 1920a, "Ein System der Sozialisierung", *Archiv für Sozialwissenschaft und Sozialpolitik* 48, trans. A System of Socialisation" in Neurath 2004, 345–370

Neurath, Otto, 1920b, Vollsozialisierung, Diederichs, Jena, trans. "Total Socialisation", in Neurath 2004, 371–404.

Neurath, Otto, 1925a, Wirtschaftsplan und Naturalrechnung, Laub, Berlin, trans. "Economic Plan and Calculation in Kind", in Neurath 2004, 405–465

Neurath, Otto, 1925b, "Sozialistische Nützlichkeitsrechung und kapitalistische Reingewinnrechnung", *Der Kampf* 18, trans. "Socialist Utility Calculation and Capitalist Profit Calculation", in Neurath 2004, 466–472

Neurath, Otto, 1928, *Lebensgestaltung und Klassenkampf*, Laub, Berlin, trans. "Personal Life and Class Struggle" in Neurath 1973, 249–298

Neurath, Otto, 1935, *Was bedeutet rationale Wirtschaftsbetrachtung?* Gerold, Vienna, trans. "What is Meant by Rational Economic Theory?", in *Unified Science* (ed. by B. McGuinness), Kluwer, Dordrecht, 1987, 67–109

Neurath, Otto, 1973, *Empiricism and Sociology* (ed. by M. Neurtah and R.S. Cohen), Reidel, Dordrecht

Neurath, Otto, 2004, *Economic Writings. Selections 1904–1945* (ed. by T.E. Ubeel and R.S. Cohen), Kluwer, Dordrecht

Neurath, Otto and Anna Schapire-Neurath, eds., 1910, *Lesebuch der Volkswirtschaftslehre* (2 vols.), Klinkhart, Leipzig

Neurath, Otto, and Wolfgang Schumann, 1919, *Können wir heute sozialisieren? Eine Darstellung der sozialistische Lebensordnung und ihres Werdens*, Klinkhart, Leipzig

O'Neill, John, 1993, *Ecology, Policy and Politics. Human Well-Being and the Natural World*, Routledge, London

O'Neill, John, 1998, *The Market. Ethics, Knowledge and Politics*, Routledge, London

O'Neill, John, 2004, "Ecological Economics and the Politics of Knowledge. The Debate between Hayek and Neurath", *Cambridge Journal of Economics* 28, 431–447

O'Neill, John, 2006, "Knowledge, Planning and Markets. A Missing Chapter in the Socialist Calculation Debate", *Economics and Philosophy* 22, 1–24

Schäffle, Albert, 1875, *Die Quintessenz des Sozialismus*, Perthes, Gotha, trans. of 8th ed., *The Quintessence of Socialism*, Sonneschein, London, 1892

Stadler, Friedrich, 1997, *Studien zum Wiener Kreis*, Suhrkamp, Frankfurt a.M., trans. *The Vienna Circle*, Springer, Vienna-New York, 2001

Steele, David Ramsay, 1992, *From Marx to Mises. Post-Capitalist Society and the Challenge of Economic Calculation*, Open Court, La Salle, IL

Streissler, Erich w., 2002, "Wirtschaftliche Entscheidungstheorie als Angelpunkt der Österreichischen Schule der Nationalökonomie", in L. Bauer and K. Hamberger (eds.), *Gesellschaft denken. Eine erkentnnistheoretische Standortbestimmung der Sozialwissenschaften*, Springer, Vienna-New York, 309–318

Uebel, Thomas, 1999, "Some Scientism, Some Historicism, Some Critics. Hayek's and Popper's Critiques Revisited", in J. Wolff, M. Stone, eds., *The Proper Ambition of Science*, Routledge, London, 151–173

Uebel, Thomas, 2003, "On the Austrian Roots of Logical Empiricism. The Case of the First Vienna Circle", in *Logical Empiricism. Historical and Contemporary Perspectives* (ed. by P. Parrini, W.C. Salmon and M.H. Salmon), University of Pittsburgh Press, Pittsburgh, 67–93

Uebel, Thomas, 2005, "Incommensurability, Ecology and Planning: Neurath in the Socialist Calculation Debate, 1919–1928", *History of Political Economy* 37, 311–342

Vaughn, Karen, 1994, "The Socialist Calculation Debate", in *The Elgar Companion to Austrian Economics* (ed. by P. Boettke), Elgar, Aldershot, 478–484

Weber, Max, 1921, *Wirtschaft und Gesellschaft*, Mohr, Tübingen, trans. *Economy and Society*, University of California Press, Berkeley, 1978

Wieser, Friedrich von, 1888, *Der natürliche Wert*, Hölder, Wien, trans. *Natural Value*, Macmillan, London, 1893

Wieser, Friedrich von, 1911, "Das Wesen und der Hauptinhalt der theoretischen Nationalökonomie Kritische Glossen", in *Jahrbuch für Gesetzgebung, Verwaltung und Volkswirtschaft im Deutschen Reich* 35, repr. in Wieser 1929, 10–32

Wieser, Friedrich von, 1913, *Theorie der gesellschaftlichen Wirtschaft*, Mohr, Tübingen, 2nd ed. 1923, trans. *Social Economics*, Adelphi, New York, 1927

Wieser, Friedrich von, 1921, "Carl Menger", in A. Bettelheim (ed.), *Oesterreichische Biographie*, vol. 2, Amalthea, Munich, repr. in Wieser 1929, 110–125

Wieser, Friedrich von, 1929, *Gesammelte Abhandlungen*, ed. by F.A. Hayek, Mohr, Tübingen

School of Social Sciences
The University of Manchester
Manchester, M 60 1QD
UK
thomas.uebel@manchester.ac.uk

Otto Neurath's Concepts of Socialization and Economic Calculation and his Socialist Critics

Günther Chaloupek

Otto Neurath was one of the most active participants in the debate about socialization that developed after the First World War. As far as this part of Neurath's work is concerned, his name is mentioned most prominently in the context of two issues: "total socialization"/"Vollsozialisierung" (as opposed to partial socialization), and "in kind accounting"/"Naturalrechnung". In both respects he is mostly seen as an advocate of strategies and concepts which aimed at changes in the economic system of a much more radical sort than those proposed by the main-stream social-democratic parties in Germany and Austria. Neurath maintained this position despite the early failure of "revolutionary" political experiments in Bavaria and Saxony in his contributions to the socialization debate which he continued to publish until 1925. In the later 1920s, when chances for realization of socialization more or less disappeared, socialization also vanished as a theoretical issue.

This contribution is confined to the debate between Neurath and his critics from the Social Democratic parties of Germany and Austria – to the part of the debate that took place "inside" the socialist movement. It makes only occasional references to contributions from "outside", which are of course much better known nowadays due to the prominence which the interventions of Mises and Schumpeter came to acquire later.[1]

In the following two sections I will not try to summarize Neurath's positions in general, because this would only duplicate a task that has been very aptly done by Thomas Uebel in his introduction to Neurath's newly published "Economic Writings" (2004, 39 ff). I will only restate some of the distinctive arguments on which Neurath based his controversial positions, and otherwise refer to details of the debate in the context of the controversies with his critics. Sections 3–5 and 7 deal with the critique of Neurath's proposals for central planning, in-kind accounting, the role of money as well as the problems of incentives and of conflicts of interest. On these issues the main interventions came from Karl Kautsky at that time still the leading theoretician of Social Democracy in Europe; from Helene Bauer, Otto Bauer's wife, who was a frequent contributor to the theoretical periodical of the

[1] For a survey of the Austrian debate on economic calculation in a socialist economy see Chaloupek (1990).

E. Nemeth et al. (eds.), *Otto Neurath's Economics in Context*.
Vienna Circle Institute Yearbook [2007]. Volume 13.

Austrian Social Democrats "Der Kampf" on economic issues; Otto Leichter, economist with a practical experience as manager in socialized enterprises formed out of former war-time production plants. Section 6 discusses Neurath's treatment of accounting problems in the light of modern accounting concepts that were emerging during the interwar years.

1 Socialization: Total or Partial?

Weissel (1976, p. 202) makes the observation that inexact or deceptive use of the terms "*Vollsozialisierung*" and "*Teilsozialisierung*" was the cause of much confusion which – also in other respects – characterizes the socialization debate. To make a proposal appear more radical, it was not uncommon to speak about "total" socialization of a branch or even of a company. Neurath's contributions are not free from such ambiguity. "Total" socialization for Neurath does not necessarily mean expropriation and nationalization of all the means of production. For him, nationalization as such does not mean socialization, because "socialization is concerned with the whole, it is always total socialization, however shallow or deep the impact of the overall measures is"(1920/2004, p. 377). To "produce and distribute the final product socialistically" (ibid.), to ensure the full use of productive resources, to eliminate the "waste" of the capitalistic mode of production, etc., "socialism tries to replace the planlessness which springs from the disconnected activities of individual entrepreneurs by an administrative economy according to a plan, by an economic order in which central institutions survey the entire economy in order to participate in decisions on work, production and consumption"(ibid., p. 381).[2] In this administrative economy "the decisions about production, distribution, wages and prices … are to be taken by the whole" (p. 382). Whereas Neurath strictly opposes any kind of market socialism, he appears to be willing to allow some degree of independence of small producers in the crafts and in agriculture. "The doctrine that there is a trend towards ever more comprehensive organisations has been confirmed fully, less so the doctrine that small businesses will be replaced by large-scale concerns"(387 f). The essential thing is that small producers of various sorts are organized in a multitude of regional and branch organization to ensure that goods and services are produced according to the central plan (ibid.). In addition, "total" socialization requires a comprehensive statistical apparatus on which the plan must be based. "Even before they begin their work all bodies … should be required to report to the Central Economic Administration which, in collaboration with the Centre for Statistics … will fit the individual results into the universal statistics" (p. 389).

[2] Notice that Neurath uses "soft" formulations (survey, participate), thereby avoiding the impression that it might be necessary to establish central control over production and consumption by command backed by force.

2 Accounting in Kind: with or Without Money?

Neurath's proposal to set up a system of "*Naturalrechnung*", i.e. economic accounting in kind, was even more controversial than total socialization. Understood as an encompassing system on which the envisaged comprehensive economic and social planning would have to be based, it was seen at best as a curiosity, and in its most counter-intuitive effect as proof of the economic impossibility of socialism (Mises 1922). Starting from his general idea that production as well as consumption would be planned in kind, Neurath never produced more than sketchy illustrations and partial examples of how the plan should be designed, not to speak of implementation. Due to his principal opposition to money, Neurath thought that "in socialism, production can never be based on calculation with one unit of any kind, not even with the help of 'labour vouchers' "(1925a/2004, p. 432). But as he goes on to discuss concrete questions of his planning system, he resorted to similar instruments which contradicts the principle stated before: to give sufficient incentives for workers and also to allow for some freedom of choice of consumer goods, provisions the system could provide that "each individual receives the right to take consumer goods from the total pool according to the number of points of his labour vouchers" (ibid., p. 435). In addition, in order to ensure an economic use of material resources, in case of a shortage "the number of points for their distribution will have to be increased beyond the number representing the work spent on their production" (p. 436). In an earlier version, Neurath had considered the possibility of keeping two accounting systems in parallel: "It does not matter .... whether money is still in use as vouchers for goods, or whether vouchers replace money entirely ... or whether money is still used in some capacity as a unit of calculation. This kind of 'monetary calculation' can remain side by side with the 'calculation in kind' of the economic plan; in such a case it is useful to speak of an economy in kind with reckoning in money" (1920/2004, p. 383).

More fundamental from a methodological point of view is Neurath's ambivalence between what Thomas Uebel has called "strong" and "weak in-kind calculability assumption" (Uebel 2005, p. 318). "Weak in-kind calculability" is a common phenomenon in the monetary market economy when resources are allocated to the provision of public goods such as roads or internal and external security, or public services such as hospitals, through the state budget, and planning is done also in non-monetary terms, e.g. kilometres of roads or number of policemen, judges, doctors and nurses, etc. In contrast, the "strong in-kind calculability assumption says that alternative uses of production goods can be assessed as fully as is required for rational decision making by quantitative in-kind labour and production technology statistics – money calculation is not even necessary for rational decision making" (ibid.). It appears that Neurath was not aware of this crucial difference, and that he unconsciously changed back and forth between these two concepts.

3 Encompassing Central Economic Planning

To consider an encompassing system of central planning of the whole economy as the essence of socialization – rather than a change in the ownership of the means of production, which was seen as a complementary element in the socialization process – was not Neurath's original insight. Of the multitude of socialization concepts put forward at the end of World War I, several had a special emphasis on overall economic planning. As early as mid-1918, well before the end of the war, Walther Rathenau, president of the famous German company AEG, who had also been in charge of the organization of raw material supplies during the war, in his pamphlet "*Neue Wirtschaft*" ("A new economy") proposed a system of comprehensive planning as a framework for "rationalization" of the whole economy in order to promote the application of the best technologies of production and a more efficient use of resources in private enterprise (p. 20). This approach was taken up by the German minister for economy Rudolf Wissel (Wissel 1920) whose plan ("*Wissel-Moellendorff-Plan*", 1919) combined overall planning with partial nationalization, e.g. of coal mining.[3]

The idea that an encompassing system of planning should be seen as the essence of socialization was strongly rejected by Karl Kautsky in his book "*Die proletarische Revolution und ihr Programm*" ("The proletarian revolution and its program", 1922). Kausky's critique was directed not only against Neurath but also against the Wissel-Moellendorff-plan. Kautsky's main argument was that it would be impossible to provide the statistical base on which such a plan would necessarily have to be based. It would take a huge bureaucracy many years "to produce a reasonably reliable set of statistics". Moreover, Kautsky criticizes Neurath for his simplified examples using a few inputs in low stages of the production process, thereby ignoring the complicated flow of goods through numerous intermediate stages to the final product. Kautsky was convinced that "it would be completely impossible to obtain a statistical survey of the infinite variety of all the products from private companies" (Kautsky 1922, p. 198). As an advocate of a socialist economy, Kautsky does not principally deny the necessity of a planned economy, which, however, "cannot be the starting point of socialization, but only its final result" (ibid., p. 202).

On a more fundamental level, Kautsky rejected Neurath's rationalist, constructivist approach to economy and society: "Society is not an edifice which is built according to a definite plan. Rather, it is comparable to an organism which grows and develops" (ibid., p. 181). In Kautsky's view, Neurath's exercises in "social engineering" were an unfortunate example of utopian thinking which had been definitely overcome by Marx's and Engels' scientific socialism. It is consistent with Kautsky's evolutionary

---

[3] An implementation of these plans would have resulted in a kind of "mixed economy"-system with indicative planning, as was developed after World War II in some countries. In Austria concepts similar to Rathenau's were put forward by Karl Pribram (1918) and Gustav Stolper (1921). For a survey of these concepts see Chaloupek (1987).

approach that the idea of maturity becomes the central concept for the envisaged transformation from capitalism to socialism. Socialization can take place only if the development of the capitalist economy has produced institutions and forms of enterprise which are ripe for socialization. For Kautsky, this is the case only in a few branches such as railways and coal mining. Socialization starts with change of ownership in these branches, to be followed by new forms of organization of the nationalized enterprises. As a necessary consequence, socialization is pushed forward step by step, whereas total socialization is impossible and bound to fail. Therefore, the leading social-democratic politicians such as Otto Bauer in Austria, and also most theoreticians of socialization[4] were advocates of "*Teilsozialisierung*" (partial socialization).

Emil Lederer, who served as secretary of the German socialization commission which was headed by Karl Kautsky, argued against Neurath along similar lines. To replace the existing market-coordinated economy with all its enormous complexity by establishing a complete system of planning "with one stroke" would be possible only if "all men wanted such a production system, i.e. if no private interests would stand against it" – a condition which evidently was not fulfilled (Lederer 1921, p. 161).

In his replies to Kautsky's critique Neurath concentrated on the most controversial part of his own socialization theory, i.e. the role of money (see Sect. 5). With respect to the specific criticisms referred to above, he admitted the enormous effort that would be necessary to produce his "universal statistics". With real prospects for socialization having become extremely dim in 1925, Neurath proposed to start "to prepare a universal statistics... The automatism of the market order for private entrepreneurs, even for nationalized autonomous economic enterprises in a capitalist order, must be paralleled by an economic plan, by calculation in kind for the socialist society.... also smaller sections... can be depicted in this way. We can, for example, show the input and output of fat for the whole country" (Neurath 1925a/2004, p. 444). A curious proposal indeed, which ironically seems to foreshadow the growing problem of over weighted people of our present time.

4 Calculation in Kind and "*Naturalwirtschaft*" (In-Kind Economy)

Among Social Democratic politicians and writers, Neurath's idea to organize an economy in its totality on the basis of an accounting system in terms of material inputs and outputs which requires the application of a multitude of different units of measurement was not considered to be a serious proposal for economic policy.

[4] For a survey of the great number of contributions which were published in the years following the war, many of them by "autodidacts," see Weissel (1976), especially 202 ff, and also Fischer/Rosner (1987, 185 ff).

The intention behind most of the negative reactions it provoked was to counteract the growing tendency in public opinion that the conditions for socialism as an alternative system could never be established. In this sense, Otto Leichter approvingly cites Max Weber's verdict, who considered Neurath's "'blueprints of a planned economy' ('*Planwirtschaftspläne*') a dilettantish, objectively and absolutely irresponsible frivolity without parallel, which might discredit socialism for hundred years" (Leichter 1923, p. 96).[5]

Karl Kautsky, who postulated freedom of choice for consumers and also "most possible freedom for producers" (1922, p. 313) in the socialist economy, argued that this would be impossible if the whole production would be organized in one single factory under central management, which assigns production tasks to each factory, which receives all the products and apportions all means of productions to factories and all consumption goods to households *in natura*. The ideal of such a state of affairs is the prison or the barracks, whose inmates get everything they need *in natura*" (ibid., p. 314). Kautsky's ironic remarks are certainly polemical, but nonetheless they illustrate the principal difficulties which Neurath refused to take seriously. If Kautsky was not able to formulate this kind of argument in general terms, the reason is because the critique would turn against socialism per se.

Compared to Karl Kautsky's criticisms, the arguments against calculation in kind put forward by Helene Bauer and Otto Leichter were of a more theoretical nature. Helene Bauer emphasized that the measurement of the value of all goods in terms of labour hours would be indispensable in a socialist economy for two reasons: (i) goods are distributed to consumers proportional to their work effort; (ii) for decisions about allocation of productive resources, it is necessary to compare the values of the different goods despite the fact they have ceased to be "commodities" (Bauer 1923a, 198 ff).[6] She also questions Neurath's idea of choosing among a variety of different plans with alternative production plans and alternative sets of conditions of life. "The socialist society... will not allow a central organ to make experiments with different conditions of life, but will calculate exactly how much labour time the production of each group of goods costs, starting from raw materials to the finished goods including distribution" (ibid., p. 200).

A major part of Neurath's articles in "*Der Kampf*" (Neurath 1923a, b), and also of Helene Bauer's reply, were not, or not directly, concerned with matters of

[5]Even more harsh was Karl Renner's reported judgement of Neurath ("Narr", engl. "fool"). (Weber 1982, p. 139). In her contribution to this volume Elisabeth Nemeth points to the fact that the concept of accounting in kind was developed by Neurath many years before the socialization debate started in the purely theoretical context of his economic research programme. This implies that, if Neurath later applied the concept for practical purposes when he engaged himself in the political debate about socialization, he misunderstood his own concept, being insufficiently aware of its limitations.

[6]To support her argument, Helene Bauer (p. 200) quotes Engels (1894, p. 335): "Die Nutzenffekte verschiedener Gebrauchsgegenstände, abgewogen untereinander und gegenüber den in ihrer Herstellung nötigen Arbeitsmengen, werden den Plan schließlich bestimmen". Engels's argument is actually based on a utility theory of value. Engels' argument is actually based on a utility theory of value.

substance, but with the question to what extent Neurath's ideas could be reconciled with the writings of Marx and Engels. It was an easy task for Helene Bauer (1923b) to counter Neurath's effort by citing other quotations from *Das Kapital,* from Marx's unpublished marginal notes to the Gotha Program, and from Engels' *Anti-Dühring.*

Otto Leichter, who proposed a socialist accounting system based on the hour of labour as basic unit, criticizes that in a system of in-kind calculation a rational use of resources would be impossible for several reasons. (i) Neurath nowhere shows how the various production units would reckon up their mutual deliveries (Leichter 1923, p. 33). (ii) Free choice for consumers is necessary to ensure that production units respond to their needs and preferences, which is not the case if goods are distributed to the final users according to conditions of life defined by the central plan (ibid., p. 73). (iii) More fundamentally still, Leichter argues against concepts similar to Neurath's developed by the Russian economist Chayanov[7] that the solution of rather simple tasks such as comparisons of economy between alternative methods of production of the same products become impossible. E.g. without a standard unit of accounting it is not possible to decide whether production of a given quantity of electricity is more economical by using coal or water power (ibid., p. 87). To this latter criticism, Neurath replied that it would be the task of technical engineers to develop the appropriate methods, "as soon as they have understood the nature of the problems, to assess the performance of individual production units" (1923a, p. 156). In return, Leichter (1923, p. 97) denied this emphasizing that, to the contrary, this would be the task of what Neurath called the "social engineers" ("*Gesellschaftstechniker*").

If Helene Bauer and Leichter were convinced that the hour of labour would be the appropriate unit of account in a socialist economy, they found themselves in contradiction with Karl Kautsky who had denied the viability of such an accounting system. Karl Kautsky (1923, p. 321) argued that, in a capitalist economy, actual market prices were hardly ever identical with "values", the latter presumably meant in the sense of Marshall's "normal supply price", with the market mechanism working as an automatic adjustment process to reduce deviations of prices from values. Since "normal conditions" never prevail in reality, it would never be possible to determine "normal" quantities of labour required for production of each good. "Instead of the futile attempt to measure running water with a sieve" a socialist government "would retain the prices with which it is confronted and which have been formed in the process of history." Adjustments would have to be made in a pragmatic way, without inflicting hardships on the working class as they do under capitalism.[8]

---

[7] Alexander W. Chayanov, 1888–1939, director of the Petowskoje-Rasumowskoje institute of agricultural economics (near Moscow) 1919 till 1930, arrested under the charge of founding a peasant's opposition party (according to Mänicke-Gyöngyösi 1981, p. 114).

[8] Apart from changes of conditions of demand and production, the proposal to use the hour of labour as common unit of accounting does not stand up against Eugen von Böhm-Bawerk's objection that labour is not homogeneous. (Böhm-Bawerk 1896/1962).

Karl Kautsky and also Leichter thought that the system of state control of the economy introduced during the war years could not be considered as a forerunner of the planned economy. These kinds of controls eventually would have to resort to coercion and forceful police action "with results which would be as poor as in Russia today" (Kautsky 1922, p. 201). Leichter maintained that it is one of Neurath's fundamental errors to characterize the war economy as in-kind economy. It is "quite ridiculous to speak of in-kind calculation in capitalism wherever calculations are not made in terms of money" – the costs of schools, hospitals, housing units are always calculated in monetary units. (Leichter 1923, p. 95)

It was Benedikt Kautsky, son of Karl Kautsky and head of the statistical department of the Vienna Chamber of Labour, who wrote "the last word" in the in-kind calculation debate. His review of Neurath 1926 was published in Rudolf Hilferding's journal "*Die Gesellschaft*", i.e. at a time when socialization had ceased to be a real issue of political debates. Apart from the aspect of the necessity of money as a common unit of account (see next section) Benedikt Kautsky's main critique of Neurath's approach is the latter's dominant concern with static aspects of the economic process. It is the "questions of socialist production which have to be posed in the first place, not least with respect to the complex relations of world markets. The issue is not distribution of existing goods,... but their production and augmentation." Creating the conditions for enhancement of civilization is primarily "a problem of technology and production policy" (Kautsky 1926, p. 95).

5 Money in the Socialist Economy

Since Neurath's treatment of money is the subject of a separate contribution by Peter Mooslechner, I will be rather brief on this aspect.

It has been pointed out above that Neurath was not wholly consistent on the issue of the necessity of money as a unit of calculation and as a means of distribution of goods to final consumers. But it appears that Neurath thought money as a common unit of account could be done away with completely at least in an advanced, not necessarily final state, of the socialist economy.

According to Karl Kautsky, Neurath's fundamental opposition to money was the consequence of a confusion of money as a means of exchange and money as "capital" that has an inherent drive for self augmentation. If for Neurath "the production of surplus value is not the function of capital, but of money as such", this is "completely erroneous" in Kautsky's view (Kautsky 1922, p. 316).[9] In the socialist economy, money would no more be transformed into capital, and would therefore only serve as a means of exchange which would be indispensable to ensure smooth circulation of goods and to give free choice to consumers.

---

[9] This argument was reaffirmed in Benedikt Kautsky's review (1926, p. 94) when he wrote that the use of money as a means of circulation does not lead to the domination of men by money.

Only a society in which all scarcity of material goods has ceased – the "stage of communism" envisaged by Marx for some distant future – could do entirely without money. But this is a theoretical possibility which Kautsky does not take into consideration seriously since "we can not even surmise today whether we ever get that far" (ibid., p. 315). The abolition of money would be a heavy setback for the division of labour and its progress on which modern material and cultural standards are based, it would be "regression into barbarism", an act of helpless destruction comparable to the destruction of machines by pauperized workers in the early phases of the industrial revolution (ibid., p. 324). Kautsky also points to historical examples of moneyless societies which were always based "not only on communism of production but also of consumption – with complete absence of freedom of person" (ibid., p. 336).

In his reply, Neurath (1923a, 136 f) tried to support his position with extensive quotations from Marx's and Engels' writings, insisting that in a socialist economy money, even if it is stripped of its capitalist character, would still preserve its inherent structural features.[10] He repeated his contention that a socialist economy would have to reckon not only without profit and loss, but also without money, and that this view was also in accordance with "the fundamental ideas of Marx and Engels." When Helene Bauer (1923a) had seriously challenged this accordance, Neurath argued that Marxism is not identical with the teachings of Marx himself but that Marxists may criticize Marx and also deviate from his views (Neurath 1923b, p. 288).

6 Misunderstandings and Anticipations

In this section I will try to evaluate several of the different arguments put forward by Neurath to support his idea of in kind calculation and the respective counterarguments of his critics.

Neurath argued that a partial in kind-economy is standard practice in the public sector when capacities of public services such as schools and hospitals are defined in natural terms. In this context, however, he disregards the aspect that all such decisions are subject to a budget constraint. The scale and the quality at which such services are made available must be weighed against the costs of each kind of service and of the total, necessarily calculated in terms of a common unit. No "rational" decision can be made independently of cost considerations. If this was the essence of Helene Bauer's critique referred to above, Neurath nowhere offered a convincing reply to it.

---

[10] Literally, Neurath's wording does not suggest exactly this, when he writes: "Denn es kann kein Zweifel bestehen, die Begriffe der kapitalistischen Ordnung, wenn man sie ihres Geldcharakters entkleidet, enthalten ihn dennoch in ihrer Struktur:" But judging from the context of the debate, I am convinced that my reformulation conveys much better what Neurath actually intended to say.

Otto Leichter was the only one who pointed to an even more fundamental aspect of the issue. There exists always more than one combination of inputs in order to produce a given quantity of output of a certain good (for final consumption, for investment in construction and equipment, for intermediate use, in Leichter's case: electric current). Without the possibility of comparing the total values of alternative input combinations it is not possible to decide which combination is the most effective. Hence, even in the unrealistic case where the plan correctly anticipates final consumption demand, the selection of the most productive processes to satisfy that demand must be based on cost comparisons in money terms, i.e. in terms of a common unit of calculation. It appears that this aspect was never understood by Neurath.

In his essay on socialist utility calculation (Neurath 1925b/2004), Neurath put forward still another argument. "It is possible for an economy to exhibit a constant upward trend in terms of its balance sheets while the production is in permanent decline and the life of everybody becomes ever worse" (ibid., p. 467).[11] The statement that "production is in permanent decline" necessarily implies that "production" by which nothing else can be meant than an heterogeneous aggregate of a variety of goods can somehow be expressed in aggregate terms to find out whether it is declining (or constant, or increasing). Evidently, this is impossible without calculating values in terms of a common unit. Apart form this unintended but inevitable implication which is inconsistent with Neurath's fundamental views on economic calculation, his statement is correct, but does not at all prove the necessity of in-kind calculation. The problem is solved by calculating the value of production at constant prices, otherwise referred to as "in real terms", as opposed to current prices, also referred to as "in nominal terms". This has become standard practice in the System of National Accounts (SNA) which has been used world wide after 1945 to measure the economic performance of nations. If in 1925 no such standard economic accounting system existed, there was a "theory of index numbers" which would have provided the tools for calculation at current and at constant prices.[12] This theory could have been used to explain what appeared as a paradox to Neurath. So much for "weak in-kind calculability assumptions".

As regards Neurath's "strong in-kind calculability thesis", it is difficult to imagine how Neurath came to believe in his "utopian" solution. Even if it were possible to draw up several alternatives of complete systems of all inputs and final outputs (thousands of equations), it is impossible to conceive of a decision making process by which a collective choice could be made *uno actu* about alternatives *in toto* for several years (the planning period) in advance. It appears plausible if Thomas

---

[11] Neurath made a similar statement in his response to comments to his lecture to the World Social Economic Congress 1931: "If one speaks, in monetary calculation, of the increase of production measured in money terms, then it is unclear whether there is an increase in kind, for the increase in money terms can mean a decrease of production." (Neurath 1931b/2005, p. 500).

[12] See Diewert (1987) and the literature listed in the appendix of his article; also Klein/Morgan (2001).

Uebel (2004, p. 66) suggests that in his later years Neurath "quietly dropped the advocacy of centrally planned economies in kind" although he somehow tried to save the idea of in-kind accounting.

In one important respect, Neurath's critique of the "capitalist money accounting system" anticipates the critique of the SNA developed during the 1960s and 1970s which became one of the theoretical foundations of the environmentalist movement. In his essays on socialization (1920a, b) Neurath introduces the "quality of life" as a concept which includes not only elements of material wealth such as food, clothing housing, etc.[13] "The ultimate aim of the economic plan, however, is the 'topography of living conditions' which shows the distribution of living conditions (made up of available food, housing, clothing, education, leisure, work, toil, etc.) according to certain types"(1920b/2004, p. 386). Several of these "non-material"[14] factors of well-being are discussed in Neurath's essay on socialist utility calculation (1925b). If the money calculation of the capitalist system "is precise in terms of money sums, ... it tells us nothing of the true wealth of a people, neither about the use made of sources of raw materials more about the distribution of goods produced; it tells us nothing about the rise or fall in the rates of deaths and diseases or about whether people feel better or worse" (ibid., p. 468). Neurath also mentions the exhaustion of coal mines, the karstification of mountains, "entertainment" – which obviously includes leisure time. In a socialist society, all these factors which determine the quality of life of the individual, would have to be taken into consideration and "represented by a figure, that of another by a second figure, such that in the end one would arrive at a sum for society. Than one could determine that in one case the totality of the qualities of life is greater than in another" (ibid., p. 469).

That the production of goods in the capitalist system also has negative side effects in the form of negative externalities, and that the distribution of income and material well-being is important for social welfare, had been analyzed systematically by the British economist A.C. Pigou in his "Economics of Welfare" which was first published in 1920. It appears that Neurath did not know about this newly developing branch of economic analysis.

Towards the end of the twentieth century, economists tried to develop a comprehensive indicator of economic welfare in order to include some of the factors whose neglect Neurath had criticized. It must be noted, however, that this overall "Measure of Economic Welfare" (MEW) (Nordhaus/Tobin 1972) was arrived at by directly adding or deducting such things as the value of leisure time, the value of consumption of durable consumer goods (e.g. cars), or the imputed money value of the impact of environmental factors ("regrettable necessities, "disamenities") in aggregate form to GDP, rather than calculating these values first at the level of the

[13] Also see Leßmann's contribution to this volume for a discussion of Neurath's concept of "conditions of life".

[14] National income not only includes tangible goods, but – to an ever increasing extent – also services of different kinds. Conventions have been developed to include private and public services in GDP on the basis of imputations which presently account for a large part of it.

individual, as demanded by Neurath. However, Nordhaus and Tobin hardly had any followers in the field of research in economics which they had opened more than 30 years ago.

More recently, a new type of "ecological economics" has emerged for which incommensurability of the different components of economic and social welfare as the starting point. With explicit reference to Neurath, the aim of this research programme is to "compare alternative decisions on a rational basis, on different scales of value, as in multi-criteria evaluation" (Martinez-Alier 1995, p. 75).

7 Conflicts of Interest, Incentives, Democracy and Dictatorship

In his tract on the proletarian revolution Karl Kautsky warns against the illusion that socialism would create a society of spontaneous social harmony. Foreseeable conflicts of interest of are seen as a key problem of organization and control in a socialist economy and are therefore discussed at great length. As the most fundamental problem of a socialist economy, Kautsky identifies the conflict of interest between producers and consumers (1922, 149 ff). If workers of different branches of production and different professions have special interests, in capitalism the dominant conflict is between capitalists and workers who are united by the existence of a common class enemy. Even so, there is "a constant danger that the solidaristic class consciousness degenerates into egotism of the professions" (ibid., p. 226). In a socialist economy, without the unifying bond of a common class enemy, the different groups of workers will develop a stronger tendency to pursue their special interest. In a socialist order, these interests must be carefully balanced against the interest of consumers in order to ensure that production of goods is undertaken for the purpose of consumption. It is in this respect where Kautsky sees the fundamental deficiency of the model of gild socialism which he rejects. Because self government of units of production by workers would give too much economic power to special interests, Kautsky (ibid., pp. 256 f) supports the model of tripartite governance of enterprises proposed by Otto Bauer (1919).

Instead of establishing a new structure of wages and incomes based on objective social and economic principles, Kautsky offers a rather sobering solution for the problem of wage formation under socialism. "The socialist society will be faced with existing conditions of production which prescribe a certain distribution, irrespective of formulas of justice which it must nonetheless implement" (ibid., pp. 166 f). Even if labour has ceased to be a commodity, wage differentials will have to be used as an instrument to allocate labour in accordance with changes in consumption demand (ibid., p. 167 f).

Kautsky frankly admits that socialism has not yet found a solution for the problem of bureaucracy. If bureaucratic management of big enterprise has become more and more characteristic of modern capitalism, it is essential to understand that "the bureaucracy which capitalism has created for its purposes is entirely different (from state bureaucracy)" (ibid., p. 209). Socialism can work satisfactorily only with flexible forms of management. Incentives for initiative action will be no less important for socialism to maintain the dynamic innovative character of capitalism (ibid., 216 ff).

If Kautsky does not directly criticize the ways Neurath treats this kind of problems, he certainly shares Emil Lederer's view that Neurath's evasive attitude towards conflicts of interest implies a regression into utopian thinking (Lederer 1921, p. 160).

Neurath does not wholly ignore the problems of interest conflicts raised by Kautsky and other non-utopian realists. With respect to the problem of special interest of factory councils, he writes: "for socialisation the power of workers is decisive not within the factory, but within the people's economy as a whole" (1920b/2004, p. 390).[15] Neurath shares Kautsky's critical position vis á vis gild socialism. The solutions he offers are centralist decision making within an encompassing system of economic and social planning where everything is to be decided *uno actu* by the population which can choose between a certain number of alternative overall plans. Experts and social scientists are assigned a crucial role in the preparation of decisions which are greatly facilitated by a general spirit of cooperation, e.g. in the field of wage formation: "The result will be a general system of wages in which all wages and salaries, including those of directors and factory owners, will be agreed according to danger, risk, comfort and exertion of work, locality and manner of work, age, etc." (ibid., p. 387).

Neurath's unshattered optimism that the socialist revolution would create a mood of enthusiasm among the masses of workers is sufficient reason for him to hope for solutions where they are not yet available nor conceivable in the early stages of transition. In this respect the politicians and intellectuals with real experience in the labour movement could not follow him. Moreover, with their a strong commitment to parliamentary democracy, German and Austrian social democrats were not prepared to take the risk that revolution would result in a Bolshevistic dictatorship. Kautsky abhorred the terrorist nature of the political system established under the rule of the Bolshevists, and he was equally critical of the poor economic performance of the command economy held together by brute force.[16] There is no doubt that Neurath did not sympathize with Bolshevism. Somehow, he entertained the hope that, "if there existed a far-reaching tolerance in the economic sphere, a peaceful kind of Bolshevism might develop that could exist together with other orders of life. For that, however, Bolshevism would have to abandon its intolerance" (Neurath 1920a/2005, p. 352). Kautsky, for that matter, never diluted his uncompromising position towards Bolshevism until his death in 1938.[17]

---

[15] Even more pronounced: "Eine Demokratisierung der Betriebe, die so weit geht, dass die technische Leitung durch Arbeiterräte, die Verwaltung ganzer Betriebsgruppen durch Ausschüsse höherer Ordnung erfolgt, bedeutet gesellschaftstechnisch eine Lähmung der Produktion" (Neurath 1919, p. 246).

[16] Compare the remarks in Kautsky (1922, pp. 165, 185, 234, 267).

[17] See his book "Bolschewismus in der Sackgasse" published in 1930.

8 Concluding Remarks

Considering the all too obvious deficiencies of Otto Neurath's concepts of socialization and of calculation in particular, the response from socialist critics, despite the many counter-arguments which were brought forward, is not entirely convincing – mainly for the lack of general aspects. With their consequent adherence to the Marxian labour theory of value, socialist economists like Kautsky and Leichter could not solve the problem of changing demand. Their socialization concepts did not provide an allocation mechanism for the socialist system because in their economics utility was not relevant for price formation.[18] In this respect, but also with respect to incentives, economic dynamics, innovation critical arguments against Neurath were not pursued as far as would have been possible – because the arguments could have been turned against socialism itself. With some of his arguments Karl Kautsky comes close to Mises's conclusion of economic impossibility of socialism, the difference being Kautsky's conviction the conditions for transition to socialism would be brought about by the long term evolutionary trends inherent to the capitalist system. Neurath, although he was a socialist, had obviously realized that the labour theory of value was untenable, but he hesitated to say this openly. It was in search of an alternative that he turned to in-kind calculation, which is even less suitable as accounting framework for a socialist economy. Except for Emil Lederer, who was not a Marxist, and a few others, socialist economists were not familiar with what was then modern economic theory, e.g. welfare economics, theory of index numbers, which could have cleared up some of the confusions, especially about accounting.

Finally, I think, a critical discussion of Neurath's concepts of socialization and of calculation demonstrates the insufficiency of his "physicalist" approach to the social sciences. To speak of "physics of society in the same sense as of physics of a machine" (Neurath 1931a/1979, p. 198), it does not suffice to have complete knowledge not only of the present, but also of the future "topography of different conditions of life, the flows of raw materials and energy" (1920a/2004, p. 362). In Neurath's general system of "Lebensboden" (foundations of life), "Lebenslagen" (conditions of life) and "Lebensordnung" (order of life) (1931a/1979, p. 200) the social structure in its totality is embedded in a causal sequence of stimulus and response.[19] Even more specifically, Neurath writes "that we speak of a higher condition of life, if it brings about a higher quality of life, ... If we possessed complete knowledge of the central nervous system we could be able to penetrate into this 'innermost' shell" (1925a/2004, p. 418). These formulations are an expression of Neurath's occasional leanings towards materialist behaviourism. On a more general level, Neurath recognized principal impredictability and rejected epistemological

[18] Rosner/Fischer (1987, p. 192).

[19] "Die gesamte Sozialstruktur einer Gesellschaft, ihre Lebensordnung ist eingebettet in den gesamten Kausalablauf, ist einerseits als Reiz, andererseits als Reaktion anzusehen" (Neurath 1931a/1979, p. 206).

fundamentalism and determinism (Uebel 2006). Judging from the viewpoint of economics, it appears to be impossible to construct a causally completely determined closed system with no scope for discretionary choice of individual and collective actors.

Neurath rightly pointed to serious flaws of both neoclassical and socialist economics. If most of the alternatives he proposed were neither convincing nor viable, the need for such alternatives has become even more urgent in the face of the dominance of market fundamentalism in economic and political thinking.

Acknowledgements The author expresses his thanks for comments on earlier versions of this contribution to Thomas Uebel and Stefan Schmitz.

References

Bauer, Helene, 1923a, *Geld, Sozialismus und Otto Neurath*, in: Der Kampf 16, pp. 195–202

Bauer, Helene, 1923b, *Sozialistische Wirtschaftrechnung*, in: Der Kampf 16, pp. 321–325

Bauer, Otto, 1919, Der Weg zum Sozialismus, Verlag der Wiener Volksbuchhandlung, Wien

Böhm-Bawerk, Eugen von, 1896/1962, *Unresolved Contradiction in the Marxian Economic System*, in: Shorter Classics of Eugen von Böhm-Bawerk, Vol. I, Libertaruan Press, South Holland, pp. 201–302

Chaloupek, Günther, 1987, *Die schwere Geburt der Mixed Economy*, in: Gerhard Fink/Günther Pöll/Martin Riese (eds.), Economic Theory, Political Power and Social Justice, Festschrift Kazimierz Laski, Springer-Verlag, Wien-New York, pp. 407–425

Chaloupek, Günther, 1990, *The Austrian Debate on Economic Calculation in a Socialist Economy*, in: History of Political Economy 22, pp. 659–675

Diewert, W. E., 1987, *Index Number*, in: John Eatwell/Murray Milgate/Peter Newman (eds.), The New Palgrave, Macmillan, London-New York-Tokyo, Vol. 2, pp. 767–780

Engels, Friedrich, 1894, Herrn Eugen Dührings Umwälzung der Wissenschaft, Verlag J. H. W. Dietz Nachf., Stuttgart, 3rd edition

Fischer, Georg, and Peter Rosner, 1987, Politische Ökonomie und Wirtschaftspolitik im Austromarxismus, Österreichischer Bundesverlag, Wien

Kautsky, Benedikt, 1926, *Rezension von Neurath, Wirtschaftsplan und Naturalrechnung*, in: Die Gesellschaft 2, pp. 92–96

Kautsky, Karl, 1922, Die proletarische Revolution und ihr Programm, J.H.W. Dietz-Verlag, Stuttgart-Berlin

Kautsky, Karl, 1930, Der Bolschewismus in der Sackgasse, Verlag J.H.W. Dietz Nachfolger, Berlin

Klein, Judy L., Mary S. Morgan (eds.), 2001, The Age of Economic Measurement, Duke University Press, Durham and London

Lederer, Emil, 1921, *Sozialisierung*, in: Ignaz Jezower (ed.), Die Befreiung der Menschheit, Verlagshaus Bong, Berlin-Leipzig-Wien-Stuttgart, part 2, pp. 159–167

Leichter, Otto, 1923, Die Wirtschaftsrechnung in der sozialistischen Gesellschaft, Verlag der Wiener Volksbuchhandlung, Wien

Mänicke-Gyöngyösi, Krisztina, 1981, *Nachwort*, in: Alexander W. Tschajanow, Reise meines Bruders Alexej ins Land der bäuerlichen Utopie, Syndikat-Verlag, Frankfurt

Martinez-Alier, Juan, 1995, *Political Economy, Distributional Conflicts, and Economic Incommensurability*, in: New Left Review 21, pp. 70–87

Mises, Ludwig, 1922, Die Gemeinwirtschaft, Gustav Fischer-Verlag, Jena

Neurath, Otto, 1919, *Wesen und Weg der Sozialisierung*, in: Neurath 1979, pp. 242–261

Neurath, Otto, 1920a, *Ein System der Sozialisierung*, in: Archiv für Sozialwissenschaft und Sozialpolitik 48 (1920/1921), English translation in: Neurath 2005, pp. 345–370

Neurath, Otto, 1920b, Vollsozialisierung. Eugen Diederichs Verlag, Jena 1920, English translation in Neurath 2005, pp. 370–404

Neurath, Otto, 1923a, *Geld und Sozialismus*, in: Der Kampf 16, pp. 145–157
Neurath, Otto, 1923b, *Geld, Sozialismus, Marxismus*, in: Der Kampf 16, pp. 283–288
Neurath, Otto, 1925a, Wirtschaftsplan und Naturalrechnung, Berlin, partly reprinted in Neurath 1979, pp. 262–287, English translation in Neurath 2005, pp. 405–465
Neurath, Otto, 1925b, *Sozialistische Nützlichkeitsrechnung und kapitalistische Reingewinnrechnung*, in: Der Kampf 18, pp. 391–395, English translation in Neurath 2005, pp. 466–472
Neurath, Otto, 1931a/1979, Empirische Soziologie, Vienna 1931, partly reprinted in Neurath 1979, pp. 145–234
Neurath, Otto, 1931b/2005, *Das gegenwärtige Wachstum der Produktionskapazität der Welt*, lecture before the World Social Economic Congress, Amsterdam 1931, English translation in Neurath 2005, pp. 475–505
Neurath, Otto, 1979, Wissenschaftliche Weltauffassung, Sozialismus und Logischer Empirismus, ed. R. Hegselmann, Suhrkamp-Verlag, Frankfurt
Neurath, Otto, 2004, Economic Writings. Selections 1904–1945, with an introduction by Thomas Uebel, Kluwer Academic Publishers, Dordrecht-Boston-London
Nordhaus, William, James Tobin, 1972, *Is Growth Obsolete*?, in: Economic Growth. Volume V of the Fiftieth Anniversary Colloquia Series of the National Bureau of Economic Research, New York
Pigou, A. C., 1920, The Economics of Welfare, Macmillan, London
Pribram, Karl, 1918, Die Grundgedanken der Wirtschaftspolitik der Zukunft, Verlag Leuschner und Lubenski, Graz und Leipzig
Rathenau, Walther, 1918, Die neue Wirtschaft, Berlin
Stolper, Gustav, 1921, Deutsch-Österreich als Sozial- und Wirtschaftsproblem, Drei Masken-Verlag, München
Uebel, Thomas, 2004, *Introduction: Neurath's Economics in Critical Context*, in: Neurath, Otto, 2004, pp. 1–108
Uebel, Thomas, 2005, *Incommensurability, Ecology, and Planning: Neurath in the Socialist Calculation Debate*, 1919–1928, in: History of Political Economy 37, pp. 309–342
Uebel, Thomas, 2006, Philosophy of Social Science in Early Logical Empiricism: The Case of Radical Physicalism (unpublished manuscript)
Weber, Fritz,1982, *Otto Neurath und die Sozialisierung*, in: Fritz Stadler (ed.), Arbeiterbildung in der Zwischenkriegszeit, Otto Neurath Gerd Arntz, Löcker-Verlag, Wien-München, pp. 133–139
Weissel, Erwin, 1976, Die Ohnmacht des Sieges. Arbeiterschaft und Sozialisierung nach dem Ersten Weltkrig in Österreich, Europaverlag, Wien
Wissel, Rudolf, 1920, Die Planwirtschaft, Hamburg

Chamber of Labour, Vienna
Prinz Eugen-Strasse 20
A-1040 Wien
guenther.chaloupek@akwien.at

Pluralism and Economic Institutions

John F. O'Neill

In a series of papers in *Economica* between 1941 and 1944 (Hayek 1941, 1942–1944) Hayek's criticisms of socialist planning were directed at a set of assumptions about the social world and social science that he took to partly underpin the socialist project. Hayek's epistemic arguments against planning and in defence of the market are deployed against the claims of 'scientism', 'objectivism' and 'physicalism' in the social sciences. These assumptions illustrate a pervasive version of the rationalist errors underlying socialist planning. They foster a form of social engineering which promises to achieve an optimal technical outcome through planning in which monetary calculation in the market place is replaced by *in natura* calculation in kind. One of the main objects of criticism was Neurath in whom, for Hayek, all these errors are gathered in one person. Neurath responded to those criticisms in a series of notes and letters to Hayek in 1945 which he hoped would form the basis for a public exchange between them (Neurath 1945a, b). Neurath's response focused on what he took to be shared epistemological assumptions and their common commitment to a pluralist alternative to totalitarianism. The response was in some ways an attempt to answer a question he formulated in his generous review of Hayek's *Road to Serfdom*: 'What would Professor Hayek answer if the tables were turned on him?' (Neurath 1945c, p. 121). Elsewhere I have looked in more detail at the epistemic arguments in this debate (O'Neill 1996, 2004, 2006). In this paper while I touch upon these arguments, I focus on the discussion of pluralism and its social and economic preconditions. I will argue that while there are internal problems with Neurath's arguments, (as someone put it to me in discussion of an early version of this paper, if Neurath is out to 'over-Hayek' Hayek, then there is also scope for 'over-Neurathing' Neurath) his defence of non-market institutional orders in the modern world raises significant problems with Hayek's position.

1 The Varieties of Pluralism

Central to the debates between Hayek and Neurath was their shared concern with the proper response to totalitarianism. In both one finds a defence of pluralism and claims about its institutional preconditions. However, before looking at their different

E. Nemeth et al. (eds.), *Otto Neurath's Economics in Context.*
Vienna Circle Institute Yearbook [2007]. Volume 13.

approaches to pluralism some initial clarification is in order. Both theorists use the concept of pluralism in a variety of different senses where these are not properly distinguished and in some cases are elided. Moreover, both theorists make a number of often implicit claims about the relations between them. In this section I will draw out some of the different senses in which the concept of pluralism is employed by Neurath and sketch the relations that he takes to hold between them.

I start with a concept of pluralism that has been at the central to recent liberalism which has started from the observation that in modern societies there is reasonable disagreement between citizens who hold different conceptions of the good life.

> *PCG* – Pluralism of conceptions of the good: There exists a plurality of different conceptions of the good, where one conception cannot be shown to be more rationally defensible than others.

While neither Neurath nor Hayek use the term 'conception of the good', both seem to hold something close to this doctrine. Neurath's discussion of pluralism, however, does not focus on abstract conceptions of the good but rather on ways of life. Neurath defends throughout his writings something like the following.

> *PNP* – Pluralism of normative practices: There exists a plurality of different ways of living a good life.

The concern for creating the conditions for a plurality of ways of living is already to be found in his early socialisation papers. In his later response to totalitarianism the need for 'an orchestration of ways of living' (1945c, p. 121) becomes a major theme. One expression of this pluralism that Neurath also addresses in his later work is linguistic.

> *PL* – Pluralism of language: Different communities with their different ways of living speak different languages not all of which are translatable into each other.

As I have noted elsewhere, pluralism in this sense raises a difficulty that is deeper and more intractable for public life that a plurality of conceptions of the good (O'Neill 2003b). Given a plurality of different conceptions of the good, if we speak the same language we can engage in a public conversation to resolve difference of to find a way of living with each other. A pluralism of language creates problems for the very possibility of such a conversation. As we shall see, the existence of a common physicalist language for Neurath makes possible such conversation at the point of common action (Neurath 1944b).

These general forms of pluralism need to be distinguished from a more specific claim that Neurath makes about welfare.

> *WP* – Welfare pluralism: There exists a plurality of different goods that that are constitutive of individual welfare.

Welfare concepts, such as standard of living or pleasure are multidimensional: "The attempts to characterize the standard of living are like those which try to characterize the 'state of health'. Both are multidimensional structures" (Neurath 1937, p. 146). Neurath develops the point from within a hedonistic framework. The pleasures that are constitutive of the good life are irreducibly plural in character (Neurath 1912). The practical expression of that pluralism is to be found in the plurality of conditions of life required for a good life (Lessman, this volume).

However, while welfare pluralism needs to be analytically distinguished from other forms of pluralism, there are relations between them. Welfare pluralism offers at least one basis for Neurath's claim that there exists a plurality of different ways of living a good life. Different ways of life express different ways in which the goods of life can be combined.

A major concern that can be discerned throughout Neurath's writings is the institutional conditions for is that the existence of a pluralism of ways of living. In particular he defends a version of the following.

IP – Institutional pluralism: A good economic order will involve a plurality of different institutional forms.

The defence of institutional pluralism is central to Neurath's criticisms of both market economies and Bolshevik models of socialism (O'Neill 2003a). Neurath makes a number of implicit claims about the relations between this institutional pluralism and other forms of pluralism which we will discuss later in this paper. In particular he takes IP to be a way of realising PCG, PNP and WP. Although the claim is to be already found in his contributions to the socialisations debates after the first world, they come still more to the fore in his later response to totalitarianism.

These forms of pluralism need to be distinguished from two other claims are defended by Neurath about cognitive and practical rationality. The first is a form of cognitive pluralism.

BP – Belief pluralism: a plurality of different beliefs is consistent with empirical evidence.

There are two versions of this claim, weak and strong. The weak version is an underdetermination thesis:

BP1 Empirical evidence does not determine a particular belief as true or false.

However, there is good evidence that Neurath defends a stronger more radical version of the claim:

BP2 There is no truth singular to be determined.

Corresponding to these forms of cognitive pluralism Neurath also defends a form of practical pluralism:

DP Decision pluralism: a plurality of different rational decisions is consistent with a given empirical base and set of rational decision making procedures.

Again this claim can take a more or less radical form. The less radical version is again an underdetermination thesis:

DP1 Empirical beliefs and procedures do not rationally determine a particular optimal outcome.

The more radial version is something as follows:

DP2 There is no optimal decision to be determined.

These forms of cognitive and practical pluralism are employed by Neurath in his discussion of pseudorationalism. Indeed, one way of characterising pseudorationalism in Neurath's later writings is the denial of these forms of pluralism. Insofar as the debates with Hayek are concerned the central claims are DP1 and DP2. However, Neurath takes these to follow from BP1, BP2 and WP. Whether one needs to defend something as strong as BP2 is I think open to doubt. Elsewhere I have suggested that Carnap was right to take Neurath to task for his defence of BP2 and for his assumption that it is required to defend his more practical claims (O'Neill 2006; see Neurath 1943–45). A defence of DP1 and DP2 is possible given BP1 and WP. However, I will not pursue the defensibility of radical belief pluralism further in this paper. My concern is with the various forms of practical pluralism that Neurath defends – DP, WP, PNP – and their institutional preconditions. In Sectis. 2 and 3 I will outline the debate between Hayek and Neurath and the claims about the relation of DP, BP and WP which emerge in those debates. In Sectis. 4–8 I then turn to the question of the institutional conditions for PNP and the differences that emerge between Hayek and Neurath on those conditions and the role of market institutions in their realisation.

2 Hayek Against Social Engineering

In Hayek's *Economica* papers the rationalist illusions of socialist planning are embodied in the figure of the social engineer. The 'characteristic mental attitude of the engineer' leads to two errors when it is extended beyond its proper scope and is employed in the social domain. The first is a rejection of pluralism of ends in social life. The engineer holds that there is a single end or hierarchy of ends which the engineer can employ to ascertain which of a set of possibilities provides an optimal means that can be directed to achieve that end: 'he will be concerned with a single end, control of all the efforts directed towards this end, and dispose for this purpose over a definitely given supply of resources' (Hayek 1942–1944, p. 167). Typical examples of such social ends are 'the general welfare' or 'the general interest'. This assumption that the resources can and should be directed towards some single end is taken elsewhere by Hayek to characterise the difference between liberalism and its totalitarian alternatives (Hayek 1944, 42 ff). The claim that social choices can be made on the basis of some single end or hierarchy of ends on which all can reasonably converge is incompatible with the existence within liberal societies of a plurality of different and competing values.

The second error of the social engineer is epistemic, the belief that it is possible to bring together all the information that is required to optimally achieve this particular end. The belief in the possibility of a technical optimum is premised on the assumption that the engineer could gather in one person or committee complete knowledge of society.

> The application of the engineering technique to the whole of society requires ... that the director possess the same complete knowledge of the whole society that the engineer possesses of his limited world. Central economic planning is nothing but such an application of engineering principles to the whole of society based on the assumption that such a complete concentration of all relevant knowledge is possible (Hayek 1942–1944, p. 173).

Social engineering fails to acknowledge the limits of knowledge that any a particular individual can possess. It is founded upon a mistaken belief in the omnipotence of reason, a belief Hayek variously terms 'rationalism' 'superrationalism' and 'Cartesian rationalism'. Against such rationalism Hayek claims, 'it may ... prove to be far the most difficult and not the least important task for human reason rationally to comprehend its own limitations' (Hayek 1942–1944, p. 162). There are two sources of human ignorance to which this argument appeals. The first is 'the division of knowledge' in society, that is, the dispersal of knowledge and skills throughout different individuals in society (Hayek 1937, 1945). Central to this argument is not simply the division of knowledge, but the nature of the knowledge that is dispersed among different agents which render it necessarily unavailable to any central planner. Practical knowledge embodied in skills and know-how, and knowledge of particulars local to time and place cannot be articulated or vocalised in a general propositional form that could be passed on to a central planning body. Consequently, any individual or planning body will be ignorant of this knowledge dispersed throughout society that is relevant to its decisions. A second source of ignorance is a necessary unpredictability of the future wants which has its basis in the unpredictability of the future development of knowledge and invention. Since future wants change with the invention and production of new objects for consumption and since the progress of human knowledge is in principle unpredictable – if we could predict the content of future knowledge, we would already have it – it follows that since human invention relies on the progress of knowledge, future human wants are also in principle unpredictable (Hayek 1942–1944, pp. 157–158; 1960 pp. 40–41; cf. Popper 1944–1945).

In contrast to central planning the market is taken by Hayek to solve the problems social coordination in the context of a pluralism of ends and the absence of the possibility of centralising all knowledge on a single agency. It is consistent with pluralism since a feature of market societies allows for social coordination without agreement on ends. Hence his later characterisation of the market order as the foundation of the 'Great Society':

> The Great Society arose through the discovery that men can live together in peace and mutually benefiting each other without agreeing on the particular aims that they severally pursue. The discovery that by substituting abstract rules of conduct for obligatory concrete ends made it possible to extend the order of peace beyond the small groups pursuing the same ends, because it enabled each individual to gain from the skill and knowledge of others whom he need not even know and whose aims could be wholly different from his own.[1]

Whereas the planned economy requires agreement on the relative ordering of different ends of the kind found in the household economy, the market is a catallactic order which allows for coordination without such agreement. The market also enables coordination without the centralisation of knowledge since the price mechanism

[1] Hayek F. A. (1976) *Law, Legislation and Liberty: Volume 2*, London, Routledge and Kegan Paul, p. 109.

imparts to actors that information that is required for the coordination of their activities without requiring the centralisation of dispersed knowledge.

> Though every party in [markets] will know only a small sector of all possible sources of supply, or of the uses of a commodity, yet directly or indirectly, the parties are so interconnected that the prices register the net results of all changes in demand or supply. It is as such an instrument for communicating to all those interested in a particular commodity the relevant information ... that markets and prices must be seen (Hayek 1942–1944, p. 176–177, cf. 1937, 1945).

Central to this market coordination is the entrepreneur who is alert to new opportunities in the market place. The entrepreneur confronts the second source of ignorance concerning the full range of future wants. However the market also solves this problem since it acts as a discovery procedure in which different hypotheses about the future are embodied in entrepreneurial acts and tested in the market place (Hayek 1978, pp. 179–190, cf. Kirzner 1985).

Scientism for Hayek is one source of the belief in the possibility of social engineering. Scientism involves the expansion of the methods of natural science beyond their proper domain and their application to the study of the social world. It offers a basis for the social engineer's corresponding expansion of the engineering mentality beyond its proper scope and its employment in social choices. This scientistic attitude is expressed in the doctrine of 'objectivism'. The concept is used in this context to refer to the view that social science requires the elimination of all terms that cannot be given a physical characterisation, in particular the elimination of all mental terms. That eliminativist programme is taken to be typified by Neurath's physicalist programme (Hayek 1942–1944, p. 78). Subjectivism in contrast is the view that the objects of the social sciences cannot be thus characterised. They are objects constituted by beliefs and ideas that individuals have about them: "Neither a 'commodity' or an 'economic good', nor 'food' or 'money' can be defined in physical terms but only in terms of views people hold about things" (Hayek 1942–1944, p. 53).

The doctrines of objectivism and physicalism are taken by Hayek to underpin a belief in the possibility of replacing economic choices through market prices by '*in natura*' calculations which make direct use of the physical properties of objects (Hayek 1942–1944, p. 170). The social engineer typically holds that it would be possible to bring together knowledge of the objective properties of resources and things that could replace the price mechanism of market coordination. "The engineer's ideal which he feels the 'irrational' economic forces prevent him from achieving, based on his study of the objective properties of the things, is usually some purely technical optimum of universal validity" (Hayek 1942–1944, p. 170). In rejecting objectivism, Hayek argues that such *in natura* calculations are not possible. There are no physical units that can be used as a basis for planning economic production.[2] Hence, to replace the price system in favour *in natura* calculation in

---

[2] That argument is aimed not just against socialist theorists but also against precursors of ecological economics such as Ballod-Atlanticus, Popper-Lynkeus Ostwald, Soddy and Solvay who claimed that energy units might serve as a basis of economic choice. (Hayek 1942–1944, pp. 90–91). I discuss this dimension of the argument in more detail in O'Neill (2004).

kind is to give up a solution to the problem of human ignorance in favour of a socialist illusion of complete knowledge that fails to acknowledge its existence.

Neurath is a central target for Hayek in that he brings together in one person the errors of scientism, objectivism and *in natura* calculation. In the work of Neurath all the errors underpinning the socialist project are taken come together: 'The most persistent advocate of … *in natura* calculation is, significantly, Dr. Otto Neurath, the protagonist of modern "physicalism" and "objectivism"' (Hayek 1942–4, p. 170; for a discussion see Uebel 2000). Hayek might have added that he is also a protagonist of the social engineer. Moreover, although Hayek does not quote specific passages one might also note that Neurath's writings on socialisation in the 1920s and the early 1930s do contain a number of passages that appear to bear out Hayek's characterisation of the epistemological assumptions he is concerned to criticise. Neurath does in places appear to assume that planning agencies are able to gather all knowledge relevant to formulating an economic plan. He writes for example of the possibility 'an economic order in which central institutions survey the entire economy' (Neurath 1920a, p. 381) and of viewing national or even world economies as 'one enormous factory' (Neurath 1931, p. 387). However such remarks do not do justice to Neurath's position even in the 1920s and early 1930s, and they certainly do not do justice to his later writings on planning which depart markedly from the picture of the social engineer that Hayek presents. Neurath's social engineer is as we shall see below a different character.

3 Neurath: Clearing the Ground

The central move in Neurath's response is to highlight what he takes to be his common commitment with Hayek to a pluralist alternative to totalitarianism, and to shared epistemic assumptions about the limits of reason and common criticisms of Cartesian rationalism. Correspondingly, he suggests that his commitments to physicalism and *in natura* calculation do not have the technocratic implications that Hayek takes them to have. Much of the response consists in Neurath clarifying his own position as a preparation for the debate he hoped to have. Physicalism does not involve the elimination of all 'mental' vocabulary or the reduction mental vocabulary to physical terms:

> I never tried to "explain mental processes by physical ones" because I do not have the means in my language to distinguish between "mental" and "physical" – all my terms are when, where how terms therefore what Professor von Hayek and others call "mental" appear manifestly in my language as "speech behaviour" or "arguing" etc. i.e. a good where, when, how item (Neurath 1945a).[3]

Neurath was not committed to the elimination of intentional vocabulary from the social science or to the absence of interpretative activity on the part of the social scientist. Neurath's own social theory is institutionalist – a form of social behaviourism which

[3]For a discussion of Neurath's physicalism see Uebel (2003).

takes public institutions and social orders for the starting point for analysis (O'Neill 2004, pp. 435–438). Physicalism is the doctrine that all statements in the sciences, social sciences, and everyday life should be capable of translation into the terms that refer to spatio-temporal particulars:

> 'Physicalism', as I suggested it, starts from everyday language, which avoids elements which the various peoples on earth do not have in common. The assumption is, that Melanesian tribes and European explorers can start to talk on cows and calves, pains and pleasures without difficulties, whereas difficulties appear when expressions like 'cause', 'punishment' 'mind' etc. enter the talk. In this part of our everyday language which physicalism acknowledges one formulates questions with 'where, when, how' (Neurath 1945a).

Similarly the doctrine of i*n natura* calculation is not the doctrine that there exist some purely physical units, like units of energy, that are independent of human use or belief that could be employed for planning. Neurath rejects the claim that purely physical units, such as units of energy, could be used for the purpose of planning (Neurath 1942, p. 427; O'Neill 2004, pp. 438–442). Planning answers to judgements about what best serves human welfare, and the concept of human welfare is both multidimensional and irreducibly social. There is no single scale of values, and in particular a physical scale of values in terms of which losses in one dimension of welfare can be measured in terms of gains in another.[4]

Neurath in part in virtue of this internally pluralist conception of welfare also rejects the technocratic idea of a social optimum that can be ascertained by experts. He defends a form of what I earlier called decision pluralism. Thus he opposes "what is called the 'technocratic' movement' which assumes there exists' one best solution with its 'optimum happiness', with its 'optimum population', with its 'optimum health', with its 'optimum working week', with its 'optimum productivity' or something else of this kind' and which "asks for a particular authority which should be exercised by technicians and other experts in selecting 'big plans'" (Neurath 1942, pp. 426–427). Neurath's rejection of the very idea of technocratic optimal solutions in the social context also has a basis in epistemic assumptions that he claims to share with Hayek:

> I am the arch-enemy of the 'illusion of complete knowledge' and from this point of view I think Professor von Hayek should praise me and appreciate my never ceasing efforts to destroy such illusions (Neurath 1945a).

Neurath like Hayek rejects Cartesian rationalism. The arguments are developed in his criticisms of 'pseudorationalism' which first appears his 1913 paper 'The lost wanderers of Descartes and the auxiliary motive'. A rationalist who believes in reason must recognise the boundaries to the power of reason in arriving at decisions: 'Rationalism sees its chief triumph in the clear recognition of the limits of actual insight' (Neurath 1913, p. 8). It is a mark of the pseudorationalist to believe that there do exist rules of insight which determine unique to all decisions. Pseudorationalism exists in the domains of both action and thought. In the sphere of theory, it is exhibited in the belief that there exist rules for the scientific method

[4] For a discussion see Leßman (this volume) and O'Neill (2004).

which if followed eliminate falsehood and lead to ever nearer approximations to the truth. What marks the philosophy of Descartes is a realisation of the limits of rules of reason in action, but a failure to recognise similar limits in the rules for the direction of the mind. Just as in action, so in theoretical matters, reason underdetermines our theories. Clearly Neurath's remarks about the limits of reason, and indeed his specific attack on Cartesian rationalism, are echoed in Hayek's later remarks in the scientism essay against Cartesian rationalism – that 'it may ... prove to be far the most difficult and not the least important task for human reason rationally to comprehend its own limitations' (Hayek 1942–1944, p. 162).

Neurath in rejecting pseudorationalism defends the forms of cognitive pluralism I outlined in Sect. 2. This cognitivist pluralism also provides grounds for his practical pluralism:

> Even before the first world war I realized that acknowledging a kind of primary 'pluralism' in our scientific approach has also its consequences for our daily life. If science enables us to make more than one sound prediction, how may we use science as a means of action? We can never avoid a 'decision', because no account would be able to show us one action as 'the best', no computation would present us with any 'optimum', whatever actions have to be discussed. Therefore 'decision' plays its part in any kind of scientific research as well as in our daily life. That is the reason why I stressed the 'unpredictability' as an essential element of empiricism thus repudiating all attempts to use unequivocal historical predictions as the basis of social actions (Neurath 1946a, p. 80).

With the rejection of the idea of a technical optimum Neurath also rejects the technocratic conception of planning through a board of scientific experts.

> [I] should think that even [though] disagree[ing] with many of von Hayek's remarks and his historical outlook, I should describe him as a research worker, who together with us physicalists, fights the pseudorationalism of our period, which tries to use science as a kind of idol, and scientists and quasi-scientists regarding as a kind of born leaders, who may direct our life according to so-called "tests". Who tests the testers? (Neurath 1945a).

Finally the rejection of pseudorationalism is also taken to underpin a commitment to pluralism against the idea that planning involves a single end that offers a single optimal solution of the kind that Hayek takes to be a feature of the social engineer.

> Of course there are people – I call them pseudo-rationalists – who try to present ONE and ONLY ONE best solution as a scientific one and I agree with you that this pseudorationalism is dangerous and may sometimes support totalitarianism. But I think that you should at least mention that there is a scientific attitude, represented by Logical Empiricism, which is PLURALIST through and through. ... (Neurath to Hayek 11.1.45, Neurath 1945b).

Neurath's social engineer is not the technocratic expert that Hayek portrays in his criticism of scientism. He is a more utopian figure that is grounded in another set of assumptions that Neurath shares with Hayek, that is the specific limits to prediction in social life that is consequent on the unpredictability of the future content of knowledge. It is a feature of human knowledge and invention that we cannot predict the content of that which will be novel (Neurath 1943, p. 148). In his reply to Hayek, Neurath points out that this rejection of social prediction is central to the final sections of the *Foundations of the Social Sciences*. The image of scientists as sailors at sea who cannot put into dock but must modify with materials at hand to shore up the vessel is here used precisely to deny the possibility of anticipating the future of knowledge:

> A new ship grows out of the old one, step by step – and while they are still building, the sailors may already be thinking of a new structure, and they will not always agree with one another. *The whole business will go in a way we cannot even anticipate today*. That is our fate (Neurath 1944a, p. 47, my emphasis).

Given this unpredictability, social engineering involves not the idea of running a whole society like a machine, but rather a form of scientific utopianism. The role of the social scientist is not to predict the future, but rather, like the engineer, to present possibilities which a democratic crew can use to attempt to bring a particular future into existence.[5]

This utopianism itself is not open to the criticisms of Popper and Berlin that utopian thought itself is incompatible with value pluralism (Berlin 2002, pp. 212–217; Popper 1966, Chap. 9). Neurath's utopianism was pluralist in two senses. First, it is plural in the possibilities it presents. He offers utopias not the utopia. Second and more significantly it is concerned with the institutional conditions for pluralism itself.

> Professor von Hayek thinks of planning exclusively as something dictatorial. I do not know why. In my articles PLANNING FOR FREEDOM I tried to stress the point that planning can be connected with a suppression of individuals hardly heard before, but also to enable us to be free to an extent hardly heard before, "free" i.e. a multiplicity of ways of life possible, non-conformism supported by planned institutions. (1945a).

Neurath's later work is particularly concerned with the institutional conditions for pluralism in ways of life. However, it is a concern that is found throughout his writing. It is with the question of the institutional conditions for such pluralism and Hayek's and Neurath's different responses to that question to which I now turn.

4 The Institutional Conditions for Pluralism: Discursive and Non-discursive

A question that both Hayek and Neurath addressed is the following: What institutional structures are required to allow individuals to live together and coordinate their activities given a plurality of conceptions of the ends of life and ways of living a good

[5] 'Similarly, any collection of historically given material would be advantageous, if we were discussing the future of social structures; but, the conception of new ways of life would be of some importance – a kind of creative "social engineering" or "scientific utopianism". We may invent new possibilities, but we shall not be able to invent all of them, because even invention is correlated to certain other social elements, which do not form part of our environment today. Unpredictability plays its part. As we are interested in the discussion of practical questions concerning a future world community, we should stick to this point and avoid dissertations on so called "historical necessity" or "historical forces which determine the fate of mankind" and similar phrases which indicate that some of our interlocutors pretend to a knowledge of a "film" which is as yet in the making. This "unpredictability" and "making decisions concerning our future way of life" are closely connected' (Neurath 1944b, p. 29).

life? Hayek's response to the question is non-discursive. The market allows individuals with quite different ends to coordinate their actions without conversation. Market institutions allow 'each individual to gain from the skill and knowledge of others whom he need not even know and whose aims could be wholly different from his own' (Hayek 1976, p. 109). Through market exchange individuals pursuing their own particular ends can by way of the price signal coordinate their activities with strangers whose ends they need not know or share. Given the non-cognitivist account of values that Hayek shared with others in the Austrian tradition, rational conversation about ends is not possible. The alternatives to market institutions are continual enmity, pre-modern social conformity or authoritarian force.

Neurath clearly rejects this market based account of the conditions for pluralism of conceptions of the good and ways of living in modern conditions. A central theme in his early contributions to the socialisation debates had been with the question of how a socialised economy could avoid the social uniformity that was a consequence of the market economy.

> Should China, India, Central Africa really get one and the same socialism? Each comparative study of different orders of life teaches us that it was the tendency to organise the economy in all civilisations after the same pattern which made the free market society so much hated. If socialism should bring liberation, it must be joined by tolerance, it must do justice to the differences in civilisations and fit each one into the economic plan and the administrative economy in its own way (Neurath 1920a, p. 402).

The market economy on this account far from providing the conditions for pluralism of ways of life is inimical to it. The alternative was to find a form of socialised economy that engendered institutional pluralism.

> [W]ithin the framework of a deliberately devised economic plan it is possible for forms of economy of various kinds to co-exist without being forced into competition: craft co-operatives, special settlements with shared work, industrial associations. In this way perhaps the intolerance of the market economy will be overcome, which destroyed everything that stood against 'laissez faire' and the wish of expansion for capitalist gain. Manchester liberalism ... treated community and guild movements with contempt (Neurath 1920a, p. 397).

The theme comes to the fore still more clearly in his later works, in particular his 1942 essay 'International Planning for Freedom'. Here the theme is developed in terms of the now familiar observation that totalitarianism is marked by the denial of any particular loyalties in civil society: 'In a dictatorial one-party state ... there is a tendency for one, and only one, loyalty to 'devour' all others, and various loyalties or not permitted to grow side by side ...' (Neurath 1942, p. 429) Conversely, the mark of freedom in a democratic society is that 'each member is permitted to have more that one loyalty' (Neurath 1942, p. 429). The institutional structures for planning which Neurath defends in this context, of a 'societas societum' that is made up of 'overlapping authorities' are aimed at providing the conditions for social 'multiplicity' (Neurath 1942, 431 ff).

Neurath's response to the problems of social coordination in this context is, unlike those of Hayek, discursive in character. Coordination of action requires the existence of 'social *lingua franca*' through which actors from different ways of life can arrive at common decisions at the point of action (Neurath 1944b, p. 30).

Neurath refers to the 'necessity for a neutral language' for the purposes of social co-operation:

> Variety within a community has to be based on some structure of a society and therefore we have to look at the social elements which enable contacts between human beings from group to group throughout the world and a communication of understanding from nation to nation. It is manifest that a certain amount of trust is needed for successful co-operation and the possibility to make contact through language. If one language should not be used, then languages which are partially translatable into one another are wanted. What we call science may be regarded as the typical branch of arguing which human beings of all nations, rich and poor have in common. Discussions on the sun, moon, stars, anatomy, geography, pleasure and pain, may be carried out in any civilization: whereas theology and legal terms ore mainly local. In the field of scientific talks all human beings can co-operate, whereby we use the term 'scientific' in a wider sense (Neurath 1945e, p. 251).

Physicalism makes its appearance here as a doctrine about the nature of the 'neutral' language required for social coordination.

There are two responses that might be made by the Hayekian to this position. The first is that this account of the physicalist basis of social coordination offers another example of the technocratic scientism that Hayek takes Neurath's work to exhibit. It offers a vision of experts inhabiting planning boards talking in the language of science. The second response is that the Neurathian position is open to the same objections that Hayek raises against centralised planning systems. The dispersal of practical knowledge that cannot be articulated in propositional form is a problem not just for centralised planning but for any discursive form of coordination that relies purely on knowledge that can be thus articulated. The first response is the weaker of the two. However, it does raise some significant questions about the nature of the common physicalist language to which Neurath appeals. The second is more serious and has been developed more recently against more deliberative models of socialism. I will suggest that there are responses to it implicit in Neurath's work which highlights important problems within Hayek's own position.

5 Physicalism, Welfare and Value

The first objection to Neurath's discursive account of the institutional conditions for pluralism turns on the potential technocratic narrowness of the basis he offers for public conversation. A purely physicalist language for social coordination raises the spectre of Hayek's social engineer, of experts inhabiting planning boards talking in the language of science. That accusation I think would be unfair. We have already noted that Hayek misinterprets what Neurath means by 'physicalism' and Neurath's own rejection of a technocratic politics of this kind. In the passage of Neurath's quoted at the end of the last section the use of the term 'scientific' in 'wider sense' is particularly significant. The term 'scientific' is being used not narrowly to refer to the language of the special sciences, in which particular persons have particular expertise. It is rather being used in a much more expansive sense to refer to all everyday terms or 'jargon' that refer to spatio-temporal particulars.

The conversations at the point of action form part of a more general conversation of citizens that stays at the level of an everyday physicalist language of particulars. The conception of physicalism that Neurath is not only consistent with democratic conversation, it aims to sustain just such conversations.

If there is a problem with physicalist language as neutral social lingua franca it does not lie in its being the language of technocratic experts. There are however, I believe other problems that I discuss in more detail elsewhere (O'Neill 2003b). First, it is not clear how neutral a physicalist language can be. Moving to a physicalist language of spatio-temporal particulars cannot in itself avoid the problems of communication across different languages. There can be misunderstandings even when talking of cows and calves, sun, moon, stars, pleasures and pains just as much as one talks of cause and punishment. The meanings of the terms will not be culturally neutral. Second, like Hayek, Neurath starts from a non-cognitivist approach to values. Where they differ is how they respond to that non-cognitivism. Where Hayek argues that this involves a move to non-discursive institutions for social coordination, for Neurath it involves an elimination of normative terms from the neutral physicalist language. Physicalism is intended to be value-neutral. I remain unconvinced that this is either possible or desirable.

Neurath makes two standard moves to eliminate a normative vocabulary. The first is that we should relativise value terms to speakers and communities and hence in the language for common conversation they are to be eliminated. A term like 'justice' is relativised – 'just according to the rules of a certain nation or tribe at a certain date' (Neurath 1941, p. 147). The second is to replace normative terms with equivalents that lack the normative force: 'we propose to avoid praising and blaming words in articles and books on history: one man 'kills' another man, he does not 'murder' or 'assassinate' him' (Neurath 1941, p. 147). The rejection of value terms here is not in terms of a failure of the physicalist test. For example, the assassination of the Archduke Ferdinand was a particular spatio-temporal event. It is rather that 'assassination' is a value-laden term.

Neither of the standard moves invoked by Neurath works for familiar reasons. The relativisation of terms to the group studied is often not possible since terms like 'justice' are themselves contested terms within groups studied. The elimination of normative terms is not possible without loss of information. Reference to the assassination of the Archduke Ferdinand does and should appear in history texts on the first world war and the same information would not be conveyed if ones replaces 'assassination' with 'killing'. It is not possible to replace thick normative concepts of this kind from our descriptions of the world. Neither does it strike me as desirable nor required by Neurath's position. The use of those terms is central to Neurath's own welfarism. As we noted above Neurath's account of the conditions of human welfare are not physicalist in the sense that Hayek understands the term. The specification of the conditions of well-being includes not just physical conditions in the everyday sense of the term but also social and institutional conditions of social esteem: 'change in a man's food and shelter is of less importance than a change in his state of being bullied or humiliated by certain institutions' (Neurath 1942, p. 425). Self-government and freedom and other human relations belong to the 'happiness conditions' of human beings (Neurath 1942, p. 427). Particular acts of humiliation on the one hand and of social recognition on the other would form a full account of the conditions of life of individuals through which we make judgements about their standard of living. Neurath's account of welfare is infused with a thick normative vocabulary. Nor should this be surprising. It is not possible to engage in the kind of discussion of welfare that Neurath envisages without the use of normative vocabulary.

Neurath does in place appear to assume one can through appeal to his hedonist account of well-being. The terms 'pleasure' and 'pain' are standard items on his list of physicalist terms. I have suggested elsewhere that there is a problem with his hedonism from his own physicalist perspective (O'Neill 2003b). However a still more basic problem is that in the context of discussion of welfare both these terms and the more generally conditions of life he specifies in making judgements about the standard of living clearly have a normative force. The point is one that G.D.H. Cole raised against Neurath in correspondence about Neurath's social silhouettes:

> I do not think the result of looking at things in this way is that one is less simply with a number of diverse patterns of which one can say "Here is pattern A" and "Here is pattern B", and so on, and leave it at that. I think that a pattern can be good or bad in the same sense that the work of art can be good or bad. What it cannot be is *the* good (or, of course, *the* bad). In other words, there may be no single thing of which one can say "This is good absolutely and in all circumstances", but there may be patterns of which one can say "This pattern is very much better than that," and this implies a standard of judgement, that he is of valuation, which I believed to be indispensable and yet incapable of being reduced to scientific terms. I am not sure how far you agree with this, which amounts in my mind to a pluralistic conception of values which still remain values, though they are not referable to a single and unique standard (Cole G. D. H. to Neurath, 26 January 1945, in Neurath (1945d)).

The point Cole makes here is a telling one. Cole retains Neurath's pluralism and his analogy with works of art is very similar to one that Neurath himself employed in his early writing (Neurath 1909, pp. 293–295). Cole also rejects the kind of non-naturalist ethical realism of the kind defended by G. E. Moore. What he denies is that we can make welfare comparisons without making normative judgements of 'better' or 'worse'.

Neurath's response to Cole is of interest I think in that in partly granting the point, Neurath does appear to open up the space for a form of naturalism about welfare values. Neurath's responds as follows:

> Should you agree with me that in any case, where we are using the terms "good" or "bad" we can use them only with the addition "for somebody", then I should add, that we have too described, what kinds of pleasure, happiness etc you want to include. Then we shall reach statements of this type: should we alter the social actions from A to B, then the Happiness of the group X will increase, the Happiness of the group Y will decrease etc. This description of increasing or decreasing happiness, as vaguely as it may be possible, is a scientific and empiricist statement as any other (Neurath to Cole, 3 September 1945, Neurath 1945d).

In insisting the 'good' always needs to addition 'for someone', Neurath appears to be appealing to a form of the general relativising strategy that we have just criticised.

However, things are not in this context so clear. The use of 'good for' in this welfare context is ambiguous. The phrase 'x is good for a' can be given either intensional or extensional readings. For example to say 'lard is good for John' could be understood as 'for John, lard is good', or 'John believes that lard is good': 'good for' is given an intensional reading. 'Lard is good for John' could be interpreted as 'lard improves John's conditions of life': 'good for' is given an extensional reading.[6] The two readings can clearly come apart. Given that John has a weight problem, then while John's love of chips fried in lard might make the claim 'lard is good for John' true on the intensional reading, it will be false on the extensional reading.

My own view of well-being would be that this extensional use of the term should be understood in broadly Aristotelian eudaimonic terms. However, the point is one that is consistent with Neurath's Epicurean hedonist account of well-being. Consider for example Kahneman's distinction between objective happiness as an average utility derived from a record of actual point by point reports of the quality of an experience during some episode and subjective happiness in the sense of people's retrospective and fallible assessment of what that utility score has been (Kahneman 1999) The two can depart. For example, Kahneman has some nice experiments that show that retrospective assessments of an episode of painful experiences are a function of the peak intensity of the experience and the intensity of the last moment of the period, and not of the duration of episodes; so an episode of painful experiences that is prolonged by additional but less intense pain produces a better global subjective valuation than a shorter episode without the additional period of pain (Kahneman et al. 1993). In those cases you would want to say on the intensional reading for some subject Jim, 'The period with the better end is good for Jim' but, given a classical version of hedonism, one would deny it on the extensional reading of the claim.

To apply the relativisation strategy that Neurath employs to eliminate normative terms from his physicalist language to the phrase 'good for' would require an intensional reading of the phrase. However, it is not that reading that does the work in Neurath's writings on welfare. Rather it is this extensional reading of the phrase. In this context Neurath in practice works within a broadly naturalistic account of human welfare. It is I think the better for doing so. As far as welfare is concerned the form of naturalism that Neurath assumes in practice is more defensible than his official non-cognitivism. Moreover this naturalist reading of the normative vocabulary of welfare also makes better sense of the possibility of reasoned conversations about the different groups about welfare conditions. It lies at the basis of the continuing power of Neurath's version of welfarism in social policy.

[6] To give another example, consider 'Glucose is good for John'. On the extensional reading it should be understood as saying something like 'glucose will improve John's conditions of life'. Given the identity statement 'glucose is $C_6H_{12}O_6$', we can infer '$C_6H_{12}O_6$ is good for John'. On the intensional reading it is understood as 'for John, glucose is good' or 'John believes glucose is good'. Given the identity statement 'glucose is $C_6H_{12}O_6$', we cannot infer '$C_6H_{12}O_6$ is good for John'.

6 Knowledge, Language and Coordination

A second Hayekian objection to Neurath's position is that any discursive institutions, however decentralised into different overlapping authorities, will share the problems that Hayek aims at centralised planning. As I noted above central to Hayek's argument against central planning is not simply the division of knowledge among different actors, but the nature of the knowledge thus dispersed. Practical knowledge embodied in skills and know-how, cannot be articulated in a general propositional form that could be passed on to a central planning body. The argument could run – and has run against more recent deliberative models of economic life – that if there are forms of practical knowledge that cannot be passed on to a central planning system in virtue of not being open to propositional articulation, then neither will they be open to articulation in a deliberative setting. Hence, any models of economic decision making that rely on purely deliberative institutions to co-ordinate activities are open to the same epistemic objections Hayek's develops against centralised planning (Hodgson 1999, pp. 48–49; cf. Pennington 2001. For a discussion see O'Neill 2007, Chap. 12). If Hayek is right then any co-ordination of dispersed practical knowledge requires mechanisms that 'rely to some significant extent on the market and the price mechanism' (Hodgson 1999, p. 49).

How powerful is this objection to Neurath's position? There are two distinct claims here that need to be distinguished. The first is the negative claim that no purely discursive institutions for the coordination of action could capture practical knowledge dispersed amongst actors. The second is the positive claim that only market institutions are able to coordinate such knowledge. The first point is one that Neurath grants in his correspondence with Hayek. He concedes that 'community life' will be based on rules of conduct that cannot be vindicated through rational reflection: 'I fully accept with Professor von Hayek that therefore the community life will be based on *common acceptance of certain rules* the results of which we cannot *prove* in a strict way' (Neurath 1945a). The claim is consistent with claims that Neurath makes elsewhere in his writing, for example the role of tradition in decision making which he contrasts to pseudorationalism (Neurath 1913), and the role of habit and custom in his empirical sociology (Neurath 1931, pp. 371–380). The significance of practical knowledge forms part of the Machian legacy in Neurath's work. Correspondingly his early socialisation plans held onto role for habitual and customary that was untypical of social democracy of the period. (Typical is the discussion of Gemeinschaft in Neurath 1920b, pp. 350–353.) The insufficiency of purely discursive procedures is also implicit in Neurath's reference to trust as a necessary condition for cooperation and public conversation. (Neurath 1945e, p. 251) What is disputed in Neurath's response is the claim that the epistemic arguments against purely discursive solutions to social and economic coordination entails market mechanisms are required. Neurath's work contains two main strands of argument against that claim: an argument from the ubiquity of the epistemic problems; an argument from the institutional conditions for the coordination of scientific knowledge.

7 The Ubiquity Problem

The argument from the ubiquity of the problem is one that Neurath states thus in his response to Hayek:

> Professor von Hayek thinks people think too much of the society as a factory, as if we were able to predict so much better in a factory. I want to stress the point that in the factory we are not able to predict as comprehensively as Professor von Hayek thinks. I have to over Hayek Professor Hayek we are not in a position of comprehensive prediction there either (Neurath 1945a).

Unpredictability and the absence of complete knowledge are general facts of social existence which in existing societies permeate non-market as well as market spheres. Hence, given successful coordination in those other spheres, it cannot be the case that markets are themselves a necessary condition for such coordination.

One can make Neurath's point more concrete here through consideration of the Taylorist model of scientific management.[7] Taylorism involved the attempt to eliminate practical knowledge from the productive process: 'the development of a science ... involves the establishment of many rules, laws and formulae which replace the judgement of the individual workman ... The workman is told minutely what he is to do and how he is to do it; any improvement which he makes upon the orders given to him is fatal to success.' The task of scientific management is that of 'gathering together all the traditional knowledge which in the past had been possessed by the workman and then classifying, tabulating and reducing the knowledge to rules, laws and formulae' (Taylor 1906). Something like Hayek's objections to centralised planning apply also here. The model of scientific management relies upon the elimination of local and practical knowledge. Complete Taylorism is not possible.

In raising this ubiquity problem Neurath highlights both a strength and a weakness in Hayek's position. The strength lies in the very generality of the problem that Hayek raises. The epistemic problem of dispersed knowledge is one that any complex organisation has to solve. The firm from the production line through to higher lines of management can operate only to the extent that it allows for some autonomy to those in the organisation to employ local and practical knowledge. Indeed

---

[7] The example is not Neurath's who certainly in his early writings did not object to Taylorism as such. However, his responses to Taylorism are interesting in highlighting the pluralism already evident in his early work. In 'The Converse Taylor System' he addresses the worry about the way in which the Taylor system requires the moulding of workers to fit a scientifically determined form of organisation. The converse Taylor system would be concerned rather to develop forms of organisation that are appropriate to the dispositions of individuals. The background worry here is one that we noted above – the forms of uniformity engendered by market economies: 'The trade economy has released men from countless local bonds and given them a far reaching freedom of decision; on the other hand it created market conditions such that individuals, on the basis of their free decisions, have to agree to a form of life which for the majority was basically the same, having only scant regard for variable inclinations and dispositions' (Neurath 1917, p. 132). The aim of planning should be to create conditions in which such uniformity is overcome in which there exist 'multiplicity of forms of life adapted to the multiplicity of men themselves' (Neurath 1917, p. 133).

Hayekian themes about the limits of centralised planning have there own history in the socialist tradition in discussions of the firm in the conflict within organisations between the need to direct and discipline the work force while at the same time allowing it sufficient autonomy to employs its own local practical skills on which the workplace relies.[8] The problem is one that has become more significant in 'knowledge economies' where the knowledge that is thus dispersed throughout an organisation can form its main productive asset. The weakness of Hayek's position is that the only institutional form through the epistemic problem is addressed is through market exchange. Hayek assumes a form of market monism. What the ubiquity argument highlights is another argument for institutional pluralism.

Both the merits and limits of Hayek's position are evident when it comes to the theory of the firm. A longstanding problem in the Austrian tradition has been the absence of a theory of the firm (Foss 1994, 1997; Lewin and Phelan 2000). The firm does rely upon forms of organisation that are non-market in form and indeed include hierarchical direction. Why should such organisations exist given Hayek's epistemic arguments for the price system as a means of coordinating knowledge? There are standard two responses within recent Austrian economic theory to the absence of a theory of the firm. One has been to appeal to the Coasian theory of the firm to fill the gap. Coase's theory appeals to the transaction costs to explain why the firm should exist within a market economy. Where the costs of market transactions in creating and enforcing contracts become greater than the costs of hierarchical management it is more efficient to substitute the hierarchical structure of the firm for the market exchanges between independent property holders (Coase 1937; Williamson 1975, 1985). Some recent theorists in the Austrian tradition have suggested that while the theory is not developed within the Austrian tradition, its insights are quite consistent with those of Austrian economics and indeed, it is only in conditions of uncertainty and the absence of market equilibrium of the kind posited by Austrian economics that Coasian arguments have their force. It is within Austrian theory rather than neo-classical theory that the insights of Coase are best developed (Foss 1994, 1997; Lewin and Phelan 2000). The Austrian epistemic arguments also give us insights, it is claimed, into the limits of the firm (Klein 1996). What is not clear about those attempts is how the appeal to the Coasian theory resolves the epistemic problems that Hayek raises. A second response is to suggest that the Coasian theory should be replaced or at least supplemented by knowledge based or competence theories of the firm which account for the existence and competitive advantage of the firm in terms of the ways in which the firm handles practical knowledge dispersed throughout an organisation (Foss 1993). Competence theories do start from some of Hayek's epistemic claims about the division of knowledge and owe something to Austrian theory. However, they offer a very different picture of the way that institutions gather and embody knowledge that found in the picture of the market coordination of knowledge

[8]The strongest version of the point is that of Cardan who takes it to form 'the fundamental contradiction within capitalism': 'The capitalist system can only maintain itself by trying to reduce workers into mere order-takers...into executants of decisions taken elsewhere. At the same time the system can only function as long as this reduction is never achieved'. (Cardan 1974, p. 45).

between individual actors central to Hayek's perspective. They focus on the knowledge gathered and embodied in the institutional routines of the firm which is not reducible to that of members (Adaman and Devine 2002; Hodgson 1998). They are Hayekian in their origins in that they take his epistemic problems seriously, but they are not at all Hayekian in their conclusions.

Neurath's ubiquity objection highlights the ways in which arguments that Hayek employs to arrive at this conclusion appear too strong. There are a variety of institutional structures that are employed to coordinate dispersed knowledge that do not rely directly upon market mechanisms. This does not detract from the importance of the epistemic problem that Hayek raises and its more general significance of understanding different forms of knowledge coordinating activity. As I noted above it offers another argument for institutional pluralism. There are a variety of different institutional forms through which the epistemic problem is resolved, including discursive institutions. There are a variety of different institutional forms through which the epistemic problem is resolved, including discursive institutions.

8 Science: Coordination Without Pyramidism

The arguments about the firm raised by Neurath's ubiquity argument are arguments that concern hierarchical forms of coordination within a market economy. The significance of Neurath's argument about science is that science involves coordinated activity without markets and central coordination. Thus in his response to Kallen's objection to the project of unified science on the grounds that it was coercive and monistic (Kallen 1946), Neurath answers that the project rather showed 'how much unity of action can result, without any kind of authoritative integration' (Neurath 1946b, p. 230). The promise of the project of unified science for Neurath is the coordination of activities without a single hierarchical' organisation. As is now widely acknowledged, the project of unified science did not involve the traditional reductionist model often associated with positivism in which all the sciences would be logically derivable via bridge-laws from physics. Neurath rejects this project of 'scientific pyramidism' completely: "would it not be preferable to treat all statements and all sciences as coordinated and to abandon for good the traditional hierarchy: physical sciences, biological sciences, social sciences and similar types of 'scientific pyramidism?'" (Neurath 1944a, p. 8). Neurath's account of unified science is rather that of an orchestration of the sciences. Neurath did see the coordination of the sciences as with the coordination of social action more generally in discursive terms. As such Neurath claims it required a unity in the language of science and physicalism appears again as the coordinating language.

The claim that the orchestration of the sciences requires unity of language has been subject to influential criticism by Suppes who notes that that the development of modern science has been marked not by any movement towards a unified language of science but rather by increasing linguistic specialisation. The division of knowledge in the scientific endeavour has gone hand in hand with an increasing division of linguistic labour. Scientists use language and terms that often only their most immediate disciplinary neighbours are able to understand. A unified physicalist language of the kind defended by Neurath is neither possible nor desirable:

> Personally I applaud the divergence of language in science and find in it no grounds for skepticism or pessimism about the continued growth of science. The irreducible pluralism of languages of science is as desirable a feature as the irreducible plurality of political views in a democracy (Suppes 1984, p. 122).

I have suggested elsewhere that the Suppes' criticisms may miss their mark (O'Neill 2003b). The role of a unified language is more minimal than Suppes suggests. The role for physicalism in the case of the coordination of scientific activity mirrors that in the case of social and political coordination more generally. Different groups have their own particular vocabularies, but at the point of action they need to speak a common language. Unification takes place at the point of action and decision (Cartwright et al. 1996). Similarly different scientific disciplines may have their own particular vocabularies, but at the point of action they need to speak a common language. However, while Suppes' particular criticism of Neurath's programme for the unification of the language of science may miss its target, the way that Neurath presents that case does provide some grounds for Suppes portrayal of his opponent. Neurath's account of the orchestration of the sciences and social action more generally does tend to focus on language as the means of coordination at the expense of background institutional conditions. What Suppes does highlight is the degree to which the co-operation of the specialised sciences is not primarily a linguistic achievement, but a social one. It depends upon institutional conditions in which the increasing division of knowledge and language across the sciences can proceed without undermining a common project. Central to that project are the social conditions for the trustworthiness of testimony across disciplines within the sciences, and where science informs public policy, trustworthiness between the sciences and citizens.[9] Neurath clearly recognised that social dimension to the problem and indeed of the role of testimony in science (Uebel 2005) and as we noted earlier he does refer to trust as a necessary condition for cooperation and public conversation (Neurath 1945e, p. 251). However, those institutional conditions are not given the prominence in Neurath's account that their significance warrants.

However, while the social dimensions of Neurath's account of coordination in the sciences are not as developed as it might be, he is right to highlight the orchestration of the sciences as a social achievement. The model of the cooperation among the sciences was of more general significance for Neurath. It provided an example a rational cooperative endeavour without a single over-riding hierarchical organisation. It is this model that informs his later accounts of socialist planning rather than the traditional image of society as a single factory that is still to be found in his earlier work. Thus for example, the criticism of pyramidism re-appears in the context of planning in the form of a rejection of social pyramidism:

> We may, for example, imagine a future order based not on 'state pyramidism', if this term may be accepted, but on "overlapping institutions", which do not coincide with any

[9] For a discussion see O'Neill (1998b).

> "hierarchic" world pattern. The area of national education need not coincide with the area of railroad administration and this area may overlap a wide area of international fuel-administration. The various world-wide plans may be correlated in various ways and some international committees may provide as much centralized direction as seems desirable (Neurath 1943, p. 149).

Neurath defends in his later writings an associational model of socialism in which both the market and centralisation of powers and functions in the state are rejected in favour of a model of society of dispersed overlapping planning authorities and associations. As we noted above this image of socialist society is to be a 'societas societum'. (Neurath 1942, p. 432) was central also to his account of the institutional conditions for pluralism.

Neurath's appeal to the coordination of scientific activity again has particular significance with respect to Hayek. It points to problems in Hayek's claims about the necessary role for markets in the coordination of knowledge. The work of Polanyi (1958) offers for Hayek an example of the role and nature of 'tacit knowledge' (Hayek 1978, p. 38). However, while the co-ordination of the scientific knowledge, both tacit and articulated, is one of the institutional achievements of the modern world, it gives little grounds for support for the necessity of markets and prices to co-ordinate tacit knowledge. Neurath is right to take the public scientific community is an example of a predominantly non-market social order within the modern world. Indeed one of the proper concerns about science in market society has been the problems raised by the introduction of market based intellectual property rights regimes (O'Neill 1998a, Chaps. 11 and 12).

Both the ubiquity problem and the appeal to science point to weaknesses in Hayek's epistemic arguments for markets, specifically on the role of market exchange as an institutional form for coordinating knowledge. Both involve a criticism of the form of market monism that is implicit in Hayek's writing. There exists a plurality of different institutional forms through which knowledge can be coordinated in modern societies. The arguments against such market monism can be traced back to his earlier socialisation plans. In his more radical plans for a socialised economy Neurath goes further in his criticism of the market and defends an institutional pluralism of non-market institutions. At least part of the worry here is the concern about the way the market colonises and corrodes other institutional forms. In his later writings a central question he still wants to raise is whether the market is a necessary part of that institutional pluralism. Now his arguments for the existence and presence of non-market institutions in the modern world do not as such vindicate his stronger claim that a non-market economy without money is possible. Both the firm and the sciences operate within a wider market context, and there are arguments to be made as to the extent to which that wider context is a condition for coordinated action in those non-market spheres. There is a sense in which Neurath in his later writings was more modest in his aims than that found in the more detailed plans for socialisation found in his earlier writings. While I think there is evidence that Neurath retained his radical vision of a moneyless non-market society, it was the failure to consider the possibility of different arrangements that became his central concern. His main aim in his later writings was to open the space for discussion of alternative possible economies to market economies.[10] That position retains real power in a world in which market fundamentalism has closed the social vision of alternatives. Neurath's scientific utopianism still has considerable virtues.

References

Adaman, F. and Devine, P. (2002) 'A Reconsideration of the Theory of Entrepreneurship: A Participatory Approach.' *Review of Political Economy*, 14, 329–355

Berlin, I. (2002) *Liberty: Incorporating Four Essays on Liberty*. Oxford: Oxford University Press

Cardan, P. (1974) *Modern Capitalism and Revolution*. 2nd edn. London: Solidarity Publications

Cartwright, N., Cat, J., Fleck, L. and Uebel, T. (1996) *Otto Neurath: Philosophy Between Science and Politics*. Cambridge: Cambridge University Press

Coase, R. H. (1937) 'The Nature of the Firm.' *Economica*, 4, 386–405

Cohen, R. S. and Neurath, M. (eds.) (1983) *Otto Neurath: Philosophical Papers*. Dordrecht: Reidel

Foss, N. J. (1993) 'Theories of the Firm: Contractual and Competence Perspectives.' *Evolutionary Economics*, 3, 127–144

Foss, N. J. (1994) 'The Theo ry of the Firm: The Austrians as Precursors and Critics of Contemporary Theory.' *Review of Austrian Economics*, 7(1), 31–66

Foss, N. J. (1997) 'Austrian Insights and the Theory of the Firm.' *Advances in Austrian Economics*, 4, 175–198

Hayek, F. A. (1937) 'Economics and Knowledge' in *Individualism and Economic Order*. London: Routledge and Kegan Paul

Hayek, F. (1941) 'The Counter-Revolution of Science' [*Economica*, 8, 1941, 9–36, 119–150, 281–320] reprinted with revisions in F. Hayek *The Counter-Revolution of Science* (Indianapolis, IN: Liberty, 1979)

Hayek, F. (1942–1944) 'Scientism and the Study of Society' [*Economica*, 9, 1942, 267–291; 10, 1943, 34–63; 11, 1944, 27–29] reprinted with revisions in F. Hayek *The Counter-Revolution of Science* (Indianapolis, IN: Liberty, 1979)

Hayek, F. A. (1944) *The Road to Serfdom*. London: Routledge and Sons

Hayek, F. A. (1945) 'The Uses of Knowledge in Society' both in *Individualism and Economic Order*. London: Routledge and Kegan Paul

Hayek, F. A. (1960) *The Constitution of Liberty*. London: Routledge and Kegan Paul

Hayek, F. A. (1978) 'Competition as a Discovery Procedure' in *New Studies in Philosophy. Politics, Economics and the History of Ideas*. Chicago: The University of Chicago Press, pp. 179–190

Hodgson, G. (1998) 'Competence and Contract in the Theory of the Firm.' *Journal of Economic Behavior and Organization*, 35, 179–201

[10] Thus for example in a letter to G.D.H. Cole he writes the following on the possibility of an economy employing only *in natura* calculation: 'This approach forces us to answer the question 'why money?' Some people may reach a different answer from mine, but the not answering the question seems to me a result of a certain habit, which in social sciences has a similar position as the habit to start metaphysical speculations in other fields... You see my monograph (*The Foundations of Social Science*) is written for the purpose that scientists feel themselves forced to answer first the question WHY MONEY before entering the question, how to use it etc.' (Neurath to Cole, 3 September, 1945 in Neurath (1945d)).

Hodgson, G. (1999) *Economics and Utopia: Why the Learning Economy is Not the End of History*. London: Routledge
Kahneman, D. (1999) 'Objective Happiness' in D. Kahneman, E. Diener and N. Schwarz (eds.) *Well-Being: Foundations of Hedonic Psychology*, New York: Russell Sage Foundation Press
Kahneman, D., Fredrickson, B., Schreiber, C. and Redelmeier, D. (1993) 'When More Pain is Preferred to Less: Adding a Better End.' *Psychological Science*, 4, 401–405
Kallen, H. (1946) 'The Meanings of "Unity" Among the Sciences Once More.' *Philosophy and Phenomenological Research*, 6, 493–496
Kirzner, I. (1985) *Discovery and the Capitalist Process*. Chicago: The University of Chicago Press
Klein, P. (1996) 'Economic Calculation and the Limits of Markets.' *Review of Austrian Economics*, 9, 3–28
Lessman, O. (this volume) 'Comparability of Well-Being: A Common Motive of Neurath and Sen'
Lewin, P. and Phelan, S. (2000) 'An Austrian Theory of the Firm.' *Review of Austrian Economics*, 13, 59–79
Neurath, O. (1909) 'Remarks on the Productivity of Money' in R. S. Cohen and T. Uebel (eds.), *Otto Neurath: Economic Writings 1904–1945*, Dordrecht: Kluwer, 2004
Neurath, O. (1912) 'The Problem of the Pleasure Maximum' in R. S. Cohen and M. Neurath (eds.), *Otto Neurath: Philosophical Papers*, Dordrecht: Reidel, 1983
Neurath, O. (1913) 'The Lost Wanderers of Descartes and the Auxiliary Motive' in R. S. Cohen and M. Neurath (eds.), *Otto Neurath: Philosophical Papers*, Dordrecht: Reidel, 1983
Neurath, O. (1917) 'The Converse Taylor System' in M. Neurath and R. S. Cohen (eds.), *Empiricism and Sociology*, Dordrecht: Reidel, 1973
Neurath, O. (1920a) 'Total Socialisation' in T. Uebel and R. S. Cohen (eds.), *Otto Neurath: Economic Writings 1904–1945*, Dordrecht: Kluwer, 2004
Neurath, O. (1920b) 'A System of Socialisation' in T. Uebel and R. S. Cohen (eds.), *Otto Neurath: Economic Writings 1904–1945*, Dordrecht: Kluwer, 2004
Neurath, O. (1931) 'The Current Growth in Global Productive Capacity' in T. Uebel and R. S. Cohen (eds.), *Otto Neurath: Economic Writings 1904–1945*, Dordrecht: Kluwer, 2004
Neurath, O. (1937) 'Inventory of the Standard of Living.' *Zeitschrift for Sozialforschung*, 6, 140–151
Neurath, O. (1941) 'The Danger of Careless Terminology.' *The New Era*, 22, 145–150
Neurath, O. (1942) 'International Planning for Freedom' in *Empiricism and Sociology*, Dordrecht: Reidel, 1973
Neurath, O. (1943) 'Planning or Managerial Revolution.' (Review of J. Burnham *The Managerial* Revolution), *The New Commonwealth*, 148–154
Neurath, O. (1943–1945) 'Neurath-Carnap Correspondence, 1943–1945.' *The Otto Neurath Nachlass in Haarlem*, 223
Neurath, O. (1944a) *Foundations of the Social Sciences*. Chicago: University of Chicago Press
Neurath, O. (1944b) 'Ways of Life in a World Community.' *The London Quarterly of World Affairs*, 29–32
Neurath, O. (1945a) 'Physicalism, Planning and the Social Sciences: Bricks Prepared for a Discussion v.Hayek.' 26th July, 1945 *The Otto Neurath Nachlass in Haarlem* 202 K.56
Neurath, O. (1945b) 'Neurath-Hayek Correspondence, 1945.' *The Otto Neurath Nachlass in Haarlem*, 243
Neurath, O. (1945c) 'Alternatives to Market Competition.' (Review of F. Hayek *The Road to Serfdom*), *The London Quarterly of World Affairs*, 121–122
Neurath, O. (1945d) Neurath-Cole Correspondence *ISOTYPE collection*, Reading University
Neurath, O. (1945e) 'Visual Education' in E. Nemeth and F. Stadler (eds.), *Encyclopedia and Utopia: The Life and work of Otto Neurath (1882–1945)*, Dordrecht: Kluwer, 1996
Neurath, O. (1946a) 'After Six Years.' *Synthese*, 5, 1946, 77–82
Neurath, O. (1946b) 'The Orchestration of the Sciences by the Encyclopedism of Logical Empiricism' in R. S. Cohen and M. Neurath (eds.), *Otto Neurath: Philosophical Papers*, Dordrecht: Reidel, 1983, pp. 230–242

Neurath, O. (1973) *Empiricism and Sociology*. Dordrecht: Reidel
O'Neill, J. (1996) 'Who Won the Socialist Calculation Debate?' *History of Political Thought*, 27, 431–442
O'Neill, J. (1998a) *The Market: Ethics, Knowledge and Politics*. London: Routledge
O'Neill, J. (1998b) 'Rhetoric, Science and Philosophy.' *Philosophy of Social Sciences*, 28, 205–225
O'Neill, J. (2003a) 'Neurath, Associationalism and Markets.' *Economy and Society*, 32, 184–206
O'Neill, J. (2003b) 'Unified Science as Political Philosophy.' *Studies in History and Philosophy of Science*, 34, 575–596
O'Neill, J. (2004) 'Ecological Economics and the Politics of Knowledge: The Debate Between Hayek and Neurath.' *Cambridge Journal of Economics*, 28, 431–447
O'Neill, J. (2006) 'Knowledge, Planning and Markets: A Missing Chapter in the Socialist Calculation Debates.' *Economics and Philosophy*, 22, 1–24
Pennington, M. (2001) 'Environmental Markets Versus Environmental Deliberation: A Hayekian Critique of Green Political Economy.' *New Political Economy*, 6(2), 171–190
Polanyi, M. (1958) *Personal Knowledge*. London: Routledge and Kegan Paul
Popper, K. (1944–1945) 'The Poverty of Historicism' [*Economica*, 11, 1944, 86–103 and 119–137; 12, 1945, 69–89] reprinted with revisions in *The Poverty of Historicism* (London: Routledge, 1986)
Popper, K. (1966) *The Open Society and its Enemies*. 5th edn. London: Routledge
Suppes, P. (1984) *Probabilistic Metaphysics*. Oxford: Blackwell
Taylor, F. (1906) *On the Art of Cutting Metals*. New York: American Society of Mechanical Engineers
Uebel, T. (2000) 'Some Scientism, Some Historicism, Some Critics' in M. Stone and J. Wolff (eds.), *The Proper Ambition of Science*, London: Routledge
Uebel, T. (2003) 'Twentieth Century Philosophy of Social Science in the Analytical Tradition' in S. P. Turner and P. A. Roth (eds.), *The Blackwell Guide to the Philosophy of Social Science*, Oxford: Blackwell
Ubel, T. and Cohen, R. S. (eds.) (2004) *Otto Neurath: Economic Writings 1904–1945*. Dordrecht: Kluwer
Uebel, T. (2005) 'Epistemic Agency Naturalized: The Protocol of Testimony Acceptance.' *Proceedings of the Aristotelian Society Supplementary Volume*, 79, 89–105
Williamson, Oliver E. (1975) *Markets and Hierarchies*. New York: Free Press
Williamson, E. O. (1985) *The Economic Institutions of Capitalism*. New York: Free Press

School of Social Sciences
The University of Manchester
PO Box 88
Manchester, M 60 1QD
john.f.o'neill@manchester.ac.uk

Neurath on Money: Some Reflections on Neurath's Monetary Thought in the Historical Context of the Birth of Modern Monetary Economics

Peter Mooslechner

Otto Neurath must have been a fascinating personality. On becoming acquainted with his writings which cover an incredible broad range of issues, one is immediately struck by his enthusiastic and stimulating way of analysing and discussing all kind of topics. Even if one is not a Neurath specialist and, moreover, unable to cover the broad range of his interests, it becomes clear that taking his thoughts as a starting point and trying to follow his line of thinking would make for an exciting intellectual journey. The focus of this contribution is on one specific aspect of Neurath's economic publications and puts particular weight on contextualizing it. It concerns the birth of modern monetary economics at the turn of the century and the question of whether and how Otto Neurath's economic though took account of it.

Leaving mostly aside the issue of "economic calculation" (which is dealt with in separate contributions in this volume), I will take as my starting point some of Neurath's comments on money and the monetary economy – spread over time and a large number of his economic papers – and confront them with the new monetary economic thinking at his time. This is, of course, somewhat unfair in that this is based on our present knowledge and understanding of these issues; moreover, all this is done from a rather narrow economist's point of view and neglects Neurath's own interdisciplinary. Nonetheless, such a procedure is indispensable for the assessment of Neurath as an economist in his time.

The structure of the paper is as follows. The first section conveys the historical economic context at the turn of the century. This is followed, in the second section, by my selection of pronouncements on money by Neurath. The third section deals with the characteristics of "modern monetary economics" (Blaug 1978 and 1995) at the beginning of the twentieth century and, once again, tries to relate these to Neurath's main arguments. Section four looks into the future, concentrating on post-Keynesian economic thinking on money and finance and on how this is connected to the debate at the beginning of the century. Finally, a tentative conclusion as well as a personal assessment are provided and – in addition – a particularly fascinating element in Neurath's economic writings is pointed out.

E. Nemeth et al. (eds.), *Otto Neurath's Economics in Context.*
Vienna Circle Institute Yearbook [2007]. Volume 13.

1 Economics and the Historical Context at the Turn of the Century: The Road to "The Years of High Theory"

In his influential book first published in 1967, Shackle (1983) characterized the period from 1926 to 1939 as the "Years of High Theory" in economics. This characterization was due to the fact that over this little more than one decade not only a revolution in economic thinking took place, but also the number of intellectual contributions establishing economics as a science clearly outperformed many if not all other periods since economics appeared on the scene with the publication of Adam Smith' "The Wealth of Nations" in 1776.

There is no doubt that this specific development and intellectual dynamic is related to the real world challenges experienced during these years – in between the First and the Second World War. These years were characterized by the experience of hyperinflation on the one hand and by the enormous economic damage caused by the Great Depression on the other. The situation was one of increasingly heightening tensions, because economic theory – followed by economic policy – still worked under the assumption of a basically orderly and tranquil world in equilibrium despite a volatile, turbulent and desasterous economic reality. It didn't come as a surprise, therefore, that these real world experiences very soon led to a considerable weakening of the then existing economic orthodoxy. Any progress provided by new ideas promising better and more efficient economic policy advice was urgently needed and, in the end, policy relevance was the crucial point in making the revolution in economic thinking successful.

As Shackle (1983, p. 5) put it: "Thus there began... an immense creative spasm,... yielding six or seven major innovations of theory, which together have completely altered the orientation and character of economics." If one would have to sort out the most important single issue or factor behind this outstanding wave of theoretical innovation, "macroeconomic dynamics" would be the obvious prime candidate. The fundamental issue of macroeconomic dynamics is the essential link between an improved understanding of real world developments, theoretical economic thinking and policy needs. Macroeconomic dynamics was at the core of the success of new economics and new economic policies. Keynes and Schumpeter can be taken as two out of many economists of this period who have shaped this new way of thinking in their personal way.

The characterization of the 1920s and 1930s as the "Years of High Theory" is nowadays widely accepted in the economic literature. In fact, this interpretation is often taken as a starting point in comprehensive books on the history of economic thought.[1] Irrespective of whether one is in agreement with this overall judgement, there seems to be one important element missing in understanding the whole issue: what were the *specific* circumstances that made this development possible?

Looking more deeply into the developments that led to the "Years of High Theory," there seems to be one element of thought that paved the way to all this,

[1] For a recent example see Screpanti and Zamagni (2005).

namely, the significant change in the understanding of the importance and role of money in a modern market economy. In a nutshell, it is the switch from considering "money" primarily as "neutral" in the mainstream of economic thinking of the nineteenth century (Spiegel 1983) to recognizing the central role of money in determining the functioning of the economy after the Second World War. In parallel with this, the understanding of "money" considerably widened during this process, shifting the focus of interest and importance from the narrow perspective of the circulation of money as a sole means of payment to a broader view of money as one specific type of asset (fulfilling a number of important functions) in a world of developed – or developing – financial markets (Glasner 2000).

When thinking about these developments more than half a century after they took place, again the names of Keynes and Schumpeter come to mind. But there are others who played a significant role in this context, for example Knut Wicksell. (Selected relevant contributions to illustrate the topic will be dealt with in Sects. 3 and 4.) What makes them particular interesting in the context of Neurath's economic writings (see Neurath 2004) is that (i) much of this intellectual development took place in advance or in parallel to his own work and (ii) there were some obvious ties between these intellectual questions and Vienna, therefore making it possible – if not likely – that Neurath would have had at least the chance to get in contact with this new line of monetary thought.

Taking these two criteria as a simplified starting point, Table 1 may help to illustrate the possible relevance of these interactions. When looking at the core features summarized in this table the presence of the development of this new line of thought, that in the end has led to a revolution in economic thinking, at the time of Otto Neurath becomes entirely clear. Note first that Mises, Keynes, Schumpeter and

Table 1 Otto Neurath's life related to the lifetime and publications of selected great economists and their publications

Otto Neurath (1882–1945)	
Carl Menger (1840–1921)	Geld (Money) – Handwörterbuch der Staatswissenschaften: 1892; revised version 1909
Knut Wicksell (1851–1926)	Geldzins und Güterpreise (Money and Interest): 1898
	Vorlesungen über Nationalökonomie (Lectures on Political Economy): 1901 and 1906
Ludwig von Mises (1881–1973)	Theorie des Geldes und der Umlaufmittel (The Theory of Money and Credit): 1912
John Maynard Keynes (1883–1946)	A Tract on Monetary Reform: 1923
	A Treatise on Money: 1930
	The General Theory of Employment, Interest and Money: 1936
Joseph A. Schumpeter (1883–1953)	Das Wesen und Hauptinhalt der theoretischen Nationalökonomie: 1908
	Theorie der wirtschaftlichen Entwicklung (Theory of Economic Development): 1911
	Vom Wesen des Geldes: manuscript available 1929; (published 1970)

Neurath were born within the short time span of 3 years only and that, second, all the important publications discussing the contemporaneous wisdom on monetary issues (apart from Keynes' writings and Schumpeter's manuscript) were available in pre-World War One Vienna (ranging from Menger's influential and widely discussed encyclopedia article to Wicksell's pathbreaking ideas and Mises' first major book). For anyone interested in the subject and participating in the lively theoretical and policy discussions of that time, their study must have been *de rigeur*.[2]

2 Neurath on Money: An Economist's Narrow View

When revisiting Otto Neurath's economic writings many years after their original publication one can clearly distinguish different lines of thought concerning money:

1. On money as a unit of calculation in the economy, in particular in a system of economic planning; this line of thought was the most important one by his own estimation
2. On money as an institution and on the productivity of money
3. The role and use of money in the functioning of a war economy
4. On the role of money in the context of the overall functioning of a market based macroeconomy

Interestingly enough, Neurath began his treatment of economic topics – at the early age of 23 – with a historical analysis of interest and money in ancient times. There he stressed that the characteristics of a monetary economy had been present since the time of Babylon and Egypt and that "Rome had a money economy from the start." (1904, p. 118). One of his main conclusions was that the core reason for creating money as a means of payment was long-distance (international) trade: "Money establishes a close link between trading nations." (ibid., p. 116). But while Neurath took note of the existence of well-developed credit systems as early as in Babylonian times, he didn't look far into the importance of the credit system for the functioning of the economy. In a similar way, his descriptive presentation seems to be rather inconclusive on the determinants of interest, mainly relating it to (long-distance) trade profit.

It is interesting that some elements of his early historical analysis show up again in his later works. In his writings, there is a significant neglect of the interaction between the domestic economy and a monetary economy. The very existence of money as well as the functions served by a system of credit financing is almost exclusively related to (international) trade, their role for domestic economic activities is not discussed. Relatedly, the early existence of monetary economies is accepted as a historical fact but its economic importance is not discussed. This compares

[2] It has to be mentioned in this context, that Neurath spent some time in Germany during his studies (Berlin) and later on (Munich) and finally left Vienna for Holland (1934) first and England (1940) later on because of the political developments in Austria leading to the "Anschluß" in the end.

badly with Neurath's critical position on money as a unit of calculation. This picture only changed later on when he got particular interested in the institutional structure, the functioning and financing of a war economy.

A second starting point for coming to understand Neurath's view of monetary economies is provided by a short intervention on the productivity of money, published only 5 years later. In the context of a symposium titled "Über die Produktivität der Volkswirtschaft" ("On Economic Productivity") he critically discussed two issues: first, the measurement and derivation of (real) productivity from monetary terms and, second, the neglect of one particular institution in the discussion of productivity, namely, money.

Let us call the first issue "Neurath's impossibility theorem" to measure (social) well-being ("... the total situation of a group of people...," Neurath 1909, p. 293) by means of money or in monetary terms. In most forceful terms ("Impossible!" Neurath 1909, p. 293), Neurath rejected any possibility of a monetary calculus to gauge "... the magnitude of pleasure, then the magnitude of pain and finally doing the sum." Conversion into money from his perspective does not help in this respect: "the calculus of value reaches its limits." It is easy to understand that this view became predominant for his rejection of money as a unit of calculation in his later work on economic planning.

The situation seems to be less straightforward concerning the second issue, the productivity of money. Neurath pointed out that money was treated as a tool to measure productivity only, whereas the productivity of the monetary system was not addressed. The formulations he used in this respect constitute a clear difference compared to his 1904 paper: "...the monetary system itself is part of the production process" and "The investigation of the productivity of money could claim at least as much attention as the investigation of the productivity of industry" (1909, p. 295). Neurath even adds that this can be done by analyzing "...whether a certain monetary organisation is more productive, more useful than another"

Compared to his 1904 paper the clear difference lies in the way how the monetary system is treated. First, the monetary system seems now to be related to the productivity of the whole economy, in particular to the (dominant) domestic part of the economy as well. Second, he added explicitly the need to "... examine systems of monetary organisation," thereby implying that different systems of this kind may exist and that they may make a difference concerning the productivity of the entire economy. Even if he is later on also talking about "exchange in kind, facilitated by an in-kind clearing bank" as an extreme case, he did not rule out at that time that differences in the type of monetary organization will lead to corresponding differences in real productivity. "The questions of productivity of monetary organisation... are thus granted full legitimacy..." (Neurath 1909, p. 296).

Putting these elements together it becomes evident that quite early in his economic writings Neurath has made up his mind on monetary issues and in his further writings he continued along these lines. In doing so he concentrated almost exclusively on two aspects of money: (i) the role of money as a unit of economic calculus and (ii) money as an economic institution. In addition, there is a small line of thought were he extended his analysis into more general questions of macroeconomics, which today are still interesting from a more general point of view.

(i) I will be extremely brief on the first aspect, the role of money as a unit of economic calculus, because other contributions in this volume (Chaloupek, Uebel) have concentrated on this issue. From an economic point of view it seems surprising that Neurath concentrated on this particular function of money only, neglecting almost entirely all the other functions of money dealt with in the literature. What he insisted on again and again is that he did not believe that a standardization of goods by any denumerator – not only by money – could comprehend and measure the welfare-creating benefits of goods and services available.

At least to my understanding, the reasons for this definite position are not entirely clear. What makes most sense is probably the concentration on some elements of external effects or the public goods character of a number of goods and services. Perhaps this "feeling" goes in the same direction as the concentration on what have been called Neurath's "ecological arguments." At first sight, this would also be in line with Streißler's (1982) point that the one feature that unites all economists of the Austrian school is that they were decision theorists. By rejecting the possibility of general optimizing behaviour based on goods value expressed in money Neurath may, on the one hand, have expressed his criticism of the Austrians and, on the other hand, have made clear his view of the existing welfare benefits of "non-market goods."

(ii) The second aspect, the role of money as an institution or economic system, can also be related to Neurath's argumentation against the use of money as a unit of calculation. If one rejects monetary valuation of goods, an entire system based on the general use of money, a monetary system, cannot be expected to produce optimal (or acceptable) results from a macroeconomic point of view. Rejecting money at a microeconomic level leads to reject a monetary regime in general.

Unfortunately, Neurath is not very clear in arguing on this issue. Perhaps he was most clear in 1920 when he wrote "If no longer sums of money, but things themselves are taken as the basis for our decisions, then we cannot speak of monetary economy" (1920, p. 383). In 1925 he singled out "... the foundations for such studies of moneyless economics" (1925, p. 446) as the most important task for creating a socialist administrative economy. On several occasions he wrote about the moneyless economy as something like the ultimate need for creating a better type of economic system. At the same time, banks would be transformed into institutions directly dealing with the administration of goods.

As far as one can judge this from his writings, Neurath never returned to the aspects of "productivity of money" or "the monetary system" he mentioned in 1909, with the exception of war financing, obviously a very particular case. May be he had something in mind like a gradual transition from the existing monetary system to an "economy in kind" thereby gradually increasing the efficiency or productivity of the economy.

(iii) Neurath showed a particular interest in the functioning of a war economy, possibly initiated by his personal experience in participating in the First World War and by several consultative functions in this respect. In a collection of writings "Durch die Kriegswirtschaft zur Naturalwirtschaft" published in 1919 on the occasion of becoming an advisor on economic planning to the Bavarian government Neurath put together many previously published pieces on the topic. Even though by then his perspective was already that of using the economic conditions and problems in a war situation as the starting point for transforming the economy into one without money as a unit of calculation, these writings contain his most extensive analysis of money in the economy. Several issues touched upon in this context at least should be mentioned here, even if they are related to the very specific background of a war economy.

First of all, it is interesting that Neurath takes a somewhat differentiated view there on the efficiency of the two different models he has in mind: whether the government should rely on issuing money or on administrative measures in order to acquire the resources it needs cannot be decided generally. His main arguments in favour of administrative measures are that a transformation from a war economy to an economy without money should be easy and that the importance of the projects to be realized (for example: railroads) makes administrative measures a more efficient tool. Once again, his arguments seem to be based on what we would nowadays call "externalities." Second, while subsequently stressing the character of money as a claim on the amount of goods produced or the resources available, Neurath also analysed in some detail the functioning of a monetary system. Some of the arguments raised sound rather modern. He argued, for example, that the amount of money necessary for the functioning of an economy depends on the behaviour of the people and not on the amount of goods in circulation. In other words, he argued that the velocity of money is always an endogenous variable and that "foreign money" and "domestic money" are two different things which have to be analysed separately, although both influence each other. But ultimately these considerations remain rather isolated and did not play a particular role in the for him dominant question of how the economic system can be transformed into one without money as a unit of calculation.

(iv) There also can be found a fourth interesting argument in Neurath's writings concerning money that goes far beyond the other points. This very modern perspective will be taken up at the very end of this paper.

3 Five (Unacceptably Short) Short Stories on the Understanding of a Modern Monetary Economy at the Beginning of the Century

To put Neurath's views on money in the context of modern monetary thinking of his time five examples will be used to illustrate same characteristics of the monetary thought at the beginning of the last century. The criteria employed in the selection are simple: (i) the ideas should be related to Vienna and (ii) should have been potentially available to him.

3.1 *Menger*

Carl Menger, in one or the other way, was a predecessor to the monetary thought of the other four economists to be mentioned here. Of course, this is particular true for his influence on Mises, but it is also visible in Schumpeter's work. Re-reading Menger's contributions to monetary economics reveals several interesting aspects. Primarily in his analysis of money included in the "Grundsätze" and in his article in *Handwörterbuch der Staatswissenschaften* first published in 1892, Menger applied the subjective theory of value to money. In the marginalist perspective, the origin of money is not to be sought in an explicit convention or in the action of public authorities. Instead, it was the interest of economizing individuals which led them to exchange their goods for other goods. Money is the most marketable good one can think of and, therefore, it has acquired a special role. But its value is determined in the same manner as that of other goods that are objects of exchange transactions. Even in its revised version of 1909, Menger's article stood very much in the old tradition of dealing with the role and nature of money in a descriptive way; by contrast, a number of arguments at least touched upon in the "Grundsätze" point in the direction of the upcoming modern monetary thought to be developed over the coming decades. Perhaps with the exception of Wicksell, all the theorists mentioned below had to struggle all of their life to escape from this old way of monetary thinking (as best illustrated by the destiny of Schumpeter's unpublished book on money).

3.2 *Wicksell*

Knut Wicksell, born in 1851 in Stockholm, published his *Geldzins und Güterpreise* (Interest and Prices) in German in 1898. Previously, his decision to become an economist was also considerably influenced by a 3-year grant he received in 1887 to study economics in Germany and Austria. In Vienna, he attended lectures by Carl Menger and he also spent some time in Berlin. When he died in Stockholm in 1926 he was working on a contribution for a book honoring Friedrich von Wieser. In general, Wicksell's contributions did not receive widespread attention during his lifetime, but the ties between him and Austrian economic thinking were straightforward and later on taken further by Mises, Hayek and Schumpeter. Wicksell's important work on the mechanics of a monetary economy, first of all, introduced a direct connection between the monetary system and real economic developments. The distinction between the natural and the money (or market or bank) rate of interest, which lead to his famous "cumulative process" model of the business cycle, made the interaction of monetary policy, financial markets and the demand for loans by investors to the central element of a theory of economic fluctuations. Money and the entire financial system became an indispensable part of our understanding of the functioning of the economy (Formaini 2005).

3.3 Mises

Ludwig Mises' *Theorie des Geldes und der Umlaufmittel (The Theory of Money and Credit)* was first published in 1912 and it immediately received widespread attention among German speaking economists. It was designed to be an encompassing volume on all aspects of money in the economy, starting with an extended discussion of the functions of money and ranging till the interaction of money, credit and the interest rate as the reason for "cyclical" economic fluctuations, thereby referring also to the work of Wicksell. Not surprisingly, Mises' special contribution consisted in an extensive microfoundation of money based on marginal utility theory.

3.4 Keynes' Treatise on Money

In Great Britain the publication of Keynes *A Treatise on Money* in 1930 summarized the status of the discussion on monetary issues since the beginning of the century. Intended to become the domestic counterpart of his *Tract on Monetary Reform* (1923) the seven books of the two volumes of the Treatise start with "The Nature of Money," cover "The Dynamics of the Price Level" to end with "The Rate of Investment and Its Fluctuations" and "The Management of Money." The impact of the Treatise in history remained limited, however, because it was overshadowed soon by the publication of his *General Theory* in 1936. Even so, it was at that time the most comprehensive exposition of the current debate on monetary theory and policy. Keynes referred to the most recent works by Wicksell and the Austrians but the substantive integration of these approaches into own his work happened only in the transition from the *Treatise* to the *General Theory*, in the process dubbed "How Keynes became Keynesian" (Screpanti and Zamagni 2005, 249ff). However, the *Treatise* contained notable contributions regarding questions like the motives for holding money, a first analysis of liquidity preference and the role of expectations for the yield of investment.

3.5 Schumpeter's Unpublished Book on Money

Perhaps the most interesting short story to tell about monetary thinking at the beginning of the last century is that of Schumpeter's unpublished book on money "Das Wesen des Geldes." During his whole lifetime Schumpeter was very much interested in the monetary system, both in theoretical and practical terms (Tichy 1984). He incorporated many elements stemming from this interest in several of his works, for example concerning the role of credit, the rate of interest or – most of all – he role of monetary factors in the determination of the business cycle in his *Theorie der wirtschaftlichen Entwicklung* (Theory of Economic Development, 1911).

Despite the prominent role of monetary factors in his economic thinking he always felt that his earlier work on monetary theory was not received well by the profession (Busch 2003). In fact, Schumpeter did work on a large volume on monetary theory since his early years as an economist (Mann 1970) and he published several pieces of this work separately, for example "Das Sozialprodukt und die Rechenpfennige" (1917). But the available completed manuscript was scheduled to be published in 1929, when on returning from a trip to the US Schumpeter decided that it will "never" be published. There are several stories about what changed his mind; the one I like most is that he became acquainted with Keynes' *Treatise*. There are some indications that he did work on an English translation of the manuscript afterwards but, in the end, the book was published posthumously in 1970 only. Whatever the true reason of not publishing it during his lifetime may have been, what the book clearly documents is Schumpeter's encompassing knowledge of the status of the international academic discussion regarding money in the 1920s, (Swedberg 1994) including Wicksell, Keynes, the Austrians and the entire discussion that took place in Germany, for example, triggered by the work of Knapp (1905).

What could be a conclusion from confronting these "short stories" with Neurath's treatment of money in his economic writings?

1. At the time Neurath was working on his economic writings there was considerable progress in monetary economics and many stimulating discussions going on.
2. Some of the most influential contributors to this discussion were present in Vienna and the community of Austrians took clear notice of the international discussions going on. It seems very unlikely that Neurath was not aware of all this.
3. At the very beginning of his career he picked out two issues of money – unit of account and monetary system – he was interested in. These two aspects were, with some fluctuations, of great importance in his writings during his whole life, but all the other issues of money and a monetary economy did not receive any further interest.
4. The overall conclusion may well be that Neurath was mainly interested in something else, in particular in the maximization of overall economic welfare, and that he did think that the other aspects of money or of a monetary economy were not or definitely less essential in this respect.
5. To make things more complicated, however, he occasionally came back to various other aspects of money on different occasions, for instance, in the context of a war economy. In doing so he touched upon a number of money related issues in a sometimes surprisingly modern way, but he didn't make any attempt to combine these elements into a consistent and convincing overall picture.

4 A Perspective on Keynes Beyond the *Treatise* and on the Development of Post-Keynesian Monetary Thought: A Monetary Theory of Production and After

Wicksell right from the beginning of his innovative work on monetary economics deviated from the mainstream classical view dominated by the quantity theory as well as the neutrality of money in the short and in the long term. He introduced a quite revolutionary approach to the money creation process, one that looks surprisingly modern even from today's perspective. One of the key aspects in Wicksell's approach is the use of two distinct rates of interest: a market rate determined by monetary policy and the banking system, and a natural rate of interest determined by the use of real capital, by the forces of productivity and thrift. This dichotomy between the market and the natural rates then plays an important role in his theory of inflation and the business cycle.

Wicksell defines the natural rate as "the rate of interest which would be determined by supply and demand if no use was made of money and all lending were effected in the form of real capital goods" (1965, p. 102). This points out clearly that the existence of money as well as the use of financial markets, in particular the financing of investment, constitutes a fundamental difference in the way the overall functioning of the economy has to be understood in his model. To make the consequences of this perfectly clear Wicksell assumed a pure credit economy. The market rate of interest is an exogenous variable under the discretion of the banking system and the money supply is completely endogenous and created by the banking system based on the credit market. And in the end, the creation of bank credit and thereby money will impact on the business cycle and on inflation in his famous "cumulative process."

Although argued in a somewhat different way, this Wicksellian line of thinking and replacing the classical mainstream quantity theory based view by a completely new understanding of the role of money and financing in a modern market economy was exactly the point taken up by the Austrians to develop their monetary theory of the business cycle. Elements of this conception can be found in Menger as early as 1892 and he added more on this in his completely revised version of that article in 1909, when Wicksell's work was certainly available to him. There is a lot of this Wicksellian thought also present in Mises (1912) and Schumpeter developed it into an important component of his business cycle theory.[3]

The central problem of a growing capitalist economy is how to finance innovative investments. Entrepreneurs who wish to exploit an innovation do not, generally, have the finance necessary to do so. Finance comes from profits, but innovations only produce profit after they have been activated, which is often quite a long time afterwards. Therefore, credit is necessary. The banking system does not limit itself to redistributing the savings from the savers to the users. The banks create new money and it is the added liquidity which allows entrepreneurs to finance innovations and society to increase the stock of capital. In real terms, credit produces a sort of forced savings, which allows entrepreneurs to appropriate tangible resources. Thus, credit serves to transfer resources from consumption to investment and from less productive to more productive investments.

It was largely neglected – and to some extent still is nowadays – that Keynes on his way from the *Treaty* to the *General Theory* as well as in several articles published after the publication of the *General Theory* (Keynes 1937a, b, c) explained the functioning of his model in a quite similar way, putting the main focus on the role of the financial system and, especially, on the central importance of investment

[3] See Mooslechner (2006) for a more comprehensive treatment of the importance of financing in Schumpeter's writings.

financing. Since that time, a number of important elements of this specific view have become basic building blocks of the post-Keynesian approach (Arestis 1992; Davidson 1978). For example, as early as in his *Treatise* Keynes stressed the primacy of the unit of account role of money which involves a complete switch of regime from a barter-exchange economy to a money-exchange economy. As a consequence, money acquires a non-neutrality character for the entire economic process and the dichotomy underlying the classical model doesn't hold any longer. Similar to Wicksell, introducing finance into the model destroys the assumption of money exogeneity at the same time. Money becomes credit driven and demand determined and credit is demanded by businesses because the production process takes time and the financing of innovation cannot rely on previously generated profits (Schumpeter 1997, first published 1912). Thus the supply of money responds primarily to the behaviour of private investment rather than to the (exogenous) behaviour of monetary authorities.

Perhaps the best example to summarize this approach, which definitely emerged as a type of Wicksellian – Keynesian – Schumpeterian view at the beginning of the twentieth century, is the way Hyman P. Minsky (1975) put these pieces together to build an integrated view of the workings of a modern financial macroeconomy. The prime mover of economic fluctuations is fluctuations in investment demand and financial forces inherent in a private market economy create the preconditions for business cycles through an interaction of investment needs and financing decisions. Investment expansion is largely financed by credit to firms, which leads balance sheets of investors to become increasingly fragile. With the balance sheets of both non-financial and financial firms becoming more risky, the danger of bankruptcy and insolvency increases, leading to a collapse of activity in the end, depending on the willingness and on the ability of the financial system to provide further credit.[4]

5 Some Concluding Remarks

Monetary economic thought may not have been the most important aspect of Neurath's work, but it was an interesting part nonetheless which provided a continuous line of argumentation in his writings and may be useful in understanding his sometimes tenuous relationship with the predominant economic thinking at his time.[5] Neurath picked out some very specific aspects of money only, first the role of money as an unit of calculation and second the importance of money as an institution, based on his early historical interest in the existence of money in ancient times. In addition to these two main topics, however, he also raised occasionally some surprisingly

[4] Perhaps it should be stressed that the entire argumentation presented here was developed and written long before the recent financial market turmoil unfolded in mid-August 2007, which underlines the recent importance of the Wicksellian – Keynesian – Schumpeterian view."

[5] See Uebel (2004, 34f) for examples of Neurath's historical erudition and familiarity with other contemporary theorists.

modern arguments related to the functioning of a modern market-based economy. But he never transformed these scattered ideas into a consistent picture.

Participating in the lively economic discussion of his time in Vienna, it seems very unlikely that he was not aware of the upcoming revolutionary ideas of creating a new monetary view of the functioning of the economy. However, despite mentioning theoretical ideas of Austrian economists sometimes, he concentrated mainly on various aspects of how to transform the existing economic system into a new one without money. The fundamental argument for this was the inappropriate approach of using money as a unit of calculation. Consequently, a deeper analysis of the problem of money may not have deemed to be necessary and, therefore, the development of new ideas on a monetary view of the business cycle was not worth any attention. The only important exception seem to have been his writings on war economics, where he studied in detail how to use money – mainly from the perspective of the government – and how to transform the existing monetary arrangements into a new moneyless economic system.

Keeping all this in mind, there are a number of interesting pieces in his work, which open a perspective beyond his usual narrow view on money and, at the same time, on his understanding of macroeconomic processes in general. In his contribution on "War Economy" (published in 1910) he wrote, for example:

> A distinction should be made between borrowing goods and borrowing money.... Loans can be taken from hoards or from circulation; the effects will be different in the two cases. The absorption of hoards by loans may have a stimulating effect; previously frozen moneys will become liquid. This can stimulate production if means of circulation were lacking previously. (1910, 174f)
>
> Though increase of money on its own cannot be said to cause increase of production, it can certainly advance a production which is at the point of increasing. If the quantity of money is increased, the consequence will be a rise of all goods and services, as well as lowering of the interest rate. (ibid., p. 190)

These lines of argumentation not only sound rather modern, they can be qualified as an early form of Keynesianism, later on developed into modern financial macroeconomic thinking by the Post-Keynesians. At the same time, these ideas also constitute a clear reference to the monetary economics of his time, but he seemed to be not particular interested in this evolving school of thought. Perhaps his impressive interdisciplinary approach and his overall interest in policy (making) together with the increasingly unfavourable political developments in the interwar period may have prevented him from putting more emphasis on this as well as on economic ideas in general.

References

Arestis, P. (1992), *The Post-Keynesian Approach to Economics*, Aldershot: Elgar

Blaug, M. (1978), *Economic Theory in Retrospect*, Cambridge, UK: Cambridge University Press

Blaug, M. (1995), *The Quantity Theory of Money*, Aldershot: Elgar

Busch, U. (2003), Joseph A. Schumpeter's 'Soziologie des Geldes', in J. Backhaus, *Joseph Alois Schumpeter*, Dordrecht: Kluwer

Chaloupek, G. (2007), Otto Neurath's Concepts of Socialization and Economic Calculation and his Socialist Critics, this volume
Davidson, P. (1978), *Money and The Real World*, London: Macmillan
Formaini, R. L. (2005), Knut Wicksell, The Birth of Modern Monetary Policy, Federal Reserve Bank of Dallas. *Economic Insights* 9(1)
Glasner, D. (2000), Classical Monetary Theory and the Quantity Theory. *History of Political Economy* 32(1) 39–60
Keynes, J. M. (1930), *A Treatise on Money*, London: Macmillan
Keynes, J. M. (1933), A Monetary Theory of Production, in D. Moggridge (1987)
Keynes, J. M. (1937a), Alternative Theories of the Rate of Interest, in D. Mooggridge (1987)
Keynes, J. M. (1937b), The 'Ex-Ante' Theory of the Rate of Interest, in D. Mooggridge (1987)
Keynes, J. M. (1937c), The General Theory of Employment, in D. Mooggridge (1987)
Knapp, G. (1905), *Staatliche Theorie des Geldes*, Leipzig: Duncker & Humblot
Mann, F. (1970), Die Neutralisierung des Finanzsystems, *Theorie und Praxis des finanzpolitischen Interventionismus*, 67–82
Minsky, H. P. (1975), *John Maynard Keynes*, New York: Columbia University Press
Mises, L. (1912), *The Theory of Money and Credit*, repr. 1980, Indianapolis, IN: Liberty Classics
Moggridge, D., ed. (1987), *John Maynard Keynes, The General Theory and After*, London: Macmillan
Mooslechner, P. (2006), Finance and Growth: The Legacy of Schumpeter to be Rediscovered? in Liebscher, K. et al (eds.), Financial Development, Integration and Stability, Cheltenham: Edward Elgar
Neurath, O. (1904), Interest on Money in Antiquity, in O. Neurath (2004)
Neurath, O. (1909), Remarks on the Productivity of Money, in O. Neurath (2004)
Neurath, O. (1910), War Economy, in O. Neurath (2004)
Neurath, O. (1920), Total Socialisation, in O. Neurath (2004)
Neurath, O. (1925), Economic Plan and Calculation in Kind, in O. Neurath (2004)
Neurath, O. (2004), *Economic Writings. Selections 1904–1945* (T. E. Uebel and R. S. Cohen, eds.), Dordrecht: Kluwer
Schumpeter, J. A. (1970), *Das Wesen des Geldes*, Göttingen (aus dem Nachlaß herausgegeben von F. K. Mann)
Schumpeter, J. A. (1997), *Theorie der wirtschaftlichen Entwicklung*, Berlin
Screpanti, E., Zamagni, S. (2005), *An Outline of the History of Economic Thought*, Oxford: Oxford University Press
Shackle, G. L. S. (1983), *The Years of High Theory*, Cambridge
Spiegel, H. W. (1983), *The Growth of Economic Thought*, Durham: Duke University Press
Streißler, E. (1982), Schumpeter's Vienna and the Role of Credit in Innovation, in H. Frisch, ed., *Schumpeterian Economics*, New York
Swedberg, R. (1994), *Joseph A. Schumpeter*, Stuttgart
Tichy, G. (1984), Schumpeter's Business Cycle Theory. Its Importance for Our Time, in C. Seidl (ed.), Lectures on Schumpeterian Economics, Berlin: Springer
Uebel, T.E. (2004), Introduction: Neurath's Economics in Critical Context, in O. Neurath, ed., *Economic Writings. Selections 1904–1945* (T. E. Uebel and R. S. Cohen, eds.), Dordrecht: Kluwer (2004)
Uebel, T. E. (2007), Otto Neurath as an Austrian Economist. Behind the Scenes of the Early Socialist Calculation Debate, this volume
Wicksell, K. (1965) *Interest and Prices – A Study of the Causes Regulating the Value of Money*. New York: Kelley

Oesterreichische Nationalbank
Economics and Research
P.O.Box 61, A-1011 Wien, Austria
peter.mooslechner@oenb.at

A Similar Line of Thought in Neurath and Sen: Interpersonal Comparability

Ortrud Leßmann

Otto Neurath and Amartya Sen have founded approaches to measure well-being. Their ultimate goal has been to find a measure of well-being that enables us to compare the well-being of different persons. Beitz[1] perceives the capability approach as "a solution to the problem of finding an adequate basis for interpersonal comparisons, or, in other words, to the problem of defining well-being."[2] Thus, a close link can be established between measurement and interpersonal comparisons of well-being.

Indeed, the question of interpersonal comparability has been at the centre of their concern right from the beginning and is still present in their advocacy of dominance orderings. The paper follows this line of thought: The first section presents their results of analysing the interdependence between measurability and comparability of utility. The second section introduces and compares their concepts of "conditions of life" and "functionings." The third section comes back to the question of interpersonal comparisons in their frameworks of conditions of life and bundles of functionings. The fourth section leaves Neurath aside and concentrates on Kurt Grelling's interpretation of the term life-situation and Gerhard Weisser's absorption of it. A parallel between Grelling's view of life-situations and Sen's idea of a capability-set is drawn. The last section concludes.

1 Comparability and Measurability of Utility

Both, Neurath and Sen, start their investigation in the measurement of well-being from the utilitarian conception which underlies standard economic theory. At Neurath's time there was still hope to find a measurement unit for utility, preferences played but a minor role, but the majority of economists already thought of utility as being only ordinally measurable.

---

[1] Charles R. Beitz, "Review of Resources, Values and Development", in: *Econ omics and Philosophy*, Vol. 2, 1986, pp. 283–291.
[2] Ibid., p. 290.

E. Nemeth et al. (eds.), *Otto Neurath's Economics in Context.*
Vienna Circle Institute Yearbook [2007]. Volume 13.

Hence, Neurath begins in 1911[3] by exploring the possibility of *social* preference orderings on the basis of ordinally measurable utility. He is concerned with identifying the maximum "wealth" of a nation or a group based on individual preferences, thereby taking up the subject of social choice theory. In congruence with traditional utilitarianism Neurath employs sum-ranking as the aggregation rule.

First he shows that it is possible to derive social preferences with regard to all those social states which are preferred by at least one person and not disliked by all others. This social preference relation is incomplete. Neurath asks further which conditions should be satisfied by a social preference relation. He discusses the anonymity (or symmetry) axiom[4] (it does not matter whose utility is regarded), he refers implicitly to the transitivity axioms[5] (if *A* has more utility than *B* and *B* has more utility than *C*, *A* must have more utility than *C*) and he searches for conditions of completeness[6] (every situation can be evaluated and ranked in terms of utility). Then he shows that even the interpersonal comparability of utility levels is not sufficient to render the social preference relation complete. Here we must remember that Neurath assumes utility to be only ordinally measurable. Even if utility levels can be compared, it is impossible to compare states that provide more utility for one person and less for another. In these cases it is necessary to compare utility differences. But that is a difficult task as Neurath points out: "It seems that a direct assessment of the intervals is not achievable. Though we have seen how to compare two *L* [levels of utility, O.L.], we do not know how to compare two utility intervals."[7]

Let us summarize what Neurath has done so far: He distinguishes the different tasks involved in arriving at a social preference ordering and shows at the same time the relation between them. First, there is the question of measurability of individual utilities. Neurath investigates how far we can get with ordinally measurable individual utilities. Secondly, there is the question of interpersonal comparability. Neurath distinguishes between level comparability and interval comparability of ordinal preferences. Thirdly, there is the aggregation task and the question of completeness of the resulting social ordering. Neurath uses the utilitarian rule of sum-ranking. He hints at the possibility of being able to obtain merely a partial ordering and searches for conditions to complete the resulting social preference ordering. Neurath concludes: "There can be little doubt that, in order to advance the problem of [calculating] wealth, further research into the comparability of utility increments is needed."[8]

---

[3] Otto Neurath, "Nationalökonomie und Wertlehre, eine systematische Untersuchung", in: *Zeitschrift für Volkswirtschaftslehre, Sozialpolitik und Verwaltung*, Vol. 20, 1911, pp. 52–114.

[4] Ibid., p. 57.

[5] Ibid., pp. 58–59.

[6] Ibid., pp. 60–61.

[7] "Eine direkte Abschätzung der Abstände scheint nicht recht durchführbar zu sein. Wir haben zwar gesehen, wie man zwei *L* miteinander vergleichen kann, aber nicht wie zwei Lustabstände verglichen werden" (ibid., p. 96).

[8] "Es ist im Interesse der Reichtumsprobleme zweifellos angezeigt, weiter zu forschen, wie man Lustzuwächse miteinander vergleichen kann" (ibid., p. 112).

The issue of the comparability of utilities is explored further by Neurath himself in his 1912 lecture "The problem of a pleasure maximum."[9] Neurath develops a way to cardinalize utilities (he calls them "pleasures") if utility intervals are comparable. However, these cardinal utilities are still not fully comparable if no assumption concerning the point of origin is made: "In order that utilities, and not only utility intervals, should be measurable quantities, one would have to be able to fix a zero point."[10] As a result, the social preference ordering after summing up utilities is not complete. But Neurath points out: "In practice it is generally less important to determine the maximum utility of a given group of individuals than to compare two sums of pleasure with each other."[11] He states further: "For many questions of legal, political and social philosophy it is sufficiently important if we can ascertain that the utility sum grows more under some conditions than under others."[12] In 1912, then, Neurath expands his analysis to encompass cardinally measurable utilities and their limitations. He confirms that the resulting social preference ordering often is incomplete while stressing that a partial ordering is sufficient for answering many questions and is – at least – a starting point for further considerations.

When Sen writes his book on "Collective Choice and Social Welfare"[13] standard economic theory still focuses on utilities but distinguishes sharply between preference relations and utility functions. Utility functions now are said to *represent* a preference relation under certain conditions. The preference relation of an individual can be *represented* by a utility function if it fulfils the axioms of reflexivity, transitivity, completeness and monotonicity. In conjunction with the distinction between preferences and utility functions the view that preferences are only ordinally measurable has gained wide acceptance.[14] Consequently, preferences can be represented by more than one utility function.

Sen explores the different kinds of measurability of preferences and their possible representations in utility functions.[15] If a preference relation is strict ordinally measurable it may be represented by a utility function and all its positive monotonic transformations. If the preference relation is cardinally measurable only the positive affine transformations of the utility function are admissible. Sen goes on to analyze

---

[9] Otto Neurath, "The Problem of the Pleasure Maximum", in: Marie Neurath and Robert Cohen (eds.): *Empiricism and Sociology*, 1973, Dordrecht, Holland: Reidel, pp. 113–122.

[10] "Utilities" replaces "pleasures" in these quotations from Neurath (1973) (ibid., p. 117) "Damit die Lüste, nicht nur die Lustabstände, meßbare Größen sind, wäre es erforderlich, einen Nullpunkt statuieren zu können" (p. 51, 1912).

[11] Ibid., p. 118. "In der Praxis kommt es im allgemeinen weniger darauf an, das Lustmaximum einer gegebenen Individuengruppe festzustellen, als vielmehr zwei Lustsummen miteinander zu vergleichen" (1912, p. 51 f).

[12] Ibid., p. 118. "Für viele Fragen der Rechts-, Staats- und Sozialphilosophie ist es von Bedeutung, wenn festgestellt werden kann, daß die Lustsumme unter gewissen Bedingungen größer werden als unter anderen" (1912, p. 52).

[13] Amartya K. Sen, *Collective Choice and Social Welfare*, 1970, San Francisco: Holden-Day.

[14] Robert Cooter and Peter Rappoport refer to this move as "the ordinalist revolution" in their "Were the Ordinalists Wrong About Welfare Economics?", in: *Journal of Economic Literature*, Vol. XXII, 1984, pp. 507–530.

[15] Ibid., p. 105.

the relationship between measurability of preferences and their comparability. If preferences are ordinally measured either utility levels or utility differences can be ranked and thus compared. But even if preferences are cardinally measurable they need not be comparable at all or only the units are comparable. For full comparability of preferences it is necessary that utilities can be measured cardinally plus unit comparability plus the comparability of origins. Then the preference ordering can be represented by a utility function and all its *linear* transformations.

Based on the distinction between a preference relation and the utility function being its representation Sen comes to the same conclusion as Neurath does: If preferences are only ordinally measurable, they cannot be compared interpersonally. Yet there are varying degrees of comparability depending in part on the measurability of preferences. We can distinguish ordinal preferences with level comparability, with comparability of differences and without comparability as well as cardinal preferences with full comparability, with unit-comparability, with comparability of utility differences and with non-comparability.

Measurability	Comparability			
	Not comparable	Only units comparable	Only levels comparable	Units and levels comparable
Ordinal	No aggregation	X	Other aggregation rule	X
Cardinal	No aggregation	Sum ranking	Other aggregation rule	Sum ranking

Following Sen/Foster (1997, p. 44)[16]

With respect to the aggregation task Sen[17] introduces a measure of the degree d of partial comparability, varying between $d = 0$ which implies non-comparability and $d = 1$ which implies complete comparability of units. He calls the resulting social preference ordering under non-comparability the Pareto ordering. (This is the incomplete ordering Neurath described in 1911 at the beginning.) The completeness of the resulting ordering can be gradually increased by moving to stricter comparability assumptions. The complete ordering can already be reached without complete unit comparability. Sen concludes: "Complete comparability is not merely a doubtful assumption, it is also quite unnecessary."[18]

Of course, Sen's analysis is more comprehensive then Neurath's and serves as a point of reference in contemporary economics, but Neurath already mentions the crucial issues: In order to arrive at a complete social ordering it is decisive to be able to compare utility differences. This kind of unit-comparability is not feasible with ordinally measurable utilities. But even with non comparable utilities we arrive at a partial ordering – the Pareto ordering – which can serve as a starting point. Often

[16] James Foster and Amartya Sen, *On Economic Inequality, Expanded Edition*, 1997, Oxford: Clarendon Press.

[17] Ibid., p. 102.

[18] Ibid., p. 102.

a partial ordering is sufficient for taking a decision on what policy to adopt. Full comparability of utilities implies unit comparability and fixing the origin.

This analysis is the first step of Neurath and Sen on their way to develop a measure of well-being. They are both dissatisfied with the idea that interpersonal comparisons are impossible. They argue that in everyday life we do compare our lives interpersonally:

> In ordinary life we make all these comparisons, by attempts at empathy with our own past or with our neighbors. We say, for example, that we are feeling happier in one year than in an earlier one, that a child at play is happier than a man who had been shot in the stomach.[19]

Or as Sen puts it more carefully:

> Behaviouristic measures of utility in terms of people's expressions include an interpersonally comparable element. It may be possible to say that person *A* is happier than person *B* by looking at delighted Mr. *A* and morose Mr. *B*. It may also be possible to make marginal comparisons.[20]

Their next step is the proposal of comparing the lives persons lead in order to get an idea of whose life is better.

2 Conditions of Life and Functionings

When Neurath and Sen introduce their notions of "conditions of life" and "functionings," they both are looking for a measure of well-being which is better measurable than utility and lends itself to interpersonal comparisons. They both propose to look at the life people lead.

Neurath introduces "conditions of life" as a substitute measure of well-being. He views conditions of life as a means to approximate utility: "We cannot directly capture the quality of life (Lebensstimmung) and we will therefore stick to the condition of life (Lebenslage), i.e. housing, food, clothing, working hours, etc."[21] This pragmatic description of conditions of life is in itself an approximation to a narrower definition of conditions of life Neurath gives in his first paper on the approach in 1917. A life-situation (Lebenslage)[22] in the narrow sense comprehend

---

[19] Otto Neurath, "The Conceptual Structure of Economic Theory and its Foundations", in: Thomas Uebel and Robert Cohen (eds.): *Otto Neurath Economics Writings. Selections 1904–1945*, 2004, Dordrecht, Holland: Kluwer, pp. 312–341, p. 314. Otto Neurath, "Das Begriffsgebäude der Wirtschaftslehre und seine Grundlagen", in: Rudolf Haller and Heiner Rutte (eds.): *Zeitschrift für die gesamte Staatswissenschaft*, Vol. 23, 1917, pp. 484–520 (reprinted in Rudolf Haller (ed.): *Gesammelte philosophische und methodologische Schriften*, Vol. 1, pp. 103–129).

[20] Amartya Sen, op. cit., p. 92.

[21] Otto Neurath, "A System of Socialisation" in: Thomas Uebel and Robert Cohen (eds.): *Otto Neurath Economics Writings*. op. cit., pp. 345–370, p. 356. Otto Neurath, "Ein System der Sozialisierung", in: *Archiv für Sozialwissenschaft und Sozialpolitik*, Vol. 48, No. 1, 1920, pp. 44–78, p. 58.

[22] In accordance with Thomas Uebel and Robert Cohen (op. cit.) "life-situation" and "conditions of life" are used interchangeably as translations of the German "Lebenslage."

the state of digestion, nutrition, the muscles, the warmth of the skin etc. For measurement purposes "we can replace the state of digestion by the bread which is just being digested, the state of the skin's warmth by the dress that influences it directly."[23] This is what Neurath calls the "condition of life in the wider sense."

In later definitions of "conditions of life" the connection to utility – here Neurath uses the expression "sorrows and joys" – is still present:

> Life-situation is the central concept of all circumstances that condition – comparatively directly – a man's mode of behavior, his sorrows and joys. Shelter, food, clothing, health, books, theatres, friendly human surroundings, all this belongs to the life-situation, even the quantity of malaria germs that menace him.[24]

As Neurath, Sen is concerned with measurability. Taking the same example as Neurath – nutrition – he argues in favour of direct observation:

> It was argued … that nutritional functionings may be rather badly approximated by information regarding food purchases (or even food consumption), because of variations in the relation between commodities and functionings due to such factors as metabolic rates, body size, etc. There is the further problem that with inequalities within the family, the market *purchase* data may be rather remote from individual *consumption*. There is, thus, a good case for looking directly at nutritional achievements.[25]

Another argument of Sen in favour of functionings is that they "lend themselves to easier interpersonal comparisons than comparisons of utilities (or happiness, pleasures or desires)."[26] In opposition to Neurath, Sen perceives of functionings not as a substitute of utility for measuring well-being, but as a more adequate concept for well-being: "The claim is that functionings are *constitutive* of a person's being, and an evaluation of well-being has to take the form of an assessment of these constituent elements."[27] Hence, his definition does not allude to utility at all: "Ultimately, the focus has to be on what life we lead and what we can or cannot do, can or cannot be. I have elsewhere called the various living conditions we can or cannot achieve, our 'functionings'. …"[28]

In summary, Neurath and Sen both propose to look directly at the lives people lead and use these data for measuring well-being. Their common argument in favour of this proposal is that lives are observable and can be compared interpersonally better than utility. However, Neurath and Sen disagree on the role of utility as a measure of well-being. Neurath suggests to approximate utility by looking at

[23] Otto Neurath, "The conceptual structure of economic theory and its foundations", op. cit., p. 316.

[24] In these quotations from Neurath and Cohen "life-situation" or "conditions of life" replace "living standard" as the translation for "Lebenslage." Otto Neurath, "Empirical Sociology", in: Marie Neurath and Robert Cohen (eds.): *Empiricism and Sociology*, op. cit., pp. 319–421, p. 401. Otto Neurath, *Empirische Soziologie*, 1931, Wien, p. 125.

[25] Amartya Sen, *Commodities and Capabilities*, 1985, Amsterdam: North-Holland, p. 47.

[26] Amartya Sen, *Development as Freedom*, 1999, Oxford: Oxford University Press, p. 76.

[27] Amartya Sen, *Inequality Reexamined*, 1992, Oxford: Oxford University Press, p. 39.

[28] Amartya Sen, *The Standard of Living*, 1987, Cambridge: Cambridge University Press, p. 16.

the life a person leads whereas Sen rejects the idea that utility measures well-being at all. Sen therefore suggests to replace utility by functionings as a measure of well-being.

Nevertheless, there is another striking similarity in the definitions of Neurath and Sen: Both define the notions of "conditions of life" and "functionings" respectively in a vague way. They do not propose a criterion for the identification of "conditions of life" or "functionings." Instead, they quote a lot of examples. Table 1 lists some examples and arranges them for comparison.

Although the similarity of their examples is striking in general, there are some deviations which are worth following. First, they put the examples differently: Neurath sticks more to an objectivist perception of the elements of a life-situation whereas Sen always uses phrases in relation to the subject who experiences the functioning. For example, Neurath speaks of "the quantity of malaria germs," "the illnesses a person faces" and "friendly human surroundings." In contrast, Sen's formulation always starts with the word "being": "being free from malaria," "being in good health" and "being able to visit and entertain friends." In Neurath's words the individual appears to be more passive than in Sen's. The elements of a life-situation are presented like data. Neurath is also more reluctant than Sen to introduce the more complex elements of a life-situation like "feeling powerful and capable." He mentions it, but he seems to prefer the more objective notions like "leisure time" even then. Sen, however, relates the functionings to the individual by whom they are achieved. He uses positive expressions like "being *free* from malaria" and "*escaping* premature mortality" whereas Neurath counts malaria germs, illnesses

Table 1 Examples of Neurath and Sen

Elements of life-situation (Neurath)	Functionings (Sen)
Nutrition, food	Being adequately nourished, nourishment
Health care	Being in good health
Morbidity, mortality, disease	Avoiding escapable morbidity and premature mortality, longevity
The quantity of malaria germs	Being free from malaria
Housing	Being well-sheltered
Clothing	Being decently clothed
Taking a drive	Vacationing, travelling
Reading books, education	Being literate
Listening to the radio, entertainment, amusement, leisure time	Cultural and intellectual pursuits
Developing an awareness of his personality	Having self-respect
Feeling powerful and capable, enlightened and enraptured	Appear in public without shame, taking part in the life of the community
	Being happy
Friendly human surroundings	Ability to entertain and visit friends, being close to people one would like to see
Work, working hours, workload	Being employed

Source: Neurath (1920 in 2004, 1925 in 2004, 1931 in 1973), Sen (1985a, b; 1987, 1992)

and workload as elements with a negative impact on the life-situation. After all functionings comprise not only the activities and states of a person but her abilities as well: "being able to entertain friends" and "being literate" may serve as illustrations for that point.

Secondly, Neurath is more concerned than Sen with the workload of people. He often speaks of "the worker" and uses examples in which work figures prominently. His choice of examples and his emphasis of work and the situation of workers is partly related to his political convictions. Neurath has put forward his life-situations approach as "A system of socialisation"[29] meaning it as a device for transforming a (capitalist) society in a socialist one. But it would be shortsighted to view this only as a political programme. He argues in favour of a planned economy because he is convinced that it will work more efficiently than a market economy in terms of providing a good life for everybody. His approach is, in fact, concerned with choosing a basis for evaluation of production. He is engaged in showing the shortcomings of a monetary evaluation and the advantages of an evaluation of the quality of life in terms of the conditions of life:

> If certain problems of social analysis are treated by means of accounting (for example, the characterization of conditions of life by money income) then only 'measurement in kind' (that is, calculations of conditions of life in the sense used here) can show whether the results actually exhibit the gradation of given conditions of life. In these conditions we would especially include working time, leisure time, rate of accident, morbidity and mortality rates, as well as housing, food, clothing, education, recreation, etc. Accounting does not show us whether a surplus production of iron was not obtained at the cost of a higher rate of accidents.[30]

Neurath does not restrict his approach to distributional questions but encompasses questions of allocation and production as well. In opposition to him Sen is convinced that the market has merits as an economic ordering but fails to be perfect: Sen devotes a chapter in his book on "Development as Freedom" to show the link between markets and freedom. Therein he mentions especially the labour market as a positive example: "The development of free markets in general and of free seeking of employment in particular is a much appreciated fact in historical studies."[31] Sen does not question the capability of markets to produce and allocate goods efficiently, but he points at the imperfections of the market. Mainly, Sen is concerned with distributional questions and it is in this context that he considers employment: "[U]nemployment is not merely a deficiency of income that can be made up through transfers by the state …; it is also a source of far reaching debilitating effects on individual freedom, initiative, and skills."[32]

---

[29] Op. cit.

[30] Otto Neurath, "Inventory of the Standard of Living", *Zeitschrift für Sozialforschung*, Vol. 6, 1937, pp. 140–151, p. 149. In this text the term "Lebenslage" is translated as "standard of living." I have replaced it by "conditions of life" in order to use the same English translation of the term everywhere.

[31] Amartya Sen, *Development as Freedom*, op. cit., p. 113.

[32] Ibid., p. 21.

Thirdly, Neurath mentions the time necessary for carrying out work and recreation which Sen does not. In part, this is due to the fact that Neurath measures the workload in time units. For example, when he explains how workload can be compensated by gratifications, he measures the workload in working hours:

> … the principle of distribution that the qualities of life – or the conditions of life causing them – are related to the work performed, namely by assigning a greater amount of products for consumption to a greater expenditure of work effort. … A man who works for six hours and reaches a quality of life of a certain level through radio performance, one cinema visit and two excursions in a certain period would perhaps reach the same quality of life if he worked seven hours and has two opera performances, one excursion and two and a half pumpkins at his disposal.[33]

This is, however, not the only context in which Neurath uses time as an important feature of a life-situation. In general, his life-situation approach is in line with his greater project of a unified science. As such it has to be placed in space and time: "Sociology deals with human behavior, i.e. with spatio-temporal events."[34] In "Inventory of the standard of living" he gives an example that shows how he considers time to influence the life a person leads:

> It is not sufficient to determine how much gardenland is available in the vicinity of the town, or how many books per person. These quantities must be related in some way to the time during which they can be used. It means more to a worker to be able to use his plot of ground for ten hours a week than only for two, and it means less than if he had thirty hours.[35]

Neurath is therefore well aware of the importance of time and its limited availability. Instead of focusing on time and its restricting nature, Sen considers other resources and individual characteristics as constraints to the opportunities a person faces. He does not introduce time as a variable to his approach and has been criticized for it.[36]

Thus, the examples for their respective approaches show three differences in emphasis: First, the kind of phrasing indicates that Neurath considers the conditions of life to be like data whereas Sen relates the achievements in functionings to the characteristics of the persons concerned. Secondly, Neurath mentions more examples relating to the working conditions because his approach includes the allocation,

---

[33] Otto Neurath "Economic Plan and Calculation in Kind", in: Thomas Uebel and Robert Cohen (op. cit.), pp. 405–465, p. 423. "…Verteilungsgrundsatz, dass die Lebensstimmungen – beziehungsweise die sie bedingenden Lebenslagen – mit der aufgewendeten Arbeit in Verbindung gebracht werden, und zwar derart, dass einer größeren Arbeitsleistung eine größere, für den Konsum bestimmte Produktenmenge entspräche. … Wer bei sechs Stunden Arbeit durch eine Radioaufführung, eine Kinovorstellung, und zwei Ausflüge in einem bestimmten Zeitraum Lebensstimmung in einer bestimmten Höhe erreicht, würde bei sieben Stunden Arbeit die gleiche Lebensstimmung etwa erzielen, wenn er zwei Opernaufführungen, einen Ausflug und zweieinhalb Kürbisse zur Verfügung hätte" Otto Neurath, "Wirtschaftsplan und Naturalrechnung", reprint in: Rainer Hegselmann (ed.): Wissenschaftliche Weltauffassung, *Sozialismus und Logischer Empirismus*, pp. 262–287.

[34] Otto Neurath, "Empirical Sociology" (op.cit.), p. 423. "Die Soziologie hat es mit menschlichem Verhalten, das heißt mit räumlich-zeitlichen Vorgängen zu tun" (Otto Neurath, Empirische Soziologie (op.cit.), p. 59).

[35] Op. cit., p. 147.

[36] The Capability Conference in Pavia in 2003 has been focused on capability in a dynamic perspective.

production and distribution of goods. He is sceptical of the effectiveness of the market. Opposed to that Sen views the market as one mode of allocation the effectiveness of which depends on certain conditions like perfect competition, complete information, absence of external effects etc. He restricts his approach to distributive questions. Thirdly, Neurath mentions time as an important aspect of the elements of a life-situation. His approach relies on the scientific concept of a unified science emphasizing the necessity to indicate the time and space of any observation. However, Sen stays in the tradition of economic theory which is content with comparative static.

3 Comparing Multidimensional Bundles

The concepts of Neurath and Sen are – while based on variables which lend themselves better to comparisons than utility – inherently multidimensional. Hence, there is no straightforward way to compare functioning achievements or life-situations interpersonally or to arrive at a complete ordering of functioning bundles or conditions of life. Neurath and Sen both use a kind of dominance ordering as a starting point, but their graphical illustrations differ substantially.

"Dominance ordering" stands for a generalization of the Pareto ordering mentioned in Sect. 2. The Pareto principle maintains that a state of affairs *a* which is at least as good for anyone and better for someone than another state of affairs *b* should be preferred to it. Originally, the states of affairs are evaluated by the utility they bring about. However, it is possible to apply the same principle to other evaluative measures like functionings or conditions of life. The resulting ordering is a dominance ranking as Sen explains it:

> Furthermore, the very identification of the set of value-objects, with positive weights, itself precipitates a 'dominance ranking' (*x* is at least as high as *y* if it yields at least as much of *each* of the valued objects). This dominance ranking, which can be shown to have standard regularity properties such as transitivity, can indeed take us some distance – often quite a long distance – in the evaluative exercise.[37]

The quotation shows, too, that Sen is quite optimistic regarding the sufficiency of this mode of ordering for the evaluative purpose at hand (see below). Neurath describes this mode of ordering as the only possible way to arrive at a ranking from early on:

> If one of the averages contains more food, clothing etc., less work, less illness, etc., than the other, we may probably say that the corresponding quality of life is at least not lower than the other. However, if one contains more food, less housing, more work, less illness

[37] Amartya Sen, Capability and Well-Being, in: Amartya Sen and Martha Nussbaum (eds.): *The Quality of Life*, 1993, Oxford: Clarendon Press, pp. 30–54, p. 32.

> than another, then a new basis for the comparison of these average conditions of life is required.[38]

However, Neurath always emphasizes the need to find "a new basis for the comparison." Later on, he proposes to set up a scale analogous to that of mineralogical hardness:

> If one wants to treat these problems more accurately, one must set up a scale of conditions of life, which would be comparable to the hardness scale in mineralogy. Other questions are: How far is there sense in ordering all life-situations by one scale, and does one use different scales according to time and situation?[39]

There are several reasons why Neurath does not present a solution to this problem: (i) he views the ordering to depend on preferences which cannot be captured from the outset; (ii) he warns against mixing up items which are measured in different units; (iii) he holds on to the view that the quality of life is what matters – and not conditions of life as such.[40] This does not, however, prevent him from suggesting a specific method of illustration. The method of arriving at "silhouettes of conditions of life" may be called the "cartographic" method opposed to the "geometric presentation"[41] of Pareto and Edgeworth. A "silhouette of conditions of life" simply shows the amounts of the different elements of a life-situation in symbols.[42] A big amount equals a high "mountain" of one element in contrast to which a small amount is perceived as a "valley." Neurath wants to use this impression for comparison and for applying the above mentioned principle of ordering:

> One can compare the levels of these peaks of conditions of life with one another by a casual glance, just as one compares the height of various mountains ranges in geography, without

[38] Otto Neurath, "The Conceptual Structure of Economic Theory and its Foundations," op. cit., p. 331. "Wenn ein Durchschnitt mehr Nahrung, Kleidung usw., aufweist, als der andere, weniger Arbeit weniger Krankheit usw., dann kann man wohl sagen, dass die dazu gehörige Lebensstimmung mindestens nicht niedriger ist als die andere; wenn aber die Nahrungsmenge größer, die Wohnungsmenge kleiner, die Arbeitsmenge größer, die Krankheitsmenge kleiner ist, so ist eine neue Abschätzung dieser Durchschnittslagen erforderlich." Otto Neurath, "Das Begriffsgebäude der Wirtschaftslehre und seine Grundlagen," op. cit., p. 120.

[39] Otto Neurath, "Empirical sociology," op. cit., p. 401. "Wollte man diese Probleme genauer behandeln, muss man eine Skala der Lebenslagen aufstellen, welche der mineralogischen Härteskala zu vergleichen wäre. Wieweit es einen Sinn hat, alle Lebenslagen mit Hilfe *einer* Skala zu ordnen, ob man nicht je nach Zeit und Situation verschiedene Skalen verwendet, ist eine andere Frage." Neurath has already drawn this analogy to the mineralogical scale of hardness in 1925. Back then, however, he referred to the qualities of life and not to the conditions of life: "The relief maps only need to differences in height; … . The steps can only be arranged according to a scale (as e. g. the mineralogical scale of hardness)." Otto Neurath, Economic Plan and Calculation in Kind, op. cit., p. 419.

[40] See my "Utility and the Measurement of Well-Being" on this issue.

[41] Neurath criticises the "geometric presentation" for several reasons. Some of the reasons apply to his "cartographic presentation" as well. On this issue see my "Utility and the Measurement of Well-being," op. cit.

[42] See Elisabeth Nemeth on Neurath's ISOTYPE system.

> necessarily being able to show exactly what definition was used for 'average height' of mountain range.[43]

Sen on the other hand presents "bundles of functionings" in the "functioning space"[44] thereby using exactly the "geometric presentation" Neurath avoids. In fact, Neurath's way to illustrate and visualize "conditions of life" has not been widely acknowledged. Standard economic theory presents results in the "geometric" fashion following the tradition of Pareto and Edgeworth. Sen does as well, but since both methods present a matrix of functioning achievements (or elements of life-situations) of many persons – albeit in a different manner – the underlying operation for establishing a dominance ordering remains the same.[45]

One argument Sen brings forward in favour of dominance orderings is that they can be seen as intersection orderings. A dominance ordering establishes an unanimity result according to a given set of criteria (in our case expressed in terms of a social welfare function). This is equivalent to looking at the intersection of the orderings[46] which are generated by these criteria because the dominance ordering ranks only those situations which are ranked in the same way by all these criteria. Though the ordering generated by one criterion is complete, the intersection of complete orderings usually results in incomplete or partial orderings since the various criteria disagree on the rank of certain situations. Thus, any step that narrows down the distance between the criteria will make the dominance ordering more complete. Sen suggests to look for areas of agreement and deduce the intersection ordering:

> More importantly, that dominance-partial ordering can be extended even without a full agreement on relative values. For example, if there are four conflicting views claiming respectively that the relative weight to be attached to *x vis-à-vis y* should be 1/2, 1/3, 1/4 and 1/5, there is, then an implicit agreement that the relative weight on *x* should not exceed 1/2, nor fall below 1/5. But even this agreement will, in general, permit us to order pairs – possibly many pairs – not covered by the dominance ranking. … The 'intersection approach', which articulates only those judgements that are *shared* implications of *all* of the possible alternative weights, can indeed take us quite a distance.[47]

That is where the story of a similar train of thought of Neurath and Sen ends. Both start with the problem of interpersonal comparisons of welfare in terms of utility, then they propose to look at the lives people lead because elements of a life-situation can be observed directly and compared more easily than utility, and finally they realize that their proposal implies multidimensionality and therefore does not implement a straightforward way to compare well-being interpersonally. As a way out of the problem they suggest to take a dominance ordering as a starting point and narrow down the ordering later-on.

---

[43] Otto Neurath, "Inventory of the Standard of Living," op. cit., p. 148.

[44] Amartya Sen, "Capability and Well-Being," op. cit., p. 32.

[45] A more thorough comparison of Neurath's mode of illustration to that of Sen is to be found in my "Utility and Well-being."

[46] James Foster and Amartya Sen, op. cit., p. 132.

[47] Amartya Sen, *Inequality Reexamined*, op. cit., pp. 46–47.

4 Life-Situation and Capability Set

Meanwhile there can be drawn another similarity between the conditions of life approach and Sen's capability approach.[48] The notion of a "life-situation" (which is commonly used in day-to-day language in its German version) has been taken up by Kurt Grelling[49] and Gerhard Weisser.[50] They mingle it with a Kantian notion of true interests and introduce the idea that the conditions of life define an opportunity set from which the individual can choose.

Grelling is the first who adopts the notion of a "life-situation." He defines it as follows:

> The totality of all the interests a human being actually satisfies during a certain period in his life I will call the *standard of living* [Lebenshaltung] of him during that period in his life. Thereby the degree to which an interest is satisfied shall be assigned for every single interest. The totality of all *possible* standards of living [Lebenshaltung] from which he can choose at the beginning of the period (e.g. when he sets up a budget plan) I will call his *life-situation* [Lebenslage].[51]

In this definition the elements of a life-situation are still present as "interests," but the concept of "life-situations" has been extended to encompass all feasible combinations of these elements at a certain point in time. Obviously, Grelling conceives interests to be measurable, if only indirectly since "interests can not be added up

---

[48] On this see my "Lebenslagen und Verwirklichungschancen (capability) – verschiedene Wurzeln, ähnliche Konzepte," in: *Vierteljahreshefte der Wirtschaftsforschung*, 1/2006, pp. 30–42 or my "Conditions of Life, Functionings, and Capability - Similarities and Differences", forthcoming in: Journal fo Human Development, 2009.

[49] Kurt Grelling (1886–1942) studied mathematics and philosophy in Goettingen and economics in Munich. He was a student and collaborator of the philosopher Leonard Nelson who stood in the tradition of Immanuel Kant and Jakob Friedrich Fries. Grelling joined a students association (Internationaler Jugendbund, IJB) which was founded by Nelson. His short texts on the conditions of life approach were written as contributions to the informal newsletter of the IJB. Later, Grelling turned his back on the epistemic base of Nelson's philosophy and joined the Berlin Society for Scientific Philosophy which formed along with the "Vienna Circle" a second group in the movement of logical empiricism. Grelling's main areas of interest consisted in symbolic logic, semantics and set-theory. Further, he translated several writings of Bertrand Russell into German.

[50] Gerhard Weisser (1898–1989) studied economics and philosophy in Goettingen and Munich. Like Grelling he was a student of Leonard Nelson and joined the students association IJB founded by Nelson. His first writings on the conditions of life approach can be found in the same informal newsletter of the IJB as Grelling's. After the Second World War, Weisser hold a chair on social policy at the University of Cologne. The notion of "life-situations" formed the starting point of his concept of social policy. At the same time he was engaged in the German social democratic party and in the protestant church of Germany. Thereby, he made the notion "life-situation" known among German politicians.

[51] Own translation of Kurt Grelling, "Zum Prinzip der Güterverteilung," *Neunter wirtschaftswissenschaftlicher Rundbrief*, 1921, pp. 1–2. taken from Kurt-Grelling archive, see http://www-fakkw.upb.de/institute/philosophie/peckhaus/grelling/id3.htm, "Die Gesamtheit der von einem Menschen in einer bestimmten Periode seines Lebens faktisch befriedigten Interessen, wobei jedes einzelne mit dem Grade zu versehen ist, bis zu welchem es befriedigt wird, will ich die *Lebenshaltung* dieses Menschen während dieser Periode seines Lebens nennen. Die Gesamtheit der *möglichen* Lebenshaltungen, zwischen denen er am Anfang der Periode (etwa bei Aufstellung eines Haushaltsplanes) wählen kann, nenne ich seine *Lebenslage*." (Grelling 1921, p. 1 f).

and are, thus, not cardinally measurable."[52] But, following his mentor Leonard Nelson, he assumes the intensity of an interest to equal the value of that interest and for measuring the intensity of an interest it is sufficient to state which interest has been satisfied. Essentially, Grelling's view on interests resembles the utilitarian interpretation of utility as desire fulfilment. The intensity of the desire indicates the value – or utility – of it. Grelling combines this view with a measurement concept that can be said to anticipate the theory of revealed preferences of Samuelson.[53] As this explanation shows, Grelling's concept is close to Neurath's in two points: First, it, too, looks at the life a person leads and aims at empirically measuring it. Secondly, it holds on to the idea that some value (utility) derives from the life people lead and that it is this value that matters in the end.

Weisser takes up Grelling's interpretation of "life-situation." He describes a life-situation as the space of an individual to act [Spielraum] in order to fulfil his interests.[54] This concept of conditions of life is the core of his conception of social policy. In contrast to Grelling, Weisser is very sceptical against empirical measurement and argues fervently against the inclination of economics to quantify everything.[55] He rejects as well the idea to take the degree of desire fulfilment as a measure of well-being because he is aware of preference adaptation and even speaks of "manipulation of psychic states."[56] Instead, Weisser focuses on determining those interests which can be said to have an intrinsic value. His problem is, once again, one of interpersonal comparability. Weisser is convinced that everyone has an individual set of interests, i.e. he does not believe in universal values. His main question, therefore, is an epistemic one: How is it possible to determine a set of interests which are relevant for individual well-being?

The similarity between these extensions of the conditions of life approach and Sen's approach is to be seen in the idea of an opportunity set. Sen defines the term "capability" as follows: "Capability is a *set* of such functionings *n* tuples, representing the various alternative combinations of functionings from which the person can choose one combination."[57] The chosen bundle of functionings Sen calls the "achieved functionings."[58] Hence he draws the same structure as Grelling does: The

[52] Kurt Grelling, "Zum Prinzip der Güterverteilung", op. cit, p. 1. "Interessen sind nicht addierbar und folglich auch nicht zahlenmäßig messbar."

[53] Paul Samuleson, "Consumption Theory in Terms of Revealed Preference", in: *Economica*, Vol. 15, 1948, pp. 243–253.

[54] This is very difficult to translate. His definition reads as follows: "Als Lebenslage gilt der Spielraum, den die äußeren Umstände dem Menschen für die Erfüllung der Grundanliegen bieten, die ihn bei der Gestaltung seines Lebens leiten oder bei möglichst freier und tiefer Selbstbesinnung und zu konsequentem Verhalten hinreichender Willensstärke leiten würden." Gerhard Weisser, "Sozialpolitik" (1972), in: Gerhard Weisser (ed.): *Beiträge zur Gesellschaftspolitik*, 1978, Göttingen: Verlag Otto Schwartz, pp. 275–283, p. 275, fn.

[55] Gerhard Weisser, "Quantifizierbares und Nichtquantifizierbares in den Sozialwissenschaften", in: Gerhard Weisser (ed.): *Beiträge zur Gesellschaftspolitik*, op. cit., pp. 602–625.

[56] Gerhard Weisser, "Sozialpolitik", op. cit., p. 278.

[57] Amartya Sen, *Inequality Reexamined*, op. cit., p. 50.

[58] Ibid.

life a person leads can be described as a combination of certain elements (Grelling calls them "fulfiled interests" and Sen "achieved functionings"). The actual way of leading a life is but one out of a set of possible such combinations. That is exactly the idea of an opportunity set.[59] The reason why Sen introduces this idea becomes obvious in his characterization of capability as "a set of vectors of functionings, reflecting the person's freedom to lead one type of life or another."[60] Sen is convinced that human well-being depends not only on the life a person leads but on the opportunity – her freedom – to choose between different ways of living as well. Thus, when he develops his approach, he is searching a conception that avoids relying solely on outcomes like utilitarianism does[61] or that takes only procedures into view.[62] Sen insists on the idea that the opportunity to choose has intrinsic value.

Hence, Grelling and Sen share the idea of an opportunity set, but they differ substantially in their interpretation of it. Grelling's approach resembles an utilitarian notion of desire fulfilment but it is rooted in a Kantian tradition. According to that tradition the fulfilment of certain interests depends on who is fulfiling them. In order to know about these interests (which are given a priori) human beings have to use their reasoning and engage themselves in fulfilment of these. Now, Grelling simply assumes that no human being can ever fulfil all his interests at once[63] and therefore has to choose. In contrast to Grelling's approach, Sen's is neither rooted in a Kantian tradition nor resembles any branch of utilitarianism. Instead, Sen's approach springs from a thorough critique of utilitarianism on the one hand and process-oriented libertarian theories on the other. As regards Neurath and Grelling, they both form an approach to life-situation that is apt for empirical application. Grelling, however, follows at this time still a Kantian tradition that Neurath set aside from early on. A few years later Grelling joins the movement of logical empiricism without, however, taking up the subject of conditions of life again.

5 Conclusion

The story I tell in this contribution is the story of a similar line of thought in Neurath and Sen which is driven by the issue of comparability. Both analyze at first the interdependence of measurability and comparability of utility. Both are discontented with the result that interpersonal comparisons of well-being are impossible on the basis of ordinally measurable utility. Thus, they propose to look at the life people lead instead and base the comparison of well-being on the description of

59 Robert Sugden, "The Metric of Opportunity", in: *Economics and Philosophy*, Vol. 14, 1998, pp. 307–337.

60 Amartya Sen, *Inequality Reexamined*, op. cit., p. 40.

61 Amartya Sen, *Development as Freedom*, op. cit., pp. 58–60.

62 Ibid., pp. 63–70.

63 Kurt Grelling, Zum Prinzip der Güertverteilung, op. cit., p. 1.

their lives in terms of conditions of life or functionings. Neurath and Sen have to admit, however, that this proposal does not solve the problem of interpersonal comparisons of well-being because of its multidimensionality. They suggest to start with dominance orderings and see how far this device takes us.

Supplementary to this story of a similar train of thoughts in Neurath and Sen, the paper considers the extension of this approach to well-being that Sen introduced. Namely it shows that Sen's idea of a capability set as the set of all ways of life feasible for a person has already been anticipated by Grelling in his interpretation of Neurath's term "life-situation."

Thus, the focus of this contribution is on the similarities visible between the conditions of life approach and the capability approach. Some differences between the approaches have been outlined in the paper, too. The following differences between Neurath's and Sen's approach certainly deserve further research efforts:

Although Neurath and Sen both propose to measure well-being by looking at the life people lead they have quite distinct reasons for doing so: Neurath maintains the objective to measure well-being in terms of utility. He views conditions of life as a means to approach this objective since they produce utility. Sen, in contrast, presents his capability approach as an alternative way of measuring well-being which is to replace the welfare economist focus on utility (or resources for that matter). Does this fundamental difference in their opinion on the role their approaches play has an impact on the story this paper has told?[64]

While this paper takes the history of the approaches with regard to the question of comparability into account, it does not refer to the approaches as a whole but restricts itself to the notions of life-situation and functionings. Neurath has embedded his notion of conditions of life in a theory on the structure of society and the way a society works.[65] He sketches an idea of how conditions of life evolve in time. Nothing similar can be found in Sen's writings. Sen argues in favour of giving the freedom to choose some weight in the assessment of well-being. Generally, Sen takes a more individualistic perspective than Neurath. Could their approaches complement each other?

Independent Scholar
associated with the Institute of Socio Economics
University of Hamburg
o.lessmann@web.de

---

[64] I take up this question in my "Utility and the Measurement of Well-being: A Similar Line of Thought and a Fundamental Dissent in Neurath and Sen" forthcoming in: Elisabeth Nemeth, Sigrid Stagl und Thomas Uebel (eds.) (in preparation): *Basic Income and Sustainability. The Other Austrian Economics and the Ecological Left*. Chicago: Open Court.

[65] See Wolfgang Voges, "The Standard of Living Approach as Conceptual frame for a reporting on Poverty and Wealth," paper presented at the International Centre for Comparative Research in the Social Sciences in Vienna on April 4th 2002.

The War Economy and the War Museum: Otto Neurath and the Museum of War Economy in Leipzig, c. 1918

Nader Vossoughian

For over three decades, scholars have been well aware of the fact that Otto Neurath's Museum of Society and Economy did not have its origins in the Museum of Settlement and Town Planning, as previously had been believed, but in the German Museum of War Economy, which Neurath directed for a brief period during the latter half of 1918, at the end of the first World War. This museum sought to furnish the public with an understanding of the social, economic, and administrative dimensions of wartime struggle. During its existence, Neurath divided his time between Vienna, where he headed the General War and Economics Section of the Scientific Committee for War Economy in the Austrian War Ministry, and Leipzig, site of the Museum of War Economy. As Wolfgang Schumann (1973) characterized the period,

> toward the end of the war when Neurath worked at the War Ministry in Vienna, he was also appointed director of the Museum of War Economy in Leipzig, which was a venture of the Chamber of Commerce there. I became its general secretary. Models and charts were in the making. This was the beginning of those activities of visualization which Neurath continued and fully developed in his Social and Economic Museum in Vienna.[1]

What was the precise extent of Neurath's involvement in the Museum of War Economy in Leipzig? Was Schumann correct in noting that it was there that Neurath began "those activities of visualization" that became more fully developed at the Museum of Society and Economy? What were the major exhibitions that the Museum of War Economy sponsored, and what significance did they have for Neurath's subsequent development? The answer to these questions are by no means clear – by the time of the publication of this article, I have still not been able to recover photographs from the period that illustrate what the museum and its exhibits looked like in their physical context. It is also unclear how the Museum of War Economy shaped the development of the Vienna Method of Pictorial Statistics specifically, if at all. What we do know, however, is that the Museum of War Economy sponsored numerous publications, including the *Proceedings of the German Museum of War Economy* [*Veröffentlichungen des deutschen Kriegswirtschaftsmuseums*] as well as countless

[1] Wolfgang Schumann, "Memories of Otto Neurath," *Empiricism and Sociology*, Marie Neurath and Robert Cohen (eds.) (Dordrecht: Reidel, 1973) p. 16.

E. Nemeth et al. (eds.), *Otto Neurath's Economics in Context.*
Vienna Circle Institute Yearbook [2007]. Volume 13.

pamphlets and articles. It left behind unpublished correspondences that can be found at the German War Ministry in Berlin and the Austrian War Ministry in Vienna, and sponsored a major exhibition, "World Blockade and War Economy," which was held in August 1918. Taken together, these events paint a picture of the Museum of War Economy that prefigure a number of themes that became more dominant in the Museum of Society and Economy during the latter half of the 1920s. Namely, under Neurath's direction the Museum of War Economy conceived of the modern museum as an instrument for planning the future, and as a tool for visualizing global forces; it sought to foster self-sufficiency and autonomy in the masses. It also helped popularize Neurath's provocative, if quixotic, understanding of the dynamics of modern-day war economies, which made a case for the role that informal communities and in-kind transactions could play in a centrally-administered socialist society.

The Museum of War Economy was born of Neurath's investigation into the discipline of war economics, a field he helped establish during the 1910s. War economics emphasized the positive role that cooperatives, cartels, trade unions, consumer associations, and other large organizations could play in administering socialized economies. It stressed the importance of barter, agricultural production, and other pre-industrial, pre-capitalist forms of production and exchange during periods of wartime struggle. It evolved out of Neurath's research into the Balkan wars of 1912 and 1913 and specifically, his account of why the Serbians and Bulgarians enjoyed a relatively high standard of living in spite of the fact that they were largely still an agrarian-based society, with a low gross domestic product. Serbians could produce "barley, oats, rice, beets, and potatoes," Neurath noted, even without the industrial infrastructure of wealthier nations.[2] Moreover, although Serbians and Bulgarians did not have access to money, they did have recourse to a common language and common religious practices (they were primarily Orthodox Christian). This dramatically improved their ability to manage and allocate resources, which suggested to Neurath two things. First, according to Neurath community and cooperation could also foster rationality and economic efficiency. Religion and rationality were not diametrically opposed, as Neurath's mentor and friend Ferdinand Tönnies believed, but were actually extensions of one another, as Max Weber argued in *The Protestant Ethic and the Spirit of Modern Capitalism* (1904–1905). Though Neurath took objection to the tacit idealism that underpinned Weber's analysis of capitalism, and while Weber regarded Neurath's economic theories as wildly utopian, both held that economic liberalism and the modern mass bureaucracy were unthinkable in the absence of organized religion. As Neurath wrote in a 1914 letter, "The Church appears to me more and more as

[2] Unless otherwise noted, all German translations were produced by the author. Otto Neurath, "Kriegswirtschaftliche Eindrücke aus Galizien," *Gesammelte ökonomische, soziologische und sozialpolitische Schriften (II)*. vol. 5. Rudolf Haller and Ulf Höfer (eds.) (Vienna: Hölder-Pichler-Tempsky, 1998) 78. Originally published in *Der österreichische Volkswirt* 5: 18 (February 1, 1913): 355–358.

a rationalist body... The Church is as rationalistic as the army, more rationalistic than the State. At least I believe so now."[3]

Second, Neurath was also convinced that the war economy could serve as a model for the peacetime socialist economy. Typically, Neurath observed, wartime conditions caused governments to curtail the flow of capital into and out of one's national borders, fostered widespread rationing and other measures that improved the way in which resources were allocated across a society, and improved a nation's efficiency and productivity. It allowed socialism to evolve organically out of capitalism without any violent or revolutionary overthrow of government. Which is to say that although war brought misfortune and political instability, it also had the paradoxical effect of helping alleviate economic crises. As Neurath stated in a letter to Ferdinand Tönnies,

> I see clearly that in the foreseeable future the peace economy will be arranged for military purposes more strictly than so far and, it seems to me, not to the disadvantage of the peace economy. For the military administration has no understanding for the restrictions of production in the interest of employers' profits. It is interested in a production that is as equally balanced and regularly increasing as possible. It also has an interest in the removal of economic crisis!! One is beginning to accept in these circles – at least in our country – that one is interested in a smoothly functioning peace economy, and one does not refrain from state socialist interference, as demonstrated by our lasts law of war performance, in which the taking over of the means of production by the state and general forced labor in the case of war appears to be established – with compensation to the owners.[4]

Neurath's analysis of the war economy won immediate and wide-spread attention. During the first World War, it gained him the support of the Austrian War Ministry, which appointed him head of the General War and Economics Section of the Scientific Committee for War Economy in the Austrian War Ministry in 1916. The mission of the Scientific Committee for War Economy was to discern "the extent of the needs of this modern war over all areas of practical science and technology."[5] Neurath's own role was to document, analyze, and synthesize materials and experiences pertaining to the war, particularly those that affected the daily lives of ordinary people. He spent much of his time amassing a vast archive of posters, coins, statistical tables, maps, and *ersatz* materials, and sought to identify ways of promoting the creation of barter associations [*Tauschhandelsorganisationen*].[6] Neurath also

---

[3] Letter from Otto Neurath to Ferdinand Tönnies, April 26, 1914, tr., Robin Kinross and Marie Neurath, Papers of Otto and Marie Neurath, Österreichische Nationalbibliothek, Vienna, Austria, 31.933.

[4] Letter from Otto Neurath to Ferdinand Tönnies, December, 1913, tr., Robin Kinross and Marie Neurath, Papers of Otto and Marie Neurath, Österreichische Nationalbibliothek, Vienna, Austria, 31.933.

[5] Otto Neurath, "Das wissenschaftliche Kommittee für Kriegswirtschaft des k. und k. Kriegsministeriums. Entwurf eines Arbeitsplanes," *Papers of the Kriegsministerium*. (Kriegsarchiv, Archiv der Republik (Vienna, Austria).

[6] Otto Neurath, "Schaffung einer Tauschhandelsorganisation," March 26, 1917, Papers of the Kriegsministerium, Kriegsarchiv, Archiv der Republik (Vienna, Austria) Box 87.

became involved in curating exhibitions, first in Serbia and later in Leipzig. In Serbia, Neurath put together an exhibit that "represent[ed] the cultural and administrative activities of the [local] government" during the Balkan conflict. In Hungary, he made plans to create an independent Institute for War Economy "in order to disseminate knowledge about the war economy through words and pictures."[7]

Neurath's contributions to the field of war economics also won him the favor of the leftist educator Rudolf Stegemann, who played a decisive role in helping establish and finance the Museum of War Economy. Stegemann headed the German Association for Mercantile Education, a progressive employment training organization based in Braunschweig.[8] In 1914, Stegemann sponsored an exhibit at Leipzig's International Exhibition for Book Publishing and Graphic Design (the exhibit was called "The Merchant" ["*Der Kaufmann*"]) and later donated its contents to the Leipzig Chamber of Commerce. Soon afterwards, he along with representatives from the local Chamber of Commerce initiated talks to open a permanent economic museum in Leizpig, and later they agreed that "The Merchant" should be utilized to help build its permanent collection.[9] In the summer of 1917, Stegemann lobbied successfully for the creation of a Museum of War Economy, winning financial and administrative support from the German War Ministry [*Deutsches Kriegsministerium*], the German Chambers of Industry and Trade [*Industrie – und Handelstag*], and the German Chambers for Handiwork and Commerce [*Deutscher Handwerks – und Gewerbekammertag*]. Initially, opposition to creating a Museum of War Economy was raised by the German War Ministry (Berlin was planning its own war museum, they argued). However, Stegemann managed to stave off critics by stressing the Museum of War Economy's scientific and sociological orientation.[10]

In order to flesh out the goals of the Museum of War Economy, in 1917 Stegemann published a pamphlet outlining the new museum's mission. Here, Stegemann declared that the Museum of War Economy's mission would be to furnish the public with a comprehensive picture of Germany's economic conditions during the course of the first World War – not just the state of its official monetary exchange economy, but its informal economy as well (its dependency on barter, for instance). The museum would feature exhibits reflecting innovations in industry and domestic life, as well as charts and graphs that furnished the public with a bird's-eye of Germany's trade and banking sectors. The Museum of War Economy

[7] Otto Neurath, "Anfrage wegen eines ungarischen Instituts für Kriegswirtschaftslehre," May 5, 1917, Papers of the Kriegsministerium, Kriegsarchiv, Archiv der Republik (Vienna, Austria) Box 87.

[8] "Besprechung betreffend die Errichtung eines Deutschen Kriegswirtschaftsmuseum im Reichstagsgebäude zu Berlin," *Veröffentlichungen des Deutschen Kriegswirtschaftsmuseum zu Leipzig* 1: 1 (1917).

[9] Internal Memo of the *Deutsches Kriegswirtschaftsmuseum*, September 7, 1918, Papers of the *Deutsches Kriegswirtschaftsmuseum*, Bundesarchiv (Berlin), R3101 617 (Band 1): 256.

[10] Minutes of the *Deutsches Kriegsministerium*, August 30, 1917, Papers of the *Deutsches Kriegswirtschaftsmuseum*, Bundesarchiv (Berlin), R3101 617 (Band 1): 33–40.

would be accessible to mass audiences, differing from peer institutions in that its collections drew from everyday life, mass culture rather than high culture. As Stegemann wrote, "[a]ccording to the resolutions decided upon up until the present moment, the entire economic life during war shall be the object of museological treatment and representation. This means that the work of agriculture, industry, trade, handy-work, and transportation must be included. Sovereign summary treatment of branches and instances of the war economy will also receive treatment – for example, substitutes used to meet shortages in raw materials, labor markets, and national help services, is entirely possible."[11]

Stegemann also made clear that the Museum of War Economy would include a gallery space, library, lecture hall, information center, and archive. Its collections would be divided into three separate divisions, corresponding (roughly) to primary, secondary, and tertiary economies. A Department of Natural Resources [*Urproduktion*] covered agriculture, mining, and farming; a Department of Manufacturing [*Verarbeitung*] explored aspects of mass industry, factory production, and artisanry; and a Department of Conditions of Life [*Lebenslage*] addressed labor, transportation, welfare, and war rationing.[12]

The Museum of War Economy opened its doors to the public in May 1918. Neurath was most likely appointed its director at this time as well, for it is during this period that his name first surfaces in the minutes of the Interior Ministry of Saxony and in the *Proceedings of the German Museum of War Economy*. In the Interior Ministry minutes, a meeting that was also attended by Stegemann and representatives from the Leipzig Chamber of Commerce, Neurath spoke extensively about the goals of the Museum of War Economy. He stressed the interactive character of the exhibits and the ways in which wartime shortages transformed the domestic economy. War brought hardship and struggle, Neurath reasoned, but it also stimulated innovation, resourcefulness, and efficiency in the populations it affected. It fostered self-reliance and economic independence, and he hoped to find ways to illustrate this fact in the Museum of War Economy:

> It will need to be shown [in the museum] how during war the scattered tin, cobalt, nickel, and copper mines can now be exploited. A diagram may show how mines that were hardly profitable during times of peace... now in times of war yield profits and have become important. In the section for manufacturing, the genealogy of German industry can be displayed pictorially. In order to show the changes in manufacturing, special attention will be given to technologies that are revived during war. So for instance beer breweries that are run out of the home are shown, or also an old village economy and its universal household industry. Instructive will be the juxtaposition of specialized manual trades during peace and wartime. Apart from room areas and other characteristic living conditions, interactive maps and models will be included that illustrate the increase in housing shortages... Occurrences such as the increase of nude labor in some industries, which take root in the interest of saving clothing, are to be valued.... But the museum will not only offer stationary interactive objects and models to the viewer; inasmuch as possible, the viewer himself should be moved to interact. He should experience speed of moving in an automobile in an appropriate

[11] Rudolf Stegemann, *Deutsches Kriegswirtschaftsmuseum* (Leipzig: O. Brandstetter, 1917) 5.

[12] "Das Deutsche Kriegswirtschaftsmuseum (Vorläufiger Überblick)," *Veröffentlichungen des Deutschen Kriegswirtschaftsmuseum zu Leipzig*: 3 (1918) 7–8.

> model. ... The viewer will be sequestered under experimental conditions and will observe how he responds to specific raw stimuli. How these aptitude tests help identify the pool of automobile drivers, telephone operators, etc., available for the war effort will be shown through statistical summaries; here one will be able to recognize how the introduction of aptitude tests helps save resources. The German Museum of War Economy will make visible to the broadest possible audiences the important issue of psycho-technologies and the very controversial Taylor system, and will bring to light the rationalization of the economy, which is progressively unfolding and developing meaningful connections through normification and typification.[13]

In his essay for the *Proceedings of the German Museum of War Economy*, which represented the second major public forum in which he discussed his ideas for the Museum of War Economy, Neurath talked about how he hoped that the museum would illustrate the varying ways in which wartime and peacetime conditions impacted people's daily lives. "The Museum of War Economy," he announced,

> ought to make visible to all how a peace-economy step-by-step becomes a war economy... All these developments ought to be represented in such a way that the individual visitor can discern the path of an individual product from beginning to end, right through to its use and consumption.[14]

Neurath felt that presenting an integrated picture of German society could help clarify to the average visitor his or her role in the German war economy and promote cultural unity and community –"*Gemeinschaft*" as theorized by Ferdinand Tönnies. Neurath was not opposed to cultural pluralism – in his native Vienna, he appreciated the rich perspectives and traditions that Czech émigrés brought to his city.[15] Yet he also believed that any citizenry needed a common vocabulary to communicate its needs as a society, and in this respect, museums could play a central role. Lantern slides, photographs, tree diagrams, information graphics, and physical artifacts could help communicate ideas and values in a way that words or images alone could not, Neurath believed. These tools did not just allow the museum to reach ever larger audiences, but also helped instill a sense of belonging and Pan-German solidarity. For although the Museum of War Economy was sponsored primarily by a regional authority (i.e., Saxony government and its Chamber of Commerce), its aspirations were national, stressing Germany and Austro-Hungary's common interests over those of Saxony proper. Admittedly, Neurath's own investment in this project of cultural reform was probably the result of his exposure to ethnic differences in the Balkans and Austro-Hungary, where the challenges posed by multi-culturalism were far more transparent. But he realized early on that

[13] Minutes of the Interior Ministry of Saxony, May 16, 1918, Papers of the *Deutsches Kriegswirtschaftsmuseum*, Berlin, R3101 617 (Band 1): 182–201.

[14] Otto Neurath, "Die Kriegswirtschaftslehre und ihre Bedeutung für die Zukunft," *Gesammelte ökonomische, soziologische und sozialpolitische Schriften (II)*. vol. 5. Rudolf Haller and Ulf Höfer (eds.) (Vienna: Hölder-Pichler-Tempsky. Originally published in *Veröffentlichungen des Deutschen Kriegswirtschaftsmuseums zu Leipzig* 4 (1918).

[15] See Letter from Otto Neurath to Ferdinand Tönnies, 1909, tr., Robin Kinross and Marie Neurath, Papers of Otto and Marie Neurath, Österreichische Nationalbibliothek, Vienna, Austria, 31.933.

German industrialists and intellectuals were similarly preoccupied by the decentralized nature of Germany's political system, as the country was hardly 50 years old and still struggled to contain anti-federalist sentiments. Like many left-leaning cultural reformers such as Walter Rathenau and Friedrich Naumann, both of whom served on the Museum of War Economy's Honorary Committee, he subscribed to a theory of cultural universalism that he believed would help modernize German society, and empower the country over and against its adversaries.[16] As Neurath stated in his May 4 lecture,

> [w]hat is it that characterizes today's economic system? In today's war economy... figures of authority play a larger role than before the war, reward and punishment take the place frequently of gains and losses. In place of the will of the individual, the will of states or associations often emerge.[17]

"World Blockade and War Economy [*Weltblockade und Kriegswirtschaft*]," an exhibition held in August 1918, only months before Germany's surrender to the Allies, was the only major exhibition sponsored by the Museum of War Economy. It took place on the premises of the German Association of Clerical Assistance in Leipzig [*Verband Deutscher Handlungsgehilfen zu Leipzig*], an employment aid agency, and included displays produced by Vienna's Army Museum [*Heeresmuseum*] and Berlin's World War Antiquariat. [*Weltkriegbücherei*], as well as the Museum of War Economy.[18] It was conceived in response to the blockade measures set in place against German trade: since 1916, British warships had imposed a virtual freeze on maritime transport, and the exhibition illustrated the impact these developments had had on select sectors of the economy. It sought to demonstrate the advantages of Germany's vertically-integrated wartime economy in which the state buffered relations between producers and consumers. It also reinforced the idea that Germany needed to see itself as an autonomous, self-enclosed body. As a rations officer in the Ukraine between 1915 and 1916, Neurath sought to remedy hunger by promoting agriculture and other forms of self-help. Similarly, "World Blockade and War Economy" tried to show that Germany needed to strengthen its ability to produce resources domestically in order to improve its standing internationally. As one observer wrote,

> [d]ue to the English blockade measures that violently disrupted its global ties, our German economy assumed the shape of a self-dependent economic organism over the course of

[16] "Führer durch die Sonderausstellung Weltblockade und Kriegswirtschaft", " *Veröffentlichungen des Deutschen Kriegswirtschaftsmuseum zu Leipzig*: 6 (1918).

[17] Otto Neurath, "Die Kriegswirtschaftslehre und ihre Bedeutung für die Zukunft," *Gesammelte ökonomische, soziologische und sozialpolitische Schriften (II)*. vol. 5. Rudolf Haller and Ulf Höfer (eds.) (Vienna: Hölder-Pichler-Tempsky. Originally published in *Veröffentlichungen des Deutschen Kriegswirtschaftsmuseums zu Leipzig* 4 (1918).

[18] "Das Deutsche Kriegswirtschaftsmuseum (Vorläufiger Überblick)," *Veröffentlichungen des Deutschen Kriegswirtschaftsmuseum zu Leipzig*: 3 (1918); "Führer durch die Sonderausstellung "Weltblockade und Kriegswirtschaft"," *Veröffentlichungen des Deutschen Kriegswirtschaftsmuseum zu Leipzig*: 6 (1918).

the war. One can even make the argument that our German fatherland has once again became a self-enclosed trading state.[19]

In keeping with Neurath's analysis of the war economy, which focused on the importance of in-kind economies and agricultural production, "World Blockade and War Economy" showed how barter, the use of recycled materials, folk know-how, and local technologies and resources could strengthen Germany in the war effort. It featured alternative mining and production methods, agricultural and farming techniques, and munitions manufacturing protocols. In order to depict the state of commerce, Neurath included a diorama that compared Leipzig's outdoor markets of 100 years ago to those of today. One wall illustrated the impact of the leather shortage on various segments of the economy; how cobblers had to make due with more abundantly available resources like wood, how rabbit skin could serve as a material for making clothing (it served as a substitute for cotton), and how home-makers were becoming more conscientious recyclers. A second exhibit looked at the rise of "nude labor in certain industries" such as coal mining in order to illustrate "how clothing is saved."[20] Still a third considered how consumers made due with the shortage of beef, and how readily-available products such as paper were being used in new and innovative ways: "[c]lothing out of spun paper... buckles made out of iron, such things give us an opportunity to show the viewer the effects of the blockade."[21]

Taken together, these exhibits documented how Germany's increased independence from global trade and the money market economy fostered socialistic conditions domestically. For Neurath, the war economy exemplified the manner in which the *Naturalwirtschaft* could be vital to the life of society as a whole: "[o]n account of such thickly packed representations, the visitor learns how one can become independent in one's own country, which is essentially tantamount to empowerment"[22] Neurath continues: "[t]he point is not to make the Museum of War Economy into a place of mummification,"[23] but to show how it could aid people's daily lives.

It is difficult to discern the reception of the Museum of War Economy, as access to periodicals of the period has been limited only to what I was able to uncover in the archives of the German War Ministry in Berlin and the Archive of the Republic

---

[19] Ferdinand Schmid, "Das Deutsche Kriegswirtschaftsmuseum und seine Bedeutung für die Wissenschaft", *Zeitschrift für Sozialwissenschaft Leipzig* (1918) 208.

[20] Minutes of the Interior Ministery of Saxony, May 16, 1918, Papers of the *Deutsches Kriegswirtschaftsmuseum*, Berlin, R3101 617 (Band 1): 182–201.

[21] "Führer durch die Sonderausstellung "Weltblockade und Kriegswirtschaft", *Veröffentlichungen des Deutschen Kriegswirtschaftsmuseum zu Leipzig*: 6 (1918).

[22] Ibid.

[23] Otto Neurath, "Die Kriegswirtschaftslehre und ihre Bedeutung für die Zukunft," *Gesammelte ökonomische, soziologische und sozialpolitische Schriften (II)*. vol. 5. Rudolf Haller and Ulf Höfer (eds.) (Vienna: Hölder-Pichler-Tempsky, 1998) 595. Originally published in *Veröffentlichungen des Deutschen Kriegswirtschaftsmuseums zu Leipzig* 4 (1918).

[*Archiv der Republik* at the *Österreichische Staatsarchiv*] in Vienna. Documentation concerning the number of visitors at the "World Blockade and War Economy" could also not be located. However, we do know that Neurath vacated his post there sometime toward the end of 1918,[24] soon after the war's official end, at which time he became embroiled in the radical political upheavals that took hold of Saxony and Bavaria in 1919. More relevant to the focus of this essay, however, is the fact that the Museum of War Economy later left an indelible effect on the Museum of Society and Economy, which Neurath established in 1925 in Vienna. A precise account of the history of the Museum of Society and Economy still lies outside the parameters of this investigation, but suffice it to say for the time being that the Museum of War Economy prefigured this latter institution in a number of critical ways: it established Neurath's interest in using the modern museum as a vehicle for social transformation and pedagogical reform; it illustrated the way in which Neurath's preoccupation with the *Naturalwirtschaft* also influenced his ideas about museum education. Finally, it also linked Neurath political concerns – his identification with organized socialism – to his economic ideas and his analysis of the war economy more specifically.

Acknowledgments I wish to thank my editors Elisabeth Nemeth, Stefan W. Schmitz, and Thomas Uebel for their very helpful critical feedback. I also wish to thank Kenneth Frampton, who helped shape this work in its early phases, and the archivists at the German War Ministry (Berlin), the Archive of the Republic (Vienna), and the Austrian National Library (Vienna), who helped me locate the materials on which this article was based.

NYIT School of Architecture and Design,
1855 Broadway, 11th Floor,
New York, NY 10023
USA
nv1@hotmail.com

[24] The last letter that I could find signed by Neurath while he was still secretary of the German Museum of War Economy was dated October 22, 1918. See Letter from Otto Neurath to Herr Major Cronbiegel-Collenbusch, October 22, 1918, Papers of the *Deutsches Kriegswirtschaftsmuseum*, Bundesarchiv (Berlin), R3101 617 (Band 1): 290–293.

Economy, Ideology and Culture: Otto Neurath's Approach to a Precarious Relationship

Günther Sandner

1 Culture and Austro-Marxism

The concept of base and superstructure has been one of the hotly debated issues in Marxist theory. Otto Neurath, who considered Marxism to be decisive for empirical sociology, accepted the significance of economic conditions as a driving force in the historical process. In contrast to Max Weber and Werner Sombart, he put the importance of ideas and the "capitalist spirit" into perspective. However, he also generally rejected the idea of economic determinism that was then very common among Marxists. In assuming a "coherence" of social structure, mode of production, way of life and (political) ideology, Neurath's approach enabled even an extensive understanding of cultural phenomena. Although he never elaborated a cultural theory (and was sceptical of then-contemporary concepts), his assumptions on this subject are worth considering.

In the preface to one of the most influential books of socialist theory, Karl Marx's "Contributions to the Critique of Political Economy" (1859), a frequently quoted phrase was established. "In the social production of their life," Marx put it, "men enter into relations that are specific, necessary and independent of their will, relations of production which correspond to a specific stage of development of their material productive forces. The totality of these relations of production forms the economic structure of society, the real basis, from which rises a legal and political superstructure, and to which correspond specific forms of social consciousness." That means that "(t)he mode of production of material life conditions the social, political and intellectual life-process generally. *It is not the consciousness of men that specifies their being, but on the contrary their social being that specifies their consciousness*."[1]

In the following decades or even the following century, the base-superstructure conception became an important problem in Marxist theory. On one hand, it has been very popular because of its focus on material life conditions, its radicalism and its anti-idealism as well; on the other hand, it raised some important and even

[1] Karl Marx, Preface of the Contributions to the Critique of Political Economy, in: Terrell Carver (ed.), *Karl Marx: Later Political Writings*, Cambridge: Cambridge University Press, 1996, pp. 159–160.

E. Nemeth et al. (eds.), *Otto Neurath's Economics in Context*.
Vienna Circle Institute Yearbook [2007]. Volume 13.

crucial questions with respect to political strategy. If the mode of production of material life conditions consciousness and even intellectuality, what could be the relevance of socialist and Marxist activities in the educational or even cultural field? Does it make sense to organize a socialist cultural life within the capitalist society – as many of the socialist parties did – if it is predominantly the social being that determines people's consciousness? Or is it a waste of political energy to focus on culture and education instead of on economy and societal order? It is well known that a number of socialist intellectuals gave sophisticated answers to such questions. Among the most culturalist ones were those brought forth by the Austro-Marxists. In a way, Austro-Marxist theory was a heterogeneous conception that was represented by a number of different socialist intellectuals. Nevertheless, they had some common ground and characteristic traits. Austro-Marxism was one of the socialist-oriented concepts in political theory that opposed a determinist base-superstructure conception; rather, in Austro-Marxist theory, education and culture played a crucial role for social, political and even economic transformation.

The Austro-Marxist idea of culture consists of different elements that cannot be expounded upon here in their entirety. Nevertheless, at least two of them should be mentioned. First, there was strong interest in working-class life. However, the question of whether there is such a thing as working-class culture in the bourgeois society was definitely not beyond controversy. Within the socialist movement, different approaches existed. Many socialists claimed that the question could not be addressed before the social revolution had taken place. Working-class culture could only be realized after a revolutionary change, they asserted. Realizing a proletarian culture, they said, is not a question for the capitalist, but rather for the socialist society. However, a number of Marxist intellectuals put forth a contradictory idea. They claimed that working-class attitudes and values such as collectivity and solidarity should at least partly be implemented even in the existing society. Austro-Marxists such as sociologist Max Adler (1873–1937) were among them. Although the conservative and pan-German academic establishment constricted his career, Adler was one of the very few socialist scholars who taught at the university. As a follower of Neo-Kantianism, he strictly opposed materialistic conceptions and was therefore convinced that parts of the socialist society could be anticipated even under contemporary conditions.[2] The concept of a counter-cultural socialist milieu in Red Vienna was based at least theoretically upon these assumptions.[3] For Austro-Marxist intellectuals such as Max Adler, there was no reason for "economic fatalism."[4]

[2] Max Adler, *Neue Menschen. Gedanken über sozialistische Erziehung [1924]*. Vienna, Munich: Jungbrunnen, 1972.

[3] Ibid., p. 17.

[4] Helmut Gruber, *Red Vienna. Experiment in Working-Class Culture 1919–1934*. New York, Oxford: Oxford University Press, 1991.

Second and in conjunction with it, there was a critical discourse on pedagogy and education within Austro-Marxism. It was again Max Adler who rejected the idea of non-partisan, status-quo-oriented education. In his view, socialist education aimed to overwhelm capitalism, even by the establishment of a socialist consciousness. He was convinced that, embedded in societal antagonisms and conflicts, socialist-oriented education could never be neutral. Young socialist intellectuals in the 1920s and 1930s such as Marie Jahoda and Paul Lazarsfeld followed this approach and tried to put it into practice. They combined their activities in the socialist youth movement with research studies that, as we know from the history of the social sciences, broke new ground. The most famous example was the Marienthal Study[5] that brought forth a rather pessimistic view. Unemployment, it said, does not lead to revolutionary attitudes and behaviour but results in passivity, apathy and depression. However, earlier studies, which focused on youth culture and were more closely connected with questions of pedagogy, followed a more optimistic approach. Among other findings, they came to the conclusion that solidarity is an essential attribute of working-class youth in particular, and this should be promoted by means of education. Already in 1924, Lazarsfeld together with Ludwig Wagner organized a youth camp that aimed to bring together proletarian and bourgeois adolescents and to establish a non-authoritarian, self-administered community. Although the experiment failed at least in part, it was nevertheless a valuable experience for both the participants and the young socialist intellectuals.[6]

Naturally, Austro-Marxism also referred to culture such as art, literature and philosophy and defined it idealistically as the best that has ever been thought and written. However, in addition to this traditional and very common understanding, culture in the socialist context had a broader meaning. On one hand, culture stood for workers' education. While appropriating the liberal and even revolutionary heritage of the bourgeoisie, the working class should assimilate culture and become qualified to form a new society. Obviously this approach did not break with the traditional and hegemonic meaning of culture but brought in a collective of new cultural agents: the proletariat, which, for a very long time, represented the opposite of culture and civilization. On the other hand, culture was considered as a way of life, even a counter-cultural one. In contrast to the bourgeois culture of individuality and competition, a new socialist culture should be based upon collectivity and solidarity. Within the socialist milieu (or "camp" as historians and political scientists later named it), an egalitarian society and the "new human being" could be partially realized.

[5] Marie Jahoda, Paul F. Lazarsfeld and Hans Zeisel, *Die Arbeitslosen von Marienthal. Ein soziographischer Versuch über die Wirkungen langandauernder Arbeitslosigkeit [1933]*. Frankfurt am Main: Suhrkamp, 1975.

[6] Paul F. Lazarsfeld and Ludwig Wagner, *Gemeinschaftserziehung durch Erziehergemeinschaften. Bericht über einen Beitrag der Jugendbewegung zur Sozialpädagogik*. Vienna: Anzengruber Verlag, 1929.

As an Austrian socialist intellectual, Otto Neurath was concerned with questions and debates like this. What was his position? To answer this question, three subjects will be addressed. First, I will (briefly) characterize Neurath's approach to Marxism. Second, I will analyse his position on base and superstructure, including the discussion about Max Weber and other "bourgeois" intellectuals. And finally, I will raise the question of whether something like a cultural theory emerged in (some of) his writings.

2 Neurath and Marxism

Initially, I want to characterize Neurath's approach to Marxism in three steps: First, Neurath's relation to Austro-Marxism; second, his "synthesis" of Marx and Epicurus; and finally his approach of Marxism as empirical sociology.

2.1 Austro-Marxism

What was Neurath's role in the political and intellectual formation of Austro-Marxism? As a young man, he had been deeply influenced by the social reform milieu of turn-of-the-century Vienna. The social philosopher Josef Popper-Lynkeus (1838–1921) and the natural scientist and monist Ernst Mach (1836–1916) crucially influenced his intellectual development. In this time, issues such as peace, women's rights, social reform and even housing played a prominent role in his political socialization. Although he also introduced socialist ideas and concepts in his writings, he blazed his own path in socialist theory. Anyway, he became a very active intellectual in the Austro-Marxist milieu. But although he dealt with highly relevant political issues such as the question of socialization, he was never an important political theoretician within the Austrian Socialist Party (SDAP). However, he was strongly integrated in the cultural and educational movement of Austro-Marxism. Among other things, he had close contacts to leading representatives of the SDAP such as Otto Bauer, the party's chief theoretician. After World War I, he "saw a chance of practical application of ideas he had been developing over the last decade"[7] in the Bavarian Revolution. But the socialist experiment failed in 1919 and Otto Neurath, its president of the central office for economic planning, was imprisoned. Beside academics such as Max Weber who pointed out that Neurath was a scholar and not a politician, it was Austrian Foreign Secretary Otto Bauer who spoke on his behalf and secured his release after a few weeks.

[7] Thomas Uebel, Introduction: Neurath's Economics in Critical Context, in: Thomas Uebel and Robert S. Cohen (eds.), *Otto Neurath. Economic Writings. Selections 1904–1945*, Dordrecht: Kluwer, 2004, pp. 1–106, p. 40.

Furthermore, there was a process of intellectual exchange that took place, for instance, among the circle of thinkers surrounding Otto Bauer (which included Otto and Helene Bauer, Otto Neurath and Edgar Zilsel),[8] an intellectual formation whose activities are unfortunately not very well known. In addition, Neurath collaborated and carried on discussions with Austro-Marxist intellectuals such as Marie Jahoda and Edgar Zilsel. Whereas Jahoda worked for a short time in his museum,[9] Zilsel was always a critical commentator on his research work, as his review of "Empirical Sociology" demonstrates.[10] To sum it up: The fact that he was part of the socialist cultural formation of Red Vienna was crucial to the development of his research projects and activities in knowledge transfer. This was not only a question of intellectual exchange. Neurath's connection to Austrian socialism also provided infrastructure and financial support that was essential for his intellectual activities. The Museum of Society and Economy probably would never even have been founded without the political support that was primarily provided by the Viennese Chamber of Labour and the City of Vienna, two institutions dominated by the socialists.

However, there were also disagreements among Neurath and Austro-Marxists such as those in the socialization debate (in which he disagreed with socialists such as Käthe Leichter, Helene Bauer and others) and, what is more important in this context, in cultural questions. As his review of the influential book "New Human Beings" (*Neue Menschen*, 1924) demonstrated, he was rather critical of the approach taken by Max Adler, who failed in his opinion to sufficiently characterize his subjects, the new people.[11] Otto Neurath as well as socialist scholars such as Edgar Zilsel rejected the paternalism that, in their view, some of the Austro-Marxists (including Adler) advocated. In contrast, they had more confidence in the autonomy of working class people, who were never disparaged as "the masses," as they were referred to by a widely accepted phrase in then-contemporary political and cultural discourse. Democratization of society also meant deconstructing a phenomenon Zilsel called the "religion of the genius" that necessarily results in the condemnation of the masses.[12] The idea that socialist educators must implement their cultural conception among the working class based on a top-down process was

[8] Wilhelm Filla, *Wissenschaft für alle – ein Widerspruch? Bevölkerungsnaher Wissenstransfer in der Wiener Moderne*. Innsbruck, Wien: Studienverlag, 2001, pp. 426–429.

[9] Marie Jahoda, Aus den Anfängen der sozialwissenschaftlichen Forschung in Österreich, in: *Zeitgeschichte*, 8, 4, 1981, pp. 133–141; Marie Jahoda, Im Gesellschafts – und Wirtschaftsmuseum, in: Friedrich Stadler (ed.), *Arbeiterbildung in der Zwischenkriegszeit. Otto Neurath – Gerd Arntz*, Vienna, Munich: Löcker, 1982, pp. 43–44.

[10] Edgar Zilsel, Rezension zu Otto Neurath: Empirische Soziologie, in: *Der Kampf*, 25, 2, 1932, pp. 91–94, p. 93.

[11] Otto Neurath, Rezension zu M. Adler, Neue Menschen [1925], in: Rudolf Haller and Heiner Rutte (eds.), *Otto Neurath. Gesammelte philosophische und methodologische Schriften*, Vol. 1. Vienna: Hölder-Pichler-Tempsky, 1981, pp. 219–220.

[12] Edgar Zilsel, *Die Geniereligion. Ein kritischer Versuch über das moderne Persönlichkeitsideal [1918]*. Frankfurt am Main: Suhrkamp, 1990.

never one Neurath advocated. In contrast, he favoured the idea of democratization of knowledge and humanization of science.[13] In this context, he explicitly rejected the philosophical approach in worker's education and juxtaposed to it his pictorial statistics approach.[14] However, in practice, these contradictory approaches were probably not in conflict and actually complemented one another.[15]

2.2 *Between Marx and Epicurus*

In contrast to Max Adler, the philosopher to whom Otto Neurath referred to most was definitely not Immanuel Kant. Neither were Gottlieb Fichte and Georg Friedrich Hegel among his philosophical favourites. Rather than Neo-Kantianism, Neurath advocated a materialistic approach (physicalism) that corresponded within Austro-Marxism, for instance, with the views of Friedrich Adler, a physicist and disciple of Mach. However, the way he defined his own Marxism was a singular phenomenon. It was based upon the idea of combining the approaches of Epicurus and Karl Marx. As he pointed out in "Personal Life and Class Struggle,"[16] he was an advocate of a theory that combined the ideas of the Greek philosopher with social reform. For Neurath, Epicurus negated transcendental ideas and theology but supported earthly things such as friendship and human happiness. Neurath wanted to transform Epicurus' doctrine of happiness into a collective programme with the help of Marx. He named his approach "Socialepicurism." "Everything is significant in so far as it is so for happiness," he concluded.[17] He was convinced that the realization of individual happiness and social reform on a collective level are the crucial elements for a future society. They could help to realize an ideal human being in a society that transcends the antagonisms between city and country, nature and culture, manual labour and intellectual activities, as he put it in a 1921 article entitled "Humanity."[18] Although he was a well-known and acknowledged intellectual, this concept of pleasure and happiness (which seems to have been influenced not only

---

[13] Neurath, Otto, Visual Education, in: Elisabeth Nemeth and Friedrich Stadler (eds.), *Encyclopedia and Utopia. The Life and Work of Otto Neurath (1882–1945)*, Dordrecht: Kluwer, 1996, pp. 245–335, p. 257.

[14] Otto Neurath, Bildstatistik und Arbeiterbildung [1929], in: Rudolf Haller and Robin Kinross (eds.), *Gesammelte bildpädagogische Schriften*, Vol. 3, Vienna: Hölder-Pichler-Tempsky, 1991, pp. 139–143.

[15] Josef Weidenholzer, *Auf dem Weg zum "Neuen Menschen". Bildungs – und Kulturarbeit der österreichischen Sozialdemokratie in der Ersten Republik.* Wien, München, Zürich: Europa Verlag, 1981, p. 87.

[16] Otto Neurath, Personal Life and Class Struggle, in: Marie Neurath and Bob Cohen (eds.), *Otto Neurath. Empiricism and Sociology*, Dordrecht: Reidel, 1973, pp. 249–298.

[17] Ibid., 290.

[18] Otto Neurath, Menschheit [1921], in: Haller, Rudolf and Heiner Rutte (1981) (eds.), loc. cit., pp. 197–201.

by Marxism but also by utilitarianism and utopianism) probably sounded a little weird (or at least too utopian) for some of the party's intellectuals.

2.3 *Marxism as Empirical Sociology*

In a number of publications, Otto Neurath tried to explain what kind of Marxism he advocated. One of these texts is "Empirical Sociology" from 1931.[19] The importance of Marxism in the field of social sciences, as Neurath put it, derives primarily from its rejection of any theological and idealistic speculation in the analysis of the historical process. The analysis of how capitalism works is closely connected with the analysis of the transformation of the status quo. That is why Marxism prepares, in a way, the synthesis of (national) economy and history, which will become an inseparable unit. And it is only Marxism that represents sociology based upon materialism. Materialism in this context means dealing with human behaviour within a spatiotemporal order. For Neurath, there was a close connection between empirical sociology, unity of science and Marxism. A Marxist, as Neurath put it, doesn't need any philosophical foundation. As a sociologist, a Marxist is interested in finding correlations among sociological events with the aim of being able to make prognoses. What sort of crises do we expect? What are the relevant preconditions for revolution? And how do the living conditions of social classes change in both war and peace? These were, he was convinced, examples of those questions that are relevant for the Marxist.

> Born of an activist outlook, Marxism starts from historical forecasts in the great manner. How did the social order of our days arise, how will it be changed and by whom? Those are the basic questions. To explain these, ethnology is not enough, nor economic history, nor social history; for this, as we saw, an economic analysis of the social apparatus is needed, with it wages, rents and amounts of goods, enterprises and associations. To the Marxist, human action appears not as the outflow of a sequence of concepts but as the result of specific preconditions.[20]

Although Neurath characterized his activities as "apolitical" (in the sense of social technological) because of their scientific orientation, he was, without a doubt, politically a socialist. His intellectual activities were meant to result in internationalization and, finally, world socialism. However, in his view, Marxism was a scientific theory and a sociological approach but not, and least of all, a philosophy of life (*Weltanschauung*).

[19] Otto Neurath, Empirical Sociology [1931], in: Marie Neurath and Bob Cohen (eds.), loc. cit.
[20] Ibid., pp. 347–348.

3 Between Economy and Ideology: Base and Superstructure

3.1 On Ideas and Ideologies

In 1931, Neurath published an article entitled "Marxism of a Jesuit" in the Social Democratic monthly journal *Der Kampf* (The Struggle).[21] At first glance, it was a review of I.B. Kraus' "*Scholastik, Puritanismus und Kapitalismus*" (Scholasticism, Puritanism and Capitalism). However, in effect, it constituted a critique of Max Weber and Werner Sombart, the "bourgeois" sociologists. As Neurath put it, they always wanted to demonstrate in what ways ideas formed social order and economy. Naturally, he disagreed with such an attitude and accused Weber and Sombart polemically of presenting an almighty spirit as an important historical force. For him, this was nothing but metaphysics. As Neurath noted ironically, he gladly welcomed the fact that a Christian scholar, a Roman Catholic by confession, was the one who disproved Weber's thesis of a Calvinist spirit that results in capitalism (Protestant Ethic and the Spirit of Capitalism [1904/1905]). Weber, who aimed to refute Marxism, had been challenged precisely by a Jesuit! Neurath recommended the book very highly to every Marxist interested in Weber's sociology of religion. To what extent was it a materialist one? Neurath summarized its basic assumptions as follows: It was not the Calvinist religion that formed the English merchant; rather, the English merchant adapted and adopted as well the Calvinist religion because they themselves were congenial to it. Those who wanted to merchandise and lend money became Calvinists. But it was not Calvinism that transformed them into merchants. Neurath appeared to be impressed by both the book and the author who, as he put it, cut his own path and established a third way between Weber and Marx. Ideas influence practice and vice versa, Neurath quoted Kraus, but it is first and foremost in the field of economics where practice and not theory has primacy.

Did Neurath ever define his concept of ideology? In any case, his understanding of ideology is not free of ambiguity. In his rather polemical review of Karl Mannheim's "Ideology and Utopia," he rejected Mannheim's interpretation of Marxism and Marxist understanding of ideology. But what was his own approach? First he claimed that ideologies are "trains of thought" in general and rejected their meaning as "falsification." Second, he brought forth a more precise concept. On the one hand, for Neurath, there were scientific and non-scientific ideologies and the former will overwhelm the latter. Therefore, he claimed that Marxism as a scientific ideology is the ideology of the proletariat.[22] However, this definitely does not correspond to Marx' approach to ideology as false consciousness. On

[21] Otto Neurath, Marxismus eines Jesuiten [1931], in: Rudolf Haller and Heiner Rutte (eds.), loc. cit., pp. 401–405.

[22] Otto Neurath, Bürgerlicher Marxismus [1930], in: Rudolf Haller and Heiner Rutte (1981) (eds.), loc. cit., pp. 349–356.

the other hand, he saw only slight effects of ideologies such as religious doctrines when he highlights the contradictions between them and reality. There are no clear consequences of religious doctrines, he was convinced.[23]

3.2 *Base and Superstructure*

How did Neurath himself define the relationship between ideas and economy and between theory and practice? In some of his writings such as "Empirical Sociology" (1931) he reflected on the way Marxism addressed the issue. In another article from 1931 entitled "Philosophy of Life and Marxism,"[24] he tried to make his position clear. First, he recapitulated his evaluation that Marxism is definitely not a philosophy of life but empirical sociology. Whoever is searching for correlations among sociological processes does not need any philosophical foundation. In contrast, he tried to prognosticate economic and social phenomena such as crises, revolutions, wars and even the development of the material conditions of certain social classes. Second, there are certain correlations that are crucial for Marxism. There are some processes that will be defined as superstructure. The Marxist demonstrates in what way they relate to processes of the order of production. The Marxist interprets even his own scientific formulations as superstructure and therefore as dependent upon the economic base. Therefore, certain theories will only emerge if social transformation has taken place. For the Marxist, societal transformations lead to new theoretical statements. However, theories as formations of physicalism are not only symptoms of changes within the order of life; they are also elements of change, as Neurath put it. In publishing and communicating certain findings, one can change the existing order and form a new basis for the advancement of theory.

The way Neurath interpreted the base/superstructure problem can be summarized as follows: Primarily, there are correlations between base and superstructure. However, a sort of primacy of the base should not be ignored. Nevertheless, this does not mean that only the base determines superstructure. Superstructural phenomena are more than mere reflections of the economic structure or the mode of production. In Marxism – which in Neurath's view was essential for the social sciences – theory and practice are closely interwoven. Consequently, the bourgeois doctrine of neutral scholars who study social relations from "outside" ought to be rejected.

---

[23] Otto Neurath, Marxismus eines Jesuiten [1931], in: Rudolf Haller and Heiner Rutte (eds.), loc. cit., pp. 401–405.
[24] Otto Neurath, Weltanschauung und Marxismus [1931], in: Rudolf Haller and Heiner Rutte (eds.), loc. cit., pp. 407–412.

4 The Approach Towards Culture

A sophisticated understanding of the relationship between base and superstructure has always been a key element of socialist theories of culture.[25] However, the base and superstructure issue is also a distinguishing feature among socialist approaches because differences in it inevitably result in different ideas of culture. For this reason, it is worth considering what concept of culture Otto Neurath advocated. He very rarely used the word "culture" and was very sceptical about its application. The number of imprecise meanings of culture, a word that is full of emotions, as he put it in 1921 in "Anti-Spengler,"[26] is unsurpassed even by those of the word capital – a remarkable argument for a Marxist. However, there are three points to characterize Otto Neurath's approach to culture. First, it can be discussed within his theory of coherence; second, the concept has significance in the context of working-class life; and finally, culture appeared as an important element in Neurath's project for democratization of knowledge.

4.1 Coherence

Coherence is a key term for Neurath's approach to culture. For him, the question of coherence of customs played a decisive role in the structure of sociology. He assumed that, in human society, there is always a coherence of mode of production, social structure and ideology. In contrast to Weber who argued that words, writings and ideas determine human behaviour, Neurath was convinced that there has been no determinism but rather coherence. The books one writes and the fairytales one tells are part of customs and traditions. They are coherent with the customs of the process of production and crucial to the lives of human beings. So even culture must be seen in the context of the theory of coherency. Modes of productions are coherent with ways of life, with technological, religious and cultural practices. Nonetheless, they are not determined. There are material relationships but there is no determinism. In the chapter on "coherence" within "Empirical Sociology," he illustrated the unpredictability of intellectual and artistic activities with the example of a painter:

> A relation through stimuli is much more ambiguous than a technical relation. If a painter painting sunny pictures is found in a foggy country, one might be inclined to explain this as compensation, based on many analogies: what he is denied in life he creates in his art. But if a painter of sunny pictures is found in a sunny country, then, based on many analogies, one might declare: this is a reflection of reality. Now a penetrating analysis might differentiate a picture painted by realistic association. It is more difficult to predict whether

[25] Raymond Williams, Base and Superstructure in Marxist Cultural Theory, in: *New Left Review*, 82, 14, 1973, pp. 3–16.

[26] Otto Neurath, Anti-Spengler [1921], in: Marie Neurath and Bob Cohen (eds.), loc. cit., pp. 158–213.

> painters will paint sunny or not-sunny picture in foggy countries than to predict that we shall find mathematics wherever we find engineering.[27]

Even the emergence of certain doctrines, Neurath was convinced, is not always to be explained one-dimensionally by the modes of production, but instead needs to be discussed sociologically or politically.

4.2 Working Class Culture

In Austro-Marxist theory, cultural and social elements were closely interwoven. In a way, Neurath's approach could be characterized in the same way. In capitalism, society is not only divided into social classes. There are also cultural contradictions that are interrelated with that. The political question is how to react to this development? In "Empirical Sociology" (1931), Neurath introduced conceptual terms such as terrain of life (*Lebensboden*), living standard (*Lebenslage*) and order of life (*Lebensordung*) to provide a more scientific approach for sociology. However, Neurath also defined borders of a class-based way of life within a capitalist economy. Socialist humans were created by a socialist order; it is not the other way around. If one wants to change housing, clothing, festivals, reading, love, everyday life, sociability and personal life in general, one must change the power structures, the social order as a whole. Without the radical change of the economic order, socialist thinking, feeling and life will not be successful and there will be no socialist democracy.

> Not until after the proletariat's victory will education and art be brought to all who today still must go without. Not until then will there arise in a greater measure an art more adapted to the socialist order. The practice of art and science today lies mainly in the hands of opponents to the proletariat. Only rarely will bourgeois recalcitrants wage single-handed war against the past or break through to the proletarian front. And in the proletariat there are, for the present, few possibilities to work in a scientifically or artistically creative field. Traditional means and forms are predominantly in use.[28]

Initially, this sounds rather incompatible with Austro-Marxist cultural theory. Nevertheless, for Neurath, these efforts, cultural activities and socialist reforms of everyday life were not in vain because the socialist transformation had already begun. As he put it, there is a conflicting field between measures that are already possible in the "democracy of enemies" (capitalism) and those that can be realized only in the "democracy of friends" (socialism). However, Neurath was doubtlessly convinced that the activities of the working class cultural movements were an important instrument for establishing solidarity within the socialist milieu.

[27] Otto Neurath, *Empirical Sociology*, loc. cit, p. 385.
[28] Otto Neurath, *Personal Life and Class Struggle*, loc. cit., p. 258.

4.3 Culture as Democratization

The best example to demonstrate the importance of culture in Neurath's conception is, of course, his approach to democratizing knowledge. According to the ideas of the Vienna Circle Manifesto (1929), it was necessary "to fashion intellectual tools for everyday life, for the daily life of the scholar but also for the daily life of all those who in some way join in working at the conscious re-shaping of life."[29] Democratization of knowledge, as Neurath conceptualized it, included both the level of literary language and that of pictorial language. He not only criticized the use of "intellectual jargon"[30] but also tried to replace it through his activities in adult and workers' education. As is well-known, the "Verein Ernst Mach" was founded in 1928 to "popularize" the ideas of the Vienna Circle by organizing lectures held mostly by association members such as Moritz Schlick, Hans Hahn, Edgar Zilsel and, of course, Neurath himself. In addition to these activities, Neurath cooperated with various institutions such as the *Volkshochschulen* (adult education institutions) and the *Arbeiterhochschule* (workers' university), where he gave courses and lectures as well. Also a considerable number of his publications (books, booklets, articles etc.) were addressed not only to the scientific community but also to the general public.

A discussion of Neurath's concept of humanization ought to include consideration of the following aspects: First, for Neurath, realizing humanization of knowledge was a necessary element in establishing and advancing democracy. "For a democratic society, it is important to have a common knowledge in a common language,"[31] he pointed out. Second, for him, pictorial pedagogy was an important instrument to extend "intellectual democracy." However, this project was not due to national borders. It was planned to create a universal language that would be independent of linguistic and cultural conditions. Visual education was an element of applied social science and international planning as well. And finally, Neurath's utopian programme defined aims that had to be achieved: Cosmopolitism, internationalism and world citizenship could be realized if cultural, social and linguistic barriers were transcended. The construction of a scientific worldview and the battle against metaphysical and theological tendencies had always to be carried on by means of social reform as well as economic and political planning. In contrast to Oswald Spengler's book "The Decline of the West" (1918, 1922), there was no clash of civilizations but rather the possibility of a common culture of mankind.

---

[29] Otto Neurath: Wissenschaftliche Weltauffassung: Der Wiener Kreis [The Scientific Conception of the World: The Vienna Circle] [1929], in: Marie Neurath and Bob Cohen (eds.), loc. cit., p. 305.

[30] Neurath, Otto, Visual Education, loc. cit., p. 256.

[31] Ibd., p. 331.

5 Culture and Institution in Comparison

Neurath never referred to a base-superstructure conception in a narrower sense. That is the reason why culture mattered; even so, he was a materialist and a socialist. To point that up, a comparative perspective could finally be helpful. Carefully considered, there are a number of parallels between the approaches of Austro-Marxist intellectuals such as Neurath in the 1920s and 1930s and early British cultural studies in the 1950s and 1960s (meaning the intellectual and educational activities of scholars such as Richard Hoggart, Raymond Williams and even E.P. Thomson within the British New Left). First of all, both referred to a broad concept of culture that was closely connected to a class-based meaning, to working-class culture. Second, and related to that, there were institutional similarities. Despite some university links, both the representatives of British cultural studies and many Austro-Marxist scholars were extra-mural phenomena. They worked in institutions of knowledge transfer and workers' or adult education. Therefore both represented models of "alternative institutionalization." This concept can be characterized along the lines of Edward Shils' well-known definition.[32] First of all, there were research institutes. Besides the institutions of adult education, there were two new types of organizations. Already in 1924, Otto Neurath founded the "Museum for Society and Economy." On one hand, this was a location of science popularization (or "humanization"); on the other hand, the method of pictorial statistics was advanced there. Furthermore, all of the Austro-Marxist intellectuals were writing in a number of socialist journals. This diversity of periodicals was typical for the Austrian socialist milieu. They were specialized in topics such as education, philosophy and politics. Perhaps the most interesting one was *Der Kampf* since it combined all of these elements. Officially, it was the Social Democrats' theoretical party journal; in fact, it was also a discussion forum for critical intellectuals associated with the party. Surprisingly, although most of them were never associated with the university system, the Austro-Marxist intellectuals also had students (according to the meaning used by Shils) in exceptional cases. The example that can be given relates to Neurath. As one of his numerous activities, he was a teacher at the workers' university that had been founded in 1925 and conducted by Josef Luitpold Stern. After World War II, one of his students, Franz Rauscher, became director of the Museum for Society and Economy, which Neurath himself had founded in interwar Austria.[33] But other elements of institutionalization should also be mentioned: The interaction between the different representatives was remarkable and included participation in

[32] Edward Shils, Tradition, Ecology, and Institution in the History of Sociology, in: *DAEDALUS, Journal of the American Academy of Arts and Sciences*, 99, 4, 1970, Cambridge, MA, pp. 760–825.

[33] Franz Rauscher, Mein Lehrer Otto Neurath, in: Friedrich Stadler (ed.), *Arbeiterbildung in der Zwischenkriegszeit. Otto Neurath – Gerd Arntz*, Vienna, Munich: Löcker, 1982, pp. 45–47.

a number of discussion circles, the reception of their respective intellectual work by reviews, and even intellectual cooperation in research projects. Undoubtedly, they also communicated with the general public, a phenomenon that has to be seen within the context of the socialist counterculture.

6 Conclusion

So finally, I would like to state some conclusions that emerge from the comparative approach I have put forth.[34] Historically considered, there is a problem of context. As a matter of course, different time frames and even national traditions need to be considered. I can only give some catchwords with respect to the British Left. In postwar Britain, the idea of class was challenged by welfare capitalism. The level of consumption rose even in the working class. In addition, mass culture and mass media provoked the question of classlessness, and even the reform of the educational system improved working class kids' chances of attaining better positions in society. In sharp contrast to this, the Austrian political situation in the 1920s and 1930s was conditioned by economic and social decline and political radicalization. Social classes and political camps were strictly divided. Nevertheless, there are comparable elements even on the level of political context. Both formations had to deal with political transformation after the war, which did not result in revolution, as some leftists hoped or even expected. On a theoretical level, this combination corresponded to the rejection of economic reductionism and the rise of leftist culturalism. The importance of culture and education within the Left was part of this phenomenon.

However, there is another interesting parallel worth mentioning. That is the idea that there is a relation between innovation in the academic field and the type of the cultural hybrid (i.e. the individual who moves between two different cultures). Interestingly, Paul Lazarsfeld formulated this idea in one of his publications on the history of sociology.[35] In a way, this hybridity applies to a number of intellectuals, either in the case of scholarship boys who came from working class families and entered academia, or at least in the case of intellectuals who were trained at the university but were active in the workers' movement and in workers' education as in the case of Neurath. The researcher who is familiar with working class life addresses different questions than the bourgeois academician who moves only within his own social class and cultural milieu. Therefore, there is a strong correlation between alternative institutionalization and the emergence

[34] Günther Sandner, *Engagierte Wissenschaft. Austromarxistische Kulturstudien und die Anfänge der britischen Cultural Studies*. Münster: Lit Verlag, 2006.

[35] Paul Lazarsfeld, Eine Episode in der Geschichte der empirischen Sozialforschung: Erinnerungen, in: Talcott Parsons, Edward Shils and Paul F. Lazarsfeld, *Soziologie – autobiographisch. Drei kritische Berichte zur Entwicklung einer Wissenschaft*, Stuttgart: Ferdinand Enke, 1975, pp. 147–225, p. 177.

of a critical intellectual discourse on culture. Among other elements I have mentioned, this is mainly due to political context, the extension of the concept of culture and new themes, and the transcending of disciplinary boarders. Certainly, institutionalization was essential to establishing critical research on culture. Obviously, though, it sometimes had to find alternative ways.

However, in this context – and even because of it – the objects and the orientation of the idea of culture changed. Culture appeared as mass culture, popular culture, class culture and even youth culture. It became the object of trans-disciplinary work that was addressed even to a non-academic audience. And finally, the political context is worth comparing. Both conceptions, the Austro-Marxists and the British intellectuals around Birmingham, were integrated in a socialist milieu that needed to deal with the fact that an expected revolution didn't happen. This was one of the reasons why culture and education became important elements of a critical, socialist discourse on societal and political transformation. In interwar Austria, Otto Neurath was one of its most original advocates. This can be summed up by stating that, although Neurath didn't share the optimism of socialist reform of everyday life and insisted on the significance of the economic and social order, he also advocated an approach that relates social change, culture and political transformation in a way that – perhaps because of its ambiguity – does not belong to any single one of those then-contemporary approaches. He found his own eclectic way which, however, has been inspiring for very different theories and practices.

Independent Scholar
Lecturer at the Department of Political Science
University of Vienna
guenther.sandner@univie.ac.at

Part II
General Part

Consensus in Art and Science

Keith Lehrer

The lecture is an argument for a marriage of theory and experience. It contains something old, something new, something borrowed and something true. The argument is that the dichotomy between science and art, between theory and experience is resolved and the components unified when the role of consensus in the acceptance of theory and the conception of experience is made clear. Moreover, the unification achieved brings with it a method for unifying the empiricism of Moritz Schlick[1] with the consensualism of Otto Neurath.[2] In earlier work, I developed a mathematical model of consensus with Carl Wagner.[3] That work concerned the aggregation of probabilities by weights of respect assigned by members of a community to each other that converged toward a consensual probability. The convergence depended on connectedness among the members of the group in terms of positive weights. We thought of the probabilities as probabilities of scientific theories or hypotheses. The process converging toward consensus was mathematically equivalent to finding consensual weights to be assigned to members of the group that could be used as a measure of competence and expertise. The consensual weights can be applied to find consensus concerning factors other than probabilities. The use of probabilities was in fact an incidental, though formally well articulated, application of the underlying aggregation of weights to obtain convergence toward consensual weights.

I argued that the aggregation model of consensus could explain how there could be revolutionary changes in what is accepted in science or in what probabilities are assigned to hypotheses as a result of the assignment of positive weights to members of the revolutionary group by leaders in the standard group. The shifts resulting from the assignment of positive weights to those formerly isolated can be revolutionary. However, my primary claim, which I defend and intend to develop, was that

---

[1] Schlick, M., *Gesammelte Aufsaetze 1926–1938*, Vienna: ND Hildesheim, 1938; Schlick, M. The Foundation of Knowledge, in A. J. Ayer, ed., *Logical Positivism*, Glencoe, IL: The Free Press, 1959.

[2] Neurath, O., Soziologie in Physicalimus, (1931) in R. Haller and H. Rutte, eds., *Otto Neurath, Gesammelte Philosophische und Methodologische Schriften*, Vienna: Hölder-Pichler-Tempsky, 1891.

[3] Lehrer, K. and Wagner, C., *Rational Consensus in Science and Society*, Dordrecht: Reidel, 1981.

E. Nemeth et al. (eds.), *Otto Neurath's Economics in Context.*
Vienna Circle Institute Yearbook [2007]. Volume 13.

the change results from the use of information, rather than from the exercise of power.[4] It is information about the competence and expertise of others, especially those in the revolutionary group. The result depended on axioms and theorems of linear algebra. I propose here that the argument can be readily extended to issues in the arts. The success of revolutionary art movements can be explained, at least in part, in terms of the acceptance of it by experts in the art world. A new consensus forms by the aggregation of acceptance and conception by weights of respect.

The reflections need the defense of argument and example. I do not claim that the consensual model is a complete explanation of the acceptance of claims in science or art. There is an input of experience in both science and art that constrains the values of what gets aggregated, and there is the test of experience that influences how much weight of respect, or more simply how much regard we have for others. Some have thought that the consensus model ignores the data of experience. It does not. The probabilities we aggregate are summaries of information, and the aggregation gives us a consensual summary of individual summaries of information. I suggested that the model of consensus could be applied to issues of meaning in collaboration with Carl Wagner (see footnote 3) and with greater concern for issues in linguistics with Adrienne Lehrer.[5] However, I did not in these applications to semantics note any direct application of the model to issues concerning the role of experience in our conceptions and interpretations in science or art. The role is more similar in science and art than one might imagine. In short, my argument is that personal and social aggregation sustain the link between theory and experience in science and art. You have to aggregate experience to render it conceptual and connect it with knowledge and theory. The aggregation of experience uses a sensory exemplar. The exemplar becomes part of meaning or content exhibiting the functional role it plays as part of the meaning. The process whereby the exemplar becomes conceptual and becomes part of a conceptual role, which I have called *exemplarization*,[6] is derived from Reid[7] and Hume.[8] It was developed further in different ways by Schlick[9] and Goodman.[10] I am indebted to these accounts.

---

[4] Lehrer, K., Social Information, *The Monist*, Oct., 1977, pp. 473–487.

[5] Lehrer, A. and Lehrer, K., Fields, Networks and Vectors, in F. R. Palmer, ed., *Grammar and Meaning*, Cambridge: Cambridge University Press, 1995, pp. 26–48; Lehrer, K. and Lehrer, A., Semantic Fields and Vectors of Meaning, in B. Lewandowska-Tomaszczyk, ed., *Lexical Semantics, Cognition and Philosophy*, Lødz: Lødz University Press, 1998, pp. 123–138.

[6] Lehrer, K., Meaning, Exemplarization and Metarepresentation, in Dan Sperber, ed., *Metarepresentation*, a volume of *Vancouver Studies in Cognitive Science*, Oxford: Oxford University Press, 2000, pp. 299–310; earlier in Skepticism, Lucid Content and the Metamental Loop, in A. Clark et al., eds., *Philosophy and Cognitive Science*, Dordrecht: Kluwer Academic Publishers, 1996, pp. 73–93.

[7] Reid, T., *Thomas Reid's Inquiry and Essays*, in R. E. Beanblossom and K. Lehrer, eds., Indianapolis, IN: Hackett, 1983 (1785FE), esp. 234–242.

[8] Hume, D., *A Treatise of Human Nature*, London: John Noon, 1739, Book. I, Part I, Sect. VII.

[9] Schlick, M., The Foundation of Knowledge.

[10] Goodman, N., *Languages of Art*, Indianapolis, IN/New York: The Bobbs-Merrill, 1968.

Let us consider an example first, and then turn to the mathematics. There was a great deal known about cells before anyone knew what the surface of a cell was like. Indeed, most of knowledge, what was accepted about the cell, though influenced by observation through light microscopes was about internal character of the cytoplasm or the nucleus. Then Palade[11] used the electron microscope to show us what the surface was like. Here is a photo of the surface of a cell (Fig. 1). The dots you see are granules and have come to be called ribosomes. The question is what the image means. Palade thought the granules were RNA packets. That is how he interpreted the image after microscopic investigation. If you want to know what the surface of the cell is like, the photo shows you. All this is striking enough scientifically, but the philosophical task is to explain it. Here is my take, influenced by Otávio Bueno.[12] There is an initial stage of observation in which the image is seen by Palade. He looks again and sees it again. Looking again, the image is re-identified. If Palade were to remain agnostic about what he is seeing, he nevertheless forms, as you do, a rudimentary conception of the image adequate for re-identification. The original image plays a role in re-identification. A photo might play a similar role. So far the conception remains ostensive. It is generalization of the image. This stage is theory neutral.

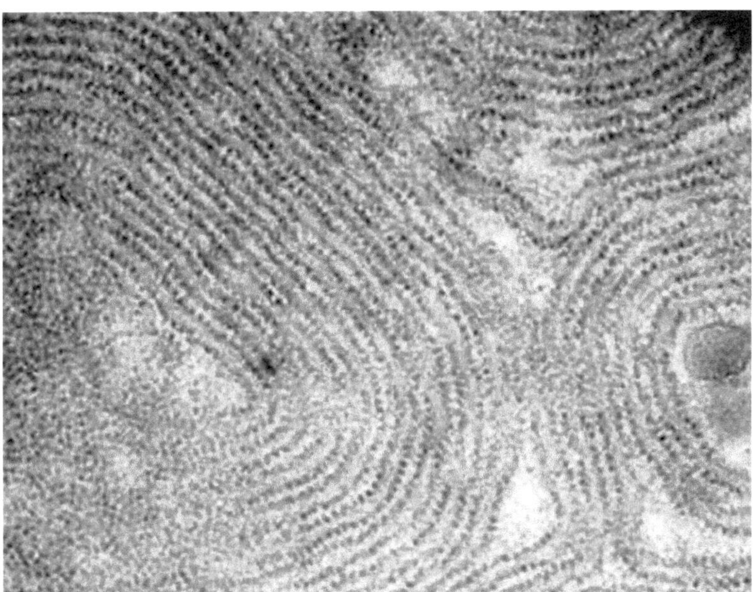

Fig. 1 Ribosomes

[11] Palade, G. E., A Small Particulate Component of the Cytoplasm, *The Journal of Cell Biology*, 1, 1955, 59–68 (abstract); *Journal of Applied Physics*, 24, 1953, 1419.

[12] Cf. Bueno, O., Representation at the Nanoscale? Forthcoming in *Philosophy of Science* 73; Bueno, O., The Drexler–Smalley Debate on Nanotechnology: Incommensurability At Work?, *International Journal for Philosophy of Chemistry*, 10, 2004, 83–98.

I know that some of you will doubt that there is such a stage. I do not claim temporal priority for this stage. Nor do I claim that it is a natural or innocent kind of perception. Nevertheless, attending to what the image is like in itself is important in science and art. What one sees in this way may, of course, be an artifact of the process, and ultimately one must ask what the object seen is and whether it is an artifact of instrumentation. To raise this question is to appeal to a level, perhaps a sophisticated one, of attending to what the experience is like in itself, to what is immediately observed. It is part of the training of both the experimenter and artist to learn to notice what one sees immediately putting aside questions of what the observed features mean.

The first stage is generalization from the exemplar to a plurality of other observable images. I call this *ostensive exemplarization* and the result *ostensive conceptualization*. The next stage in the process of converting an exemplar to a concept is to conceptualize it inferentially as the surface of a cell. At this stage, however, one might not have any further background theory about what the surface of a cell is like. The image exhibits our ostensive conceptions of the surface of the cell. We might add other vectors of inference, for example, that the granules are packets of RNA after further microscopic observation and analysis. The photo exhibits to us something about what the granules are like prior to analysis that cannot be known in another way.

Let me take an example from the arts. Here is a photo of a work of mine (Fig. 2). You see the image, and you could re-identify it. You have exemplarized the image.

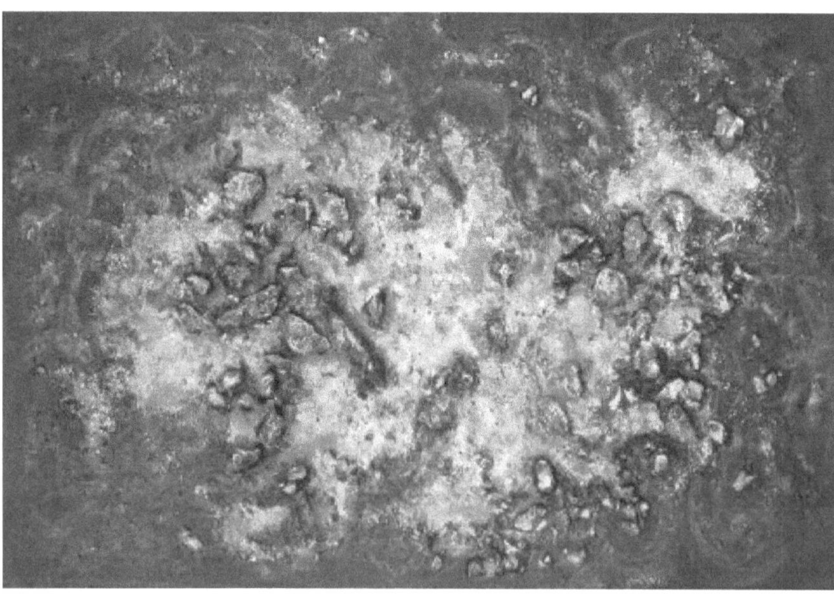

Fig. 2 Nebula

You have a general ostensive conception of what it is like using the exemplar to stand for it and to exhibit this. You may go further. Some of you may think of it as an abstract painting. Some of you may see it as an astronomical image, a nebula, perhaps, and others as some odd microscopic image of some living thing. In the case of the ribosome photo and the artwork photo you begin with ostensive exemplarization using the exemplar to remind you of something you will know when you see it.

You find yourself, like Palade or the art receiver, conceptualizing the exemplar ostensively and then building inferential meaning upon it. I do not claim that the process has to break down into the initial ostensive generalization and the subsequent inferential conception, for the brain secretes meaning as sensory information is received. There are deep lessons in these experiences, however. The first is that even ostensive generalization, how we generalize, depends on our cognitive structure, innate or learned. The second, more interesting lesson, is that there is semantic security at the ostensive stage. Schlick[13] claimed that there was a kind of meaning of some expressions such that the meaning of the expression guaranteed the truth of the expression. He may have overstated the semantic security of the guarantee. However, at the level of ostension, where the exemplar stands for or represents a class of instances as Hume suggested earlier, the exemplar is one of the instances which it stand for. So the exemplar, used to generalize to a class of instances loops back onto itself referentially. It refers to itself as it refers to instances of the class it is used to identify. This is not a logical guarantee, however, because the referential looping is a psychological process that can fail to succeed. Successful exemplarization yields content of an ostensive variety exhibited by the exemplar, however, and the exemplar is an instance of the exemplarized concept as the result of simple uncorrected generalization. Once the exemplarization becomes inferential, the truth guarantee is compromised by the loss of ostensive simplicity.

What does any of this have to do with aggregation and consensus? Consensus effects the transition from personal observation to scientific result. Consider Palade. He makes an observation. There is a consensus about how to test the result for the possibility of errors, including most saliently, the introduction of artifacts. He compared the results using oxides and formaldehyde to check whether the granules were introduced by the stabilizing substance. Notice, however, that the inferential exemplarization of the observed exemplar gives it a functional role in an inferential network, for example, one that leads to inferences about the character of the granules. Inference leads to the conclusion that what is perceived are granules observed in the surface of the cell. Indeed, the primary inferential networking of the exemplar is simply connecting it with the cell so that the exemplar represents a cell. The experimental setup may seem to guarantee that, but there are no guarantees in microscopy. This is not the place to survey the role of microscopes or their reliability. See Otávio Bueno[14] for a useful analysis. What replaces a guarantee?

---

[13] Schlick, M., The Foundation of Knowledge.

[14] Bueno, O., Perceiving Nanoscale Phenomena: Interpreting and Disseminating Nanoscale Images. Online at http://www.masspolicy.org/pdf/workshop/bueno.pdf

Consensus concerning the exemplarized conception replaces it. The robustness of the results, the possibility of replication, is, of course, of great importance. But there is the question of how much weight to give to the conception of an observer, Palade, for example, for artifacts may be replicated. The reason this is important is that there will be differences in the way in which the images are exemplarized. The details are important, but this is not the place for them. I want to offer, instead, a picture of the formal role of the process of aggregating diverse exemplarizations of individuals to obtain a scientific consensual account.

The account of consensus concerning exemplarizations resulting from aggregation of individual exemplarizations may be modeled on the simpler account of consensus resulting from the aggregation of individual acceptances of hypotheses. I want to clarify my assumptions concerning both exemplarization and acceptance. These assumptions concern indeterminacy. I assume the following about hypotheses and concepts. Scientific hypotheses, even those we accept with the greatest confidence, are only probable. We may know that they are true, and they may be true, but this kind of knowledge, though knowledge of truth, is fallible and probabilistic. It is essential not to confuse justification that contains no error with justification that guarantees truth. Even in the case of the exemplar looping back onto itself, the fallibility of the process leaves us with some risk of error. The problem is that we are fallible, and our fallibility exports a risk of error to whatever we do and whatever method we use. There is no possibility of eliminating the risk of human error however successful we may be in reducing it.

So the consensus concerning hypotheses is assumed to be a consensus concerning probabilities. That is my way of representing indeterminacy, and other ways are worth considering. I insist on indeterminacy, but I do not insist on representing indeterminacy in terms of probability. We have a formally articulated model of probability that is useful for mathematical modeling. That is my reason for choosing it. Consensual probabilities are, simply stated, weighted averages of the probabilities of individuals. It should be noted, however, that the probabilities of individuals are themselves aggregations by the individual of earlier probabilities. The question of which comes first in the process of aggregation, the individual probabilities or the consensual probabilities, is like the question of which comes first the chicken or the egg. They fly and fry together. We can form some abstract notion of individual probabilities that are prime probabilities free of social influence. But they are fictions, we have no way of calculating them, and they are nowhere to be found in reality.

Consider Palade, for example, as he accepts the ribosome hypothesis. The image may be one that only he has observed, when he first observes it. The background of accepted hypotheses that constitute his inferential network, however, are based on his aggregation of the probabilities others assign to hypotheses about cells and how to observe them. To be sure, there is a personal component in the hypothesis resulting from the role of the exemplar in exemplarization and conceptualization. I shall return to this issue of the role of exemplar. For now, suffice it to notice that the probability of the ribosome hypothesis for Palade is an amalgamation of a personal observation and exemplarization aggregated into a socially shaped inferential network concerning cells and microscopy.

The aggregation model is one in which an individual assigns weights to the probabilities of others, normalizing the weights so that they are nonnegative and sum to one. So, suppose there are a sequence of probabilities p_1, p_2 and so forth to p_n for a hypothesis *h* considered by an individual *i* to which he or she assigns some nonnegative weights w_1, w_2 and so forth to w_n. One of the probabilities is the probability *i* assigns to his or her own probability. Call the original probabilities assigned by individuals to *h* the initial state 0. I propose that if the individual is rational, he or she will average the initial state probabilities, p^0_i of all the individuals *i*, to arrive at a new stage 1 probability as follows:

$$p_i^1 = p_1^0 w_1 + p_2^0 w_2 + \ldots + p_n^0 w_n$$

The justification for the claim that aggregation is rational is simply that the refusal to aggregate is mathematically equivalent to assigning everyone else a weight of zero in the aggregation. I note in passing that averaging is only one mode of aggregation. The person assigning weights, however, must assign them some meaning, and the use of averaging is the computational meaning I assumed. I acknowledge that there is another kind of respect one might have for another that does not involve aggregation respect. I have called this communication respect,[15] and it might be called evaluation respect, instead. It is the kind of respect one shows to another by listening to the communication of another, perhaps evaluating what they communicate, while refusing to modify ones own view. In short, one may receive communication from another and even evaluate the information, for example, the probability assigned and reasons for assigning it, but refuse to modify ones own views, or, at least, ones own probabilities. One shows the other respect but refuses to aggregate the probability of the other with one's own. This amounts, however, to respecting the communication of the other while refusing to assign the other any positive weight, or, equivalently, assigning the other a weight of 0. It is, perhaps, the stance of the iconoclast in science. I do not claim that iconoclasm is unreasonable, but I note it is a refusal to aggregate information received from others.

Suppose that one finds enough merit in the views of others to assign them some positive weight. In that case, the stage 1 probability may differ from the stage 0 probability. Notice, moreover, to return to the issue of the personal and social components of probability, that the stage 1 probability of *i* incorporates the probabilities of others. So, there is already a social component in the aggregation to stage 1 in the personal probability of *i*. The social component deepens at the next level of aggregation.

Consider the situation of person *i* at stage 1. Imagine that at this stage, others have also aggregated and have new probabilities. The new stage 1 probabilities contain some new information not contained, at least in a transparent way, to *i* at stage 0. The new information is articulated in the weights that others assign to the probabilities of others representing the respect they have for others concerning the subject matter of the hypothesis *h*. So our subject needs to reconsider what weight to assign to others.

---

[15] Lehrer, K., A Mathematical Model for Resolving Conflict, *Initiative*, 5(2), 1993, 1–3, 11–13.

The reason is that he may have greater or lesser respect for views of others concerning the weight that they give to others than he had for their views about the subject matter of *h*. Again, if *i* assigns positive weight to the probabilities of others at stage 1, consistency argues for aggregating because refusing to do so is equivalent to assigning a weight of zero in the aggregate. The transition to stage 2 is as follows:

$$p_i^2 = p_1^1 w_1 + p_2^1 w_2 + \ldots + p_n^1 w_n$$

Once again, the new probabilities contain some new information. You can see this by noting that the stage 2 probabilities of *i* now incorporate information about how *i* implicitly respects the way in which others have assigned weights to others, for the stage one probabilities of members of the group are the result of their aggregations based on the weights they assign to others. At this stage, it is clear that the probabilities of members of the group are socially embedded in the probabilities of other members of the group while at the same time retaining the contributions of individual members. The contribution of individuals and the importance of it may become obvious if the process leads to all members of the group assigning a high weight to some expert, Palade, for example, whose initial probability may dominate in the group after stage 2.

Each stage brings in some new information. The first brings in information about the subject matter. The second brings in information about the weights given to others as experts. The third brings in information about the weights given to the weights of others and so forth. Consider the general transition formula taking a member from stage x to stage $x + 1$ in the aggregation:

$$p_i^{x+1} = p_1^x w_1 + p_2^x w_2 + \ldots + p_n^x w_n$$

Suppose that the aggregation is continued from stage to stage indefinitely, or mathematically formulated, as x goes to ∞. The probabilities that are assigned by all members of the group will converge toward a consensual probability p_c for all members of the group under the following three conditions. Condition one is that the weights remain constant for each person throughout the process. Condition two is that members of the group give positive weight to themselves. Condition three is that they are connected by a positive respect vector. The connectedness condition three does not require that each member of the group assign positive weight to all the others, only that there is a sequence of all members of the group such that each member in the group assigns positive weight to the next member in the sequence. This theorem was noted by others and is, in effect, a Markov chain. We also noted that the mathematical process just described is mathematically equivalent to finding the consensual weight, w_{ci}, for members of the group and multiplying these times the original probabilities to yield the same consensual probability assignment p_c.

$$p_c = p_1^0 w_{c1} + p_2^0 w_{c2} + \ldots + p_n^0 w_{cn}$$

Moreover, the set of consensual weights is a fixed-point theorem. It contains a kind of mathematical loop as the consensual weights may be used to average the stage 0 weights that people assign to a given member of the group *i* to obtain the consensual weight assigned to that member of the group by the aggregation process. The formula is as follows:

$$w_{ci} = w^0_{1i} w_{c1} + w^0_{2i} w_{c2} + \ldots + w^0_{ni} w_{cn}$$

The mathematical loop becomes obvious when one specifies which member of the group *i* is, for example, member 2, for then the formula tells us that

$$w_{c2} = w^0_{12} w_{c1} + w^0_{22} w_{c2} + \ldots + w^0_{n2} w_{cn}$$

and w_{c2} occurs in the formula for computing itself in a mathematical loop. The loop is not a defect. It is, instead, a way of characterizing the consensual weights as that unique set of weights that when used to average the initially assigned weights yields the consensual weights.

So much for the mathematics of the simple case of connectedness and constancy of weights. Wagner and I noted that the requirement of constancy was unrealistic and explored convergence conditions under change in weights. Convergence still occurs under quite general conditions, and, again, the process is mathematically equivalent to finding a set of consensual weights.

What are the philosophical conclusions to be drawn from the mathematics? First of all, there are two applications of the model that were not sharply distinguished in our early work. One application is a dynamic model of probability shifts in science. People often shift probabilities in response to information they receive from others. This is characteristic of social institutions, both science and art, in which expertise is recognized and evaluated. Radical shifts will occur when groups that are not connected become connected as the result of some members of the divergent groups giving positive weight to members of the other group. The connection may be accomplished by a single person. Consider, for example, Arthur Danto as an art critic successfully defending Mapplethorpe's sexual photographs,[16] who receives positive weight from members of a group, the art world, for his positive esthetic evaluation of the photographs contrary to a standard paradigm of photographic esthetics. Roger Fry[17] once remarked, in reply to the objection that postimpressionist art, Matisse's, for example, was not beautiful, "It will be," and Fry was right. The objects exemplarized by the experts changed the consensus concerning the beauty of the objects and concerning beauty itself. That consensus influenced the perception of the artworks in turn. The consensus model, construed as a dynamic model of probability shifts, explains what is accepted as art and in what is accepted as beautiful art. The consensus theory explains radical shifts as the result of respected members of one group, art critics like Danto, for example, assigning positive weight to members of some outlying group, Mapplethorpe and related artists, creating a new consensus.

---

[16]Danto, A. C., *Playing with the Edge: the Photographic Achievement of Robert Mapplethorpe*, Los Angeles: University of California Press, 1996.

[17]Fry, R. and Reed, C., The Grafton Gallery: An Apologia, in C. Reed, ed., *A Roger Fry Reader*, Chicago: University of Chicago, 1996.

The second application of the consensus model is to yield an idealized conception of consensus at a time. We assume that there is a consensus in science and art about some matters including who the experts are. Some receive great respect and weight in that consensus even if we cannot specify in any exact numerical way what it is. The consensus viewed in this way is like our conception of certain mathematical fictions, like the amount of money the average car purchaser in Tucson spent on a car in June. Looking around, we may have some idea of what he is buying, but the average may never be computed. Nevertheless, there is a fact of the matter about that average sum even it is not calculated. This is a factually grounded fiction. I have proposed that when we think of meaning in a communal language, the meaning is similarly a factually grounded fiction. The fiction is a weighted average based on the consensual weights that could, if the values were known, be calculated from the individual weights.

Now I want to turn from consensual probabilities of hypotheses to the issue of relationship between theory and experience. Let us return to Palade and the ribosomes. No one knows what the cell of a surface is like until Palade obtains the microscopic image. The image must be examined for how it appears. I do not contend that the process of attending to how it appears is unselective. But attention to immediate appearances is an important part of expertise of the observer. The less expert observer is only concerned with what the appearances mean or are about, and rushing to conclusions in this matter as well as others leads to ignoring information that is scientifically important. Palade accepts hypotheses about the surface of the gene and what it is like based on the exemplarization of his microscopy. Firstly, he can recognize the image that is used as an exemplar to represent images of a certain kind. Secondly, the exemplar is used to represent the surface of the cell. Finally, the word "ribosome" is introduced to stand in for the exemplarized meaning and to refer to the plurality of things for which the exemplar stands. It is crucial to recognize that the exemplar is part of the meaning of the word. It is not simply a vehicle of representation. The reason is that exemplar provides us with an exhibit of what a ribosome looks like. It is part and parcel, vehicle and exhibit, of the meaning or concept of a ribosome, that is, it is a part, a crucial part, of the functional role that the word "ribosome" plays scientifically.

So far, we have considered the role of the word "ribosome" and the exemplarized meaning in the idiolect of Palade. The meaning consists of the reference *r* of an expression *e* and the semantic relations of the word *e* to other words *f*, which may be considered the semantic sense of the expression. The meaning is a function $m_i(e)$ for a person, Palade in this case, which is an ordered pair of relationships of reference and sense for the person. So

$$m_i(e) = \langle s_i(e,f), r_i(e,o) \rangle$$

Now, already at the individual level, there is indeterminacy that might be represented by probabilities. In the case of reference, the probabilities are those that the person will apply the word *e* to various objects *o*. In the case of sense, the probabilities are those that the person will relate the word *e* to other expressions *f*. Following the lead of Adrienne Lehrer and John Lyons, I would restrict the sense to the probabilities of relationships between words in the same field, that is, as describing the same subject matter. In the case in question, the probabilities of reference are those of Palade applying the word "ribosome" to various objects. Those probabilities articulate his dispositions to apply the word. The probabilities of sense are those of inferential relations between "ribosome" and "contains granules" as well as other expressions concerning cells and articulating his dispositions to draw inferences from "ribosome."

The foregoing account of sense and reference is refined in the work of Adrienne Lehrer and Keith Lehrer cited above, but the oversimplified version will, nevertheless, enable us to capture the role of consensus in scientific meaning. Palade is an expert who has achieved a kind of consensus for his results. It is worth noting that in other uses of microscopes, exemplarization of exemplars aimed at discovering the surface of DNA, for example, was a kind of misexemplarization of the exemplar because the image was an artifact of the carbon plate on which the DNA was placed. The exemplar was not appropriate for the representation of the surface of DNA.[18] The correct way to view Palade is not only as an expert with a microscope, but also as a person whose conception of the ribosome, and meaning of "ribosome" in his idiolect, receives the dominant weight in the scientific conception and meaning.

The scientific meaning, $m_s(e)$ of an expression, "ribosome" for example, is the ordered pair of the weighted average of the probabilities constituting the reference functions of an individual *i* for an expression *e* to an object *o*, $r_i(e,o)$, and the weighted average of the probabilities constituting the sense function of an individual *i* for inferentially relating *e* to another expression *f*, $s_i(e,f)$. The weights are the consensual weights for individuals considered above. The mathematical representation of the weighted average of reference articulating the scientific reference, $r_s(e,o)$, is

$$r_s(e,o) = r_1(e,o)w_{c1} + r_2(e,o)w_{c2} + \ldots + r_n(e,f)w_{cn}$$

while the representation of scientific sense, $s_s(e,f)$, is

$$s_s(e,f) = s_1(e,f)w_{c1} + s_2(e,f)w_{c2} + \ldots + s_n(e,f)w_{cn}$$

to obtain

$$m_s(e) = <r_i(e,o), s_i(e,f)>$$

Further mathematical refinements are desirable to capture other features, but the present somewhat simplified account will enable us to articulate the philosophical implications of the mathematics. The implications may be articulated in terms of a famous Vienna Circle contrast and disagreement between Schlick and Neurath.

[18]Cf. Bueno, O., Perceiving Nanoscale Phenomena: Interpreting and Disseminating Nanoscale Images.

Neurath emphasized the role of social consensus in the construction and acceptance of scientific meaning and theory, while Schlick emphasized the role of empirical evidence in scientific meaning and theory. The present account of the role of consensus in science enables us to transcend the consensus versus experience opposition.

Consensus concerning the acceptance of hypotheses and meaning in science incorporates the evaluation of experts, members of the scientific community, to obtain theories and meanings that aggregate the information the community has about the expertise of members within. This information includes information about success in scientific undertakings of various sorts from the appropriate thought experiments to the most precise use of experimental instruments. The result of aggregation, whether dynamic or idealized, is that it finds the appropriate weights to give the meanings and theories. Does this ignore experience? It does not. Instead, it explains the relationship between theory and experience. Experience gets exemplarized in the conceptions of individuals who experience the exemplars. Different people exemplarize different exemplars, and they do so in different ways. The scientific meaning and theory are the weighted aggregate of exemplarized experience in meaning and theory.

The individual exemplarization, ostensive generalization, yields a kind of meaning that results in a semantic loop to obtain truth. The exemplar functions in exemplarization to stand for a class of instances of which it is a member. Indeed, the exemplar exhibits what it is like to be a member of the class and is a kind of paradigm. It is, however, a sign, a vehicle, though not only a vehicle, of representation, at the same time that it is one of the instances signified, indeed, a special instance that shows us what instances look like. Indeed, that is the crucial semantic function of the exemplar. Exemplarization reminds us of Schlick as he attempted to find a kind of sentence that was true by virtue of the meaning of the words. His project was criticized. However, exemplarization as I have used it, based on exemplification introduced by Goodman,[19] supports Schlick's project. Exemplarization contains a loop of reference as the exemplar loops referentially back on to itself in the process of exemplarization to refer and apply to itself. It is not a logical guarantee of truth because the process of exemplarization yielding the loop contained therein is a psychological process of representation confronting the hazard of loops that fail to close. Nevertheless, the closed loop, a truth loop, is part of what is accomplished by the process of exemplarization. Successful ostensive exemplarization contains a truth loop. That is the good news for Schlick.

Once the individual proceeds beyond the security of the truth loop of ostension to obtain linguistic articulation and inferential connection the security is compromised. Palade knows what his microscopic image is like. That knowledge is restricted to the immediate experience of the image and the ostensive exemplarization of it. In that process, the image loops back onto itself in a truth loop. However, once the exemplar is given a name, the risk of applying a word to an experience faces the

[19] Goodman, N. *Languages of Art*, Indianapolis, IN: The Bobbs-Merrill, 1968 (op. cit.).

problems of misapplication and the vicissitudes of memory. The next step is, however, the most important. It is the creation of inferential connections between the word naming the exemplar as well as other instances of the exemplarization, "ribosome" for example, and other expressions, most notably, those of theory like "cell" and "RNA packets." The sentences that articulate these inferential connections are the bridges or interpretations of theory in terms of experience. The connections between the exemplars of experience and the terms of theory are effected by the consensual probability vectors of reference and sense.

It is important, however, to see that the probabilities of reference, which articulate the dispositions to apply the word under the exemplarized meaning, are directed by exemplarization. The exemplar is part of the functional role of the meaning of the words connected to the process of exemplarization. These words connected to exemplarization are related systematically to the terms of theory. That ties theory to experience. It provides a non-reductive connection of theory to experience. These ties are sometimes called bridge sentences, correlation sentences, interpretative sentences or meaning postulates. But such sentences, connecting the terms of theory with those of experience, leave us with a puzzle. For the acceptance of such sentences connecting theory with experience seem arbitrary. It appears that an individual intent on saving a pet theory from refutation need only undo the ties, that is, reject the inferences from theory to experience and the sentences that articulate them, to protect theory from refutation by experience. We are given the reassurance, for example, by Quine,[20] that theory, if not tied to experience by individual sentences, must confront experience as a whole. The nature of the confrontation remains open, however. That openness suggests that unwanted confrontation leading to the rejection of theory may be replaced with another way of confronting experience that saves the theory. We may, of course, just postulate the truth of the connecting ties, but that looks arbitrary. So where are we to find the some information to strengthen those ties between theory and experience?

The solution to the problem of theory and experience is to be found in the consensual theory articulated above. It is a theory that shows us why Schlick needs Neurath and how Neurath incorporates Schlick. Consensual probabilities, whether the probabilities of hypotheses or the probabilities of meaning, are summaries of information that we have about the expertise, including the truth finding and error detecting skills, of scientists. If a scientist leads us to correct descriptions and prediction, the way he accepts hypotheses and forms concepts deserves and receives our respect. That respect results in weights assigned to them aggregated to find consensual weights. Those consensual weights are summaries of information that individuals have about other individuals. The resulting consensual probability vectors, including those of the connecting ties, the bridges or correlations, are equivalent to the result of giving each member of the scientific community his or her appropriate or consensual weight based on our information about expertise,

[20] Cf. Lehrer, K., Quine, Coherence and Justification, in A. Orenstein and P. Kotatko, eds., *Knowledge, Language and Logic: Questions for Quine*, Dordrecht: Kluwer, 2000, pp. 57–62.

competence and success. The consensual weights are an ideal summary of the total information contained in the group, the scientific community, and so are the consensual vectors of scientific probability, scientific sense and scientific reference.

Should we consider the consensual vectors reasonable and worthy of our trust? We begin with self-trust,[21] with the assumption that we are reasonable and worthy of trust in how we proceed. The consensual vectors are an ideal aggregation of the results of our self-trust and the reasonableness thereof. They tie together the exemplarization of experience with the construction of theory. Does this guarantee that we shall obtain truth? There is no guarantee. We are fallible. But we do have a theory about how to obtain truth. We aggregate our total information in an ideally rational way to obtain a consensus about truth. Here is a bonus. If we do reach truth, our theory explains why, namely, that we have placed our trust in the aggregation of total information, including our exemplarized information about experience, our social information about the expertise of others, and theoretical extrapolation. Our theory contains a subtheory that this is the way to reach truth. If it and we obtain truth, we have an explanation of why. The explanation is a loop of trust, beginning with self-trust and extended through consensual aggregation, which applies to itself. There is a loop in this theory, as it explains why it succeeds. It is that a defect? It is a desideratum. If we seek to maximize explanation, our theory must contain a subtheory about how to obtain truth. Why? Otherwise we shall lack an explanation of why we obtain truth when do and we shall have left the thing that most concerns us unexplained. An explanation maximizing theory must explain why it succeeds in obtaining truth, and, of course, the explanation must itself be true. So the theory must be true to explain why it is true. Is the explanation in the theory, then, or in the truth of it? The explanation is in the loop. The loop is a fixed point looping truth back onto itself to explain how the consensual aggregation of exemplarized experience leads us to truth.

Department of Philosophy
University of Arizona
Tucson, Arizona 85721-0027
USA
lehrer@u.arizona.edu

[21] Lehrer, K., *Self-Trust: A Study of Reason, Knowledge and Autonomy*, Oxford: Clarendon Press, 1997.

Analyticity and the A Priori: Fifty Years of "Two Dogmas"

Paolo Parrini

Fifty Years of Quine's "Two Dogmas", ed. by H.-J. Glock, K. Glüer and G. Keil, *Grazer Philosophische Studien. Internationale Zeitschrift für analytische Philosophie*, Vol. 66, 2003, Editions Rodopi B. V., Amsterdam – New York, NY, 2003, pp. 297, ISBN 90-420-0948-9.

2001 marked the 50th anniversary of the publication in the *Philosophical Review* (January 1951) of W. V. Quine's "Two Dogmas of Empiricism". Since Quine reprinted the article in *From a Logical Point of View* (Cambridge, MA, 1953; second edition, revised, 1961), the editors of this number of the *Grazer Philosophische Studien* saw the year 2003 as 'a good occasion to celebrate 50 years' of "Two dogmas" (p. 1) and collected the ten papers presented at the conference "50 Years of Empiricism without Dogmas" (Berlin, 13–15 September 2001) adding to the volume a paper by Donald Davidson who could not attend because of the September 11 events.

The editors' intention is undoubtedly a very worthy one. The discussions Quine's article arose go well beyond the criticism to the Neoempiricistic conception of analyticity and deeply affect the destiny of the analytic approach to the philosophical problems in the fields of Epistemology, Philosophy of Science and Philosophy of Language. The editors rightly underline how the Quine/Carnap contrast on the analytic-synthetic dichotomy ultimately influenced also the problem of the nature and task of philosophy. Quine's refusal of analyticity put into discussion the 'idea that philosophy is an *a priori* discipline which differs in principle from the empirical sciences' (p. 1). Since this idea has characterised not only early analytic philosophy, but also many aspects of the Kantian tradition, Phenomenology and Philosophical Hermeneutics, one can say that the 'mixing of cards' caused by "Two Dogmas" affected various lines of thought and a large set of questions. Quine himself developed this refusal of analyticity to the point of questioning the a priori/a posteriori knowledge distinction, the separation between science and philosophy and the traditional criticism to psychologism. Abandoning these dichotomies and views led, in its turn, both Quine and other analytical philosophers to a kind of naturalism according to which philosophy is part of natural science, or at least in line of continuity with it.

Thus there is more than one reason to welcome this collection that intends 'to reconsider the semantic, epistemological and methodological questions raised by "Two Dogmas" ' (p. 3) highlighting Quine's attack 'on analyticity, apriority and necessity' and at the same time evaluating the 'implications of that attack that far transcend the limits of Quine scholarship, and lie at the heart of the current self-understanding of philosophy' (p. 3). The editors deserve also the merit of having included essays written by both opponents and proponents of the views attacked by Quine.

The first paper is by Herbert Schnädelbach, "Two Dogmas of Empiricism. Fifty Years After" (pp. 7–12). As well as underlining the importance still enjoyed today by Quine's essay, Schnädelbach examines Carnap's conception of philosophy as a *logische Analyse der Wissenschaftssprache*, G. E. Moore's paradox of analysis, Quine's criticism to the analytic/synthetic dichotomy, Wittgenstein's conception of philosophy, and Kant's explanation of analytic judgement as *Erläuterungsurteil* in order to support a pragmatic conception of philosophy as practice of explication and clarification. For Schnädelbach analytic philosophy 'has its identity in the pragmatics of elucidation, and not in some sort of special knowledge incorporated in special philosophical statements' (p. 12). This way of doing philosophy still needs the notions of analyticity and synonymy even if 'they cannot be defined in terms of something else' (p. 12).

The other ten essays have been grouped into three sections. The first one entitled *Analyticity Revisited* includes the works by Paul A. Boghossian, Kathrin Glüer, Verena Mayer, Christian Nimtz and Åsa Maria Wikforss. They introduce in various ways the question of analyticity either to defend such notion from Quine's attacks, negate it in line with Quine or clarify its various historical interpretations.

In "Epistemic Analyticity: a Defense" (pp. 15–35), P. Boghossian develops the project that he started in the 1996 essay "Analyticity Reconsidered" (*Noûs*, 30, pp. 360–391). He intends to salvage a notion of analyticity from Quine's widely accepted critique and explain the a priori via the notion of meaning or concept possession. This project rests on the distinction between a metaphysical and an epistemic version of analyticity. According to the *metaphysical* version, "a sentence is analytic if it owes its truth entirely to its meaning and without any contribution from the 'facts' " (p. 15); according to the *epistemic* version, a sentence is 'analytic if grasp of its meaning can suffice for justified belief in the truth of the proposition it expresses' (p. 15). Boghossian affirms that Quine 'was deeply right to insist that there are no metaphysical analytic sentences'. He also thinks that, though, Quine's objections against metaphysical analyticity do not regard epistemic analiticity and that 'it is possible to provide a model of how some sentences might be epistemically analytic' (p. 16).

In this paper Boghossian better specifies his conception and defends it against some objections moved to previous formulations. In particular, he tries to reply to the objection that 'there can be no epistemically analytic sentences that are not also metaphysically analytic, and that the notion of implicit definition cannot explain a priori entitlement' (p. 15). He thus introduces the distinction between an *inferential* and a *constitutive* way in which 'facts about meaning might generate facts about entitlement' (p. 15) and concludes his paper by outlining a theory of the constitutive way that modifies some of his preceding ideas.

A contrasting view is presented in the paper by K. Glüer that immediately follows Boghossian's: "Analyticity and Implicit Definition" (pp. 37–60). Glüer criticises Boghossian's analytic theory of a priori knowledge using only arguments independent of the thesis of the indeterminacy of translation presented by Quine in *Word and Object* (1960). Such strategy was chosen because in the above-quoted 1996 essay on analyticity Boghossian states that Quine's criticism to analyticity is ineffective as long as it does not depend on the extremely controversial thesis of indeterminacy.

For Glüer, Boghossian underestimates the power of the classical Quinean objections to the analytic/synthetic distinction and the linguistic doctrine of the a priori, in particular to the conventionalistic account of logical truth. By taking again the argument from epistemological holism presented in the concluding pages of "Two Dogmas", she shows how difficult it is to maintain the dichotomy between empirical and non-empirical sentences, and thus the distinction (defended by Boghossian) between meaning-constitutive and non meaning-constitutive sentences. Moreover, Glüer also refers back to "Truth by Convention" in order to attack the conventionalistic account of logical truth via the idea of implicit definition. To obtain this she appeals not only to the well known infinite regress argument, but also to an overlooked objection expounded in this essay, the objection according to which there are no *sentences* such that 'stipulating them to be true would result in the meaning assignment' to the logical constants. In fact, in order to perform this function the sentences used 'would have to be general, that is they would have to contain already interpreted expressions of the very kind they are to implicitly define' (55 f).

To develop her criticism, Glüer does not limit herself to rehearsing Quine's arguments. Using an argument criticised by Boghossian in this very volume and linked to an analogous remark by Laurence Bonjour (see p. 22), she tries to show that even if implicit definers for the logical constants existed, their epistemic analyticity would be doubtful, since knowing 'their meaning does not provide justification by virtue of meaning alone, for knowledge of meaning itself turns out to already require knowledge of facts about the world' (p. 58). Glüer concludes thus: 'the distinction between metaphysical and epistemic analyticity' does not seem to be defendable: 'at least on the Boghossian model, the facts do return, and with a vengeance' (p. 58).

V. Mayer's essay ("Implicit Thoughts: Quine, Frege and Kant on Analytic Propositions", pp. 61–90) brings a change of scenery: the purely theoretical discourse is supplemented by historical elements. Mayer tries to show that the *semantic* conception of analyticity presupposed by Quine and attributed to Kant, Frege and Carnap, has nothing in common with the one effectively maintained by Kant. Kant actually had a distinctly *pragmatic* conception according to which 'analytic propositions elucidate certain presuppositions of our conceptual scheme, thereby serving the anti-metaphysical project of transcendental philosophy' (p. 61). Differently from what has been suggested by Quine, this conception is not connected to metaphysical essentialism and an essentialist theory of meaning. It regards instead the explication of our conceptual apparatus: 'analytic sentences are not true "in virtue of meanings and independently of facts" but in virtue of conceptual relations within our web of beliefs' (p. 88).

Meyer's analysis leads to a Wittgensteinian conclusion similar to the one advanced by Schnädelbach: 'Analytic propositions in the sense of Kant do not spell out the literal meaning of their subject terms, but are rather similar to Wittgenstein's grammatical sentences in that they elucidate or describe the use of a concept' (p. 88). In Meyer's perspective, freeing Kant's conception from the essentialist vision of meanings presupposed by Carnap and criticised by Quine should not lead 'to stop the analysis of language or concepts, or to blur the analytic/synthetic distinction', but 'to restore' a 'pragmatic notion of analytic judgments' such as the one developed by Kant 'against the methods of bad metaphysics' (p. 89).

This conclusion certainly contains valid aspects and can be useful in order to individuate the presence of metaphysical elements in Carnap's philosophy; nevertheless it does not take enough into consideration the fact – as it emerges especially from the 1950 essay "Empiricism, Semantics, and Ontology" – that Carnap's reference to conventionalism, semantic rules, meaning postulates, and in general the idea of linguistic frameworks is the very basis of his refusal of ontology and metaphysical realism.

C. Nimtz ("Analytic Truths – Still Harmless after All These Years?", pp. 91–118) defends Putnam's thesis of analyticity advanced in "The Analytic and the Synthetic" that was published in 1962, i.e., about 10 years after "Two Dogmas". Nimtz finds Putnam's deflationist thesis essentially correct according to which (*pace Quine*) there are analytic truths, but these analytic truths are *harmless*, since 'they are trivial and hence ill-suited to play any exceptional epistemological or methodological role' (p. 91), such as the one assigned to them by Logical Empiricists. Thus Nimtz elaborates a semantic approach to analyticity similar to Putnam's, but without its defects, that he calls "sophisticated Kripkeanism" (p. 100). Nimtz states that this approach can show the harmless nature of analytical truths and rebut the thesis, recently propounded mainly by David Chalmers and Frank Jackson, that 'analytic truths are the means as well as the aim of philosophy' (p. 92). Notice that Nimtz is the first to recognise that this approach leaves out mathematical and logical truths and regards mainly 'purported analyticities' involving terms such as "crow", "energy" and the like (p. 92).

The last essay of the first section is "An a posteriori Conception of Analyticity?" (pp. 119–139) by Å. Wikforss. The question here is whether it is possible to use the *de re* conception of necessity resuscitated by S. Kripke in order to free 'analyticity from its epistemic ties' and propose by means of such transformation 'a notion of analyticity that is immune to Quine's attack, and compatible with his epistemic holism' (p. 119). With this aim in mind, Wikforss examines Tyler Burge's externalist idea 'that truths of meaning depend on features of the external environment and are a posteriori' and highlights some of the problems arising from both this idea and the attempt of transferring 'Kripke's strategy with respect to necessity' to analyticity (p. 121). Wikforss so achieves an interesting result: Burge's externalist neo-rationalism 'rests on unusually strong essentialist assumptions' according to which 'not only natural kinds have underlying essences, but almost everything – artefacts, events, natural phenomena that do not constitute natural kinds, etc.' (p. 132).

For Wikforss this strengthening of essentialism 'is not an accident. If one rejects analyticity in the positivist sense, and tries to replace it with an a posteriori notion of analyticity, one needs to endorse a form of generalized Aristotelian essentialism. The essentialism simply replaces conventionalism. We have, as it were, come full circle' (p. 132). As a matter of fact the circle is really full because the whole Neoempiricistic construction, with the distinction between analytic and synthetic and the grouping of the necessary and the a priori with the analytic and the contingent and the a posteriori with the synthetic, played an important role within the project of *Überwindung der Metaphysik durch logische Analyse der Sprache.* Wikforss's conclusion, anyway, ends up favouring Quine's rejection of analyticity: 'To the extent one agrees with Quine and is wary of the traditional, a priori conception of analyticity, [...] one is better off giving up analyticity altogether than trying to reconstrue a non-epistemic, a posteriori conception of it' (p. 137).

The second section titled *Necessity, Synonymy, and Logic* includes the papers by Hans-Johann Glock, Peter Pagin and Tyler Burge. H.-J. Glock ("The Linguistic Doctrine Revisited", pp. 143–170) explores 'the possibility of rehabilitating' a 'limited version' of the linguistic doctrine of necessary truth supported by both Wittgenstein and Logical Empiricists. He starts off from the thesis that there is a distinction between analytical assertions and synthetic assertions, in other words – as it had been maintained in various ways by A. Naess in 1953 (*Interpretation and Preciseness*, Oslo) and P. Grice and P. Strawson in 1956 ("In Defense of a Dogma", *Philosophical Review*, 65, pp. 141–158) – between assertions that provoke reactions of *disbelief*, or *belief disagreement*, and assertions that provoke reactions of *non-understanding*, or *linguistic disagreement.* Following Boghossian and Wolfgang Künne, Glock characterises analytic assertions by saying that in their case 'the mere grasping' of their meaning 'suffices for being justified in accepting' them (p. 147). Then he argues for the following two theses: (i) Analytic propositions like "All vixens are female" 'do *not* describe a special kind of reality (whether it be abstract entities beyond space and time or the most abstract or general features of physical reality)'; (ii) rather, 'their special (necessary, a priori) status has to be explained by reference to *language*, and, more specifically, by reference to the meaning of expressions and hence to the way they are used' (p. 143).

For Glock, this conception far 'from being grotesque' has a 'respectable philosophical pedigree and chimes with commonsense, as Quine came to realize' (p. 143). Glock tries to protect this thesis from the 'powerful objections' advanced against the original version of the linguistic doctrine 'by reconciling Wittgenstein's claim that' analytic statements 'have a normative role with Carnap's concession that they are true' (p. 143): 'Analytic propositions can be said to be true, but their truth consists in their having a normative status within a certain linguistic practice' (p. 144). An interesting aspect of Glock's proposal is that while the truth is 'a feature of what is expressed by sentences', maybe analyticity 'is best regarded as a feature of sentences: it indicates that they have a special, normative, function. And this role is obviously something that sentences can lose, subject to the vagaries of our linguistic practice. The price to be paid for this manoeuvre is the acknowledgement that talk of analytic *propositions* and analytic *truths* is strictly speaking elliptical. *Au fond* it is sentences that are analytic, namely if they are used to express a rule that is constitutive of the meaning of a word' (p. 168).

Pagin ("Quine and the Problem of Synonymy", pp. 171–197) takes "Two Dogmas" as his starting point in order to discuss not the notion of analyticity but one closely linked to it: synonymy. His poignant considerations mainly aim at underlining the difficulties that prevent us from satisfactorily solving the problem.

Burge's essay ("Logic and Analyticity", pp. 199–249) is the longest in the volume under review; in some ways it can stand on its own and would be worthy of separate treatment. It comes with three appendixes, two of which are of a historical nature. In the first one, he sketches the key intuitive notions of logical validity and logical consequence in the history of logic with particular reference to Aristotle, Abelard, Duns Scotus, Buridan, Leibniz, Bolzano and Tarski. The second one shows the dependence of logic on mathematics in Poincaré's philosophy. For Burge, 'Poincaré's insight is that a systematic reflective understanding of logic must invoke mathematics' (p. 246), and this understanding 'is synthetic, not analytic' (p. 246). The reference to Poincaré is connected to the main theoretical thesis that Burge supports by taking again into consideration the arguments developed by Quine, not only in "Two Dogmas" but also, and mainly, in "Truth by Convention" (1935), "Carnap and Logical Truth" (1954) and *Philosophy of Logic* (1970) against the existence of assertions that, like logical truths, are analytical in the sense that are true in a vacuous way, in other words independently of a subject matter.

For Burge, 'full reflective understanding of logic and deductive reasoning' reveals some a priori relations and 'requires substantial commitment to mathematical entities' (p. 199). Such relations 'emerged only slowly in the history of logic', but 'they can be recognized retrospectively as implicit in logic and deductive reasoning'. This leads to an image of logic different from traditional conceptions. For Kant both logic and mathematics are a priori; logic is analytic, since its truths are contentually empty, whereas mathematics should be considered as synthetic similarly to sciences (sciences which in their turn have an a priori and an empirical component). For Carnap, like Kant, both mathematics and logic are a priori; differently from Kant, though, Carnap thinks that they are both analytic in the sense that they are empirically and factually vacuous: only sciences have an empirical value and are thus synthetic. For Quine, differently from both Kant and Carnap, there are no vacuously analytic sentences and all knowledge is a posteriori. Burge proposes a different interpretation altogether. He thinks that Quine was right in negating the existence of vacuously analytic statements; he also thinks, though, that Kant and Carnap were right when arguing for the existence of a priori statements. His idea is that there is a synthetic a priori knowledge – in the sense of "synthetic" that contrasts with the vacuousness concept – and that such synthetic a priori knowledge is represented at best by both logic and mathematics.

Differently from Kant, Burge denies not only the analyticity of Logic but also the confinement of synthetic knowledge to the world of appearances. Regarding this problem, Burge is prepared to acknowledge that how 'to bridge the feared gap between thought and subject matter without causal-experiential relations still needs explanation' (p. 240), but thinks that he has given an at least partial answer to Kant's question: How is a priori knowledge of a subject matter possible? He thinks in fact that he managed to show that the possibility of synthetic a priori knowledge of mathematics 'is implicit in conditions on the possibility of relatively elementary propositional thinking. Such knowledge is necessary to explaining conditions on the possibility of such thinking' (p. 239). Burge's discourse, accordingly, is 'parallel to the aspect of Kant's answer that claims' that synthetic a priori cognition 'is possible because it is necessary to the possibility of explaining and justifying sense experience' (p. 239).

The third and last section entitled *"Two Dogmas" and Beyond* includes two papers that see "Two Dogmas" 'in the perspective of Quine's overall philosophy' (p. 4).

The first one is by Geert Keil, " 'Science itself Teaches'. A Fresh Look at Quine's Naturalistic Metaphilosophy" (pp. 253–280). As it is well known, for Quine, the refusal of the analytic/synthetic distinction is connected to the thesis that there is no clean-cut difference between philosophy and natural science, a thesis that, starting from the late 1960s, Quine began to indicate as a form of "naturalism". Keil's paper deals with the question 'of what exactly Quine's claim means that philosophy is continuous with natural science' (p. 254). Following Jonathan Cohen's suggestion ("The Importance of Quine", *London Times Literary Supplement*, November 1987), Keil tries to sort out Quine's 'scientistic avowals from his philosophy at work' (p. 254), in other words (quoting Cohen) 'to investigate closely the extent to which Quine's ideas about the method of his philosophical enterprise are coherent with the substance of his philosophical doctrine'. Aiming at this, Keil takes up one of Quine's preferred phrases (found in the paper's title, 'Science itself teaches that ...') and follows its development in Quine's works.

For Keil, Quine, differently from Wittgenstein, does not specify what distinguishes philosophical and scientific investigations and the analysis of his metaphilosophy shows that naturalism and the use of naturalistic language are some kind of a 'rhetoric' that has very little influence 'on the way he actually does philosophy' (p. 253). Keil's clear cut conclusion is that there is a 'real' (p. 278), 'unresolved' (p. 270) tension between Quine's empiricist definition of science as a game whose aim is the '*prediction of observations*' (p. 268) and 'the non-empirical nature of mathematics, logic, and major parts of philosophy. These parts of the scientific enterprise enable us to knit our web of belief more closely without contributing additional empirical checkpoints" (p. 278).

The last essay of the volume is Donald Davidson's "Quine's Externalism" (pp. 281–297). Here Davidson (to whose memory the volume is dedicated) credits 'Quine with having implicitly held a view' that Davidson himself 'had long urged on him: externalism'" (p. 281). Quine had the merit of defending a behaviourist approach to language that explains the meaning of verbal utterances on the grounds of observed usage. For Davidson, such approach as well as destroying the myth of meaning – as Quine has always stated, theorizing the possibility of the indeterminacy of translation – entails also a powerful form of externalism. In Quine, though, this externalism finds 'a counter-current' in the idea of stimulus meaning and in his reluctance to take the final step from the proximal to the distal stimulus as the relevant cause of a mental state.

On the whole the volume maintains the promises made by the editors in the Introduction. All the essays fully show the importance and wide ramification of the problems raised by Quine in his seminal 1951/1953 paper and both the works that preceded (in particular, "Truth by Convention") and followed it (in particular, "Carnap and Logical Truth" and "Word and Object"). As I will say later on, the only area left untouched is the one of philosophy of science.

First of all, the essays confirm the editors' idea that the reasons 'for a philosophical retrospective of 50 years of "Two Dogmas"' and its wide repercussions are not 'purely or even predominantly historical'. As a matter of fact these reasons, of a strongly theoretical nature, are mainly three and emerge from all the essays. The first one is that on closer scrutiny the apparently broad consensus on what "Two Dogmas" has demonstrated 'proves to be deceptive' (p. 2). For the editors, Quine's aims are not yet clear, and it is not clear either how the rejection of the analytic/synthetic distinction relates to Quine's thesis of the indeterminacy of translation and his general semantic holism. Personally, I think that this is also true for Quine's criticism to logical conventionalism elaborated in "Truth by Convention" (1935).

Secondly, since the days of Paul Grice's and Peter F. Strawson's article ("In Defense of a Dogma", *Philosophical Review*, 65, 1956, pp. 141–156) various attempts have been made to disentangle the criticism to the 'dogma' of reductionism from the criticism to analyticity and rehabilitate distinctions such as synthetic/analytic, a priori/a posteriori and contingent/necessary by recurring, to clarify their nature, to tools different from the ones criticised by Quine. For example, since the 1950s and 1960s, David Hamlyn ("Analytic Truths" and "On Necessary Truths", *Mind*, 65, 1966, pp. 359–367; 70, 1961, pp. 514–525) tried to clarify and defend the notion of analyticity using Wittgenstein's theories on meaning. Along with Wittgenstein's followers also other philosophers contested the cogency of Quine's original arguments or suggested ways of tracing the distinctions attacked by Quine in a way that made them immune from his criticisms. As for their names, I would mention not only Hilary Putnam (to whom the volume gives a particular relevance), but also, for example, Arthur Pap, Jaakko Hintikka and Laurence Bonjour. The wide variety of theoretical stances testified by this volume can only confirm how Quine's negation of analyticity and a priori cannot be considered – differently from what some people think – the last word on the subject.

As far as this aspect of the problem is concerned, I will add that these papers prove not only the existence of a wide disagreement on Quine's theses, but also something more. That is, they prove also that both rejections and acceptances of the distinctions between the analytic and the synthetic, the a priori and the a posteriori have been, and are, an integral part of alternative philosophical projects of a global nature and that for this reason it is extremely difficult to evaluate both rejections and acceptances outside the wider theoretical context in which they are inserted. For example, from Mayer's paper there clearly emerges the link between Kant's conception of analyticity and the a priori and his transcendental idealism. Some recent papers have shown how the disagreement between Quine and Carnap on analyticity should be seen as a contrast between two extremely different epistemological projects. Such projects, in fact, share the intent to eliminate the reference to intuition from epistemic justification, but Quine's argument mainly centres on a holistic evaluation of the way in which our beliefs change, whereas Carnap's aims at understanding not so much the dynamics of knowledge but the logical structure of epistemic justification.

Thirdly, this volume confirms the important stimulus given to the debate by S. Kripke's conception that 'resuscitates the traditional idea of *de re* necessities and thereby challenges both the Kantian analytic/synthetic distinction and its empiricist debunking' (p. 2). Kripke has in fact advanced the thesis that 'some necessary truths, truths about the essence of things, are discovered a posteriori by empirical science' (p. 2). In this way his 'essentialism has forcefully revived the view', rejected not only by Quine (as the editors remind us), but also by Logical Empiricists' Machian anti-absolutism, 'that necessity is an intrinsic and perhaps *sui generis* feature of reality, rather than a product of our thought and language' (p. 3).

From this point of view, Burge's essay seems to me of pivotal importance. If we look at Quine's work we can see that he draws contrasting consequences from his refusal of analyticity and the linguistic doctrine of the a priori. At the beginning of "Two Dogmas" he says that such refusal brought with itself a blurring of the science/metaphysics distinction and a coming closer to pragmatism; in the later writings, though, he ends up underlining mainly the realism involved by such blurring, stating – against the antimetaphysical Carnap – that the elaboration of an efficient canonical notation must not be distinguished from the 'limning of the most general tracts of reality' (see, in particular, *Word and Object*, The M.I.T. Press, 1960, Sect. 35, p. 161). It is also true, though, that Quine never developed his approaching to realism and metaphysics to the point of accepting the adoption of the modalities *de re* and the essentialism that such acceptance involves. Moreover he always stated that his 'Empiricism without Dogmas' had to be seen as a form of empiricism not weaker, but more radical than the one supported by Logical Empiricists in which a certain dose of apriorism was still implicit. In order to understand the historical-philosophical climate that followed "Two Dogmas", it is interesting that Burge, now, puts aside all of Quine's pragmatistic, empiricistic and anti-essentialistic components and explains the importance of his criticism to analyticity since this has helped analytical philosophy to free itself of the 'prohibitions' of Neo-Empiricistic origin: 'Quine's arguments, albeit primarily ones outside the famous paper, – Burge writes at the beginning of his essay – subverted the notion of analyticity that had buttressed the positivist view of mathematical logic. This notion had functioned to close off mathematics and logic from philosophical reflection, and to sever a main route to rationalism and metaphysics. Quine reopened the route, but declined to develop it. The route invites development – especially its epistemic branch' (p. 199). Personally I still prefer an empiricist attitude to a rationalistic and metaphysical one. On the historical level, though, Burge's description seems to be substantially correct.

With Burge's reference to the epistemic branch I will pass on to another relevant aspect of the volume and also to what I deem an omission. The essays collected here show very clearly the weight of the epistemological dimension of the problem of analyticity and the a priori along with the weight of the ontological and metaphysical dimension. Almost all the defenders of the analytic/synthetic distinction and the a priori/a posteriori one state, in one way or the other, the importance of looking at such dichotomies from the point of view of epistemic justification. This idea is in line with what has been stated also by other scholars whose views are not represented in this volume but that equally have insisted on the epistemic aspect not so much from the point of view of general epistemology but from the point of view of the philosophy of science.

In the 1950s and 1960s, an important place in the discussion on analyticity, a priori and necessity was held by the following question: do we have to attribute a role to these notions within the Standard Conception of Scientific Theories and the description of the scientific method? It was on this very question that Carnap parted ways not only with Quine, but also with Hempel. This aspect of the problem was significantly present also in the recent philosophy of science where it appeared again not only in relation with the historical revision regarding the meaning of the Neo-Empiricistic criticism to Kant's theory of synthetic a priori judgements and in relation to the relationship between Logical Empiricism and the New Philosophy of Science. Think of Kuhn's thesis according to which 'normal science' includes as its integral parts some 'paradigmatic propositions' characterised by the fact of being neither analytic nor empirical in the usual sense. They are rather propositions that despite not being eternal truths play a constitutive role in the structure of scientific thought.

Such idea has behind itself a complex story regarding not only the New Philosophy of Science and Logical Empiricists' criticism to Kant's synthetic a priori, but also Poincaré's conventionalism, Carnap's conception of the theory/experience relationship starting from *Die logische Syntax der Sprache*, the 1960s and 1970s discussions on geocronometric conventionalism and the logical structure of empirical control (an important aspect of the epistemic justification of our beliefs) and finally the adoption, in various sectors of contemporary epistemology, of the theories of the so-called *contextual*, *relativised* and *functional* a priori. Similar conceptions generally accept a more or less strong version of the thesis of the holistic dependence of the network of our beliefs, but state at the same time that within the network we cannot assign to all assertions the same role or function when evaluating the way in which empirical evidence relates itself to this or that specific belief. Some beliefs, hypotheses or assertions – but not others – have a presuppositional role, contextually or relatively a priori. We can find no traces of this debate in this volume. On p. 151 Glock quotes as 'still unsurpassed' Arthur Pap's *Semantics and Necessary Truth* (New Haven 1958); nowhere, though, we can find mention of the fact that, for example, Pap also wrote *The A Priori in Physical Theory* (1946; reissued, Russell & Russell, New York, 1968) that is today seen by some scholars as an interesting step towards a functional theory of the a priori.

Apart from this omission, the volume seems to me a significant contribution to the discussion on analyticity and a priori; among the numerous merits already mentioned, I wish to add another. As I said, the editors insist (rightly) on the theoretical rather than the historical aspect of the debate started by "Two Dogmas" in the last 50 years; nevertheless some of the essays contain very interesting historical observations. So, the volume has the additional merit of showing how productive the interplay between historical and theoretical research can be when they are both carried out in full accordance with their respective methodological principles and do not impinge on each other.

Dipartimento di Filosofia
Via Bolognese, 52
I-50139 Firenze
Italia
parrini@unifi.it

A Second Appraisal: New French Literature on Logical Empiricism

Christoph Limbeck-Lilienau

Christian Bonnet / Pierre Wagner (eds.), *L'âge d'or de l'empirisme logique, Vienne-Berlin-Prague 1929–1936, Textes de philosophie des sciences*, Paris: Gallimard, 2006.
Mélika Ouelbani, *Le Cercle de Vienne*, (Philosophies vol. 189), Paris: Presses Universitaires de France, 2006.
Jacques Bouveresse, Delphine Chapuis-Schmitz, Jean-Jacques Rosat (eds.), *L'empirisme à la limite. Schlick, le langage et l'experience*, Paris: CNRS Editions, 2006.

In recent years, one can discern an increasing interest in the philosophy of the Vienna Circle and logical empiricism in France, an interest that is vividly testified by the mere fact that three books on the subject have appeared in a single year. Before addressing them one by one, let me give a brief overview of the history of this reception. After a long time of ignorance, renewed interest in this philosophical movement slowly began already in the 1980s, when the first books appeared, mainly those by Pierre Jacob (1980) and Antonia Soulez (1985). Till the seventies French philosophy of science not only ignored logical positivism, but often consciously rejected it. Different reasons can be given for this attitude. A first phase of reception initiated in the thirties by the two Congresses for the Unity of Science in Paris (1935 and 1937) was interrupted by World War II and did not continue afterwards. After the Second World War, French philosophy of science was dominated by a historically oriented "épistemologie" highly critical towards the logical reconstructions and the ahistoric attitude of analytic philosophy. Following Auguste Comte, philosophers like Gaston Bachelard and Georges Canguilhem analyzed science through a historical reconstruction of the products of science and refused to suppose a unified scientific method that could explain scientific rationality, and they ignored the instruments of modern logic. In their books, we find only some negative remarks about logical positivism without any substantive confrontation with this philosophy or its later analytic developments. In the sixties, this negative attitude towards logical positivism was fueled by the usual political clichés against "positivism," especially by Marxist philosophers such as Louis Althusser who was strongly influenced by the "épistemologie" of Bachelard.

E. Nemeth et al. (eds.), *Otto Neurath's Economics in Context.*
Vienna Circle Institute Yearbook [2007]. Volume 13.

But already in the sixties there were some exceptions to this negative view of logical positivism: Jules Vuillemin (1920–2001) and Gilles Gaston Granger (b. 1920) were two philosophers strongly interested in the philosophy of mathematics. They were both students of Jean Cavaillès (1903–1944), one of the main figures of the first phase of the reception of logical positivism in the thirties, who was strongly, albeit critically, interested in Carnap's *Logical Syntax of Language* and in Reichenbach's work on probability and who was among the first in France to publish an extensive review on the Vienna Circle in 1935. Vuillemin, after an existentialist and phenomenological phase, began in the sixties to publish on the foundations of mathematics and wrote a book on Bertrand Russell in 1968. Granger published, one year later, a book on Wittgenstein and organized in southern France (at the University of Aix en Provence) seminars on philosophy of science that were important for many young philosophers interested in analytic philosophy. Jacques Bouveresse remarks on their view of the philosophic situation in France in the sixties: "As his colleague and friend Granger, Vuillemin was convinced that the divorce which happened at a certain moment between philosophy and the sciences was a catastrophe for the first and that our time which can be called the "age of science," does not have the type of philosophy and of philosophers it would merit." ("Hommage à Jules Vuillemin" (3)) For them, the interest in logic and analytic philosophy was a means to close this gap.

Bouveresse continued these efforts to interest French philosophers in analytic philosophy and particularly drove the attention to its continental origins. Besides his several monographs on Wittgenstein, he published, to my knowledge, the first extensive description of the philosophy of logical positivisme in French ("La théorie et l'observation dans la philosophie des sciences du positivism logique," 1973). These efforts were followed by the first monographs on logical positivism in the early eighties: Pierre Jacob's *L'empirisme logique* (1980) described analytic philosophy from Russell to the debates on scientific realism in the seventies. Despite the title, the book covers a topic much larger than logical empiricism, but it contained two chapters on the Viennese origins of logical empiricism and the liberalization of empiricism in the years of the main protagonists' emigration from Europe. Jacob was still strongly influenced by the "received view" on logical empiricism then common in analytic philosophy in America (Jacob's book is the published version of his PhD thesis he wrote in Harvard). Antonia Soulez, in her long introduction to her reader on the Vienna Circle (*Manifeste du Cercle de Vienne et autres écrits*, 1985), gave a historically much more accurate image of logical empiricism. Her book was already influenced by the historical studies on the Vienna Circle that showed a quite different image of logical empiricism and underlined that it developed in a quite different social and political context than did anglo-saxon analytic philosophy.

The last 10 years showed a high increase of French studies on and translations of logical empiricism. The translations published to date have mainly centered on Carnap and Schlick: Carnap's *Meaning and Necessity* was translated in 1997, the *Aufbau* finally appeared in French in 2002, and a translation of the *Logical Syntax of Language* (by Bouveresse) will appear soon, as will Schlick's *Allgemeine*

Erkenntnislehre (translated by Christian Bonnet, his translation of Schlick's *Fragen der Ethik* already appeared in 2000). Several collections of papers appeared recently, among them two on Carnap (Laugier (ed.), 2002; Lepage, Paquette, Rivenc (eds.), 2003), one on Neurath (Soulez, Schmitz, Sebestik (eds.), 1997) and on Feigl's philosophy of mind (Andrieu (ed.), 2006). The interest in logical empiricism which was marginal till the eighties is thus becoming much broader and we can only guess the reasons for this change: An important factor is certainly that French historically oriented post-war philosophy of science (what Jean-François Braunstein calls the "French style" in "épistemologie" represented by Bachelard, Canguilhem and Foucault, in: Wagner, 2002) has lost its main figures. Also the crucial influence of Heidegger's criticism of science and technology on French philosophy is losing its importance since the controversies over Heidegger's political involvements in the Third Reich (mainly since the book of Victor Farias on Heidegger in 1987). Another reason is the general endeavor for an internationalization of French philosophy and the desire to obtain a better knowledge of the philosophical debates in analytic philosophy (a sign for this are not only the books by Pascal Engel, Claudine Tiercelin, Joëlle Proust or Sandra Laugier, but also the increasing importance of the "European Society for Analytic Philosophy" founded in 1991). Finally a better awareness of another tradition of French philosophy of science, the conventionalism of Poincaré and Duhem (and more generally the different philosophies of science before the dominance of Bachelard), as well as the international reception of these philosophers, plays a role in the presently growing interest in logical empiricism. Especially the recent volume on *Épistemologie française 1830–1970* (Michel Bitbol, Jean Gayon (eds.), 2006) analyzes this tradition and its early involvements with the Vienna Circle and analytic philosophy. Let me now come to the three volumes.

I

Bonnet and Wagner present a thick and very useful anthology of texts of logical empiricists that provides an excellent overview of the different discussions and positions. The editors have chosen to include only complete articles which are not already available in French (the exception being two papers translated in the thirties and not reprinted since). Chronologically they limited their choice to the period between 1929 and 1936, which corresponds to the public phase of the Vienna Circle from the publication of the "manifesto" to the end of the Circle with Schlick's death. But they did not limit the anthology to the Viennese members, with articles by Schlick, Carnap, Neurath, Feigl/Blumberg and Frank, but also included the Berlin group with two articles by Reichenbach and one by Hempel. With this presentation of fifteen texts, the anthology makes accessible for the first time in French a comprehensive overview of the discussions inside logical empiricism.

The book has obvious advantages over three earlier readers in French, which were published in the eighties. The anthology of Antonia Soulez (1985) was the first extensive publication in French on the Vienna Circle and it had the merit to initiate a larger interest in this field; it was till now the essential reference for French readers interested in logical empiricism, but it contained besides the "manifesto" only four, though essential articles by Carnap, Neurath, Schlick and Hahn, which mainly exemplified the criticism of metaphysics in the Circle. The other anthology on logical empiricism by Pierre Jacob (*De Vienne à Cambridge, l'héritage du positivisme logique*, 1980, 2nd edition 1996) mainly included the anglo-american controversies over logical empiricism after Quine and did not reprint the original texts of the Viennese period. In 2004 Pierre Wagner has already edited a reader in philosophy of science, where half of the texts are penned by philosophers of the Vienna Circle, but these six articles could not amount to a comprehensive view of the Circle's debates. Bonnet and Wagner's volume is an indispensable complement to these older anthologies, it has the advantage to introduce in detail the essential positions in logical empiricism, but by the chronological order of the articles it also shows the internal controversies and the pluralism within logical empiricism and the evolution of the positions over these essential 7 years.

The reader is preceded by a comprehensive introduction showing the historical development of the Vienna Circle and the internal dynamics of the philosophical debates. The authors analyze the development of the Vienna Circle out of a tradition of "scientific philosophy" deriving from Bolzano, Brentano and Mach and underline the influence of French conventionalism on the so-called "first Vienna Circle." For Bonnet/Wagner, logical empiricism can more accurately be characterized by a common philosophical tradition than by any agreement on a common set of theses, but they remain critical towards the characterization of this tradition as "Austrian philosophy," as did Rudolf Haller following Neurath's historiography. But it seems to the reviewer that the Neurath-Haller thesis is not so much contestable because it would overrate the opposition to idealist philosophy in "Austrian philosophy," as Bonnet/Wagner say, (after all, of the four Viennese chairs in philosophy before 1936, only Reininger was clearly a Kantian, while the other two besides Schlick, namely Gomperz and Bühler, were quite close to the Vienna Circle), but because the Haller thesis postulates an exaggerated unity inside the so called tradition of "scientific philosophy," for example between followers of Brentano and logical empiricists (a counter example for this is the strong hostility between Carnap and the local follower of Brentano, Oscar Kraus, in Prague).

The authors rightly emphasize that even the "fundamental thesis of logical positivism" (11), verificationism, is not shared by all logical empiricists and is liberalized or even abandoned in the debates of the thirties. Bonnet and Wagner accurately underline that logical empiricism cannot be conceived as a philosophical school, but rather as an informal group undertaking a collective and critical reflection. Evoking the controversies over the name of the philosophic movement, they opt for "logical empiricism" as a larger denomination which includes not only the Berlin group, but also Popper and contrast it with the narrower "logical positivism," whose association with phenomenalism is more strongly linked to the members of the Vienna Circle.

The authors then give brief and clear presentations of the main themes in the philosophy of science of logical empiricism: their conception of logic and mathematics, the analysis of language, the philosophic questions raised by the theory of relativity, quantum mechanics and the question of causality, the different interpretations of probability. Finally they describe the internal debates on protocol-sentences, unity of science and the concept of truth. These are also the themes covered by the chosen original papers. The authors mention in a note that their choice is limited to philosophy of science, while they underline that the logical empiricists also debated social and ethical issues. As already Antonia Soulez strongly emphasized in her book, Bonnet and Wagner insist on the dimension of social emancipation implicit in logical empiricism, describing its members as "heirs of the enlightenment" (23). But this social aspect is only exemplified in the selected papers by Neurath's "Soziologie im Physikalismus." It would still be a desideratum to publish a collection of texts showing especially this aspect, particularly in France, where the reception of logical empiricism was for a long time heavily biased for political reasons and where the Vienna Circle was more seen in the context of the American atmosphere of cold war than in the context of the liberal and left groups of Red Vienna.

The always accurate general presentation of logical empiricism in the introduction is accompanied by very useful smaller introductions to each of the translated texts. The choice of the texts is quite suitable to get a comprehensive picture and it avoids the usual over-emphasis on Carnap and Schlick. The anthology begins with two general presentations of the "scientific world conception," one by Frank (1929) and one through a paper by Feigl and Blumberg (1931). The comment on this last paper testifies how some elements of a distorted American reception of logical empiricism was already pre-figured by this paper, which entirely ignored Neurath and appeared too early to include the controversial discussions on physicalism, verificationism and the foundation of knowledge. Three papers of the volume deal with physicalism. Besides Carnap's seminal paper of 1932 and Neurath's already mentioned essay, one finds Hempel's early attempt to situate psychology in the physicalist program ("The logical analysis of psychology," 1935). In the otherwise excellent translation of Carnap's paper ("Die physikalische Sprache als Universalsprache der Wissenschaft"), it is somewhat misleading not to mention in a note that the French word "constatation" (p. 337) does refer to the German "Feststellung" and not to Schlick's concept of "Konstatierung," which is generally also translated by "constatation." Although the origin of physicalism is closely associated with a materialist conception of science and society, a fact that is accurately stressed in the introduction to Neurath's paper, it seems to us somewhat exaggerated to postulate the equation: "physicalism = materialism" (259) or to define physicalism as a "non-metaphysical materialism" (260), because Carnap and Neurath do not want to define what matter is, but only want to avoid entities which are not in space and time, they do not take an ontological position on what these entities are. Thus they avoided the term "materialism" precisely in virtue of its ontological connotations. The debate on protocols begun in Carnap's paper is supplemented by a translation of Schlick's paper on the foundation of knowledge (1934). In the context of the protocol sentences, Neurath's attack on Popper is reprinted (1935). Three translations present the consequences Carnap draws from his logical syntax, concerning the relation between formal and empirical science, the transition from theory of knowledge to the logic of science and his first presentation of a semantic concept of truth (all of 1935–1936), as well as Schlick's late response to Carnap's conventionalism (1936). More concerned with the consequences of contemporary physics are the papers of Schlick on causality (1931) and Reichenbach's two papers. Finally the difference of Neurath's conception of the unity of science and encyclopedism is presented with his paper on the "Encyclopedia as 'model'" (1936). The volume concludes with a careful and extensive bibliography of primary and secondary literature and with a very useful "Index rerum" in French and German (The only mistake noticed by us in the book concerns there the name of the Polish philosopher Jan Woleński, instead of twice "Woleski"). The always excellent translations and presentations by the editors and a young group of philosophers (Alexis Bienvenu, Ronan de Calan, Delphine Chapuis-Schmitz, Céline Vautrin) give quite a good instrument for a new appraisal of logical empiricism in France.

II

The book on the Vienna Circle by Mélika Ouelbani is a short introduction of 150 pages to the main themes of logical empiricism. It appeared in a collection of small books allotting only this little space to present one philosopher or one philosophic topic. It is quite difficult to compress into this small space the different problems touched by the Vienna Circle and it is necessary to make difficult choices and limit the presentation to some aspects which appear crucial, and obviously the choices made can be questioned. Within the limitations of this collection, Ouelbani gives a substantive and well argued discussion of the central positions of Schlick and Carnap, of the debate in the thirties on protocol sentences and the unity of science.

In her introduction, she gives a brief historical description of the Circle and his evolution, from the first Vienna Circle and the constitution of the Schlick-Circle in the twenties to the phase of disintegration in Vienna and the concomitant internationalization. She follows here the chronological distinction in five different phases given by Hans-Joachim Dahms. Then Ouelbani gives a brief philosophical characterization of the Circle, insisting that there is no common doctrine and even less a common dogma. She underlines the diversity of the Circle and criticizes the still common fallacy to reduce the Circle to one philosopher, usually Carnap. While not of a "doctrine", Ouelbani thinks we can speak of a "neo-positivist program" (11). She describes this program by "the realization of the unity of science" (11) and a certain idea about the function of philosophy. Ouelbani gives a closer characterization of this "program" through the manifesto of 1929: the opposition to metaphysics and to pseudo-problems, the disintegration of the Kantian a priori, but she adds that "all the neo-positivist program" is centered around "the question of *foundation*" (18). It is right that this aspect is stressed in the manifesto, but it seems questionable to the reviewer to unify the positions of the Circle in a foundational program, even if this foundation is not metaphysical, as the author adds. While the historical description in this introduction is mainly correct, there intruded some small errors: Neurath did not leave for England in 1938, but in 1940 and he died in 1945 (not 1946). The last Congress of Unity of Science movement was not the one in Cambridge 1939, but it took place 2 years later in Chicago.

In a first chapter the author refines her characterization of the Circle as "scientific philosophy" and "philosophy of meaning." She discusses the problematic status of the first label, especially for Schlick's therapeutic conception of philosophy as linguistic elucidation and clarification in which philosophy cannot itself produce scientific propositions. But Schlick pleaded for a "theory of knowledge" defined as an "analysis of the concepts and the principles of knowledge" (28). Similarly, Ouelbani interprets Carnap's paper "Von der Erkenntnistheorie zur Wissenschaftslogik" (1936) as an argument for a purified and exclusively logical "theory of knowledge" identified with the logic of science (25). It is not quite clear in Carnap's paper, to what extent he wants to keep any theory of knowledge or whether he simply wants to dissolve it. But it seems that Ouelbani interprets Carnap's position as a renewal of "purified" "empirical theory of knowledge" without metaphysics. She interprets Carnap's plea for a transition from the "empirical theory of knowledge" to the "logic of science" as a continuation of theory of knowledge by only logical means and not as an abandonment of the foundational ambitions of *Erkenntnistheorie*, as would seem more accurate to us. Concerning the Circle's "philosophy of meaning," the author analyzes the evolution from Wittgenstein's explanation of the meaning of words and propositions to Carnap and rightly shows that from Carnap's *Scheinprobleme in der Philosophie* on, verification was defined as a notion much larger than is often supposed, namely as a "verifiability" going already in the direction of the later liberalization of empiricism in "Testability and Meaning."

After this description of the "program" of logical empiricism, the author gives a close look to the "sources of the Vienna Circle." Ouelbani mentions mainly three sources: the classical empiricism from Hume to Mach, Russell's and Wittgenstein's logical atomism and Frege's logicism. This is a more classical description of the sources compared to Friedman's insistence on neo-Kantian origins. For Ouelbani, especially Carnap continues Frege's foundational efforts and tries to realize Russell's program of a "scientific philosophy," which extends these efforts from the foundation of mathematics to empirical knowledge. More generally logical empiricism is seen by the author primarily in connection to the analytic tradition deriving from Frege, Russell and Wittgenstein, and the second part of her chapter analyzes the *Aufbau* as a continuation of this tradition. It must be said that this emphasis on the *Aufbau* highly undervalues other sources, for example all the philosophic reflections raised by physics, especially by Einstein. It is quite defendable in a short book to put so strong an emphasis on the early Carnap, but it seems to the reviewer that in this way also a main source of the early Carnap and of the *Aufbau* is highly underrated, namely conventionalism, which is only mentioned in two sentences in connection with Neurath's holism (66 and 114) (and briefly in the introduction in connection with the first Vienna Circle, 5). As a consequence, Ouelbani stresses the "foundationalist project of Carnap in his *Logische Aufbau*," the "foundationalist method of a logicist type" being used there even to give "logical foundations" to the "sentences of the empirical sciences" (62). It seems to us that the conventionally chosen (material or phenomenal) bases for the constitutional system strongly relativize Carnap's "foundationalism" and, more generally, that the growing influence of conventionalism on Carnap, at least until the *Logical Syntax*, prevents him from being a "foundationalist." The author suggests a relativization of the distinction between the analytic and the synthetic, which seems to her too rigidly drawn by Carnap, with the intention to permit a logical foundation of empirical sentences (62). It seems to us that Ouelbani desires a stronger foundation than the empty analytic propositions of logic would permit.

The next two chapters are clear and careful descriptions of Schlick's *Allgemeine Erkenntnislehre* and of Carnap's *Aufbau*. The analysis of Schlick's book reveals his general conception of knowledge, which Ouelbani sums up by two principles Schlick never abandons: the observational foundation of knowledge and the necessity to reduce knowledge to the smallest possible number of concepts (89). Similarly the *Aufbau* is then seen as a first attempt for a unified language of science, achieved by the reduction to basic concepts and by a theory of knowledge giving a "unique" and "common foundation for all the sciences" (92). Ouelbani describes the constitution of objects and concepts in the constitutional system of the *Aufbau*, which should permit a unified system for science. The rise of discussions on the unity of science is described here from the perspective of Carnap and not from the controversial internal discussions conducted by the Circle about this notion. Quite different views on the "unity of science" are therefore underrated, for example Neurath's and Frank's defense of unity, which comes from a clear refusal of the need for a foundation of the sciences and from a profound distrust towards Kantian theory of knowledge and any attempt of a "philosophical" foundation of the science. This defense of "unity of science" is quite opposed to the author's picture of Carnap.

The internal debates and the internal pluralism of the Circle are only analyzed more closely in a chapter on "basic sentences." In this description of the protocol sentence debate, the author analyzes the relation of Carnap to Neurath, the former's acceptance of physicalism and of Neurath's holism as well as his changing attitude concerning the foundational character of protocol sentences. Despite these changes of Carnap's position, Ouelbani stresses a general continuity within Carnap's philosophy. While Carnap gets nearer to Neurath's anti-foundationalism and coherentism, there still remains between them a profound divergence on the way to conceive the language of science and, accordingly, on the unity of science, so Ouelbani. For Carnap this language is an ideal and formal language, while for Neurath it is a universal slang full of vague concepts. It is not quite clear in this chapter, how much Carnap, with the described changes and continuities, maintains his original "foundational program." Finally Schlick's position on the debate is shown and the author concludes that the protocol sentence debate showed three different conceptions of the unity of science represented by the three philosophers. A final chapter concerns Quine's and Popper's "criticism of logical positivism" as well as a general evaluation of their relation to the Circle.

It is understandable that Ouelbani, who is a Carnap specialist and has published a monograph on him in 1992, carefully analyzes mainly Carnap and Schlick, given the concision of the book, but it seems to us that a very strong emphasis is put on texts mainly written before these two philosophers joined the Circle. It seems for this reason, that the strong criticism of foundationalism and of the ambitions of a traditional Kantian theory of knowledge are not given a central role, while many texts of the Vienna Circle can be read as a demise of this foundational program, including Carnap's *Logical Syntax*. It seems to us that the central turn in philosophy – initiated by the Vienna Circle around 1930 and symbolized for example by Schlick's announcement of a linguistic turn in his "Wende der Philosophie" and the consequences following from there for the conception of protocols, truth, the role of philosophy and for the criticism of traditional *Erkenntnistheorie* – is given a too small a share from the little space available in the volume (i.e., mainly one chapter, pp. 107–125). But the early texts emphasized by the author are always carefully explained and analyzed and they form an interesting introduction to the early positions in the Circle. The author's sometimes provocative interpretations require already a certain acquaintance with different interpretations given in the secondary literature. Some inexactitudes occur in the names and dates (so Feigl is spelled "Feigel" at p. 6 and Gomperz as "Comperz", p. 154, the years for the same reference change, p. 31)

III

The last volume reviewed here is an anthology of papers centering around one text of Schlick and the problems addressed in it: Schlick's lectures *Form and Content* given in London in 1932. In this central text for the understanding of his late philosophy, Schlick develops his conception, that what can be expressed in language and what can be communicated – and hence be called knowledge – is only the structure of a fact, not the material, only the form and not the content of an experience. Schlick sharply counterposes form and content and defends the thesis that knowledge concerns by definition only the form and that the content of experience is wholly excluded from it. The papers of this volume put Schlick's conception in the broader context of the Kantian question of the relation between concepts and experience, or more precisely between the formal and structural aspect of concepts and of what Kant called "intuition." In virtue of Schlick's strong opposition between these two aspects, the difference between the empirical aspect and the logical aspect is pushed to its limits. These limits would be, on the one side, the idea of immediately given data of intuition and therefore the danger to fall under the criticisms raised against the myth of the given, and on the other side, a conception analyzing only the logical relations between expressions, a coherence theory of knowledge losing any relation to experience. The different papers explore the historic questions of the relation of Schlick's position to earlier Kantian or neo-Kantian solutions (Bonnet, De Calan), to contemporary positions such as Carnap's "logical structuralism" and to later philosophers, among them Sellars (Chapuis-Schmitz, Grellard); they also explore specific problems, such as the possibility to know something about new qualities in experience (Benoit) or the thesis of incommunicable content (Rosat, Bouveresse). The papers are very valuable for a closer understanding of Schlick and the contemporary implications of his late philosophy.

Christian Bonnet studies Schlick's relation to Kantianism and explores in detail Alberto Coffa's and Michael Friedman's argument that Schlick before Vienna was neo-Kantian or at least mainly involved with Kantian questions. To the contrary, Bonnet stresses that Schlick was already in 1913 opposed to the Kantians by his rejection of any material aspect of the a priori and therefore of any a priori intuition of space or time (see his "Gibt es intuitive Erkenntnis?", 1913). Schlick rejects the central role Kant attributes to intuition in knowledge and for him the Kantian thing-in-itself cannot be known, not because the intellect does not have an intuition of it, but because knowledge by definition just never is intuitive. Bonnet develops in detail Schlick's opposition to Kant concerning the synthetic a priori. But finally, he stresses one point of convergence between the two philosophers on the issue of realism: Schlick compares his realism to Kant's empirical realism because Kant already asserted that reality is a "category." Kant showed that reality and existence are not properties and when we attribute reality to something, we mean that it is subjected to a lawlike order. Hence for Schlick, the Kantian concept of reality is similar to his own, defining reality as a regular lawlike connection between our perceptions.

A closer look to the differences and similarities between Schlick and the neo-Kantian movement is given in the article by Ronan de Calan, which examines the impact of non-Euclidian geometry and of the theory of relativity on neo-Kantian revisions of Kant's original position, especially concerning his "transcendental aesthetics." For De Calan, Schlick's clear rejection of the Kantian synthetic a priori and his position that the a priori is strictly formal is paralleled by the evolution of neo-Kantianism, which goes in the same direct as Schlick. De Calan analyzes this evolution of neo-Kantianism over two generations (from Cohen to Cassirer) and shows that it gradually deprives the a priori of its intuitive content and adopts, especially in the case of Cassirer, a formal a priori close to Schlick's own. In a careful analysis of the impact of science on Kantianism and on Schlick, De Calan shows how gradually Riemann's and Helmholtz's conceptions of non-Euclidian geometry and the "second crisis of neo-Kantianism" caused by Einstein led to the abandonment of Kantian intuitive space. Schlick and Cassirer stress the conceptual nature of physical space strictly separated of any psychological, intuitive content. De Calan concludes that in this "neo-Kantianism and positivism go hand in hand" (48), but he concedes that Schlick remained opposed to the neo-Kantians in one respect, namely concerning his conventionalism: the intuitive spaces, given by our senses, are coordinated to the objective physical space by conventions.

A third paper, by Florent Grellard, explores Kantian themes by a comparison of Schlick with the "analytic Kantianism" of Sellars as regards the question of the relation between concepts and experience. Schlick is, strangely, absent from Sellars's criticism of logical positivism, so the author argues. Both Schlick and Sellars emphasize the separation of form and content, but they give different answers to the question, how conceptual form can connect with experience. Schlick's conception of observation permits a connection between signs and the world, but he gives observation a privileged status and attributes to observational statements a "self-justifying" (57) role, so Grellard. Thereby he cannot avoid the criticisms Sellars directed against the myth of the given. A second part of the paper analyzes how Sellars tried to avoid the danger of coherentism and foundationalism in his explanation of the relation between form and content. Grellard shows that for Sellars any *justification* of knowledge must be inferential (and hence part of the logical space of reason), but that knowledge cannot be reduced to logical, inferential relations. The myth of the given is avoided only if this non-inferential knowledge is not "self-justifying." In the theory of Sellars the causal relation between objects and sensations is distinguished from the logical relations between inferences, but hereby the nature of the relation between sensations and non-inferencial knowledge remains problematic. Grellard shows how Sellars makes a distinction inside content between "descriptive content" and "propositional content" and, in opposition to Schlick, introduces a "descriptive content" as a mediation between form and content, knowledge and sensation and hence between the logical spaces of reason and of causes.

After these papers on different types of Kantianism, two papers are concerned with the relation of Schlick's empiricism to realism and to "logical structuralism." One essay by Joselyn Benoit confronts Schlick's formal conception of knowledge with the problem of a new, not yet classified experience, as would have been the Humean example of the taste of a pineapple after its discovery. Knowledge communicates only the relation of the sensation to other sensations and not what it is like to see "green" or to taste an "apple"; only the place of green towards other colors, the logical structure of the color "green," can be the object of knowledge. For Schlick, the power of language lies in its capacity to express new facts by the syntactic recombination of available terms. But Benoit insists that a new experience reshapes the corresponding logical space of meanings, the taste of the pineapple reshaped the logical space of the tastes. He criticizes that Schlick's sharp distinction between form and content does not acknowledge this dependence of the structural space of meanings on experience. For the author, Schlick passed from an "empiricism of content" to an "empiricism of the form" (84), but in both empiricisms the "massive reality of reference" (84) is ignored and hence the fact that the "real" goes beyond the framework of our concepts. This provocative paper reproaches Schlick still a dependence on a Kantian idealism and an "intellectualization" of experience (85) ignoring the "real" aspect of experience.

Delphine Chapuis-Schmitz gives a close look at what Gustav Bergmann has called the "logical structuralism" in Schlick's and Carnap's philosophy, according to which only the structure of our experience can be an object of knowledge and linguistic expression. But this logical structuralism as formulated by Bergmann implies that an inexpressible, subjective and private quale of experience remains and hence implies a dualism. Chapuis-Schmitz calls this dualism of knowledge and private experience a "naïve version" of the logical structuralism (88), and the purpose of her paper is to show how Schlick and Carnap try to escape this naïveté. Schlick wants to express by content only the trivial fact that we cannot avoid experiencing the unique world, but that this does not amount to any knowledge. Only when we express its order or its structure can we speak of knowledge. Schlick's intention is to avoid suggesting two distinct spheres (form and content). The author shows, however, that Schlick identifies structure with a form that has to be interpreted and applied to experience and that this interpretation is conceived by him as a private act of filling in with substantial private and incommunicable content. Therefore Schlick, so Chapuis-Schmitz, does not avoid the naïve dualist implication of Bergmann's logical structuralism and he does not avoid the arguments against the myth of the given. To this view the author opposes Carnap's quite different "logical structuralism" in the *Aufbau*, where Carnap starts with the structure of the lived experience. For him structure is found as well in the conceptual forms as in experience, such that he avoids the problem to fill in forms with a private content. Finally the author critically discusses Carnap's abandonment of any reference to phenomenal experience in physicalism.

The last part of the volume presents two papers, by Jean-Jacques Rosat and Jacques Bouveresse, who critically discuss Schlick's thesis of the inexpressibility of content by confronting it with other analytic philosophers, with Wittgenstein's private language argument in the case of Rosat, and with more recent criticisms of Schlick's thesis by Bernard Harrison and Sidney Shoemaker. Rosat criticizes by means of Wittgenstein's private language argument Schlick's conception that meaning is given through private interpretation and the author argues that Schlick rests attached to a metaphysical idea of a pure and inexpressible experience although he radically criticized the metaphysical implications of Kantian intuition. Bouveresse carefully discusses Schlick's thesis in the context of newer arguments raised in philosophy of mind concerning qualia and the communicability of color experience. First he emphasizes that Schlick's thesis follows from the conception of meaning in the *Tractatus*: a proposition shows the arrangement of things, hence the structure of a fact, it can only designate these things but not describe them. The meaning of a proposition is therefore completely separated from any content. As a consequence, content becomes incommunicable, but this thesis does not mean, as Bouveresse shows, that there are no qualia, no content in our experience. Neither does it mean that only I myself can know the content of my experience, but no-one else. Only the structure of experience can be known, even from the perspective of the first person, and in this regard there is no difference to the perspective of the third person. After this clarification, Bouveresse confronts Schlick's thesis with more recent objections to it from analytic philosophy. He discusses the criticism of Bernard Harrison according to which Schlick and Wittgenstein without justification presuppose an identity between the structure of our experience given before language and the structure of our syntax, of the linguistic subdivisions and categories. Then Bouveresse confronts, in a detailed analysis, Schlick's thesis with the arguments of Harrison and Sidney Shoemaker about the possibility of the inversion of the color spectrum. He discusses the serious objections against the possibility that another person has a different spectrum without being able to know and communicate it. But if the spectrum inversion argument is rejected, this would be a serious challenge for Schlick's thesis of the independence of knowledge and content.

The well argued essays in this book represent a very valuable contribution to the understanding of the later Schlick and put his philosophy in interesting historical and contemporary perspectives. With the two introductory volumes discussed first, this book is a very positive sign of the lively reception of logical empiricism in France.

References

Bernard Andrieu (ed.) *Herbert Feigl. De la physique au mental*, Paris: Vrin, 2006

Michel Bitbol, Jean Gayon (eds.) *L'épistemologie française, 1830–1970*, Paris: Presses Universitaire de France, 2006

Jacques Bouveresse "La théorie et l'observation dans la philosophie des sciences du positivisme logique", in: François Châtelet *La philosophie au XX*[e]*siècle*, vol. 4, Paris: Marabout, 1973

Jacques Bouveresse "Hommage à Jules Vuillemin", Paris: Collège de France, published on: www.college- de-france.fr/media/ins_dis/UPL53971_necrovuil.pdf

Pierre Jacob *L'empirisme logique*, Paris: Editions de Minuit, 1980

Pierre Jacob (ed.) *De Vienne à Cambridge. L'héritage du positivisme logique de 1950 à nos jours*, Paris: Gallimard, 1980

Sandra Laugier, Pierre Wagner (eds.) *Philosophie des sciences. Théories, experiences et méthodes*, Paris: Librairie philosophique Vrin, 2004

Sandra Laugier (ed.) *Carnap et la construction du monde*, Paris: Vrin, 2002

François Lepage, Michel Paquette, François Rivenc (eds.) *Carnap aujourd'hui*, Paris: Vrin, 2003

Antonia Soulez (ed.) *Manifeste du Cercle de Vienne et autres écrits. Carnap-Hahn-Neurath-Schlick-Waismann-Wittgenstein*, Paris: Presses Universitaire de France, 1985

Antonia Soulez, François Schmitz, Jan Sebestik (eds.) *Otto Neurath, un philosophe entre science et guerre*, Paris: L'Harmattan, 1997

Pierre Wagner (ed.) *Les philosophes et la science*, Paris: Gallimard, 2002

Institut Wiener Kreis
Spitalgasse 2-4, Hof 1
A-1090 Wien
Austria
christoph.limbeck@univie.ac.at

Reviews

Moritz Schlick, *Über die Reflexion des Lichtes in einer inhomogenen Schicht* and *Raum und Zeit in den gegenwärtigen Physik*. Gesamtausgabe. Abt. I, Bd. II. Fynn Ole Engler and Matthias Neuber, eds. (Wien: Springer-Verlag, 2006). Ix + 412pp. $98.27.

In the early 1970s, when the leading lights of academic Philosophy were solemnly declaring that the hegemony of Logical Positivism had ended, a few lonely thinkers realized that our understanding of the movement, especially its origins and early development, was distressingly incomplete. Much of the published record from the formative years of Positivism – the 1930s and earlier – remained beyond the reach of English speakers. True, some prominent articles had been translated in the 1950s, and collected in anthologies like Feigl's and Sellars' *Readings in Philosophical Analysis*, Feigl's and Brodbeck's *Readings in the Philosophy of Science*, and A. J. Ayer's *Logical Empiricism*. But the few items translated and published did not, by any means, exhaust the broad range of the extant literature or the proliferation of viewpoints it represented. If anything, the selections reflected editorial judgments of what was most significant about Logical Positivism and – looking to future book sales – what would continue to be in demand. Soon this situation was corrected, and important works were translated and published in English editions. By the end of the 1970s, the second edition of Moritz Schlick's monumental *Allgemeine Erkenntnislehre* became available in English, and D. Reidel began publishing volumes of the Vienna Circle Collection, making the major publications of Schlick, Otto Neurath, and other leading lights of early Positivism available to English scholars. At the same time as these results began to appear, efforts were also initiated to carefully collect, organize, and store the literary remains of early figures of the movement. The Archives for Scientific Philosophy at the University of Pittsburgh gathered, inventoried, and made available to the public the papers, notes, and correspondence of Rudolf Carnap and Hans Reichenbach, while the Vienna Circle Foundation in Amsterdam collected the papers of Moritz Schlick and Otto Neurath, eventually depositing them with the Achief voor Noord-Holland. By the end of the 1980s, scholars could access much of the original published record of early Positivism and numerous efforts were underway to make available more recondite materials.

These early efforts were accompanied by the interest of a broad range of scholars, not only in German- and English-speaking countries but across the continent of Europe.

E. Nemeth et al. (eds.), *Otto Neurath's Economics in Context.*
Vienna Circle Institute Yearbook [2007]. Volume 13.

Numerous conferences were organized to provide forums for the scholarly discussion of early Positivism, accompanied by a flood of full-length works on the philosophical, economic, sociological, and mathematical thought of Vienna Circle figures and their affiliates.

In 1991, a major benchmark was reached, with the establishment of the *Institut Wiener Kreis* at the major conference *Wien, Prag, Berlin*. The *Institut* was the brainchild of Friedrich Stadler, who immediately undertook numerous projects, ranging from hosting conferences to various publishing activities. Of these, one of the most important was announced in 2002 as the *Schlick Projekt*, involving scholars from the *Institut* as well as from Rostock and Graz. Their goal is to produce critical editions of Schlick's published works (forming *Abteilung I*), selections of a philosophical nature from his *Nachlass (Abteilung II*), correspondence (*Abteilung III*), as well as miscellaneous items with an index (*Abteilung IV*). The formation of the *Projekt* and the production of critical editions of Schlick's major works represents a significant advance on all previous efforts in the scholarly study of the Vienna Circle and allied philosophical groups.

For it marks an achievement, not only in advancing scholarship on the early development of Logical Positivism, but for singularly expediting the availability of resources to serious researchers. If the volume described in the current review is indicative of what is to come, scholars have much to be thankful for, and even more to look forward to.

The first *Abteilung* of the *Moritz Schlick Gesamtausgabe* consists of three volumes: the first, to appear later in 2007, will be Schlick's classic epistemological text, *Allgemeine Erkenntnislehre*. The third – which has just been released – contains his principal ethical writings, including his youthfully enthusiastic ethical tract – *Lebensweisheit* (of 1910) – and his later, better-known work, *Fragen über Ethik* (published in 1930). The second volume, which is the focus of the current review, contains Schlick's major works in physics – his dissertation *Über die Reflexion des Lichtes in einer inhomogenen Schicht* and the classic *Raum und Zeit in den gegenwärtigen Physik*.

The present volume is nothing less than superlative. The editors have provided a substantial introduction to set the biographical, historical, and philosophical background. Additionally, they have provided separate prefaces for each of the texts, providing even more details concerning the conditions under which it was written and published. The evolution through subsequent editions is carefully documented for *Raum und Zeit* ..., and indices of names as well as subjects have been added. The texts are accompanied by a multitude of editorial footnotes – nearly 200 for *Raum und Zeit* ... alone! – referring readers to other literature, further publications by Schlick, as well as items from his *Nachlass*. Of course, the difficulty faced by editors providing such a rich storehouse of ancillary information is the tendency to interpret the original texts themselves, thereby providing a perspective which might mislead the reader. In this regard, special care was taken to avoid editorial interpretation and the end-result is a surfeit of helpful information without any introduction of bias.

The first item in the volume is Schlick's dissertation in physics, *Über die Reflexion des Lichtes in einer inhomogenen Schicht*. Defended on 8 February 1904, it resulted in the awarding of the doctorate degree with the distinction "magna cum laude" on 20 May of the same year. The degree was the culmination of efforts begun in 1900, when Schlick first enrolled in the University of Berlin. He supplemented his work in Berlin by attending Heidelberg and Munich in the summers. Although his studies were dominated by coursework in mathematics and physics, the "striving for generality" which drew him to these sciences also attracted him to philosophical studies, which he pursued mainly on his own. Schlick found mathematical-physics especially attractive because of its combination of generality with precise attention to details. As is well-known, his thesis supervisor was the celebrated physicist Max Planck, who later commended him for the "thoroughness" of his dissertation. The focus of Schlick's work is a difficulty in optics created by the behavior of light-waves traveling through non-homogeneous media. The question Schlick addresses is whether the discontinuous behavior of light-waves in such media is to be attributed to the light-waves themselves, or the effect of the media. The answer, Schlick reasoned, lay in the application of Maxwell's equations, thus making the problem of the dissertation a purely theoretical rather than experimental one. The question boils down to whether or not the transition of light in a non-homogeneous medium is analyzable into component cases of the transmission of light in distinct homogeneous media. If so, the discontinuity of the transition of light through a non-homogeneous medium would be due to properties of the medium and not to properties of light-waves themselves. Thus the problem Schlick addresses is not a recondite physical puzzle, a physicist's trick for treating anomalous phenomena with his pet theory, for it sheds light on the more general question of the nature of light-waves and the answer to the question bears manifold implications for the general understanding of the nature of light. In this respect, Schlick's dissertation exemplifies the "striving for generality" which he considered the guiding principle of his scholarly life.

The highlight of the volume is Schlick's classic *Raum und Zeit in der gegenwärtigen Physik*. Certainly, this was the most successful publication of Schlick's entire career: originally appearing in Die Naturwissenschaften in 1917 with three subsequent editions published over the next 5 years. The work was translated into 11 languages and is still available in English in an inexpensive paperback. At the time of its appearance, Einstein himself commended it for its perspicuous grasp of the underlying physics, praising it as one of the best treatments of the topic. Certainly *Raum und Zeit* ... is one of Schlick's finest pieces of philosophical writing.

The work itself defies easy categorization. On the one hand, it is subtitled *Zur Einführung in das Verständnis der Relativitäts- und Gravitationstheorie*, suggesting a popular work, one which could be picked up and perused by the interested layperson willing to devote an evening to the topic. And, indeed, most of the text is so clearly and patiently explained, it might – for the most part –be a primer on the latest theory of space and time. Yet Schlick does not hesitate to rely on mathematical symbolism, when it enhances the effectiveness of his prose explanation. And while the work certainly does possess a definite appeal for popular readers, it nonetheless ventures into territory which would be *terra incognita* even for the philosophically trained. The most remarkable feature of the work, however, is not its deft combination of scientific and philosophical topics, nor its masterful treatment of complex matters – of both physics and philosophy – at an introductory level. Rather, the achievement of *Raum und Zeit* … is that it conveys a wealth of information, in readily understandable terms, about some of the most complex matters facing professional physicists and philosophers. At the same time, the thoughtful reader, though satisfied with what he has learned from the book, yearns to further broaden his understanding of the physics Schlick explains, and reflect more deeply on the philosophical issues he raises.

Much of Schlick's treatment is familiar simply because so much of it has become standard fare in philosophy of science lore. Indeed, the narrative of the early chapters definitely seems old-hat, so often has it been repeated, especially the treatment of late nineteenth century classical physics and the anomaly presented by the Michelson-Morley experiment. In particular, Schlick's logical representation of the historic state of affairs anticipates many later illustrations of the hypothetico-deductive model. But it should be kept in mind that *Raum und Zeit* … is the point at which these common elements entered the literature. And Schlick relates these matters in a such a convincing manner, that one cannot help wonder, "Whatever were physicists thinking?". But Schlick does not dawdle over the historical background, moving quickly into the details of the Special Theory, how it resolves the difficulty raised by the Michelson-Morley experiment, and how it incorporates the Lorentz-Fitzgerald contraction. From this point, Schlick approaches General Relativity through the avenue provided by geometry, introducing the traditional debate over the nature of space and then explaining its relevance by means of one of Poincaré's charming examples. Schlick further explains spatial relativity mathematically, in terms of coordinate-systems, explaining how, without physical objects only the presumption of absolute space can distinguish a coordinate-system from its (Gaussian) transformation. On this basis, Schlick argues the holistic thesis that geometry and physics are inseparable in experience, relying on Helmholtz' famous example of the space of the image in a convex mirror. As an example, he recalls Gauss' observation of the angular sum of the triangle formed by three mountain-tops, reiterating that a deviation of the sum from that of two right angles could easily be accommodated by assuming that light-rays are curved or that the geometry of space is non-Euclidean. From these considerations, Schlick draws Poincaré's conclusion that geometry is conventional, that the choice of geometry to be used in conjunction with physical theory is simply not determined by the facts of experience. Notably, Schlick departs from Poincaré's contention that physicists will always choose Euclidean geometry because of its simplicity, insisting that the appropriate desideratum is not the simplicity of the underlying geometry, but of the form of the laws of physics. The terrain through which Schlick next guides his reader is the most difficult encountered in the text, as he tries to explain – in the simplest of terms – the intricate details of the theory, including covariance and general relativity. To master the middle chapters of the work, the reader must do more than casually peruse the material, he must study it assiduously. Epistemologically speaking, Schlick's explanations continue to excel, as he carefully points out how various features of Einstein's work were guided – and confirmed – by empirical considerations. At the same time, he also painstakingly indicates when experience was irrelevant to the theoretical development and guided other factors guided Einstein's choice of approach. Schlick completes his explanation of General Relativity by drawing out its cosmological implications. Of course, cosmological questions concerning the extent, shape, and density of the universe receive quite different answers from Relativity and Newtonian physics. And Schlick explains these differences in straightforward terms, arguing for the greater plausibility of the Einsteinian cosmos compared to the classical one.

The very last chapter draws out the philosophical implications of the new physics, in particular how the leading philosophies of the day – the critical philosophy of Kant and Machian positivism – fare in the light of Relativity. To students of Schlick's thought, these are familiar refrains, first suggested in his earlier essays and fully adumbrated for the first time in *Allgemeine Erkenntnislehre*. Schlick's philosophical debts are obvious throughout, as he describes the construction of physical space from sensory intuition in a manner reminiscent of Helmholtz, and then arguing, *a la* Poincaré, that space and time are conceptual constructions which serve as referential systems for ordering experiences. Here there is much that is worthy of further study, especially the conventionalist thesis that was to play such a central role in subsequent philosophical theorizing. Not only did conventionalism play figure prominently in discussions of the relativistic physics throughout the twentieth century, the understanding of conventionalism first suggested by Poincaré and subsequently developed by Schlick – in *Raum und Zeit* ... (as well as numerous later writings) – applied well beyond physical geometry to any representational system whatsoever. Of course, discussion would eventually turn to the role of conventions in logic and language and it is in this form that the doctrine decisively shaped mature Logical Positivism. Still, despite all the years and countless heated discussions, there are still unanswered questions about the exact nature of Schlick's contribution to the discussion. While it is recognized that Schlick departed in some details from the conception suggested by Poincaré's remarks, scholars have yet to determine the extent to which Schlick extended and enriched the doctrine by contributing original elements and combining conceptions developed by other authors. Nor has there ever been a full discussion of the extent to which there is a genuine consensus between all those who invoked conventionalism in their explanations of the epistemological role of geometry in physical theory. And it would be a grievous philosophical error to simply associate, without attention to specific details, the conventionalist views of thinkers ranging from Einstein and Eddington to Reichenbach and Carnap. Yet this is what frequently passes for the current wisdom on conventionalism. Given its long and influential history – to say nothing of the troubles conventionalism has seen in the last half-century – it is surprising indeed that its nuances have not drawn more attention from serious historical scholars. Hopefully, their hesitation was only due to the lack of reliable sources for their research. But that situation is changed now, as a new milestone in philosophical scholarship, the Schlick *Gesamtausgabe*, establishes a new standard for research materials on early Logical Positivism.

Thomas Oberdan (Clemson)

George A. Reisch, *How the Cold War Transformed Philosophy of Science. To the Icy Slopes of Logic*, Cambridge, NY: Cambridge University Press, 2005

This is a very interesting and remarkably well-written book. It addresses an important and clearly expressed *problem*: "What, precisely, was logical empiricism originally all about? And, the main topic of this book, How did philosophy of science evolve into the very different form it takes today?" (2) Or, answering the first question already in part and phrasing the rest a little bit differently: "Knowing as we do now that logical empiricism was originally a philosophical project with cultural and social ambitions, the time is ripe to inquire how the discipline was transformed and how these cultural and social ambitions were lost." (6)

In answering the second question the author proposes an plausible but disputable *thesis*: "The answer defended here is that it [the discipline] was transformed during the 1950s at least partly, if not mainly, by political pressures that were common throughout civic as well as intellectual life during the Cold War following World War II. In large part, these pressures led logical empiricism to shed its cultural and social engagement by shedding Neurath's Unity of Science movement."(6)

Later on (xi) the time-span, during which the transformation in question is said to have occurred, is given more exactly:

"Logical empiricism was originally a project that self-consciously sought engagement not only with science but with progressive social and cultural developments (both in Europe of the 1920s and in North America of the 1930s and1940s). In the space of about 10 years, however, from roughly 1949 to 1959, it became the scrupulously nonpolitical project in applied logic and semantics that most philosophers today associate with the name "logical empiricism"or "logical positivism". (XI)[1]

This implies of course – and that has to be kept in mind, when we go on to a critical discussion of Reisch's main theses – that neither processes or events outside that decade nor those within that decade but without connection with the transformation, can serve as explanations for it.

Furthermore we are informed about the *kind of transformation* that brought about the change in question. Reisch sees this transformation as a selective process that fundamentally changed the power-relations among subgroups of Logical

[1] Later on in the book, even some dates within that time-span are given: "If the death of the Unity of Science movement is to be dated, one candidate would be 1955, the year that concluded Frank's second 3 year grant for the Institute of Science, The year 1959 is also an appropriate date. In that year Feigl followed Reichenbach in delineating a firm, logical gulf between philosophy of science and social and ethical discourse; Frank was cryptically attacked in Philosophy of Science as a neo-Thomist; and Reichenbach's image appeared in Science to promote an image of logical empiricism in the service of the RAND Corporation and military science. Perhaps the most useful date would be 1966, not only because in that year Frank died and Richard Rudner emphatically demarcated philosophy of science from social philosophy, but because during the 1960s the Unity of Science movement must have been remembered as something of a monster: an awkward patchwork of technical philosophy of science, on the one hand, and public writing contests, vague proposals for studying sociology of science, and interest in society and values of all kinds, on the other." (370)

Empiricists. Those who defended a broader conception of philosophy of science alongside the goal of social enlightenment and cultural and political change (termed by me in the following: the left wing of Logical Empiricism) and who led the movement until the end of the 1940s were from then on overturned by another subgroup (termed the right wing) who had in mind a narrower, apolitical, value-neutral, more formalist and professional philosophy of science. Thus the explanation is, so to speak, given mostly in terms of elite-change.

In order to establish the image of Logical Empiricism as a progressive movement, which preserved much of its former European heritage from Vienna, Berlin and Prague, Reisch presents a wealth of material. Beginning with some champions of early philosophy of science in the USA, he portrays Albert Blumberg, the co-author (together with Herbert Feigl) of the manifesto "Logical Positivism"of 1931 and also a communist theoretician, and the left-wing William Malisoff, the founder and first editor of the journal "Philosophy of Science" (Chap. 5). He also describes in detail the reception of the movements' teachings and actions among liberals and leftists in the USA (Chap.s 6, 7). This material will be in large part new for anyone interested in the history of Logical Empiricism. It shows that the progressive aims of the Vienna Circle were not forgotten after most of its members had emigrated to the USA and the difficult process of their acculturation to their new environment.

Turning, in the second half of the book, to the years of the Cold War, Reisch presents again very interesting new material that he often himself unearthed from the archives. I found especially interesting the FBI-records of leading exponents of Logical Empiricism and the Unity of Science Movement, among them Philipp Frank and Rudolf Carnap (268ff.). It was these chapters in particular which make the book a really compelling reading. That Carnap, a man otherwise famous for his formalistic and detached writing, joined the Waldorf-peace-conference and defended his participation against the vehement criticism of Sidney Hook, supported the acknowledgment of Red China in 1949, protested against the death-sentences of the Rosenbergs, and took part in a whole number of leftists activities, all this was mostly new to me. Taking all this together, I recommend the book as urgent reading for everyone interested in the more contemporary history of philosophy of science and analytical philosophy and its social and political background.

But does Reisch also prove his theses? Here I have some doubts. Reisch's above-mentioned selectionist thesis consists of two parts:

1. The decline of the left wing (like Philipp Frank and Charles Morris and their project of the Unity of Science, Chaps. 15 and 16)
2. The rise of the right wing (including Hans Reichenbach and Herbert Feigl, Chap. 17) with their defense of a narrower, formalist project of philosophy of science

The leftist good guys are characterized as enlightenment-driven, interested in the theme of values and sociology of science: "Together, logical empiricism and Neurath's Unity of Science movement were in the business of *Aufklärung*... They sought nothing less than to specify and to help fulfill the promise of the eighteenth-century French Enlightenment while taking full advantage of twentieth-century developments in science, logic, social thought, and politics." (3) They also had a lively interest in the *sociology* of science: "Some, such as Otto Neurath, Philipp Frank, and Charles Morris, shared the belief that logical empiricism, or philosophy of science more broadly, should embrace not only formal, abstract studies of scientific theory and scientific language, but also socially and politically relevant topics (such as the study of values in science, the sociology of science, and the logical structure and evidentiary content of ideologies and ideological claims."(2)

Let me begin by discussing how these criteria are applied for the left wing, so to speak, of Logical Empiricism. Yes indeed: Otto Neurath repeatedly mentioned the *tradition of the French Enlightenment* and Diderot's and d' Alembert's Grand Encyclopedia, when he tried to persuade candidates to participate in his International Encyclopedia of Unified Science (IEUS) and when he presented the IEUS to the public. But, as I have learned only recently, the idea of this ancestry in French Enlightenment was originally not Neurath's, but Einstein's, whom Neurath asked in 1921 (that is: even before Moritz Schlick's call to Vienna and long before the formal foundation of the Vienna Circle) to participate in a forerunner-project of the IEUS. It was Einstein's idea to use this tradition as a sort of advertisement to eventual publishers of a *Lese-Lexikon* ("reading-dictionary") aimed for workers and trade-unionists.[2] This project, and others Neurath had in mind in Vienna from then on, did not materialize. Nevertheless he used Einstein's letter of recommendation quite often, although the IEUS in the end was already far from the original project. It is telling for the IEUS that no one except Neurath himself used the Enlightenment-rhetoric there any longer.

The topic of "*values*" was far from being common ground to all the participants of the IEUS. Reisch makes this clear himself when he follows in some detail the debates about Johns Dewey's contribution to the Encyclopedia. First of all already the use of the very term "value"was something that Neurath vehemently opposed as a component of the title of the monograph. He instead proposed "Empirical Axiology", expressing thereby his conviction that the only thing that could be done in an empiricist context was to study empirically which values and system of values are actually held by different groups of people. The exchange of letters about the "ejaculatory theory" of ethics that Dewey criticized in his monograph, shows that Neurath and Carnap were far from accepting any substantial ethical theory, although they distanced themselves rhetorically a little bit from the non-cognitivist approach of Ayer.

It is true, some Logical Empiricists had a lively interest in the *sociology of knowledge*. The Chicago-based sociologist Louis Wirth was expressly hired for writing the respective monograph, and he gave a paper bearing a similar title at the 1939 Cambridge (MA) Congress for Unified Science. But he did not deliver, partly because he was drafted for the war, partly because he had more important things to do afterwards (like the presidency of the International Sociological Association, or the work on his monumental unfinished monograph "The City"). I find it surprising to learn from Reisch's book that Philipp Frank was in contact with some sociolo-

[2] Dahms (2005).

gists of science in the 1950s (like Merton or Barber), but that no one was asked to step in for Wirth.

Other no-shows could be added, such as the Aesthetics-monograph not delivered by Meyer Shapiro, or the unwritten history of logic-monograph farmed out to Łukasiewicz.

Had all these things indeed been published, the IEUS would have assumed a strikingly different shape. But there is no indication that this petering-out of the impetus of the Unity of Science-movement had anything to do with the Cold War. Taking all this together I would put some question marks behind Reisch's characterization of the left wing of Logical Empiricism before the Cold War.

According to Reisch, the left wing declined during the fifties, a process he exemplifies with Philipp Frank and Charles Morris. Frank indeed had made efforts to continue the movement of unified science by accepting the chairmanship of the newly-founded Institute of Unified Science in Boston. Furthermore he propagated an activist positivism and acted on many occasions in that direction.

Reisch now cites the discontinuation of the Rockefeller Foundations financial aid for Frank's Institute (308ff.) and an enigmatic critical article against Frank by a Charles Kegley (325ff.), who charged him as an ally of the neo-Thomists, as main points of the decline. But the evidence that the institute's financiation was discontinued not only during but because of the Cold War is not convincing. It could as well have been the case that Frank's erratic way of leadership, already visible during the 1940s, was the real reason. And the article criticizing Frank for alleged neo-Thomists alignment was perhaps a motive for him not to publish anything else, but certainly nothing which could exhibit Franks *"pink"* reputation.

The case of Charles Morris is no more convincing: that his book "Signs, Language and Behavior" was not well received (especially among pragmatists) is certainly true. But publication and reception of that book *predated* the Cold War. Other books by Morris, like *Paths of Life*, had an even worse reception. But that – according to Reisch himself – has to do with Morris' – doubtful liaison with William Sheldon and his "somatotypes" (338ff.).This alliance was surely disliked by any empiricist, be it of the left or right wing, and had nothing to do with the Cold War. So once again the conclusion is: Morris' fall in disrepute took place (in small part) in the years 1949–1959, but it was not *caused* by the Cold War.

Reichenbach had, as Reisch rightly notes, a reputation as a socialist and critical spirit long before he came to the USA: he opposed the First World War in public, when it started and afterwards, he was not only the founder of a socialist students party in Berlin after the revolution of 1918/1919, but continued his engagement in left-wing literary circles around Bert Brecht, Walter Benjamin, Alfred Döblin, Karl Korsch and others in Berlin. This, by the way, did not prevent his appointment at the university of Berlin in 1926, as Reisch asserts (353), but "only" arose violent, but in the end unsuccessful, opposition against it from right-wing members of the faculty, among them Ludwig Bieberbach who after 1933 would become a leading propagandist of a "Deutsche Mathematik." (3)

Reisch does not seem to know that Reichenbach reestablished ties with the Brecht group (now including Hans Eisler, the composer), the Mann brothers and even the exiled members of the Frankfurt School living in Los Angeles at that time (like Theodor Adorno, Max Horkheimer and Friedrich Pollock).[3] The minutes of some of their discussions about political and aesthetic question have been published in Horkheimer's Collected Works.[4] Perhaps these materials are less known to the American philosophical public because most of these meetings involved poets, novelists and composers rather than philosophers, most of whom went back to Europe shortly after the Second World War (many to East Germany, some to the West or to Switzerland). Seen in a broader cultural perspective, Reichenbach, accordingly, was at least as active as Carnap had been in Chicago or Philipp Frank in Boston in the cultural field.

What makes Reichenbach, in Reisch's eyes, a representative of the right wing, are mainly two points: his non-cognistivist theory of value contained in his popular "Rise of Scientific Philosophy" published in 1951 and a strange advertisement in "Science" in 1959. Now, as Reisch repeatedly notes himself, a non-cognitivist attitude towards ethics was common to all the Logical Empiricists (Carnap, Neurath, Schlick – in stark contrast to the pragmatists). In the case of Reichenbach, it is however already contained in his short popular book "Ziele und Wege der Naturphilosophie" published in 1931,[5] long before the Cold War. In my view, this common stance even precedes the formal foundation of the Vienna Circle and the Berlin Group by at least a decade and has to do with the "Werturteilsstreit" within German social science that took place before the World War I. From these academic discussions the debate spread to liberal and leftist student circles like the *Freistudentenschaft* already before 1914, of which Carnap and Reichenbach were leading members. Nevertheless the non-cognitivist stance towards ethics did not hamper their political interest and activist impetus. As Reichenbach repeatedly emphasized, insight into moral principles is not gained by reading philosophers' books but by involving oneself in political parties, trade unions, civic groups etc.

Now the only point in which Reichenbach view of ethics and values differs from the non-cognitivist empiricist mainstream is the idea that value judgments are not (as Carnap or Alfred Ayer maintained) expressions of emotions, but can be seen as hidden imperatives or commands.[6] That Feigl seems to have adopted this view, does not make him any more a right-winger than Reichenbach.

Reisch places an astonishing emphasis on an advertisement by the Rand Corporation in "Science"associating Reichenbach in this way with the military (352). This move I cannot understand at all: the advertisement was published long after his death and only merits the commentary that back then celebrities' portraits and names were not safer from being high-jacked than they are now. To print two

[3] See Brecht (1973), Dahms (1994), and Hecht (1997).

[4] Horkheimer (1985). (eine Diskussion über die Theorie der Bedürfnisse)

[5] Reichenbach (1931) 59 f.

[6] See for a more systematic presentation (including some introductory remarks which show that it was Walter Dubislav who developed the main tenets of this view already in Dubislav (1937)), Rescher (1966) and a discussion of Reichenbach's meta-ethical theory in Dahms (1994).

pages later an anticommunist advertisement one of an anonymous asking for money for Radio Free Europe, I find an especially weak idea on Reisch's part.

A special problem is indeed posed by the classification of Rudolf Carnap, as far as his belonging to one of the wings mentioned above is concerned. Reisch devotes a chapter to his FBI-files and discusses him again towards the end of his book (382–384). On the one hand, he certainly belongs to the political left since his student years and never gave up this orientation including, at least to a certain degree, the activism in that direction. On the other hand, Carnap is a representative of that formal mode of doing philosophy of science that gained domination in the late 1940s and 1950s (XII, put together there with Reichenbach and Feigl and again 345). Reisch acknowledges, rightly, that Carnap himself was not intimidated by loyalty oaths, FBI-spying etc. He simply stuck to his characteristic approach that he had already developed when entering philosophy with his very first published writings, namely to adopt tools taken from mathematical logic to develop themes in the philosophy of science, be it Russell's logic of relations, Hilbert's meta-mathematics, or Tarski's results in semantics. Therefore Reisch asserts correctly:

> It would be a mistake ... to take Carnap's postwar work in semantics, probability, inductive logic, and confirmation in the last decades of his life as the result of a substantive change in his philosophical work that was driven by political caution. (383)

To which one perhaps has to add that Carnap published besides these topics some articles about thermodynamics prompted by Reichenbach's last book "The direction of time" which were mostly neglected by philosophers of science and *did not* publish the original much longer version of his autobiography which was instead dramatically shortened, among others by Feigl. I suppose that the forthcoming publication of the original version will give an enormous amount of information about the change philosophy of science and analytical philosophy as a whole underwent from Vienna to Chicago and Los Angeles.

Reisch himself presents his main theses about the transformation of *wissenschaftliche Weltanschauung* into philosophy of science with some caveats:

"Politics, *in part*, is what went wrong. This book does *not* pretend to offer a *complete account* of all the events and circumstances of intellectual, social, economic and other kinds of history that bear on postwar trends in philosophy of science. But it does propose that any convincing account must include the politics of anticommunism that... wind through and in a sense, unify some of the experiences and circumstances marking the rise and fall of the Unity of Science movement during the Cold War." (IX f., emphasis added)

I think that part of what goes wrong with this explanation, is the exclusive focus on that special decade between 1949 and 1959 (let alone Reisch's efforts to present special dates of catastrophes within this span). There were processes on a much longer time scale at work here. First of all, one has to recognize that philosophy of science was not invented in the Vienna Circle (and Reichenbach's Berlin Group). It originated as an attempt by eminent physicists since the last half of the nineteenth century (among them Kirchhoff, Helmholtz, Hertz, Planck, Mach, Boltzmann) to make their achievements understood not only in their own profession, but also to a wider academic and also an educated lay public. This "Philosophie der Physiker," as Erhard Scheibe has justly called it,[7] made its first steps of professionalization as a discipline within philosophy when philosophers (like Schlick, Reichenbach, Carnap) took up the task of explaining the revolution in physics caused by relativity theories and quantum mechanics. In the 1920s the emerging "Wissenschaftliche Weltauffassung" presented itself as a progressive cultural project. For a while it formed a number of alliances with modernist extra-scientific movements (with modern architecture e.g.).[8] Little wonder: its main heroes – named in the programmatic manifesto of the Vienna Circle – like Russell or Einstein were both pacifist and progressive thinkers and had many enemies inside and outside science. And the members of the Vienna Circle and the Berlin Group had a history of leftist leanings of their own. Was this alliance between philosophy of science and progressive forces something "natural"and perhaps even inevitable, as Carnap asked Russell in a letter? I doubt that. Think only that Planck or even Frege had achieved what the others did. What then about the political alliances of philosophy of science?

In any case: a full professionalization of philosophy of science was not achieved in the years before the Nazi seizure of power despite various efforts[9]: Schlick's was and remained the only chairholder for philosophy of science, the journal "Erkenntnis" preceded 1933 only by 2 years. A full professionalization (with the foundation of a proper journal, society, textbooks, centers etc.) was achieved only in a different environment, mainly in the USA. And the question is whether the process of professionalization and its results would have been much different, had they taken place in Europe. In any case, I think that the history of the philosophy of science cannot be properly understood in isolation from the conflicts and struggles that went along with this new discipline's efforts of *professionalization*.

Second, this professionalization took place in an altogether different environment and was accompanied and in part achieved by alliances with the inborn culture and philosophy (especially the pragmatists and the New York Intellectuals). This process led to an *acculturation* of the former *wissenschaftliche Weltauffassung* to the new climate, especially to a liberalization of empiricism.[10] During this process of penetration and acculturation the IEUS and the unity of science movement played an important role. Later on, when Logical Empiricism and philosophy of science were firmly established, *all* the leading figures of the movement lost their initial interest in it. Even Otto Neurath, instead of delivering a good up-to-date

---

[7] Scheibe (2006).

[8] Reisch mentions in particular, following Galison, the Dessau Bauhaus. But one has to keep in mind, that this alliance was in place only in the short period from April 1929 to August 1931 under the directorate of Hannes Meyer. To this one may add that Neurath and Josef Frank were very active in the Austrian Werkbund from November 1928 onwards and in the internationale of modern architects, the CIAM, which, by the way, was founded in Switzerland (La Sarraz) and had its headquarter there as well (in Zürich) and no special relation to Belgium, as Reisch (2, 32) has it.

[9] See for an example Peckhaus (1990), 219ff.

[10] Described in Carnap (1963).

monograph, had published only a relatively poor contribution (which received only very few reviews). He decided instead to concentrate his efforts in the last years of his life on a long manuscript about "brotherhood and prosecution."

Third, even if Reisch's characterization of the transformation were entirely correct (namely: that of the leading historical figures of logical empiricism the left wing declined and the right wing rose), the question remains: why, when presented with a choice between these options, did the younger *generation* mostly choose the formalist, apolitical brand of philosophy of science?

Hans-Joachim Dahms (Berlin)

References

Bertolt Brecht (1973), *Arbeitsjournal 1938–1955* (ed. Hartmut Hecht), Frankfurt am Main (2 vols.)

Rudolf Carnap (1963), "Intellectual Autobiography", in: Paul A. Schilpp (ed.), *The Philosophy of Rudolf Carnap*, La Salle, IL, 3–84

Hans-Joachim Dahms (1994), "Hans Reichenbachs Beziehungen zur Frankfurter Schule – nebst Bemerkungen zum Wahren, Schönen und Guten", in: Lutz Danneberg/Andreas Kamlah/Lothar Schäfer (eds.), *Hans Reichenbach und die Berliner Gruppe*, Braunschweig, 333–349

Hans-Joachim Dahms (2005), "Die "Encyclopedia of Unified Science" (IEUS). Ihre Vorgeschichte und ihre Bedeutung für den logischen Empirismus", in: Elisabeth Nemeth/Nicolas Roudet (eds.) *Paris – Wien. Enzyklopädien im Vergleich*, Wien/New York, 105–120

Walter Dubislav (1937), "Zur Unbegründbarkeit der Forderungssätze", in: *Theoria* 3, 330–342

Hartmut Hecht/Dieter Hoffmann (1982), "Die Berufung Hans Reichenbachs an die Berliner Universität", in: *Deutsche Zeitschrift für Philosophie* 30, 651–662

Werner Hecht (1997), *Brecht Chronik 1898–1956*, Frankfurt am Main

Max Horkheimer (1985), *Nachgelassene Schriften 1931–1949* (ed. Gunzelin Schmid Noerr), Frankfurt am Main (Gesammelte Schriften vol. 12)

Volker Peckhaus (1990), *Hilbertprogramm und Kritische Philosophie*, Göttingen

Hans Reichenbach (1931), *Ziele und Wege der heutigen Naturphilosophie*, Leipzig

Nicholas Rescher (1966), *The Logic of Commands*, London

Erhard Scheibe (2006), *Die Philosophie der Physiker*, München

Rudolf Carnap, *Scheinprobleme in der Philosophie und andere metaphysikkritische Schriften*, ed. by Thomas Mormann (2004).

Michael Stöltzner and Thomas E. Uebel (eds.), *Wiener Kreis. Texte zur wissenschaftlichen Weltauffassung*, von Rudolf Carnap, Otto Neurath, Moritz Schlick, Philipp Frank, Hans Hahn, Karl Menger, Edgar Zilsel und Gustav Bergmann (2006).

It is a delight to notice that there are now two collections of original Vienna Circle articles which serve not only experts but can also be used in academic education. The background of both of them is recent research. They are part of the process in which a new and more articulate picture of the Vienna Circle is dawning. They go back to an astonishingly dynamic philosophical period in Vienna and present some of the most memorable shorter writings, including some earlier texts of the founders, their manifestos and a great amount of later developments in close connection with natural science. There is no overlap. The books should actually be read and used together.

Thomas Mormann has put together and elegantly introduced what could be called Carnap's *Wiener Antimetaphysik*. In addition to the published classics the anthology contains also one piece that was intended to be printed but remained in the archives against the will of the author, "Von Gott und Seele. Scheinfragen in Metaphysik und Theologie" (1929). The article "Über den Charakter der philosophischen Probleme" which opened the new journal *Philosophy of Science* in 1934 as a translation is also published for the first time. It is a presentation of Carnap's positive program, already looking forward from his stations in Vienna and Prague. In line with his earlier research, Mormann introduces briefly the geometrical origins of Carnap's thought and presents him in general terms as a "philosopher of possibilities."

The texts by Carnap are all from the crucial period of 1928–1934, but Michael Stöltzner and Thomas E. Uebel give a broader picture, including especially what is now called the "First Vienna Circle" of Otto Neurath, Philipp Frank and others in the beginning of the twentieth century, together with a number of Viennese interventions in later scientific controversies from quantum mechanics to biology and social science, all under the cover of the unity of science and its factually pluralistic, non-hierarchical interpretation, well known from numerous publications of the editors. The fascinating spectrum of the Vienna Circle is documented so excellently that there should be no longer any room for the stereotypical prejudices that dominated much of the earlier literature.

The small book of Carnap's papers and the bigger one are both of a manageable size. However, the Vienna Circle was a so many-faceted phenomenon that one must ask whether there is still something important that is left out.

There are respectable philosophers who think that the Vienna Circle was a school of thought with shared beliefs, interests and concerns, values and goals and methods of inquiry. However, Schlick did definitively not see himself as a head of such a school, nor did others perceive the Circle as a school. Otto Neurath coined the designation with a reference to Vienna, probably because he did not like the earlier talk of "Schlick's Circle." It was his wish to have the matters anchored to Vienna.

Stöltzner and Uebel emphasize correctly on the first page of their introduction that the Circle was "a heterogenous movement of independent philosophers" engaged in developing the scientific world view. Still, they continue, the Circle was "a coherent historical phenomenon." It is possible to characterize the Circle on both ways.

Already the first public appearance of the Circle in Prague 1929 was the joint effort of Neurath, Philipp Frank and Hans Reichenbach. In addition to Vienna it included also Prague and Berlin. The same geographical plurality was behind the book series of the Circle and the journal *Erkenntnis*, only with slightly different combinations, and the same persons were active in organizing the Unity of Science movement, although Reichenbach and Neurath already were in exile. As concerns Schlick, he had his own international contacts, especially in the U.S.A., but he was not enthusiastic about the organizational activities of Neurath, and one can say that these feelings were mutual.

A broad name for this movement is of course Logical Empiricism. It includes without doubt Reichenbach and his followers. It was used in print already 1926 by Eino Kaila as a designation of his own position, before his visits to Vienna, and today one speaks usually of the "Vienna Circle of Logical Empiricism." There was a phase of extreme positivism in Carnap's development, but it eroded soon, and "positivism" became a target and label of criticisms against the Logical Empiricists.

Whatever names are used, it is a fact that the movement was created by many independent philosophers in different locations. Against this background it is difficult to agree with Stöltzner and Uebel when they tell us that the Vienna Circle ended when Schlick was murdered in 1936. For this reason, they include to their anthology no papers after that date. But the *Erkenntnis* was published still for 2 years, although not in Germany, the conferences of the Unity of Science movement continued, there were the monograph and book series published in the Netherlands and the new encyclopedism. The death of Schlick was a great tragedy especially for Vienna, but the Vienna Circle never was a locally restricted phenomenon. It did not end with Schlick. The Circle in exile cannot be compared to the exiled Frankfurt School, for instance, but there is no reason for such a comparison even in the period in Vienna.

There was a specific continuity between the First Vienna Circle and the better known unique one, kept up mainly by Neurath and Frank. When we accept this, I see no reasons to deny that there was also a continuity after 1936, in the sense suggested by Friedrich Stadler. There was actually a small "Third Vienna Circle" after the war around Viktor Kraft and his followers and visitors. The names of "Vienna Circle" and "Logical Empiricism" did not survive in the new conditions, but the varieties of philosophical orientations and methods developed under these labels are alive as ingredients of the broader phenomenon of analytic philosophy.

The talk about the "European phase" of Logical Empiricism needs a comment. It suggests that all of Europe became empty of this movement, apparently continuing only in the North American exile. However, Neurath always remained an European philosopher, publishing the *Erkenntnis* on the continent as long as it was possible. Towards the end of the war Neurath was planning how empiristic and pluralistic rational education could be restored in the countries where they had been excluded. Kraft and Bela Juhos could continue in Austria, although badly marginalized. The Austrian born Wolfgang Stegmüller succeeded in making an important career in Germany. Sadly, the powerful exiles were not called back. But this is hardly the whole story.

In Finland, Norway and Denmark there was a direct continuity, in some sense also in Sweden. The centers of the movement had supporters and counterparts in the North European "peripheries" very early. The northern networks actually acquired dominating positions in their own geographical areas and their social impetus was not lost in the course of time. The Nordic welfare states could hardly have been built without the empirical, politically relevant research advocated in the teachings of the heirs of Logical Empiricism.

Who was invited to the meetings held in the Boltzmanngasse was for Schlick more a matter of keeping the business going on and avoiding diplomatic errors than a matter of acceptance or non-acceptance. Schlick felt free to express his own ideas, but he could not press these on others. For this reason, we need both a very broad and a very strict definition of the phenomenon around him.

The strict definition concerns, of course, Schlick's meetings. It is a pity that Stöltzner and Uebel have not included Felix Kaufmann and some other "untypical" personalities in their anthology. Kaufmann participated in the meetings as one oriented towards phenomenology and Hans Kelsen's school of law, but now these important dimensions of the Circle remain neglected. Schlick's Circle was open to different orientations and circles. In this respect, the bridge-building activity of the Unity of Science movement was not an innovation.

The book contains Gustav Bergmann's reminiscences of the Circle, expressed in 1938 (not yet 1936) in a letter to Neurath. The letter is lively and informative, but it also has a bias. Schlick's and Friedrich Waismann's reception of the new ideas of Ludwig Wittgenstein is presented as a kind of mysticism that split the Circle. The good point in this description is that Wittgenstein's influence on the Circle is not restricted to the effects of a reading of the *Tractatus*. Wittgenstein's new teachings were also gaining ground in Vienna, especially among the young generation. Schlick's death and the changed political conditions made their further development impossible.

Wittgenstein sometimes called his influences "influenzas." There was one kind of Wittgensteinian influenza in Vienna and a very different one later in Cambridge. The heirs of these influenzas had very different profiles in the later history of analytic philosophy which has made it difficult to understand Wittgenstein's decisive role in the history of the Vienna Circle. The Circle began with a reading of the *Tractatus* and soon there was a constant communication with Wittgenstein which continued much longer than is usually thought.

Waismann not only presented his well-known theses on Wittgenstein's *Tractatus* to the Circle. He lectured to the Circle and to his students on the new developments of Wittgenstein's ideas. As regards the circulation of ideas, Wittgenstein was certainly a member of the Vienna Circle, although he did not attend the meetings in the Boltzmanngasse. At least Waismann, Schlick, and probably also Carnap, profited in different ways from these communications. The frequent meetings presented also new questions to be digested by Wittgenstein.

Stöltzner and Uebel record correctly Wittgenstein's claim in a meeting in December 1929: "Der Sinn des Satzes ist seine Verifikation." This is only one example of Wittgenstein's new ideas that did not remain hidden. In the proceedings of the Prague conference Waismann published a remarkable paper on the logical interpretation of probability, actually a development of Wittgenstein's ideas. In the form in which it was printed in 1930 one can find the following: "...der Sinn eines Satzes ist die Methode seiner Verifikation" (*Erkenntnis* 1930–1931, p. 229). When Carnap later adopted this strict verificationism, he referred both to Wittgenstein and Waismann, but Mormann observes only that the lived experiences (*Erlebnisse*) of Carnap's *Aufbau* "became" later methods of verification.

Conventionalism is not the only background of Carnap's philosophy of possibilities. To it belong also the Tractarian possible states of affairs, Carnap's state-descriptions, and what could be made of them by means of modern logic.

Carnap never denied Wittgenstein's crucial importance for the development of his thought. In fact, when he had completed his *Habilitationsschrift* and came to Vienna to hold lectures, one of his first tasks was to get acquainted with Wittgenstein's philosophy like the rest of the Circle. It was Wittgenstein that made the Vienna Circle unique within Logical Empiricism. If one looks at Reichenbach and the Berlin group, no similar interest in Wittgensteinian topics can be found. The influenza in Vienna was certainly very different from what was later known as "Wittgensteinianism." Nobody, not even Wittgenstein's official expositor Waismann, accepted uncritically all of his ideas. On the other hand, everybody had to tackle somehow with the presence of Wittgenstein that always took new forms.

The careers of Wittgenstein and Waismann do not fit into Carnap's and Neurath's programmatic ideas, but still Waismann's exposition of Wittgenstein's philosophy was planned to be the first volume in the Circle's book series edited by Schlick and Frank, eagerly awaited – in vain. Much later Waismann's manuscript was already set in type in the series edited by Neurath in the Netherlands, only to be destroyed by bombs. However, without the "discovery" of Wittgenstein in Vienna there would not have been the Vienna Circle as we know it now. If we could ask Moritz Schlick, he would not be completely satisfied with the reviewed two books, exactly for this reason.

In the bigger book, there is a curious error in the contents and on the first page of Neurath's "Soziologie im Physikalismus." It has the date of 1931. The correct date 1932 is given in the catalogue of sources. Neurath's idea of physicalism was earlier than Carnap's, but they were published together.

These books are intended for German-speaking readers, but it is to be hoped that they will be used also by others.

Juha Manninen (Helsinki)

Jan Radler, *Victor Krafts konstruktiver Empirismus. Eine historische und philosophische Untersuchung.* Berlin: Logos, 2006.

Whoever is concerned with philosophy of science, the philosophy of the Vienna Circle or epistemology of the twentieth century sooner or later gets acquainted with Victor Kraft (1880–1975). He is known for being a member of the Vienna Circle and for philosophical activities beyond, esp. after World War II. A detailed view of his thoughts – besides the simple estimation of Kraft as an empiricist – is not easy to obtain since there is still no compendium on the philosophy of Kraft. This was the motivation for Radler's "historical and philosophical inquiry". The 280-pages book is meant as a general introduction into, and evaluation of the thoughts of Kraft, i.e. the origin of his empiricist attitude, the historical development that includes the influence of Kraft's teachers such as Friedrich Jodl, as well as his concerns about Neokantianism, Popper's rationalism, and the is-ought problem. All in all Victor Kraft for a long time has been a witness of many items in theoretical and practical philosophy. Still his thoughts are a manageable theme in respect to his published output and to the already existing secondary literature. Thus, Radler addresses any philosopher of science, of epistemology, and any historian who is interested in a further detail of Austrian philosophy, and, besides, Radler addresses anyone capable of the German language in which the book is written.

This investigation, based on a Ph.D.-thesis finished at the University of Frankfurt (Oder), Germany, in 2006, contains chapters on the relationship of Kraft's philosophy to the thoughts of other philosophers and chapters on some systematic issues like realism, conventionalism and the already mentioned is-ought problem. The book starts with some introductory considerations on fallibilism and the epistemology of Popper, and on Kraft's constructive realism in a nutshell. The main thesis is that Kraft has always been an empiricist and a realist concerning the existence of a world beyond our sense data. He defended this attitude during his lifetime against several philosophical antagonists, and although he was, according to Radler, not always on the right track, Kraft's thinking seems to be worth a deeper reconsideration.

The book's opening consists of two chapters. The first chapter deals with some crucial epistemological concepts that are mostly known in connection with Popper's falsificationism. These concepts are fallibilism, empirical background information and the so-called epistemological problem (Erkenntnisproblem). The second chapter is a summary of Kraft's philosophy in general.

Radler takes quite some time to lay down a decent piece of preliminary work on epistemology before starting with his analysis of Kraft. Popper's critical rationalism is contrasted with William Bartley's pancritical rationalism and Gerard Radnizky's version of the distinction between questions of fact and questions of justification or validity (Tatsachenfragen vs. Geltungsfragen). This is done to get a more detailed view of Popper to which Radler continuously comes back in his comments on Kraft.

Returning to Kraft, Radler develops his constructive realism on the basis of his *Erkenntnislehre* of 1960. Radler motivates that Kraft deals with Kant's transcendental epistemology in several respects. Perception seems to be the result of raw sense data that are structured by further ingredients. These ingredients are for Kraft, according to Radler's discussion, connections of different sense data and constructions of these connections as mind-independent objects. The very important assumption of an objective and mind-independent external world is the second point of contact between Kraft and Kant. Following Radler, this assumption is a condition for explanation and lawlikeness of nature.

Although these points of contact between Kraft and Kant do exist, Kraft remains an empiricist and a scepticist concerning metaphysical assumptions. Therefore Kraft competes with neo-kantianism, namely the Marburg and the Southwest neo-kantianism, about realism and the problem of reliable knowledge about the external world. Radler dedicates two chapters to these schools. He shows that Kraft and Cassirer differ in their opinions about the applicability of intuition in mathematics. For Kraft, intuition is restricted to the purpose of making knowledge of the empirical world possible. The comparison of Kraft and the Southwest Neokantianism shows lots of similarities while the basic attitudes differ. For Radler, the most important similarity is that both Kraft and the Southwest philosophers vote for a normative epistemology. That is, there are purposes that guide our judgement. For Kraft, the assumption of an external world is indispensably fixed in order to fulfil the mere pragmatic purpose of gaining knowledge at all whereas, e.g. Heinrich Rickert describes the ought as a transcendental principle.

Turning to Popper, Radler studies the history of some of his concepts developed apparently by Kraft, too, and maybe even earlier. These concepts are the deductive method and the probabilistic theory of induction. In the end there is no reason to accuse Popper of infringing a copyright but by reading Radler's investigation we get quite a picture of the close interaction between the thoughts of both philosophers. In his already mentioned manner, Radler now works out differences and similarities between the philosophy of science of Kraft and Popper. Radler argues mainly for a discrepancy with respect to their appraisal of basic statements. While Popper takes basic statements with a conventional touch, Kraft insists on their immanent truth. According to Radler, Kraft needs this assumption to prevent epistemology from the danger of psychologism or relativism.

Radler then starts investigating Paul Feyerabend. This is meant not only as a case study about the impact of Kraft's work on Feyerabend as a presumably better known philosopher. It is also supposed to sharpen the concepts of Kraft's philosophy, since Feyerabend's (relativistic) variation of Kraft's (non-relativistic) preliminary work may show some yet ignored fractures of the latter. Radler identifies a common normative decision in Feyerabend's and Kraft's epistemology: it is the conventional fixation on practical purposes. Since Radler finds it justified to criticise Feyerabend in this respect, a critical point is discovered in Kraft as well.

The culmination of Radler's work takes place in a final chapter on the so called is-ought problem and its connection to Kraft's main commitment: constructive realism. On the basis of the main parts of the book Radler motivates and structuralises the "meta-ethical principles" in the merely theoretical philosophy of Kraft. These are the "ought-implies-capability principle" ("Sollen-impliziert-Können-Prinzip") and the "principle of purpose and means" ("Zweck-Mittel-Prinzip"). Radler tries to unfold the subtle dependencies between this cornerstones of Kraft's very epistemological basis and is able to benefit from a rich and still ongoing debate that he takes into account, too.

The title of Radler's inquiry borrows a prominent expression of one of Kraft's latest publications, a paper called "Constructive Empirism" (Konstruktiver Empirismus) of 1973. Today's readers are immediately reminded of Bas van Fraassen's concept of constructive empirism. This newer concept is, to my knowledge, not related to preliminary works of Kraft. Therefore, it may have been adequate to evaluate shortly the relation or non-relation of Kraft to contemporary philosophers, who also call themselves constructive empiricists. This might have been even more interesting since Kraft – although certainly a constructive empiricist – was, according to most passages in the book, a constructive realist.

Radler's investigation, however, is gaining importance due to its respect for and critical distance to Victor Kraft and his thinking. The multiple connections of a doyen of analytical philosophy to other persons and branches of the philosophical business are quite impressive, and they are displayed almost completely in this volume. Since Kraft is known first of all as one of the earliest commentators of the Vienna Circle, one might have wished to learn something about Kraft's impetus to the "Vienna Circle research" and possible reactions of, say, Rudolf Carnap or Herbert Feigl.[11] All in all this book remains a reliable basis for future research on Kraft as well as for readers who wish to get an easy and broad overview about his philosophy.

Tobias Fox (Wien)

Jutta Schickore and Friedrich Steinle (eds.), *Revisiting Discovery and Justification. Historical and Philosophical Perspectives on the Context Distinction.* Dordrecht: Springer, 2006.

If there is one conceptual distinction that not only defines logical empiricist philosophy of science but also casts a long shadow over its self-consciously post-positivist successors, it is surely that of the distinction between the "context of discovery" and the "context of justification." When it was codified in these terms by Reichenbach in 1938, a previously implicit and therefore considerably amorphous practical understanding of what distinguished specifically philosophical analyses from other investigations of science was cast in a form that opened a seemingly unbridgeable gap between these different disciplinary approaches. The search for methodological autonomy of philosophy of science quickly led to its isolation from science. Increasingly so therefore since Kuhn's *Structure of Scientific Revolutions* (but not only since then) the distinction between the two contexts has been viewed with suspicion – if it was not rejected outright – by practitioners of historically and sociologically informed philosophy of science. With the advent of what the editors Jutta Schickore and Friedrich Steinle in their helpful introduction call the "new experimentalism" – the turn of philosophical attention from high theory and its confirmation to issues arising from experimental work in science and its bearing on concept and theory formation – this pressure has become even stronger. So far, however, a solution of this conflict at the very centre of philosophy of science has proved elusive, and entrenched opposition still seems the order of the day. To investigate how philosophers have come to reach this impasse and how they might overcome it is the avowed aim of this volume. Without quite putting it this way, Schickore and Steinle seek to counteract the further Balkanisation of their discipline such that specialists with different methodological orientations utterly disregard each other's work. We may all bid "good riddance" to the old false consensus, but without a new and better shared understanding the philosophy of science is hardly going to recapture the place it once had in the general and non-specialist discourse

[11] see Kraft's Der Wiener Kreis: der Ursprung des Neopositivismus, Vienna 1950.

about the nature of public reason. Yet even if their aim were more academically circumscribed, their project possesses considerable urgency.

Stemming mostly from a 2002 conference at the Max Planck Institute for the History of Science in Berlin, the papers are organised into three parts dealing with various aspects of Reichenbach's distinction, the issue of its forerunners and the issue of its applicability and possible revision, respectively. While all are worth studying in detail, I have space only for comments on the papers in Part 1 and the first half of Part 3.

Let me note explicitly therefore that Part 2 features interesting essays by Schickore on the difference between Whewell's distinction between the generation and validation of knowledge claims and the orthodox context distinction, by Lothar Schäfer on the distinctive use in defending the autonomy of science (not philosophy of science) to which Duhem put the context distinction, and by Volker Peckhaus on the role of the context distinction in Frege's and Husserl's attacks on psychologism and, previously, in Fries' philosophical anthropology. Likewise, the second half of Part 3 features interesting investigations by Steinle of the discovery of the bipolarity of electricity, by Thomas Potthast of the emergence of the concept of an eco-system and the discipline of ecology and by Theodore Arabatzis of the discovery of the Zeeman-effect and of unobservable objects like electrons, each considered as a test case for the context distinction. It is a common conclusion of all these papers – whether they are case studies of philosophical conceptions or of scientific episodes – that the orthodox context distinction erects oversharp boundaries between closely related inquiries and prompts the misleading postulation of the existence of distinct processes of discoveries and justification. Discovery and justification are much more intimately related with each other than the orthodox context distinction allows for.

But what of Reichenbach's distinction itself? (Do we possess more than a superficial understanding of it yet, e.g. does his understanding of it agree with the orthodoxy?) Three papers in Part 1 consider it from different angles.

Alan Richardson seeks to reconstruct the context which Reichenbach's philosophy of science as a whole provided for his context distinction. As a realist for whom all scientific claims were rarely if ever certain but mostly merely probable, Reichenbach was concerned to delimit the areas of the scientific enterprise that left freedom to the researchers and to understand the relevant processes of decision making without impugning the objectivity of science. Richardson argues that the distinction between mere conventions which led to empirically equivalent formulations and "volitional bifurcations" which had lasting differences as consequences, as well as the concept of "entailed decisions," served this function. Distinguishing the context of discovery from that of justification likewise played such a role: while the strictures of logic and the demand for evidential support reigned supreme in the context of justification, human creativity remained unfettered in the context of discovery. In light of the many criticisms which Reichenbach's distinction received, it is surely salutary to have Richardson's wider perspective on it. It also notable that viewed at this level of abstraction, Reichenbach's distinction says as yet very little to restrict what considerations may count as pertaining to justification proper.

Somewhat more concretely, Gregor Schiemann sets out to show that for Reichenbach the issue of the justification of induction forms the immediate background of the context distinction, providing the distinctive field of the philosophy of science. Again the reader is prompted to note a certain flexibility that Reichenbach's concept of justification possesses, encompassing not only deductive validations of hypotheses and probabilistic reasoning about their probity, but also merely pragmatic vindications of entire methodologies. Schiemann nevertheless criticises Reichenbach for an impoverished vision of the plurality of goals that science may pursue and points out that with goals other than prognosis, his vindication of induction may fail.

While both Richardson and Schiemann are thus concerned to retrieve a lasting positive message from Reichenbach's own employment of the context distinction, Don Howard seeks to show that one of the features that appears most objectionable from the perspective of theorists aiming for a culturally engaged, "critical" philosophy of science – its establishment of a morally and politically neutral zone of purely cognitive claims to be evaluated by purely epistemic criteria – can be traced back directly to Reichenbach himself. The context distinction, Howard argues in his exegetical *tour de force*, represents Reichenbach's in his day successful attempt to contain and counteract Otto Neurath's campaign to have the socio-political dimension of theory choice recognised as such by scientists and admitted as legitimate by philosophers. (For Neurath as a philosopher of social science this was far more of a bread-and-butter issue than it was for Reichenbach as a philosopher of physics.) Howard's own sympathies clearly lie with Neurath and he urges advocates of a socially engaged philosophy of science to rediscover and critically develop his long-neglected perspective.

It may be wondered whether all three analyses of Reichenbach's own employment of the context distinction could possibly be right together. I am inclined to think so. That Reichenbach sought to delineate legitimate areas of freedom of choice for researchers (both individually and collectively) in an attempt to contain the threat of relativism to an enterprise recognised to proceed by necessity both fallibly and with the aid of conventions only, does not at all contradict the view that he would draw the line when it came to socio-political determinants of theory choice – indeed, it may well support it. It is also not unlikely that Reichenbach's stance was prompted at least in part by his taking empirical reasoning to be factually more constrained than Neurath: for Reichenbach, the underdetermination of theory choice concerned mostly empirically equivalent theories. Once factual knowledge was at issue, volitional bifurcations no longer had a role to play. For Neurath, by contrast, it was underdetermined even what the set of protocol sentences should be that provided the primary orientation for an empirical research programme. For Reichenbach, the choices which scientists faced were far more restricted and he could plausibly claim that for these socio-political considerations were irrelevant. (On this account, Reichenbach's reasoning paralleled Carnap's defence of the neutrality of his strictly formal "logic of science.") Whether Neurath's holism prevents drawing the distinction between epistemic and non-epistemic considerations for theoretical choices at all, as Howard suggests, is yet another matter. It does not even seem necessary, for already the choices faced by scientists in Neurath's perspective were much more extensive and quite plausibly involved socio-political considerations.

Even if he did not reject standard distinctions like those between analytic and synthetic statements, descriptive and normative questions and epistemic and non-epistemic considerations, Neurath had good reasons to object to the way Reichenbach delineated the scientist's choice situation.

Readers are quickly led to the question of what all this historical scholarship may mean for philosophers of science today: is the distinction of the contexts alive and relevant still? The essays in the first half of Part 3 face this question squarely and, given the negative results concerning the orthodox distinction reached in other papers (as reported above), investigate whether an alternative formulation might still do useful work.

Paul Hoyningen-Huene continues where an earlier contribution of his to the debate left off (Context of Discovery and Context of Justification, *Studies in History and Philosophy of Science* 18 (1987) 501–515). Cataloguing five ways in which the orthodox context distinction has been understood and finding arguments for any of these less than convincing, Hoyningen-Huene now renews his proposal for a "lean" version of it as one that has never been attacked (with any plausibility) by anyone in the debate. Foremost among the standard interpretations stands that of the contexts as temporally distinct processes (version 1); other interpretations either distinguish the process of discovery from the methods of justification such that the latter is contrasted as normative (version 2) or logical (version 3) or they distinguish empirical disciplines dealing with discovery from logical disciplines dealing with justification (version 4) or they distinguish the type of questions asked in the two contexts as factual and normative (version 5). Noting that versions 1–4 are often conflated with each other (though some can be held jointly), Hoyningen-Huene points out that they all embody assumptions typical of logical empiricist philosophy of science that are far from innocent. One of these is that "rational disagreement about justification is conceptually impossible," an assumption which renders justification a "one-person game" and leaves "no fundamental epistemic role for scientific communities as opposed to individually working scientists." Just that, of course, was what irked Kuhn; what Kuhn never challenged, however, was the distinction we can draw between two perspectives that can be taken towards scientific knowledge, a factual and a normative one. Simply drawing this distinction entails nothing, Hoyningen-Huene argues, concerning an absolute separation between facts and values nor does it proscribe a strongly individualist approach to justification. Being unloaded with unwanted assumptions and controversial theories, Hoyningen-Huene recommends this new construal of the distinction of the contexts of discovery and justification as drawn simply between factual and normative inquiries concerning science as suitably "lean" and defensible.

Thomas Sturm and Gerd Gigerenzer then explore the applicability of this lean context distinction between issues arising from what they call the "generation" of knowledge claims and their evaluation. Concerned to show that the lean distinction fares rather well against the so-called Strong Programme in the sociology of knowledge, they first distinguish the arguments against the orthodox context distinction that were given by Kuhn and advocates of the Strong Programme and then argue that the latter are committed to rejecting even the lean context distinction. As so often in refutations of its blatantly anti-philosophical claims, a central role here is played by the interpretation of the Strong Programme's "symmetry requirement" as precluding any consideration of reasons, so nothing new emerges here. Far more instructive is Sturm and Gigerenzer's case study of the generation and acceptance of new theories, even paradigms, in cognitive science, e.g. that of the mind as a computer. Noting that superficially it looks as if social factors do after all play a determinative role in the wide-spread acceptance of new models and paradigms, they show that even though the invention of metaphors and new theoretical notions escapes more familiar ways of justification, it is possible to discern and evaluate reasons for doing so. The lean context distinction thus survives in inhospitable terrain and allows that – contrary to the Strong Programme's more extravagant claims – normative evaluations of the role of exemplars and metaphors in theory development can be sustained.

Thomas Nickles has long been an advocate of philosophical studies of discovery and so viewed the orthodox context distinction with considerable misgivings; here he considers whether the lean distinction can do justice to a division that can be drawn within the context of justification, between what he calls "epistemic appraisal" and "heuristic appraisal." Whereas the former "attends to the truth-conducive features of justification and decision-making," the latter "attends to a variety of heuristic and pragmatic considerations relating to economy of research." Nickles convincingly argues that truth and purely epistemic justification only forms part of the evaluative work done by scientists and that heuristic appraisal is not reducible to epistemic appraisal. Given that heuristic appraisal is essential to innovation in science in that it assesses, among others, the likely fruitfulness of roads not yet taken, it should have but has not been much considered in philosophy of science, a state of affairs for which Nickles blames the orthodox context distinction. Since, by contrast, the lean distinction is not committed to ruling out heuristic appraisals as external to the context of justification, carries no other undue philosophical commitments and also continues to promise genetic fallacies in justification (the one thing that bestows merit on the orthodox distinction in his view), Nickles welcomes its introduction.

Since the orthodox context distinction is often held to characterise the position of logical empiricism generally, let me briefly address, before closing, a question which the contributions to this book leave open. This is the question of where the rejection of the orthodox distinction and the acceptance in its stead of its new "lean" version leaves the narrative of logical empiricism. Is this but another nail in its coffin? Again the different trends and tendencies within logical empiricism need to be recognised. Following Howard's reconstruction of the confrontation between Reichenbach and Neurath, we must ask therefore whether Neurath would have rejected the new lean distinction just as he evidently rejected Reichenbach's. As far as I can see, he would not have done so. In fact, his and his colleague Philipp Frank's incorporation of sociological and political considerations into the philosophy of science, their rejection of the sharp distinction between internal and external criteria of theory choice and particularly their rejection of the orthodox opposition between the rational and the social, strongly suggest that their understanding of the context distinction – which they did not dispute as such – largely approximated to the new "lean" way of drawing it. Since I argued the case for this elsewhere (Logical Empiricism and the Sociology of Knowledge, *Philosophy of Science* 67 (2000) Proceedings S138–S150), albeit without quite this terminology, I will not repeat myself here.

To conclude, already this brief survey of its contents should make evident that Schickore and Steinle have provided us with a substantial volume. Anyone concerned to see how attention to the history of philosophy of science can profit its future, need look no further than this book.

Thomas E. Uebel (Manchester)

Galavotti, Maria Carla, *Philosophical Introduction to Probability*, Stanford: CSLI Publications, 2005. [=CSLI Lecture Notes Number 167]

In September 1998, an American hedge fund called Long Term Capital Management suffered losses so colossal that the Federal Reserve had to organize a gigantic bailout, unseen in the history of Wall Street and most controversially discussed.[12] The impending threat of a financial collapse could have resulted in a major financial meltdown. Yet, the fund's trading strategies heavily relied on nothing less than highly esteemed models by Nobel Laureates.[13] What went wrong? Why were the calculated probabilities in their models not reliable? How sensitive are statistical models to the domain in which they are employed? Is there a fundamental difference in the application of statistical models between capital markets and, say, statistical mechanics, where many ideas employed in modern finance once originated? Are the law of large numbers resp. the central limit theorem, that suggest a normal distribution for a sufficiently large sample of random events, applicable in a universal way or is it true that "life always has a fat tail"[14]? Does the social realm undermine true independence of events and thus allow for contagious congenial phenomena like "rational bubbles"?

Many burning questions in all kinds of scientific and social endeavors today seem unresolvable without better knowledge about the concepts of statistics. Galavotti's *Philosohpical Introduction to Probability* is the right place to get

[12] The discussion concerned the application of a "too-big-to-fail"-status for a hedge fund and the resulting adverse incentives; cf. "Decade of Moral Hazard," *The Wall Street Journal*, September 25, 1998.

[13] Cf. Lowenstein, Roger, *When Genius Failed*, Fourth Estate: London, 2001.

[14] Eugene Fama quoted by Lowenstein, p. 72.

started. The book is organized around different standpoints of thinkers who contributed to the history of probabilistic thought. After a short historical sketch and an introduction to the probability calculus, five interpretations of probability are presented: the classical interpretation, the frequency interpretation, the propensity interpretation, the logical interpretation and the subjective interpretation. (The prior Italian version of the book contained an "empirical interpretation" conjoining Popper's propensity view with von Mises' frequentism.[15] The Vienna Circle adept happily finds them separated in the new "expanded and completely revised" English version.) Each chapter is segmented into subsections containing for the most part individual mathematicians' versions of that interpretation. Also, Galavotti reports on criticisms as well as further developments of each standpoint.

There are varying choices as concerns the sciences' respective ways of applying probabilities. This point isn't made until the end of the book in the "closing remarks," though it might be a helpful guideline at the outset. On a very superficial note, the natural sciences seem to favor a rather objectivist interpretation,[16] whereas the social scientist is more inclined to make use of a subjectivist interpretation.[17] Yet, needless to say that any kind of association of the taxonomy of interpretations with the respective sciences must be very complex. Even the most clear-cut cases turn out to be more intricate than it may seem at first sight.[18]

First, the classical interpretation, of which Laplace is the sole representative, is juxtaposed with the so-called "Bertrand paradox." His principle of insufficient reason stands as the most simple approach for finding about one's way if no other hints are available as to how one should come up with probabilities. Galavotti mentions his achievement of the central limit theorem. Also, the rule of succession and its problems are discussed.

Next, the frequentist approach plots the story of von Mises and Reichenbach, among others. Emphasis is put on von Mises' notions of collective and randomness, as well as Reichenbach's "posits," his probabilistic view on causality, and his attempt to pragmatically justify induction, an attempt he shares with Feigl's "vindication."

---

[15] Galavotti, Maria Carla, *Probabilità*, R.C.S. Libri S.p.A.: Milano, 2000.

[16] Cf. e.g., Fließbach, Torsten, Statistische Physik, Mannheim et al.: BI Wissenschaftsverlag, 1993, p. 15.

[17] Cf. e.g., Hirshleifer, Jack and John G. Riley, *The Analytics of Uncertainty and Information*, Cambridge et al.: Cambridge University Press, 1992, pp. 9–11.

[18] E.g., even if one agrees that "financial markets are a pure case of the social," as Galavotti (p. 235) quotes Donald Gillies (*Philosophical Theories of Probability*, London & New York: Routledge, 2000, p. 194), this judgment about the *domain* does not at all imply that the *statistical methodology* employed in academia and practice is purely subjectivist. cf. e.g., Lowenstein, p. 69: "Merton's entire oeuvre depended on his assumptions about random walks, with their close tie-in to the physical world. As the unassuming Rosenfeld described it, he and his fellow Merton protégés used to run to the physics library looking for formulaic solutions that they could 'jam into finance'." As concerns the normative side, a pragmatic-subjectivist approach is being promoted in the field, e.g., explicitly in Holton, Glyn A., "Defining Risk," *Financial Analysts Journal 60 (6)*, 2004, pp. 19–25. However, Holton's views on a scientific world conception in general and the Vienna Circle philosophy in particular appear rather one-dimensional, since he only identifies Vienna Circle philosophy on a more-or-less-operationalist scale.

After that, Popper's propensity interpretation is presented. His view is a reaction to the demand for probability assignments in single case experiments, especially in quantum mechanics, where, we are told, the arrangement or set-up of the experiment plays an important role and therefore enters the assignment. A lengthy discussion follows, featuring protagonists like Miller, Fetzer and Gillies; each arguing for a different shade of Popper's original understanding of probability as a disposition.

The logical interpretation comprises the works of, above all, Keynes and Carnap. Both argue for a role of rationality against pragmatic approaches justifying probabilistic inferences on success. Although Keynes criticizes Laplace for the principle of insufficient reason, there is a side to Keynes' work, an epistemological disclaimer, which subscribes to a kind of probabilistic underdetermination of our theories: probability measures might sometimes miss important points. This is why he argues for an important role of intuition, certainly under the influence of Moore. This, in turn, is comparable with Knight's distinction, around the same time, between risk and uncertainty (not described by Galavotti), which serves as an epistemological justification for discretionary policies. Carnap first comes up with a justification of the inductive method, where calculated probabilities can explain progress on the basis of accumulated experience, but in his later work probability is interpreted as a basis for rational decision theory. Carnap also explicitly accepted the frequentist approach in his early work.

The final chapter introduces subjectivism, understanding probability as degree of belief. Here the main character is de Finetti, who deems a non-psychological justification of induction impossible. He himself finds the roots of his pragmatist approach in Mach and Hume. However, let me supplement Galavotti's account of de Finetti's somewhat peculiar philosophy of science by one fine detail. Probability is denied any kind of objective existence. Therefore, de Finetti explicitly associates probability with "misleading misconceptions"[19] in the history of science like phlogiston, which means that he must, at bottom, expect the concept of probability to vanish from the current field of scientific endeavors. One waits in exhilaration for the prophecy to come true. However, Galavotti reports that de Finetti has shifted his viewpoint a little in his later career, allowing for a "special meaning" (p. 217) of the assignment of probabilities within accepted scientific theories. Alas, Galavotti concludes that "subjectivism has never been taken very seriously by scientists" (p. 217).

Quite naturally, the volume is much richer than can be outlined here. Many other intellectual figures are introduced. Galavotti always includes references to the latest literature, current discussion standpoints and other historical works are mentioned accordingly in the portraits of the individual interpretations.

It is remarkable how much of the history of probability theory is indebted to considerations about betting systems, e.g., Dutch book arguments (better known as arbitrage arguments in some circles), and their implications concerning not only the relation between belief and action, but also the supposed restriction probabilities impose on the degrees of belief of rational agents. This influence seems especially important in the cases of Ramsey and de Finetti, although there is no rational belief

---

[19] De Finetti, Bruno, *Theory of Probability*, London: John Wiley & Sons, 1974, p. X.

for de Finetti in any strict sense, as there is for a Carnapian logicist. Galavotti reports that it was Jimmy Savage, who first put de Finetti's ideas on the map of statisticians. This is not surprising at all: ever the broker of the unknown, it was around the same time that Savage also brought the forgotten work of Bachelier, who was a student with Poincaré, to the attention of scholars.[20]

Galavotti has written a very rich and insightful introduction with a strong historical orientation. The volume is very structured and the subsections are thus very short and smooth to read, the explanations are clear and simple and the biographical notes are compact. But what is most surprising about this book is how little symbolism can be used in writing a philosophical introduction to probability theory.

It follows that some basic concepts even a bachelor in psychology or business or physics might have encountered in his studies will not pop up in the book. I recommend additional reading if applications are crucial or mathematical bedrock is expected.[21] It might be helpful nevertheless to have some basic technical knowledge in statistics *before* reading the book; otherwise the differences in philosophical interpretations of probability might shadow the actual success in using the probability calculus, i.e., the philosophical ingredient in probability theory might be overestimated. In other words: this book is solely concerned with the "foundational problems" (p. 4) of probability; i.e., the question of how *initial* probabilities (or "priors") are assigned. This is where the different interpretations give different answers. Having read Galavotti, you are not able to calculate the probability that X+265 pages from CSLI Publications actually contain 17 typos, yet, you know what it takes to discuss in which various general ways a probability for such an amount could be introduced.

Edwin Glassner (Wien)

[20] Bachelier, Louis, Théorie de la Spéculation, Gauthier-Villars: Paris, 1900. Bachelier was *avant-garde* in that he was the first who tried to give a probabilistic account of the movement of stock prices. The re-discovery by Savage is reported in Bernstein, Peter L., *Capital Ideas. The Improbable Origins of Modern Wall Street*, Free Press: New York, 1992, p. 23.

[21] For a more mathematically oriented sketch of the different interpretations, cf. e.g., Hájek, Alan, "Interpretations of Probability", *The Stanford Encyclopedia of Philosophy (Summer 2003 Edition)*, Edward . Zalta (ed.), URL <http://plato.stanford.edu/archives/sum2003/entries/probability-interpret/>.

Activities of the Institute Vienna Circle

http://www.univie.ac.at/ivc

Activities 2005

Fifth Vienna International Summer University
Scientific World Conceptions (VISU/SWC)
"Chance and Necessity"
Location: University Campus Vienna, Court 1, Kapelle, and Institute for Contemporary History
Date: July 18–29, 2005
Lecturers: Ted Porter (University of California, Los Angeles, USA), Wolfgang Spohn (University of Constance, Germany)
Assistant Lecturers: Deborah R. Coen (Cambridge, Mass., USA), Franz Huber (University of Constance, Germany)
In co-operation with the Austrian Ludwig Wittgenstein Society:
28. Internationales Wittgenstein-Symposium/28th International Wittgenstein Symposium

"Zeit und Geschichte/Time and History"
Location: Kirchberg am Wechsel
Date: 7–13 August, 2005
Scientific direction: Friedrich Stadler (University of Vienna, Institute Vienna Circle) and Michael Stöltzner (University of Wuppertal)
International Conference

Neurath's Economics in Context
Location: University Campus Vienna
Date: September 29–October 1, 2005
Lecturers: Guenther Chaloupek (Wien), Robert S. Cohen (Boston), Albert Jolink (Rotterdam), Thomas König (Wien), Robert Leonard (Montreal), Ortrud Leßmann (Hamburg), Peter Mooslechner (Wien), Elisabeth Nemeth (Wien), John O'Neill (Lancaster), Hermann Rauchenschwandtner (Wien), Günther Sandner (Wien), Roman Stolzlechner (Wien), Thomas Uebel (Manchester), Nader Vossughian (New York)
Moritz Schlick Project

E. Nemeth et al. (eds.), *Otto Neurath's Economics in Context.*
Vienna Circle Institute Yearbook [2007]. Volume 13.

Moritz Schlick (1882–1936): Critical Edition of the Complete Works and Intellectual Biography
First phase 2002–2005, Funded by the Austria Science Fund (FWF)
In co-operation with *Universität Rostock* (D) and *Universität Graz, Institut für Philosophie* and *Forschungsstelle für österreichische Philosophie*
Stegmüller-Carnap-Project

Banishment and Return of the Philosophy of Science Before and After World War II
Together with Research Institute Brenner Archiv, University of Innsbruck
Funded by the Austrian Science Fund (FWF), 2005–2007

Publications
Paris – Wien. Enzyklopädien im Vergleich
Elisabeth Nemeth und Nicolas Roudet (eds.)
Vienna, New York: Springer, 2005 (Veröffentlichungen des Instituts Wiener Kreis, Bd. 13)

Activities 2006

In cooperation with the Austrian Kurt Gödel Society, Institut für Experimentalphysik, Institut für Mathematik der Universität Wien
International Symposium celebrating the 100th birthday of Kurt Gödel

Horizons of Truth. Logics, Foundations of Mathematics, and the Quest for Understanding the Nature of Knowledge
Location: University of Vienna
Date: April 27–29, 2006

6th Vienna International Summer University/Scientific World Conceptions (VISU/SWC)
"Philosophy and Economics"
Together with: University of Bayreuth, Institut für Philosophie und Volkswirtschaftslehre and University of Wien, Institut für Zeitgeschichte
Main Lecturers: Geoffrey Brennan (Duke University), Hartmut Kliemt (Universität Duisburg)
Guest Lecturer and 14th Vienna Circle Lecture: Rainer Hegselmann (Universität Bayreuth)
Venue: University Campus Vienna
Date: July 17–28, 2006
Meeting of the International Program Committee: July 7–9, 2006
6th International Workshop

Moritz Schlick Project: Critical Edition of the Complete Works and Intellectual Biography
Together with: University of Graz, Department of Philosophy and University of Rostock, Department of Philosophy
Location: Institute Vienna Circle
Date: January 27–29, 2006
International Meeting and book presentation
(on the occasion of the 70th anniversary of the death of Schlick)

Moritz Schlick: Critical Edition of the Complete Works
Vols. 2 and 3
University of Vienna: June 22, 2006
Austrian Embassy in Berlin: June 1, 2006

On the Banishment and Return of the Philosophy of Science After World War II
As part of the 6th International Congress of the International Society for the History of Philosophy of Science (HOPOS 2006)
Location: Paris, Ècole Normale Supérieure
Date: June 14–18, 2006
14. Wiener Kreis Vorlesung/14th Vienna Circle Lecture
Rainer Hegselmann (University of Bayreuth)

Truth and Cognitive Division of Labor – First Steps Towards a Computer Aided Social Epistemology
as part of VISU 2006
Location: Universitätscampus
Date: July 25, 2006

Wissenschaftsphilosophisches Kolloquium
Weekly lectures by Austrian and international as well as younger scholars on scientific philosophy and philosophy of science
http://www.univie.ac.at/ivc/koll

Publications
Cambridge and Vienna. Frank P. Ramsey and the Vienna Circle
Ed. Maria Carla Galavotti
Dordrecht/Boston/London: Springer 2006 (Vienna Circle Institute Yearbook 12/2004)
Paul Feyerabend (1924–1994) – Ein Philosoph aus Wien
Hrsg. von Kurt Rudolf Fischer und Friedrich Stadler
Wien, New York: Springer 2006 (Veröffentlichungen des Instituts Wiener Kreis 14)
Proceedings of the 28. International Wittgenstein Symposium
Time and History
Ed. by Friedrich Stadler und Michael Stöltzner

Frankfurt am Main: Ontos Verlag 2006
Moritz Schlick Gesamtausgabe
Hrsg. von Friedrich Stadler und Hans-Jürgen Wendel
Wien, New York: Springer 2006ff. Vols. 1–3, 6
Über Reflexion des Lichtes. Raum und Zeit in der gegenwärtigen Physik. Hrsg. von Flynn Ole Engler und Matthias Neuber
Lebensweisheit/Fragen der Ethik. Hrsg. von Mathias Iven

Research projects
On the Banishment and Return of Philosophy of Science Before and After World War II: Rudolf Carnap and Wolfgang Stegmüller
Together with: Brenner Archiv of the University Innsbruck
Funding: FWF

Moritz Schlick Project: Critical Edition of the Complete Works and Intellectual Biography
Phase 2: 2006–2008
Abteilung II. Nachgelassene Schriften und intellektuelle Biografie

Wissenschaftliche Weltauffassung und Kunst: Kunsttheorie und Kunstforschung im wissenschaftlichen Diskurs/Scientific World Conception and Art: Art, Theory of Art and Studies in Art in the Scientific Discourse
Scientific direction: Martin Seiler
Library/Documentation/Archives
The Robert S. Cohen Collection and The Robert S. Cohen Archives at the Institute Vienna Circle
(Boston Studies and Boston Center for the Philosophy of Science)

Activities 2007

7th Vienna International Summer University
Scientific World Conceptions (VISU/SWC)
"Consensus in Science"
Main Lecturers: Naomi Oreskes (University of California, San Diego, USA), Miriam Solomon (Temple University, Philadelphia, USA), Andrzej Wróblewski (Warsaw University, Poland)
Guest Lecturer: Keith Lehrer (University of Arizona, Tucson, USA)
Location: Universitäty Campus
Date: July 16–27, 2007
Together with: University of Vienna/Department of Contemporary History
15. Wiener Kreis Vorlesung/15th Vienna Circle Lecture
Keith Lehrer (University of Arizona, Tucson)

Consensus in Art and Science
As part of VISU 2007
Location: University Campus
Date: July 24, 2007
Affiliated Meeting

West Meets East in the Philosophy of Science: Moritz Schlick and Tscha Hung (Hong Qian)
Location: Tsinghua University, Beijing
Date: August 13, 2007
As part of the 13th International Congress of Logic. Methodology and Philosophy of Science, organized by the IUHPS/DLMPS
International Symposium

The Vienna Circle in the Nordic Countries
Networks and Transformations of Logical Empiricism
Together with the Helsinki Collegium for Advanced Studies und Centre for Nordic Studies at the University of Helsinki
Location: Helsinki Collegium
Date: September 2–5, 2007
International Symposium

Rethinking Popper
Organised by the Department of Philosophy at the Czech Academy of Sciences
Location: Prague, Academy of Sciences
Date: September 10–14, 2007
International Workshop

Moritz Schlick Project: Critical Edition of the Complete Works and Intellectual Biography
Phase 2: 2006–2008
In co-operation with *Universität Rostock* and *Universität Graz, Institut für Philosophie* and *Forschungs- und Dokumentationsstelle für Österreichische Philosophie*
Location: Institute Vienna Circle
Date: February 2007
Workshop

Vertreibung und Rückkehr der Wissenschaftsteorie: Rudolf Carnap und Wolfgang Stegmüller
Together with: Universität Innsbruck, Brenner-Archiv
Location: Institute Vienna Circle
Date: January 2007
Internationales Austauschprogramm im Rahmen des ÖAD

Österreich-Ungarn: Am Beispiel der Wissenschaftsphilosophie
Location: ELTE Budapest and University of Vienna
Date: Several bilateral workshops in 2007 and 2008

Wissenschaftsphilosophisches Kolloquium
Weekly lectures by Austrian and international as well as younger scholars on scientific philosophy and philosophy of science

Publications
Otto Neurath's Economics in Context
Ed. by Elisabeth Nemeth, Stefan W. Schmitz, Thomas Uebel
Dordrecht: Springer 2007 (Vienna Circle Institute Yearbook 13)
Moritz Schlick Gesamtausgabe: Vol. V: Vienna, 1923–1937. Ed by Heiner Rutte and Johannes Friedl. Springer: Wien-New York 2007

Research Projects
Vertreibung und Rückkehr der Wissenschaftstheorie vor und nach dem Zweiten Weltkrieg: Rudolf Carnap und Wolfgang Stegmüller/The Banishment and Return of the Philosophy of Sciences: Rudolf Carnap and Wolfgang Stegmüller
In co-operation with: *Brenner Archiv* der *Universität Innsbruck*
Moritz Schlick Project

Moritz Schlick (1882–1936): Critical Edition of the Complete Works and Intellectual Biography
Second phase 2006–2008
In co-operation with *Universität Rostock* and *Universität Graz, Institut für Philosophie* and *Forschungs- und Dokumentationsstelle für Österreichische Philosophie*

Wissenschaftliche Weltauffassung und Kunst: Kunsttheorie und Kunstforschung im wissenschaftlichen Diskurs/Scientific World Conception and Art: Art, Theory of Art and Studies in Art in the Scientific Discourse
Scientific direction: Martin Seiler
Library/Documentation/Archives
The Robert S. Cohen Collection and The Robert S. Cohen Archives at the Institute Vienna Circle
(Boston Studies and Boston Center for the Philosophy of Science)
In preparation:
Adolf Grünbaum Collection (University of Pittsburgh, Center for Philosophy of Science)

Index

VIENNA CIRCLE INSTITUTE YEARBOOK

The *Vienna Circle Institute* is devoted to the critical advancement of science and philosophy in the broad tradition of the Vienna Circle, as well as to the focussing of cross-disciplinary interest on the history and philosophy of science. The Institute's *Yearbooks* provide a forum for the discussion of exact philosophy, logical and empirical investigations, and analysis of language. Each volume centers around a special topic which is complemented with a permanent section with essays arising from the scientific activities at the Institute and reviews of recent works in the history of philosophy of science or others with a particular relation to the tradition of logical empiricism

1 [1993] F. STADLER (ed.), *Scientific Philosophy: Origins and Developments*. 1993.
ISBN 0-7923-2526-5

2 [1994] H. PAUER-STUDER (ed.), *Norms, Values, and Society*. 1994.
ISBN 0-7923-3071-4

3 [1995] W. DEPAULI-SCHIMANOVICH / E. KÖHLER / F. STADLER (eds.), *The Foundational Debate. Complexity and Constructivity in Mathematics and Physics*. 1995.
ISBN 0-7923-3737-9

4 [1996] E. NEMETH / F. STADLER (eds.), *Encylopedia and Utopia. The Life and Work of Otto Neurath (1882-1945)*. 1996.
ISBN 0-7923-4161-9

5 [1997] W. LEINFELLNER / E. KÖHLER (eds.), *Game Theory, Experience, Rationality. Foundations of Social Sciences, Economics and Ethics. In honor of John C. Harsanyi*. 1998.
ISBN 0-7923-4943-1

6 [1998] J. WOLEŃSKI / E. KÖHLER (eds.), *Alfred Tarski and the Vienna Circle. Austro-Polish Connections in Logical Empiricism*. 1999.
ISBN 0-7923-5538-5

7 [1999] D. GREENBERGER / W.L. REITER / A. ZEILINGER (eds.), *Epistemological and Experimental Perspectives on Quantum Physics*. 1999.
ISBN 0-7923-6338-X

8 [2000] M. RÉDEI / M. STÖLTZNER (eds.), *John von Neumann and the Foundations of Quantum Physics*. 2001.
ISBN 0-7923-6812-6

9 [2001] M. HEIDELBERGER / F. STADLER (eds.), *History of Philosophy of Science. New Trends and Perspectives*. 2002.
ISBN 1-4020-0509-1

10 [2002] F. STADLER (ed.), *The Vienna Circle and Logical Empiricism*. 2003.
ISBN 1-4020-1269-1

11 [2003] F. STADLER (ed.), *Induction and Deduction in the Sciences*. 2004.
ISBN 1-4020-1967-X

12 [2004] M.C. GALAVOTTI (ed.), *Cambridge and Vienna. Frank P. Ramsey and the Vienna Circle*. 2006.

13 [2007] E. NEMETH / S.W. SCHMITZ / T.E. UEBEL (eds.), *Otto Neurath's Economics in Context*. 2007.
ISBN 978-1-4020-6904-8

FSC
www.fsc.org
MIX
Papier | Fördert
gute Waldnutzung
FSC® C083411

Kolibri 360 GmbH
Ferdinand-Jühlke-Straße 7
99095 Erfurt, Deutschland
produktsicherheit@kolibri360.de